Beyond the Quagmire

Beyond the Quagmire

New Interpretations of the Vietnam War

EDITED BY

Geoffrey W. Jensen and Matthew M. Stith

Denton, Texas

10 9 8 7 6 5 4 3 2 1

Permissions:
University of North Texas Press
1155 Union Circle #311336
Denton, TX 76203-5017

The paper used in this book meets the minimum requirements of the American National Standard for Permanence of Paper for Printed Library Materials, z39.48.1984. Binding materials have been chosen for durability.

Library of Congress Cataloging-in-Publication Data

Names: Jensen, Geoffrey W., 1975- editor. | Stith, Matthew M., editor.
Title: Beyond the quagmire : new interpretations of the Vietnam War / edited by Geoffrey W. Jensen and Matthew M. Stith.
Description: Denton, TX : University of North Texas Press, [2019] | Includes bibliographical references and index.
Identifiers: LCCN 2018054806| ISBN 9781574417487 (cloth : alk. paper) | ISBN 9781574417586 (e-book : alk. paper)
Subjects: LCSH: Vietnam War, 1961-1975--Causes. | Vietnam War, 1961-1975--Diplomatic history. | Vietnam--Politics and government--1945-1975. | Politics and war--United States--History--20th century. | United States--Politics and government--1969-1974.
Classification: LCC DS557.6 .B49 2019 | DDC 959.704/3--dc23

The electronic edition of this book was made possible by the support of the Vick Family Foundation.

This volume is dedicated to the memory of Marilyn Young (1937-2017), whose work on Vietnam has influenced a generation of scholars, including our efforts here, and will continue to enhance studies of the conflict for years to come.

Table of Contents

List of Images

Acknowledgments

We met years ago in the history graduate program at the University of Arkansas, Fayetteville. While there, we struck a fast friendship that grew during office hours, graduate seminars, lunches on Dickson Street, and while we commiserated about the art of history. It was also in those nascent years of our career that we began to scheme toward a collaborative project on the Vietnam War. Almost a decade later, *Beyond the Quagmire* represents the fruits of that effort. And frankly, we could not be prouder of it.

But we hardly did this alone. Eleven authors joined us to help make this collection happen, and it was our good fortune to serve as their editors. We express our sincere thanks to them for their outstanding contributions as well as their positive attitudes, good humor, and support throughout the process. We sincerely thank UNT Press Director Ron Chrisman for his patience and encouragement from the earliest discussions through publication. Thanks also to Ben Abercrombie who copy-edited the collection and helped make it a better volume from start to finish.

Geoffrey W. Jensen would like to specifically thank the following: At Embry-Riddle Aeronautical University, Prescott, thanks to friends and colleagues in the College of Security and Intelligence, most importantly,

Dean Phil Jones and Department Chair Thomas Field who ensured that I would have the time to complete revisions throughout the process. Thanks also goes out to my wife, Beth, and our daughter, Aurora. Both provided energy, encouragement, laughter, and when it was necessary, drug me away from the computer long enough to relax.

Matthew M. Stith would like to thank the following. At UT-Tyler, thanks to friends and colleagues Misty Holmes, Vicki Betts, Marcus Stadelmann, Eric Lopez, Mark Owens, Mandy Link, Colin Snider, and Randy LeBlanc for their support and friendship throughout the project. Thanks also to old friends and outstanding historians Madeleine Forrest, David Schieffler, Scott Cashion, and Alan Thompson for their perpetual encouragement and good-natured advice. Teacher, historian, and friend Betsy Moore at Walnut Hills High School in Cincinnati, OH, proved enormously helpful in the final weeks of the project and helped make the final editing process both fun and rewarding. And special thanks to Robert Forrest in Charlottesville, VA, for his interest and participation in this project— and for his service in Vietnam. Finally, thanks to Lorelei and Wyatt, both of whom make everything worthwhile.

Geoffrey W. Jensen

Associate Professor of History

Embry-Riddle Aeronautical University, Prescott, AZ

Matthew M. Stith

Associate Professor of History

University of Texas at Tyler

Beyond the Quagmire

Introduction

Geoffrey W. Jensen and Matthew M. Stith

Lyndon Johnson was perplexed. He had spent the better part of six months wrestling over what to do in Vietnam. Johnson had inherited the presidency and the crisis in Southeast Asia that came with it. As a "can-do" warrior, he naturally sought a solution. So, as Johnson was apt to do, he called on an old friend, sometimes rival, for help: Georgia Senator Richard Russell. But after a long conversation, the avid-anticommunist and head of the Senate Armed Services Committee proved equally flummoxed, as was the president, by the riddle of Vietnam:

> I wish I could help you. God knows I do, because it's a terrific quandary that we're in over there. We're just in the quick sands up to our very necks. And I just don't know how, what the hell is the best way to do about it.[1]

From that conversation, the historical narrative emerged of Vietnam as an inescapable trap, a foreign policy and military quagmire, that would ensnare Americans in a war of which neither they, nor their leaders— including Johnson and Russell— wanted any part. Right or wrong, and despite recent works that have deepened our understanding of the particulars of the matter, the historical narrative of Vietnam as a quagmire has overshadowed other aspects of the war and remains firmly entrenched. *Beyond the Quagmire* brings together scholars from across disciplines to provide a series of provocative and timely essays designed to help dislodge Vietnam War historiography from this morass by providing new ideas and directions about the politics, combatants, and memory of the war.[2]

It was a time of deep introspection as questions over the legality of American involvement, political dishonesty, civil rights, countercultural ideas, and American overreach during the Cold War congealed in one place: Vietnam. Just as Americans fifty years ago struggled to understand the nation's connection to the war, scholars today, across disciplines, are working to come to terms with the long and bloody affair. Perhaps the best-known collection of essays on Vietnam is Marilyn B. Young and Robert Buzzanco's *A Companion to the Vietnam War* (2002). Young and Buzzanco's compilation contains twenty-four essays from some of the conflict's most renowned scholars, and has remained a benchmark for recent scholarship. That volume, however, is sixteen years old. In the interim, new discoveries, ideas, and authors have emerged and challenged some of its findings, while others have crafted regional specific compilations, such as Marcia A. Eymann and Charles Wollenberg's *What's Going On?: California and Vietnam War* (2004), which examines the war and the trappings of the 1960s from a California perspective. Others have looked abroad, for instance, Nathalie Huynh Chau Nguyen's *New Perceptions of the Vietnam War* (2014) provides a much-needed international perspective on political and social issues.[3]

So why another collection on the Vietnam War? *Beyond the Quagmire* opens new lines of debate while also providing focused and original essays that both individually and as a whole advance our understanding of a variety of troublesome and complicated interpretive threads regarding the conflict in Vietnam and in America. The authors of *Beyond the Quagmire* examine issues both within and outside of Vietnam and do so through the crafting of essays on antiwar activism, race, gender, warfare, nature, and memory. The thirteen distinct chapters are organized in three parts. The first contains four chapters by scholars who explore the high and low politics of the Vietnam era. To this end, in the opening chapter, Geoffrey C. Stewart examines nation-building programs in Ngo Dinh Diem's First Republic of Vietnam. Stewart shows how land reform, agrovilles, and several other programs developed by Diem's government and supported by the United States were used by the regime as a way to convince South Vietnamese citizens to remain, or become, loyal to his government. But Diem's First Republic of Vietnam (1955-1963) had broader and more ambitious goals, namely an effort to become a viable nation in a global context. In sum, Stewart effectively shows that Diem's efforts, though ultimately unsuccessful, serve as a valuable example for how developing nations, like South Vietnam, agitated for their own, singular in the global arena with goals independent from world powers. Stewart argues that Diem took a middle path to navigate between communism and liberalism toward a policy of "Personalism," which allowed for a level of self-sufficiency and gradual separation from the bounds of American aid.

In Chapter 2, Nengher N. Vang sheds light on the evolving dynamic between Hmong and American cooperation in Southeast Asia. Vang moves America's Secret War in Laos and the tumultuous aftermath squarely to the center of what has long been a historiographically marginalized topic. After American forces left Laos, ethnic Hmong continued to fight the Lao People's Democratic Republic (PDR) in the country just as Hmong exiles agitated for liberation from their positions in the United States and Thailand. Vang's valuable analysis provides context to American intervention in Laos and traces the volatile evolution of the Hmong struggle through the twenty-first century. He examines, for example, Hmong Gen. Vang Pao's criminal trial along with a dozen others who, as late as 2007, had been accused of conspiracy to overthrow the PDR with alleged American connections. In so doing, Vang provides insight into a dimension of the Vietnam War and its aftermath that helps develop a more complete picture of the contemporary and ongoing struggle with America's involvement in Vietnam.

In Chapter 3, Martin G. Clemis moves the discussion toward the geopolitics of American involvement during Richard M. Nixon's presidency. Clemis conveys geography's central and paramount role in shaping military strategy, diplomacy, and Vietnamization. The American war in Vietnam cannot be fully understood without recognizing the primacy of geographical boundaries at every level— from political borders with political and diplomatic liabilities like Laos, Cambodia, and North Vietnam, to the myriad of geographical "patchworks," as Clemis calls them, across the jungles, highlands, and mountains of South Vietnam. These boundaries— some static, some fluid— played a critically important role in shaping the American war from the beginning, but they were hardly as vital as they were during Nixon's tenure. Clemis's chapter, then, provides an important and valuable new interpretation of how we might rethink the geographical and spatial dimensions of Nixon's Vietnam.

Moving from Southeast Asia to the American South, Jeffrey A. Turner refocuses our attention on the antiwar movement among university students in a region of the United States that is often overlooked with respect to Vietnam protests. Turner offers a compelling argument that the conflict reshaped southern universities by offering students a platform on which to agitate for reform not just regarding the war in Indochina, but issues on southern campuses and the South as a whole. In the end, the southern student movement during, and because of, the Vietnam War helped diminish those disparities between southern universities and those throughout the nation. Vietnam, Turner shows, made the South less "southern" and more, perhaps, American.

In the second part, five chapters engage the story of Vietnam combatants through the lenses of race, gender, environment, and fighting. Geoffrey W. Jensen's contribution delves into issues of race, the military, and the Great Society during the war by examining the contentious and heavily politicized Project 100,000. Here, Jensen explores the origins, politics, and criticism— then and now— of Daniel Patrick Moynihan, Lyndon B. Johnson, and Robert McNamara's quest to uplift America's poor during the Vietnam War. This "Guns and Butter" approach, as Jensen calls it, set its sights on enabling approximately a third of draft age men who had been educationally disqualified to meet the requirements for induction. In addition to swelling the ranks during the always potentially volatile Cold War, Moynihan and company believed that these underqualified recruits would benefit from the rigorous discipline and training provided by the military. Recruits would not only help buttress the American effort during the Cold War, most notably in Vietnam, but they would gain character and a step up on the theretofore slippery socioeconomic ladder. While situating it within the greater discussion of the Great Society and Christian Appy's analysis of the Vietnam conflict as a "working-class war," Jensen, in contrast to some of the existing historical literature, determines that Project 100,000 was less about avoiding the political fallout of calling up the reserves or yanking male students out of college by way of the draft to go to war in Southeast Asia, and instead about Johnson, Moynihan, and McNamara's desires to wage the War on Poverty with the United States military.

In Chapter 6, Heather Marie Stur tackles the question of women, gender, and victimhood in Vietnam. Stur balances the traditional sympathetic narrative that espouses a dramatic and heartbreaking American loss in Southeast Asia with the combatants'— both men and women— that benefited from, and misused, a myriad of services offered by South Vietnamese. Stur questions the viability of this narrative in the context of so many stories about American men and women who lived the "good life" in Saigon. More than freewheeling adventures in the busy streets of Saigon, though, Stur explains that we must adjust our interpretation of the war with a new lens on how women participated directly as combatants. Just because women did not go on patrols in enemy territory hardly meant they did not experience a brand of combat. There were no front lines in Vietnam, and women in most military positions routinely came under enemy fire, cared for damaged and destroyed bodies, and experienced the same level of trauma as any of their male counterparts. Our understanding of Vietnam has for too long centered on the trauma experienced by male troops at the expense of marginalizing, or even forgetting, women. In the end, Stur makes clear, we must reorient our view through a fresh lens untainted by the traditional victimhood narrative.

No robust consideration of the Vietnam War is complete without a close look at China's role in the conflict. Xiaobing Li's innovative chapter provides scholars with the one of the first analyses of Chinese military aid in Vietnam from 1965 to 1968. Li's work emphasizes the impact of the more than 300,000 Chinese troops who directly participated in the conflict on behalf of North Vietnam. Using newly available archival sources, Li lays to rest uncertain speculation regarding Chinese intervention and provides readers with a powerful new overview of China's actions in the war. Moreover, he illuminates the turbulent relations between the Communist powers in Beijing and Moscow and how they struggled to deal with Hanoi and the war; here, we see a hint at what historians such as Lien-Hang T. Nguyen and Qiang Zhai, among others, have long known—the war was often a competition for all parties, whether Russian, Chinese, or Vietnamese, involved as they sought to obtain some semblance of supremacy in the communist pecking order.[4] American diplomatic efforts with China during Richard Nixon's presidency, spearheaded by Henry Kissinger, had been as much about easing China's support for North Vietnam as helping mitigate the broader Soviet threat. China, then, served as a lynchpin in the Vietnam War specifically and the international Cold War generally, ultimately, if indirectly, aiding American interests in the latter if not the former.

Ron Milam brings the conversation back to the jungles and highlands of South Vietnam with his study of American military advisors in Chapter 8. He examines advisors' multifaceted role with a variety of allied groups in South Vietnam. In so doing, Milam examines their selection, actions, and overall aptitude in the field. He draws not only on careful research but also upon his own personal experience as a Mobile Advisory Team Leader and Assistant Team Leader in 1970-1971. For the reader, it will strike a unique chord between personal recollection and the skilled acumen of a scholar striving to situate it within the era. At its heart, Milam's contribution shows how advisors, whose jobs continued to evolve throughout the war, worked with ARVN units, Regional Forces, and Popular Forces (Ruff-Puffs) to affect the course of Vietnam as well as draw lessons for future American military efforts when employing advisory units.

In Chapter 9, Matthew M. Stith moves the discussion deeper into the brush by exploring the natural environment's role in shaping the American military experience in South Vietnam. Stith starts his chapter with a general examination of military strategy and perception associated with the challenging environmental contours. American commanders saw their fight as not just one against the VC and NVA but against the forests, mountains, mud, and myriad of other natural forces they leveraged as a defensive force multiplier. Stith then transitions to the combatant-environment dynamic and makes clear that soldiers and support personnel on the ground faced this reality directly. Americans found nature to be a powerful and omnipresent enemy that muddled, slowed, and frustrated their attempts to get the upper hand. In sum, he concludes, we can hardly understand the Vietnam War until we recognize nature's ubiquitous and paramount part in the American experience.

In the final section, four innovative and unique essays tackle the meaning of the war in history and memory. Susan L. Eastman's chapter starts the section with an innovative look at how *The 'Nam* comic book series interpreted the conflict in the late 1980s and early 1990s. She shows that unlike the prevalent nature of protest-style film and music, the comic series focused on the daily drudgery of regular soldiers. Created by veterans, *The 'Nam* explored the war's brutal reality via a nontraditional, even palliative platform that helped veterans and nonveterans alike to understand the war through a new lens; though, as she demonstrates, the author's view of the war faced real scrutiny for its desire to adhere to the firm restrictions of the Comics Code that governed the industry, and in the opinions of some of its readers, white-washed aspects of the story. While it struggled to appease all of its audience and to make sense of the war, Eastman argues that the comic's timing— at the end of the Cold War and in the midst of the First Gulf War— served to underscore America's transition into a new political, diplomatic, and military era less bound to Vietnam and the Cold War. So, while films such as *First Blood,* in particular, *First Blood Part II*, *Missing in Action*, and others celebrated the avenging American hero returning to Southeast Asia "to win this time," *The 'Nam*, despite its failings, sought to tell it as it was.

In Chapter 11, Sarah Thelen analyzes President Richard M. Nixon's contentious and far reaching conflict against the anti-war movement. By labeling protestors and their cause un-American, Nixon attempted to delegitimize agitators. He simultaneously encouraged the "Silent Majority" to launch counter protests in an effort to reframe the conflict as a patriotic endeavor. She argues that beneath the veneer of these competing movements, Nixon's administration attempted to redefine what it meant to be patriotic. The new definition centered on those who were, in her words, "uncritical" of the administration's goals and policies. Americans who voiced their opposition to official policy could not, in this new order, also be patriotic. In the end, Thelen ably contends, the Nixon Administration's war against those who differed ultimately yielded long lasting ramifications about the meaning of being American. They also, she shows, exacerbated and, to an extent, solidified divisions within the United States. Thelen's contribution ultimately makes direct and provocative connections to current debates within our own era with respect to patriotism, presidential politics, and the legacy of Vietnam.

As perhaps the most prominent and visible manifestation of Vietnam War memory, the Vietnam Veterans Memorial in Washington, D.C., serves as the fulcrum point for William Thomas Allison's examination of cultural, social, and political forces emanating from the United States' struggle to memorialize the war. Allison offers a penetrating analysis of not only the growth of physical veteran memorials across the country, but also on their deeper cultural meaning in a nation struggling to both remember and forget Vietnam. The memorial building "frenzy," Allison argues, reflected American guilt and a collective attempt to forget and move on, while at the same time, hinting at the lucrative possibilities for some towns that a memorial could generate. To an extent, he suggests that by relegating the remembrance of the war to physical memorials, Americans sealed their feelings of culpability in the same stone that memorialized those who lost their lives in Vietnam.

In Chapter 13, Douglas J. Bradley shows how music of all kinds— country, rock and roll, pop, and soul— served as a multifaceted cultural platform connecting every part of American society to the war in Vietnam. A veteran of the conflict, whose writing in the chapter intertwines the personal with the professional, Bradley makes clear that music is among the most universal of all popular representations and memories of Vietnam. It directly or indirectly reflected visceral reactions to the conflict from both pro-war and anti-war Americans, and, as he conveys, connected soldiers, through a musical tether of sorts, in the field with their generation back home. Bradley ultimately argues that it gave a voice to a diverse generation who struggled to come to terms with the war as it happened— and as it happened to them— and helped the survivors heal in the subsequent decades.

Americans are coming to terms with the Vietnam War. As of 2018, relations between the United States and Vietnam are more amicable than they have ever been. Ken Burns and Lynn Novicks' 2017 *The Vietnam War: A Film*, though it has its critics, reflects the renewed popular interest in the conflict and how we might remember it. With popular, if not powerful, representations and reinterpretations of the war, such as Burns and Novicks' work, it is imperative that scholars and veterans of the conflict continue to probe the edges of the American experience in Vietnam to understand what have long been sideshows, or no shows at all. Taken together, the essays in this volume do just that. They adjust and broaden our understanding of one of America's least understood conflicts. They push accepted interpretations in new directions, and create fresh lines of inquiry that will be fleshed out by a new wave of scholarship. Taken separately, each chapter stands alone as an important inquiry into specific subfields of Vietnam historiography. In sum, they go beyond the quagmire.[5]

Notes

1. "Lyndon Johnson and Richard Russell on 27 May 1964," Tape WH6405.10, Citations #3519, #3520, and #3521, *Presidential Recordings Digital Edition* [Toward the Great Society, vol. 6, ed. Guian A. McKee] (Charlottesville: University of Virginia Press, 2014–). URL: http://prde.upress.virginia.edu/conversations/9060283, accessed on 12/21/2017.
2. See David Andrew Biggs, *Quagmire: Nation-Building and Nature in the Mekong Delta* (Seattle: University of Washington Press, 2010), 7-8.
3. Other notable volumes include: James Olson's *Dictionary of the Vietnam War* (Westport, CT: Greenwood, 1988); Spencer C. Tucker's *Encyclopedia of the Vietnam War: A Political, Social, and Military History* (New York: Oxford University Press, 2001); David Anderson's *The Columbia Guide to the Vietnam War* (New York: Columbia University Press, 2002); Jayne Werner, ed., and Luu Doan Huynh, *The Vietnam War: Vietnamese and American Perspectives* (New York: Routledge,1994); Marc Jason Gilbert, ed., *Why the North Won the Vietnam* War, *Second Edition* (New York: Palgrave Macmillan, 2002); David L. Anderson and John Ernst, eds., *The War That Never Ends* (Lexington: University Press of Kentucky, 2007); Mark Philip Bradley and Marilyn B. Young, eds., *Making Sense of the Vietnam Wars* (New York: Oxford University Press, 2008); David L. Anderson, *The Columbia History of the Vietnam War* (New York: Columbia University Press, 2010).
4. Lien-Hang T. Nguyen, *Hanoi's War: An International History of the War for Peace in Vietnam* (Chapel Hill: The University of North Carolina Press, 2012); Qiang Zhai, *China and the Vietnam Wars, 1950-1975* (Chapel Hill: The University of North Carolina Press, 2000).
5. *The Vietnam War: A Film* by Ken Burns and Lynn Novick (PBS, 2017).

Part I

The Politics of War

Rural Development and Revolution in Ngo Dinh Diem's Vietnam

Geoffrey C. Stewart

In recent years, scholars of Vietnamese studies have been using Vietnamese archival and vernacular sources to reassess our understanding of the Vietnam War. This "Vietnamese turn" in the scholarship has resulted in interpretations that go well beyond the Cold War as a root cause of the conflict to include internecine struggles between myriad Vietnamese factions— both communist and noncommunist— over what a postcolonial Vietnam should look like.[1] This chapter attempts to cast the regime of South Vietnamese President Ngo Dinh Diem in such a light.[2] It seeks neither to demonize nor exult his administration, rather it looks to comprehend it in a manner that accounts for Diem's aspirations, shortcomings and the realities he faced as a postcolonial leader in a Cold War world. Though, the South Vietnamese state that Ngo Dinh Diem ascended into power occurred within an international system governed by the geopolitical contest between the East and West; it was also a product of the French imperial project.

Roughly eighty years of French rule and a brutal war of decolonization had left southern Vietnam's agricultural sector stagnant. Once a source of economic strength, it had been exploited by a few for personal gain. Tenancy and dire inequality had become a way of life for much of the peasant class while French-owned rubber and rice monopolies diverted the profits from their Indochinese ventures to the metropole rather than invest in the colonial economy. War had added a further hardship to certain segments of the population as it disrupted livelihoods and exacerbated existing political tensions.[3]

Between 1955 and 1963, Ngo Dinh Diem's government sought to ameliorate these problems in the countryside by implementing several rural development measures including land reform, community development, land development, the Agroville Program, and the Strategic Hamlet Program. This chapter will argue that they were all part of a larger effort to fashion a politically viable and economically self-sufficient nation in the southern half of Vietnam that would be capable of pursuing its own destiny in the international realm. It will demonstrate that in order to achieve this, Diem's rural development policies attempted to exploit the two resources his state had in abundance: its land and its people.

As an agrarian society, the Vietnamese people were heavily dependent on the land which supported the livelihood of roughly eighty percent of the population.[4] Ngo Dinh Diem hoped to capitalize on this sector to revitalize South Vietnam's economy. But it was more than a simple pragmatism that motivated him. He believed the countryside had once been a sociocultural source of Vietnam's national strength. Diem was particularly enamoured by the corporate village structure that had been predominant in central Vietnam where he had grown up.[5] This network of "decentralized" and relatively autonomous rural settlements, Diem contended, had provided his people with a "moral cohesion" and "strong spiritual unity" that, for "centuries," had enabled them to avoid "destruction" by Vietnam's "more powerful neighbors."[6]

As a leader of a postcolonial state in an age where the old imperial edifice was crumbling, this national solidarity was particularly important to Diem. He was extremely wary of trading one form of imperialism for another. Though he placed his state firmly in the camp of the so-called "free world," he was determined that it would not be beholden to it. Diem wanted to avoid becoming overly dependent on foreign aid. Though necessary in the short-term, he feared undue reliance on foreign powers would sap the will of his people and lead to a devastating cycle of debt and dependency, which would jeopardize South Vietnam's newfound independence.[7] With the right motivation, Diem believed, he could "tap" the "deep roots" of the village, unify the South's disparate groups and marshal this latent energy toward the social and economic development of his country, minimizing the need for foreign assistance.[8]

To motivate the South Vietnamese people, Diem sought to propagate a revolution that would be rooted in the philosophy of Personalism (*nhan vi*).[9] This was a set of principles associated with the French Catholic thinker Emmanuel Mounier that Ngo Dinh Diem's brother, and later chief political consul, Ngo Dinh Nhu discovered while he was studying in France in the 1930s. Personalist thought took a holistic view of the person as more than just a human being. Whereas the human being was physically manifest in the corporeal body, the total person included a spiritual component. Personalism placed great emphasis on the development of the spiritual over the material to empower the individual to achieve his or her maximum potential, which could be achieved by working collectively for the common good. This had the dual benefit of providing the people with a social safety net while tightening their communal bonds.

At the same time, there was an ideological element of Personalism that appealed to the South Vietnamese leader. Emmanuel Mounier developed his philosophy during the Great Depression: a period of political uncertainty when leaders throughout the world experimented with new doctrines to organize society. Mounier was a leftist who viewed liberal capitalism as a source of the global economic crisis, but he was also a Catholic who opposed both the impersonal and atheistic aspects of communism. So, he conceived Personalism as a middle way that would balance one's commitment to social justice with one's liberal rights as a citizen. This resonated very much with Diem's own world view. As a postcolonial leader, he feared adopting the liberal-capitalist model of development promoted by the West might make his burgeoning state subject to an aid regimen that would leave it, in the words of one scholar, a "permanent mendicant" of the West.[10] At the same time, Diem was a vehement anticommunist who very much appreciated Personalism's rejection of Marxist-Leninism.[11]

This, then, was the basis of the revolutionary thought that underpinned Ngo Dinh Diem's approach to nation building. It offered "a balance between economic, social and political development" that would help to "create a society" where the entire population could enjoy "the necessary conditions to fulfill its material, cultural and spiritual needs."[12] It would establish a new polity of civic-minded citizens willing to selflessly sacrifice their own interests for the greater good of the community. This would help mobilize the grassroots for the larger task of building a self-reliant nation while also providing the peasantry with a shared sense of belonging to a state that appeared genuinely concerned with its wellbeing. Just as importantly, it could be used to counter the Marxist-Leninist revolution being promoted by his communist opponents in both the northern and southern halves of Vietnam.[13]

LAND REFORM

For Ngo Dinh Diem to realize his vision of making South Vietnam an economically viable and self-sufficient nation, he would first have to deal with the problem of land tenancy. An estimated one million farmers in South Vietnam did not own the land they farmed.[14] Rights to the land were often unprotected, leaving them vulnerable to ejection at the whim of the landlord.[15] The lot of many peasants temporarily improved during the war with the French, when landlords fled to the urban centers to avoid harassment and possible assassination at the hands of the Viet Minh, a nationalist front organization clandestinely led by the communists who were fighting against the French colonial forces and their Vietnamese supporters.[16] In some cases, rents went unpaid and the Viet Minh offered the tenants rights to the land if they won the war.[17] In other cases, the land was abandoned altogether, leaving roughly 162,000 hectares of land fallow in the Mekong Delta alone.[18] The reprieve was short-lived, however, as following the war some landlords returned, expecting to be paid the "arrears."[19]

The government attempted to tackle these problems with two ordinances issued in early 1955. Ordinance number 2, promulgated January 8, sought to protect tenant rights through written contracts outlining the tenant-landlord relationship.[20] It established a minimum lease period of five years and set maximum rates at a value of 25 percent of the value of the principle crop.[21] Ordinance 7, decreed February 7, 1955, required owners of abandoned land to declare their intentions for it.[22] They could either cultivate the land themselves or lease it to the tenant of their choice.[23]

While Ordinances 2 and 7 effectively protected the rights of the tenants, they did not contend with the tremendous disparity in land ownership—a particular problem in the Mekong Delta, where, in 1954, approximately 2.5 percent of the landowners owned nearly half of all cultivated land.[24] On October 22, 1956, the Diem government promulgated Ordinance number 57 to deal with this.[25] According to this regulation, all rice landholdings in excess of one hundred hectares were to be sold directly to the government.[26] The government, in turn, would sell the excess land in lots of three to five hectares to farmers.[27] For the landlords who had to sell their lands to the government, they were encouraged to use the bonds they received in payment to contribute to the national economy. They could be used either as legal tender to pay mortgage debts or land and inheritance taxes, or they could be exchanged for shares in specific industrial enterprises set up by the government as part of its program of national economic development, such as coal mining and cement or sugar refinement.[28]

Consistent with the social aspects of Ngo Dinh Diem's revolution, the overall objective of these measures was to create "a new category of small landowners cultivating their own lands." [29] According to David Elliott and Edward Miller, this would be the basis for a new peasant middle class of freeholding farmers that Diem envisioned in the South Vietnamese countryside.[30] This took the anti-feudal measures of Ordinances 2 and 7 to the next level by creating a large peasant base who would be beholden to no one but themselves. The land would provide a source of income and a social safety net for the family, while the crops grown could be used to contribute to the national economy. As the farmers were tilling their own land, they would theoretically have a vested interest in being as productive as possible, contributing to the overall development of South Vietnam's agrarian sector.[31]

While well-intentioned, the results of these measures were mixed. Ngo Dinh Diem was not as invested in land reform as he was other rural development programs. In terms of its tangible effects, less than half of the land surveyed was transferred and roughly one hundred thousand "farming households" actually enjoyed any benefits from the program.[32] Those who did profit from the reforms were rice farmers because the ordinances only applied to rice lands. Vast tracts of land used for other crops, like rubber, that could have been redistributed were exempt.[33] As for the intangibles, the government could claim more success. The tenant farmers benefited tremendously from the written contracts guaranteeing them tenure of land for a fixed rate and renewable term which, arguably had a psychological impact consistent with the palace's social goals of nation building. As Wolf Ladejinsky, Ngo Dinh Diem's land reform expert concluded, land reform represented "the first breach in the traditional view of landlordism as the basis of wealth, political power, and social prestige."[34] This break from Vietnam's feudal past was essential if Diem wanted to create a productive citizenry capable of contributing to the national economy— a necessary step in establishing a freeholding society of peasants.

Community Development

At the same time Ordinance 57 was being promulgated, Ngo Dinh Diem's government was in the process of developing a Five-Year Plan for Social and Economic Development.[35] This plan was designed to harness the energy of the new freeholding peasant middle class for the physical and ideational construction of Diem's nation. In many ways, it was a concrete manifestation of the Personalist Revolution. This plan attempted to forge a middle path between socialism and liberal-capitalism to exploit South Vietnam's agricultural sector for the development of the "productive capacity of the country." According to Vu Van Thai, the Director-General of Budget and Foreign Aid, it anticipated a "stage of social capitalism" where South Vietnam's land, including the redistributed land from Ordinance 57, would be used to diversify the country's agrarian output. This, in theory, would lead to a rise in both income and purchasing power that could be translated into increased demand for manufactured goods produced by small local industries. Over time, this "complementary industrialization" would be fueled by an increased labor force made available by technological advancements in agricultural production. Ideally, Vu Van Thai contended, this would allow the South Vietnamese to "accelerate" their "capital formation without passing through a phase of concentration of capital in the hands of the few."[36] Or, as Diem put it, it would enable South Vietnam to "quickly" achieve "the industrial revolution without the evil consequences" of either capitalism or communism.[37]

The concept of community development (*phat trien cong dan*) was an integral component of the Five-Year Plan.[38] This was a transnational phenomenon that swept the developing world at the midpoint of the twentieth century. It had its roots in New Deal urban renewal projects that had been transposed to India following the Second World War. Under community development, an advisor with both sociological and technical training would be sent out to a community to help it determine its most pressing needs. They then assisted the local population in coming up with the resources and means to meet those needs.[39] This concept gained considerable traction in the developing world as a way for the governments of newly formed states to reach out to the rural population and demonstrate their concern with the people's well-being, allowing them to increase their legitimacy as political institutions that ostensibly represented the popular will.[40] This was part of community development's appeal to Diem as was its reliance on local human and material resources.

The palace selected the Special Commissariat for Civic Action to oversee this effort.[41] According to its community development plan, civic action cadres underwent training in community development techniques and were then assigned to a team and sent out to a village to organize the people in various community development projects designed to improve the welfare of the community. This involved anything from erecting bridges and buildings to improving livestock production and crop diversification. The local population did the bulk of the community development work with financial and material support from the village, province, and relevant government organ where necessary. As more cadres were trained, new projects could be implemented in other districts, while those teams already in the field began to circulate to other communities once their initial project became self-sustaining, theoretically permitting all of South Vietnam's 135 districts to have their own community development projects.[42]

More than just a rural development initiative, however, the community development plan had a psychological aspect to it. Some cadres selected for community development work went to the Ministry of Information for instruction in "the theory of community development" along with "the doctrine of personalism" (*chu nghia nhan vi*) in order to "mobilize the consciousness" of the people for "community development."[43] This consciousness referred to the spirit of self-sacrifice that Diem believed was necessary to build his nation from the ground up. Land and agricultural development would be combined with revolutionary thought to mobilize the people to work collectively to make their communities self-sufficient.

Gradually, this would free up capital that would otherwise have been devoted to rural development to be directed at other more ambitious light industrialized projects such as rice milling or textile production. South Vietnam would become increasingly dependent on its own resources for its continued viability theoretically, at least, giving it greater control over its own destiny in the international arena.[44]

Land Development

While land reform and community development had been intended to make more productive use of the existing farm lands, they did not address the pressing matter of overpopulation. Urban centers like Saigon had swollen as refugees sought to escape the fighting in the countryside during the war with the French and the dictates of the communist government in the North afterward.[45] The regime believed this was a potential resource that could be used to develop South Vietnam's vast tracts of unclaimed and uncleared land for the larger benefit of the state. Using its surplus population to develop the land excited Diem to a far greater degree than land reform as it appealed directly to his romanticism of Vietnam's pioneering heritage.[46] As mentioned previously, Diem believed these earlier settler generations embodied the attributes of voluntarism, communal solidarity, and self-sufficiency that he considered the essence of a new, model South Vietnamese citizenry.

In April 1957, Saigon launched the *Dinh Dien* land development program, which aimed to satisfy several aspects of Diem's nation building effort at once.[47] Politically, the program could ease some of the overcrowding in urban areas like Saigon and the coastal plains of central Vietnam, which were home to some of the state's most impoverished subsistence farming families who had barely enough land to survive. This would alleviate their dire circumstances and theoretically engender loyalty to the state. Economically, it increased the overall productivity of the land. Unused land in the fertile plains of the southern provinces could be reclaimed for rice growing, while fresh territory could be clawed back from the dense jungle and mountainous regions of central Vietnam for cultivation. New farming techniques, fertilizer, and improved seed selection could be used to help expand South Vietnam's agricultural sector and diversify its output.[48] Strategically, the land development centers could bolster security along the countryside with pockets of loyalty in territory subject to the influence of the government's opponents: a veritable "human wall" to protect against communist infiltration from Cambodia or Laos.[49]

As for their social impact, land development centers served two very important ends. First, by providing land to the landless and increasing "individual peasant proprietorship," they furthered the aims of establishing a new peasant middle-class of freeholding farmers.[50] Second, they helped bring the ethnic population of central Vietnam's highland plateau into the body politic. The Saigon government viewed their nomadic existence and reliance on "swidden agriculture" as backward and inefficient.[51] They intended to settle much of the highland population in these centers where they could introduce them to supposedly more modern cultivation and animal husbandry techniques, as well as provide them with greater healthcare and sanitation. Not only did this allow the government to improve their standard of living, but it also made them subject to civil administration and education. This allowed the authorities to counter the threat of communist subversion while enabling the regime to gradually assimilate them to what Diem conceived to be the Vietnamese way of life. Finally, there was the ideological aspect of the land development program. By harkening back to Vietnam's pioneering past and drawing on the idea of community development, Ngo Dinh Diem believed, the new settlements could serve as incubators for his new polity.[52]

The Diem government initially established three settlements in the politically contested areas of the Mekong Delta, and it inaugurated a much larger project in the Central Highlands, which stretched across several provinces along the borders with Cambodia and Laos.[53] Each settlement contained a headquarters, storehouses, medical dispensary, maternity ward, information center, school, marketplace and, in the cases of some of the more remote settlements, a radio receiver. They also received regular visits from medical teams and mobile propaganda units, which arranged films and theatrical productions for the people.[54]

Given the potential the palace saw for the program to promote its revolutionary agenda and bring stability to the countryside, it moved forward at a relentless pace. The four initial settlements were followed by seventeen more by February 1958, and another sixty-three were created over the ensuing eighteen months.[55] Unfortunately, this led to coercion, ill-prepared settlements, and tensions between the ethnic minorities subject to assimilation and the officials sent out to relocate them. Though these were not insurmountable problems, American advisors found them quite disconcerting. The United States aid mission in Saigon had helped in the planning and implementation of the program, including an offer of $10 million of funding, which the regime accepted out of necessity. The Americans were alarmed at what they saw as poor planning and inept execution, which led to waste and the inefficient use of US funds. The matter became so acute that US-South Vietnamese relations deteriorated to the point where the US mission effectively broke with the program in 1958. It ceased offering direct financial aid and limited its involvement to some technical advice and assistance. Relations improved and the land development program went on to be seen as a moderate success.[56]

The Agroville Program

The tensions that emerged between the Diem government and the United States aid mission reflected some of the more systemic problems that hampered Ngo Dinh Diem's rural development policies. For him, as we have seen, rural development was as much about changing the relationship between the state and the society as it was rehabilitating the South Vietnamese countryside. His intention to use South Vietnam's human and material resources to fashion a self-reliant nation would require the citizenry to develop the appropriate attitude. Rather than rely only on the state for their well-being, which would be costly, particularly for a developing nation, in Diem's mind, they needed to be capable of providing for themselves. The self-help that underpinned community development and land development spoke directly to this.

The United States saw this somewhat differently. The South Vietnamese government's priority should have been to ensure the people's welfare. Instead of compelling the people toward a greater level of self-sufficiency, the Diem regime should offer aid and material support, so they could secure a better standard of living. If the South Vietnamese government proved more incapable of providing for the people than its opponents, American advisors feared the peasantry would have little reason to support it.[57]

American fears were not unfounded. Significant segments of the population remained deeply unsatisfied with the Diem government; particularly those groups it considered its opponents and those affected by the draconian measures it employed to combat them. From the earliest days of his leadership, Ngo Dinh Diem encountered individuals and groups who he perceived to be threats to his position in power. These included officials he inherited after assuming power: independent politico-religious sects like the Cao Dai and Hoa Hao; members of a Saigon-based organized crime syndicate, the Binh Xuyen; and clandestine communist agents that remained in the South to agitate on behalf of the Hanoi government following the war with the French. Diem was not opposed to clamping down on real or suspected opponents by restricting their freedom of speech, arbitrary arrest or other forms of intimidation. To contend with the Cao Dai, Hoa Hao and Binh Xuyen, Diem employed his security forces in the spring of 1955, nearly pitching the South into a civil war.[58] As for the communist "stay-behind" agents, the regime launched its denounce the communist (*To Cong*) campaign that summer to try to weed them out of the general population.

In theory, this campaign was intended to provide a forum for local communities to report subversive activity and denounce suspected communist operatives in their midst. In practice, it was often abused by corrupt officials and citizens looking to settle old scores or curry favor with the regime. Those branded as communists or even sympathetic to their cause were subject to harassment and abuse by both the regional authorities and local population, while their families were effectively ostracized by the village community.[59] In the short-term, the denunciation campaign proved to be brutally effective, neutralizing a significant proportion of the southern communist apparatus. In the longer-term, however, it had the unintended consequence of driving many non-communists who were either unjustly denounced, or friends or relatives of those who were targeted, into the enemy camp where they could join other elements of the South Vietnamese population who felt alienated by the regime's abuses like the remaining members of the Cao Dai, Hoa Hao, and Binh Xuyen.[60]

This kind of corruption was emblematic of the bureaucratic deficiencies of the Saigon government. Its malevolence toward communism, which included the endorsement of torture and "extrajudicial killings," combined with the cloistered nature of the ruling clique (where power was becoming increasingly centralized in the hands of Diem, Nhu, and a small circle of trusted officials) enabled the self-serving action of overzealous and corrupt officials.[61] All of this contributed to a rising discontent in the countryside that stood to undermine whatever noble intentions the government may have had with its rural development programs.[62] In the midst of this ferment, the government looked for new ways to promote the economic and social development of the country while keeping the people protected from the enemies of the regime. One measure, which drew on an earlier experiment with regroupment, was the Agroville Program.

During the winters of 1958 and 1959, a district chief in Phong Dinh province had experimented with two types of regroupment, or "agglomeration," centers to deal with this threat. One type was intended for families whose loyalty to the regime was suspect. The other was designed for those who were believed to be loyal to the government, but under threat because they lived in remote locations that were "inaccessible to government control." In both cases, families would be relocated to these centers where they could live under the watchful eye of the government's security apparatus.[63] Inspired, Diem sought to make this the basis of a new regroupment scheme that would bolster security and serve the developmental aims of his regime.[64] Unlike the land development program, which moved the people from densely populated areas to remote settlements where the government wished to increase its presence, the Agroville Program moved families living in insecure areas to new complexes located within a few kilometers of their homesteads. There they would be provided with a plot of land to build a home and live on as well as a host of modern amenities and social services to improve their standard of living under the watchful eye of the government's security apparatus.[65] The palace anticipated each family purchasing the plot of land they had been allotted and developing it for subsistence farming while retaining their original property to tend for their livelihood.[66]

Like the land development centers, the relocated families were supposed to be as self-reliant as possible and use the agrovilles to contribute to the overall development of the country. Experts provided training in "modern methods of agriculture," artisanal work, and small-scale manufacturing. They developed new crops to increase the diversity of the agricultural yield. Public lands were used to grow fruit trees while ponds were stocked with fish to provide added village revenue. And central markets bolstered the inhabitants' income which would then be taxable for the government.[67] At the same time, these centers served as crucibles for social development as the establishment of a residential section and the construction of its communal buildings and infrastructure occurred by the "community development principle."[68]

Unfortunately, just as with the land development centers, the importance the regime placed on agrovilles to increase the security of the countryside led it to set overly ambitious goals for the program. Ground was broken on the first complex in December 1959 and the government expected to complete eighty complexes by 1963. This created problems as ambitious officials forcibly relocated families in order to keep up with or even surpass the government's relentless pace. Unsurprisingly, this bred resentment that fed on the other indignities the people felt the program imposed on them. Many bristled at being uprooted from their existing farms to be moved into the new resettlement centers with little to no compensation from the government and then be expected to purchase a new plot of land, construct a new dwelling, and commute anywhere from one to five kilometers to farm their fields each day.[69]

The peasants' biggest grievance, however, was the seemingly forced labor that went into constructing the agrovilles. As the community development idea was central to the agrovilles' role in South Vietnam's social and economic development, the palace had lofty expectations for what its new inhabitants should be contributing. From the government's perspective, the privilege of living in these new sites should have been more than enough compensation for whatever sacrifices were asked of their inhabitants. But the size, scope, and ambition of the program ensured that establishing each agroville would be a massive undertaking, which would require far more than the supposedly "idle" time the government anticipated the peasants volunteering out of their day. To provide the necessary manpower for agroville construction, farmers found they had to forego tending crops essential to their own continued survival.[70] Rather than improve the standing of the regime in the eyes of a seemingly vulnerable peasantry, agrovilles "aroused considerable discontent."[71]

Despite these grievances, Diem held firmly to the belief that the spirit of community development would carry through and the people would come around to all of the potential benefits the agrovilles had to offer. What actually concerned him was the financial cost involved in establishing and maintaining each one. Equally troubling, as one author suggests, were the reports Diem was receiving of communist penetration of the program. When coupled with its expense, this potential breach in security called the whole endeavor into doubt in Diem's mind. After roughly one year of operation, the program was quietly shelved.[72]

THE STRATEGIC HAMLET PROGRAM

As the Agroville Program sputtered along throughout 1960, resistance to the regime increased precipitously to the point where the communists formed the National Front for the Liberation of South Vietnam (NLF) in December.[73] The rise in insurgent activity was due, in no small part, to the increasingly severe measures the regime employed against its opponents. In the spring of 1959, just as the government was experimenting with the forerunner to the Agroville Program, the regime passed Law 10/59. This measure surpassed the communist denunciation in its brutality while broadening the scope of treasonous activity from past association with any suspected communist activity to any form of political opposition. Those accused would appear before special military courts that circulated throughout the countryside and possessed the power to immediately sentence any potential offender to life imprisonment or death. Rather than merely face the kangaroo courts of the communist denunciation campaign, those who stood accused under Law 10/59 could be summarily executed on the spot.[74] Those moderate elements in the South who may have previously stood on the margins of the communist-led revolutionary movement began to draw the conclusion that their political fortunes would be better served by aligning with the militants than the government, particularly when it appeared increasingly like a police state.[75]

Under these circumstances, the insurgency faced by the regime took on a more sustained level of violence and community development began to falter. In some areas, the civic action cadres who were responsible for implementing the community development plan were forced to retreat from the villages where they were assigned during the day to the sanctity of urban centers at night to avoid harassment or assassination. In others, they were attached to security details whose mission was to "lead the people" to denounce and "exterminate the communists."[76]

Despite the increasingly reactionary nature of the regime, the palace still maintained its faith in community development. It just needed a more secure environment in which to promote it. During the autumn of 1961, the Saigon government began developing a new program to do just that.

The Strategic Hamlet Program (*Ap Chien Luoc*) was launched on April 17, 1962. While much of the early scholarship on the Strategic Hamlet Plan suggests it was indebted to the "New Villages" employed by the British in the Malayan Emergency (1948-1960), more recent work indicates that it owes far more to local South Vietnamese initiatives to separate the peasantry from the insurgents and French counterinsurgency doctrine from the First Indochina War and the war in Algeria.[77] According to the plan, each of South Vietnam's existing hamlets would be fortified by hedges, ditches, and sharpened bamboo stakes and defended by the local population in a bold effort to try to separate the insurgents from the peasantry. At the same time, the local population would be trained and armed to defend each hamlet in the event of an attack. These security measures, however, became only one part of the strategic hamlet's function. Ngo Dinh Diem saw the hamlets as the "foundation" of a new "Vietnamese society where values are reassessed according to the spirit of the personalist revolution where social, cultural and economic reform will improve the living conditions of the large working class down to the remotest village."[78] Socially, strategic hamlets were designed to establish a new breed of citizen along the lines of the hardy peasant that Diem believed had been the lifeblood of the nation prior to the arrival of the French. Making the villagers responsible for their own protection was one element of this process. Another was the Hamlet Self-Help Program. This embodied the spirit, if not tactics, of community development. The governing council of the hamlet would organize a mass meeting where members of the village community would be able to discuss their social and economic needs and then vote on what they felt was most pressing. The people would be mobilized to meet these needs with help from either the province or the US aid mission.[79]

This communal action formed the basis of the economic component of the Strategic Hamlet Program. Although this was the least developed aspect of the program due to the focus on counterinsurgency efforts, the palace envisioned village agriculture and local cottage industries that required little external support as the basis of the hamlet economy. Once the insurgents had been defeated and peace had returned to the countryside, Diem's government hoped these self-reliant communities would be able to flourish on the initiative of their rugged and enterprising inhabitants. In all, the palace had great expectations for the Strategic Hamlet Program.

The South Vietnamese government made the Strategic Hamlet Program its priority. But, like the land development and Agroville programs before, it started out at a pace that threatened to overstretch it.[80] In some cases, officials, rushing ahead to complete their hamlets, emphasized the security components of the program at the expense of the less tangible social aspects.[81] In others, hamlets were reported as secure even though they remained under NLF control.[82] Nevertheless, it appeared to be having the desired effect in the grand scheme. Within four months of the Strategic Hamlet Program's implementation, the palace could boast moderate success. In August, a foreign observer stated that the mood among the Western embassies in Saigon was one of "qualified optimism."[83] Two months later, that "guarded optimism" had become "optimism." Roughly one-third of the rural population was reported to be safely ensconced in strategic hamlets with another third expected to be secured by the end of the year.[84] The following April, an American official closely related to the program even contended that the tide might have been turned.[85]

Unfortunately, just as it appeared to some that the fortunes of the Diem government might be improving, it was struck by the Buddhist Crisis. In May, militant Buddhist leaders seized upon the repressive actions of Diem's security forces at a demonstration in Hue to launch a political campaign against what they claimed to be religious persecution. Throughout the spring and summer of 1963, the internal turmoil wrought by the activism of the Buddhists prompted Diem's American allies to endorse a coup that resulted in his assassination in November.[86] By this time, the NLF had launched a massive, coordinated campaign against the strategic hamlets that had brought about its "collapse" throughout much of the countryside.[87]

It is unclear what impact the Buddhist Crisis had on the Strategic Hamlet Program.[88] At the very least, both the violence that precipitated the Buddhist Crisis and the repressive measures the regime took to quash it must be counted. These measures included a countrywide crackdown on the pagodas where the Buddhist leadership were gathering. The regime's reprisals, though harsh, were consistent with measures it had employed against its other opponents. Just like the abuses of the communist denunciation campaign and the severity of Law 10/59, the pagoda raids would have called into question the sincerity of the humanistic ideals that lay at the heart of the Ngos' Personalist Revolution. With confidence in the government's goodwill eroding, it is hard to imagine the people risking their lives to stand behind it and defend the strategic hamlets. Unsurprisingly, Diem's successors began distancing themselves from the Strategic Hamlet Program. Construction on new hamlets was halted during the month following the coup that ended with the death of Ngo Dinh Diem. In March, they suspended the program altogether.[89]

Conclusion

From 1955 to 1963, Ngo Dinh Diem's government implemented a number of rural development programs intended to employ the land and people in a massive effort to fashion a viable and self-sufficient nation in the southern half of Vietnam. At the heart of these efforts lay a revolution which, Ngo Dinh Diem and his brother Ngo Dinh Nhu believed, would mobilize South Vietnam's peasantry to selflessly volunteer their time and effort to this ambitious undertaking. In some regards, these efforts were remarkably successful. Land reform helped to establish tenant rights, reducing the crushing grip the landlords had been able to place on the peasantry. Land development had managed to establish some relatively self-reliant communities while alleviating some of the overcrowding that had plagued South Vietnam's urban centers and lowland areas. The Strategic Hamlet Program had, temporarily at least, brought a significant portion of the countryside under the government's control and slowed the pace of the mounting insurgency. In other regards, they were failures, particularly in terms of Diem's broader goal of building a politically unified and self-reliant nation. Land reform, though it endeavored to establish a middle class of landed, peasant farmers, could never compete with the sweeping land transfers promised by the Viet Minh during the war with the French. Land development had alienated portions of the ethnic highlanders with its efforts to assimilate them to a Vietnamese way of life. The agrovilles had been particularly unpopular in what was seen as forced regroupment into settlements that took the farmers away from their livelihoods. And neither community development nor the Strategic Hamlet Program could ultimately withstand the challenges posed by the communist-led insurgency.

Laying at the root of these failures were the Ngos' assumptions about peasant attitudes toward the state. The Ngos firmly believed they were acting in the best interests of the peasants. Their nation building plans were going to completely transform South Vietnamese society for the better by establishing a nation of hardy and self-reliant citizens who would work collectively for the well-being of each other and the nation. Virtue would be its own reward. Though this may not be evident to the peasantry at the outset, the Ngos felt the benefits would become apparent in time and the people would fall in line behind the regime. Unfortunately, as the standard of living of much of the rural population was barely removed from a subsistence-level, the peasantry could ill-afford to sacrifice their own livelihoods for the betterment of the state. They complained at having to volunteer their time and labor for projects that kept them from earning a living.[90] For these peasants, Diem's vision of a postcolonial Vietnam was wholly incompatible with their interests, particularly when it was undermined by the actions of corrupt and self-serving government officials and his indiscriminate and increasingly repressive security measures.

Despite the failings of Diem's rural development policies, they offer an enlightening window through which to view his South Vietnamese regime. They suggest that rather than understand his regime as an anticommunist chess piece in the Cold War, we should consider it a postcolonial entity in its own right. Diem's rural development policies demonstrate that he had a distinct vision of a postcolonial Vietnam and some ideas about how to achieve it. This offers us alternative ways to conceive of the Vietnam War. Though it was certainly a conflict that became tied up in the global Cold War, its causes lay more in internal questions about national identity and state formation, which were the products of the French colonial experience. Ngo Dinh Diem's rural development policies posed one set of answers, but they were not the only ones. Diem's rivals offered the people of South Vietnam a vision of what they perceived to be a brighter future. As the competition increased, all sides proved willing to employ violence to make their voices heard. It was this escalating cycle of violence, rooted in these competing postcolonial visions that led to the Vietnam War.

NOTES

1. For a discussion on the "Vietnamese Turn" see Edward Miller, "The Postcolonial War: Hue-Tam Ho Tai and the 'Vietnamese Turn' in Vietnam War Studies," *Journal of Vietnamese Studies* 12(3) (Summer 2017): 14-22; and Edward Miller and Tuong Vu, "The Vietnam War as a Vietnamese War: Agency and Society in the Study of the Second Indochina War," *Journal of Vietnamese Studies* 4(3) (Fall 2009): 1-16. For a survey of the Vietnam War that is representative of the "Vietnamese Turn" see Mark Philip Bradley, *Vietnam at War* (New York: Oxford University Press, 2009).
2. In this chapter, I use South Vietnam to refer to both the Republic of Vietnam, established by Ngo Dinh Diem in October 1955, and the southern territory lying below the seventeenth parallel administered by the Saigon government following the 1954 Geneva Accords.
3. Milton C. Taylor, "South Vietnam: Lavish Aid, Limited Progress," *Pacific Affairs* 34(3) (August 1961), 243; Robert Scigliano, *South Vietnam: Nation Under Stress* (Boston, Houghton Mifflin Company, 1964), 102-107; David L. Anderson, *Trapped by Success: The Eisenhower Administration and Vietnam, 1953-1961* (New York: Columbia University Press, 1991), 140.
4. Scigliano, *Nation Under Stress*, 107.
5. Dennis J. Duncanson, *Government and Revolution in Vietnam* (New York: Oxford University Press), 313; and Philip E. Catton, *Diem's Final Failure: Prelude to America's War in Vietnam* (Lawrence, KS: University Press of Kansas, 2002), 49.
6. Presidency of the Republic of Vietnam, *Toward Better Mutual Understanding*, vol. 1, *Speeches Delivered by President Ngo Dinh Diem during his State Visits to Thailand, Australia, Korea* 2d ed. (Saigon: Presidency of the Republic of Vietnam, Press Office, 1958), 20-1.
7. Catton, *Diem's Final Failure*, 32-4.
8. Quoted in Marguerite Higgins, *Our Vietnam Nightmare: The Story of U.S. Involvement in the Vietnamese Tragedy, with Thoughts on a Future Policy* (New York: Harper & Row Publishers, 1965), 166; See also Catton, *Diem's Final Failure*, 33, 49, 209.
9. Dai Cuong ve Viet Nam [General Overview of Vietnam], June 1959, Folder 371, Phu Tong Thong De Nhat Cong Hoa [Office of the President

of the First Republic] (hereafter PTTDICH), Trung Tam Luu Tru Quoc Gia II [National Archives Number 2] (hereafter TTLTQG2).

10. Catton, *Diem's Final Failure*, 31.
11. Emmanuel Mounier, *Personalism*, translated by Philip Mairet (London: Routledge & Kegan Paul, 1952), 3-53; and John C. Donnell, "Politics in South Vietnam: Doctrines of Authority in Conflict," (PhD dissertation, University of California, Berkeley, CA, 1964), 86-7, 108, 578-83; See also Catton, *Diem's Final Failure*, 41-4; Edward Miller, *Misalliance: Ngo Dinh Diem, the United States, and the Fate of South Vietnam* (Cambridge, MA: Harvard University Press, 2013), 43-6; and Jessica M. Chapman, *Cauldron of Resistance: Ngo Dinh Diem, the United States, and 1950s Southern Vietnam* (Ithaca, NY: Cornell University Press, 2013), 121-24.
12. Our Concept of Development: An Address by The Honorable Vu Van Thai, Director-General of the Budget and Foreign Aid, October 23, 1959, Item number 1780612031, Texas Tech Virtual Vietnam Archive, www.virtualarchive.vietnam.ttu.edu (hereafter referred to as TTVVA), accessed February 2, 2007.
13. Dai Cuong ve Viet Nam [General Overview of Vietnam], June 1959, Folder 371, PTTDICH, TTLTQG2.
14. Gilbert Jonas, Agricultural and Land Development Achievements in the Republic of Vietnam since 1956, ND, Item number 0720608009, TTVVA, accessed July 24, 2017.
15. Wolf Ladejinsky, "Agrarian Reform in the Republic of Vietnam," in *Problems of Freedom: South Vietnam since Independence*, ed. Wesley R. Fishel (New York: The Free Press of Glencoe, 1961), 155.
16. The Viet Minh (*Viet Nam Doc Lap Dong Hoi Minh Hoi*, Revolutionary League for the Independence of Vietnam) was created by Ho Chi Minh during the Second World War to resist the Japanese occupation of Vietnam and continued its efforts against the French following their return in 1945. Fredrik Logevall, *Embers of War: The Fall of an Empire and the Making of America's Vietnam* (New York: Random House, 2012), 35.
17. Ladejinsky, "Agrarian Reform in the Republic of Vietnam," 157,161.
18. Scigliano, *Nation Under Stress*, 104.
19. Duncanson, *Government and Revolution in Vietnam*, 245.
20. English Translation of Basic Vietnamese Land Tenure Legislation, September 30, 1960, Item number 2390211003, TTVVA, accessed July 24, 2017.
21. Ibid. In addition, Ordinance 2 fixed interest rates for loans for seeds and fertilizer at the cost of the supplies plus a 12 percent interest rate per

annum. It also provided greater protection to the tenants by removing any obligation to pay the rent in the event of a major crop failure and laying out specific conditions under which the landlord could terminate the lease or cancel its renewal, such as providing proof that he intended to cultivate the land himself or nonpayment of rent by the tenant.

22. Ibid.
23. If they chose the latter option, they were obligated to sign a three-year contract where the tenant paid no rent the first year, no more that 50 percent of the rent the second year, and a maximum of 75 percent of the rent in the third year. After that they had to provide the tenant with a five-year lease. Tenant selection would occur on a priority basis where existing tenants farming the land would be offered a contract first followed by refugees, relatives of deceased combatants, veterans, and the poor. Secretariat of State for Land Property and Land Reform, Land Reform Program Before 1954, and Land Reform Programs and Achievements since July 1954, July 21, 1959, Item number 1780614025, TTVVA, accessed July 24, 2017.
24. Conversely, more than 70 percent of the people held title to roughly 12.5 percent of the cultivated land. Ladejinsky, "Agrarian Reform in the Republic of Vietnam," 155.
25. English Translation of Basic Vietnamese Land Tenure Legislation, September 30, 1960, Item number 2390211003, TTVVA, accessed July 24, 2017.
26. The landlords were permitted to retain an additional thirty hectares of land, provided they cultivated it with paid labor, as well as fifteen hectares for ancestor worship if it was the site of the ancestral tombs. Ibid.; and Ladejinsky, "Agrarian Reform in the Republic of Vietnam," 166.
27. In purchasing the land, the government would pay the landowner 10 percent of the cost of the land in cash and the remainder in twelve-year government bonds, which yielded 3 percent annually in interest. The peasants who purchased the land from the government would pay for the land over six annual installments, interest-free. Additionally, the new landowners were forbidden to sell, lease, or mortgage their land for a minimum of ten years after purchase. English Translation of Basic Vietnamese Land Tenure Legislation, September 30, 1960, Item number 2390211003, TTVVA, accessed July 24, 2017; Secretariat of State for Land Property and Land Reform, Land Reform Program Before 1954, and Land Reform Programs and Achievements since July 1954, July 21, 1959, Item

number 1780614025, TTVVA, accessed July 24, 2017; and Ladejinsky, "Agrarian Reform in the Republic of Vietnam," 166.

28. Secretariat of State for Land Property and Land Reform, Land Reform Program Before 1954, and Land Reform Programs and Achievements since July 1954, July 21, 1959, Item number 1780614025, TTVVA, accessed July 24, 2017; and Ladejinsky, "Agrarian Reform in the Republic of Vietnam," 166.
29. Secretariat of State for Land Property and Land Reform, Land Reform Program Before 1954, and Land Reform Programs and Achievements since July 1954, July 21, 1959, Item number 1780614025, TTVVA, accessed July 24, 2017.
30. David Elliott, *The Vietnamese War: Revolution and Social Change in the Mekong Delta, 1930-1975*, vol. 1 (Armonk, NY: M.E. Sharp, 2003), 166, 180; and Miller, *Misalliance*, 160-61.
31. Dai Cuong ve Viet Nam [General Overview of Vietnam], June 1959, Folder 371, PTTDICH, TTLTQG2.
32. Miller, *Misalliance*, 159.
33. Ladejinsky, "Agrarian Reform in the Republic of Vietnam," 169.
34. Ibid., 162.
35. Airgram from USOM/Saigon to ICA/W, April 15, 1957, Subject Files 1954-1958 (hereafter referred to as SF 54-58), Box 2, Record Group 469 (hereafter RG 469), National Archives and Records Administration (hereafter referred to as NARA).
36. Our Concept of Development: An Address by The Honorable Vu Van Thai, Director-General of the Budget and Foreign Aid, October 23, 1959, Item number 1780612031, TTVVA, accessed February 2, 2007. See also Dai Cuong ve Viet Nam [General Overview of Vietnam], June 1959, Folder 371, PTTDICH, TTLTQG2.
37. Quoted in Donnell, "Politics in South Vietnam", 113.
38. Airgram from USOM/Saigon to ICA/W, April 15, 1957, SF 54-58, Box 2, RG 469, NARA.
39. Daniel Immerwahr, *Thinking Small: The United States and the Lure of Community Development* (Cambridge, MA: Harvard University Press, 2015), 66-85. See also Nick Cullather, *The Hungry World: America's Cold War Battle Against Poverty in Asia* (Cambridge, MA: Harvard University Press, 2010), 76-94
40. Francis X. Sutton, "Nation-Building in the Heyday of the Classic Development Ideology: Ford Foundation Experiences in the 1950s and 1960s,"

in *Nation-Building: Beyond Afghanistan and Iraq*, ed. Francis Fukuyama (Baltimore: The Johns Hopkins University Press, 2006), 53-4.

41. For a more extensive discussion of the Special Commissariat for Civic Action and community development in South Vietnam see Geoffrey C. Stewart, *Vietnam's Lost Revolution: Ngo Dinh Diem's Failure to Build an Independent Nation, 1955-1963* (New York: Cambridge University Press, 2017), especially 88-161.
42. Ibid., 145-152.
43. For details about the cadres being sent to the Ministry of Information and the two quotes regarding "the theory of community development" and the "doctrine of personalism" see Ban Tom Luoc ve Van De tai Phien Hop Hoi Dong Noi 4.8.1958 [Summary of Issues from August 4, 1958 Meeting], August 6, 1958, Folder 1725, PTTDICH, TTLTQ2. See also Phieu Trinh ve Viec Phan Boi Can Bo Cong Dan Vu [Report on the Distribution of Civic Action Cadres], ND, Folder 16921, PTTDICH, TTLTQ2. The quotes regarding mobilizing the people's "consciousness" for community development comes from Chuong Trinh Hoat Dong Phu Dac Uy Cong Dan Vu nam 1958 [Program of Action for the Commissariat for Civic Action in 1958], March 3, 1958, Folder 16560, PTTDICH, TTLTQG2.
44. Chi Thi [Instructions] Draft, April 1958, Folder 16560; and Dai Cuong ve Viet Nam [General Overview of Vietnam], June 1959, Folder 371, PTTĐICH, TTLTQG2.
45. One of the provisions of the 1954 Geneva Accords, which ended the war with the French, allowed Vietnamese civilians to choose under which government they wanted to live: Ho Chi Minh's communist government in the North or Ngo Dinh Diem's government in the South. They initially had three hundred days to relocate if they desired. Nearly one million refugees left the North to live under Ngo Dinh Diem's government. Agreement on the Cessation of Hostilities in Vietnam, July 20, 1954, *Foreign Relations of the United States, 1952-1954* Vol XVI, *The Geneva Conference* (hereafter *FRUS*) (Washington, DC: US Government Printing Office, 1981), 1505-20; and Miller, *Misalliance*, 161.
46. Catton, *Diem's Final Failure*, 56-7; and Miller, *Misalliance*, 161-62.
47. *Dinh Dien* was the Vietnamese name of the program. It means "to nourish ricefields." Miller, *Misalliance*, 171.
48. This was particularly appealing as diversification of crops with industrial applications, such as rubber and jute, would help facilitate import substitution, thereby promoting South Vietnam's economic independence. William Henderson, "Opening of New Lands and Villages: The Republic

of Vietnam Land Development Program," in *Problems of Freedom*, 133; and Miller, *Misalliance*, 163.

49. Henderson, "Opening of New Lands and Villages," 123-25.
50. Ibid., 124
51. "Swidden" refers to practices of raising crops on tracts of land cleared by controlled fire. Miller, *Misalliance*, 173.
52. Gilbert Jonas, Agricultural and Land Development Achievements in the Republic of Vietnam since 1956, ND, Item number 0720608009; Commissariat General for Land Development, Activities Performed by the Commissariat General for Land Development, ND, Item Number 0720608001, TTVVA, accessed July 24, 2017; Henderson, "Opening of New Lands and Villages," 123-5; Catton, *Diem's Final Failure*, 57-60; and Miller, *Misalliance*, 171-73.
53. Miller, *Misalliance*, 171. See also Henderson, "Opening of New Lands and Villages," 123-24.
54. Commissariat General for Land Development, Activities Performed by the Commissariat General for Land Development, ND, Item Number 0720608001, TTVVA, accessed July 24, 2017; Henderson, "Opening of New Lands and Villages," 132.
55. Miller, *Misalliance*, 172, and Henderson, "Opening of New Lands and Villages," 130.
56. Henderson, "Opening of New Lands and Villages," 127; Catton, *Diem's Final Failure*, 60-3, 71; and Miller, *Misalliance*, 173-77.
57. Miller, *Misalliance*, 164-65.
58. Chapman, *Cauldron of Resistance*, 72-115; Miller, *Misalliance*, 95-123; and Anderson, *Trapped by Success*, 77-119.
59. Elliott, *The Vietnamese War*, 189.
60. Jeffrey Race, *War Comes to Long An: Revolutionary Conflict in a Vietnamese Province* (Berkeley, CA: University of California Press, 1972), 19; Chapman, *Cauldron of Resistance*, 119-121; Miller, *Misalliance*, 132-33; Neil Sheehan, *A Bright Shining Lie: John Paul Vann and America in Vietnam* (New York: Random House, 1988), 186-193; Anderson, *Trapped by Success*, 166; and Robert K. Brigham, *Guerrilla Diplomacy: The NLF's Foreign Relations and the Vietnam War* (Ithaca, NY: Cornell University Press, 1999), 9; and George McT. Kahin, *Intervention: How America Became Involved in Vietnam* (New York: Alfred A. Knopf, 1986), 96.
61. See Miller, *Misalliance*, 197-201 for a discussion of the malevolence of the Diem regime; and Duncanson, *Government and Revolution in Vietnam*, 228-9 for mention of its cloistered nature.

62. Catton, *Diem's Final Failure*, 64-65; Chapman, *Cauldron of Resistance*, 173-188; Nu-Anh Tran, "Contested Identities: Nationalism in the Republic of Vietnam (1954-1963)," Ph.D. diss. (University of California, Berkeley, CA, 2013), 74-7.
63. Joseph J. Zasloff, *Rural Resettlement in Vietnam: An Agroville in Development* (Washington, DC: Department of State, Agency for International Development, 1963), 6.
64. Some earlier literature attributes the Agroville Program to French efforts to separate the peasants from the Viet Minh insurgents; see, for example, David Halberstam, *The Making of a Quagmire* (New York: Random House, 1964), 184; and Robert Shaplen, *The Lost Revolution: The Story of Twenty Years of Neglected Opportunities in Vietnam and of America's Failure to Foster Democracy There* (New York: Harper & Row, Publishers, 1965), 142-43. Recent work demonstrates, however, that Diem was far more inspired by the efforts of the Phong Dinh province chief than any previous French program. These new settlements were referred to as "dense and prosperous areas" (*khu tru mat*). The term "agroville" originated with some Vietnamese officials who referred to the centers as "agricultural towns" and then "agrovilles." Miller, *Misalliance*, 178-180.
65. These included a hospital or dispensary, a school, a centralized market, shops, hotels, and electricity— a novelty experienced by many of the new inhabitants for the first time. Zasloff, *An Agroville in Development*, 1; Memorandum from Wesley R. Fishel to Senator Mike Mansfield, November 12, 1960, Item number 6-20-1907-116-UA2-1-12_000114, TTVVA, accessed September 22, 2017; and Miller, *Misalliance*, 180.
66. Zasloff, *An Agroville in Development*, 15-17. See also Memorandum from Wesley R. Fishel to Senator Mike Mansfield, November 12, 1960, Item number 6-20-1907-116-UA2-1-12_000114, TTVVA, accessed September 22, 2017.
67. Zasloff, *An Agroville in Development*, 10.
68. Ibid., 16.
69. Ibid., 9, 24-5; Memorandum from Wesley R. Fishel to Senator Mike Mansfield, November 12, 1960, Item number 6-20-1907-116-UA2-1-12_000114, TTVVA, accessed September 22, 2017; and Miller, 181.
70. Zasloff, *An Agroville in Development*, 18-19; Catton, *Diem's Final Failure*, 68; and Miller, *Misalliance*, 181-82.
71. Memorandum from Wesley R. Fishel to Senator Mike Mansfield, November 12, 1960, Item number 6-20-1907-116-UA2-1-12_000114, TTVVA, accessed September 22, 2017.

72. Miller, *Misalliance*, 183-84.
73. The National Front for the Liberation of Vietnam was established in Tay Ninh province. Though a front organization intended to unite all southern opponents of the Diem government, like the Viet Minh, it was organized by the southern communists to advance their political agenda. Brigham, *Guerrilla Diplomacy*, 9-11; William Duiker, *Ho Chi Minh: A Life* (New York: Theia, 2000), 523-27.
74. For a copy of Law 10/59 see Appendix A in Luther Allen and Pham Ngoc An, *A Vietnamese District Chief in Action* (Washington, DC: Department of State, Agency for International Development, 1963), 69-71. See also Kahin, *Intervention*, 97-8 and Duiker, *Ho Chi Minh*, 518.
75. Elliott, *The Vietnamese War*, 196-97; and David Hunt, *Vietnam's Southern Revolution: From Peasant Insurrection to Total War* (Amherst, MA: University of Massachusetts Press, 2008), 34.
76. Bao Cao Thang 4 nam 1960 [April 1960 Report], May 18, 1960, Folder 17180 PTTDICH, TTLTQ2. For a discussion of the increasing violence in the countryside and its impact on community development see Stewart, *Vietnam's Lost Revolution*, 175-91.
77. Edward Miller has demonstrated that while the Ngos used the Malayan Emergency as "a useful source of ideas and support," Ngo Dinh Nhu appeared to have been far more inspired by the French counterinsurgency expert Roger Trinquier, who had developed his own theories on local population control from his experiences in the First Indochina War and Algeria including the concept of *hameaux stratégiques* (strategic hamlets). Miller, *Misalliance*, 232-33. See page 238 for a discussion of local South Vietnamese efforts to deal with the insurgents.
78. Quoted in Milton Osborne, *Strategic Hamlets in South Vietnam: A Survey and a Comparison* (Ithaca, NY: Cornell University Southeast Asia Program), 28.
79. A Report on Counter-Insurgency in Vietnam, August 31, 1962, General, 1961-63 (2), Subject File: Vietnam, Box 49, Edward G. Lansdale Papers (hereafter ELP), Hoover Institute (hereafter HI); and Bert Fraleigh, "Counterinsurgency in Vietnam: The Real Story," in *Prelude to Tragedy: Vietnam, 1960-1965*, eds. Harvey Neese and John O'Donnell (Annapolis, MD: Naval Institute Press, 2001), 103.
80. Catton, *Diem's Final Failure*, 133-34.
81. John B. O'Donnell, "The Strategic Hamlet Program in Kien Hoa Province: A Case Study of Counter-Insurgency," in *Southeast Asian Tribes, Minori-*

ties and Nations, ed. Peter Kunstadter (Princeton, NJ: Princeton University Press, 1967), 720.

82. Memorandum from Assistant Director for Rural Affairs of the United States Operations Mission (Phillips) to the Director of the United States Operations Mission in Vietnam (Killen), September 7, 1964, Box 34, Charles T.R. Bohannan Papers (hereafter CBP); and Some Comments on the Counterinsurgency Program of Vietnam and USOM, March 1964, Counterinsurgency, Box 46, ELP, HI and Colby, *Lost Victory*, 101-2.
83. Memorandum from Canadian Delegation ICSC, Saigon to the Under-Secretary of State for External Affairs, Ottawa, August 14, 1962, Folder 50052-A-1-40 pt 3, Box 4639, RG25, LAC.
84. Memorandum from Canadian Delegation ICSC, Saigon to the Under-Secretary of State for External Affairs, Ottawa (part 1), October 19, 1962, Folder 50052-A-1-40 pt 3, Box 4639, RG25, LAC.
85. Miller, *Misalliance*, 245.
86. For a detailed account of the Buddhist Crisis and its impact on US-South Vietnamese relations see ibid., 260-318; and Edward Miller, "Religious Revival and the Politics of Nation Building: Reinterpreting the 1963 'Buddhist Crisis' in South Vietnam," *Modern Asian Studies* 49(6) (November 2015): 1903-1962.
87. Memorandum from Assistant Director for Rural Affairs of the United States Operations Mission (Phillips) to the Director of the United States Operations Mission in Vietnam (Killen), September 7, 1964, Box 34, CBP, HI; and Catton, *Diem's Final Failure*, 192.
88. The NLF decision to strike at the Strategic Hamlet Program was made independent of the Buddhist's actions. Both the southern insurgents and the politburo in Hanoi were as surprised by the eruption of the Buddhist Crisis as the Ngos. It was not until well into the crisis that the insurgents attempted to capitalize in the regime's difficulties. NLF Document, June 29, 1963, VC Docs 1962-1963, Box 5, CBP, HI; Douglas Pike, *Viet Cong: The Organization and Techniques of the National Liberation Front of South Vietnam* (Cambridge, MA: The M.I.T. Press, 1966), 352-353; and Catton, *Diem's Final Failure*, 205.
89. Telegram from the Central Intelligence Agency Station in Saigon to the Agency, November 5, 1963, General 11/3/63-11/5/63 CIA Reports, Countries: Vietnam, Box 20; Telegram from the Embassy in Vietnam to the Department of State (2), November 9, 1963; and Telegram from the Embassy in Vietnam to the Department of State, November 12, 1963, General 11/6/63-11/15/63 State Cables, Countries: Vietnam, Box 202,

National Security Files, John F. Kennedy Library; and Osborne, *Strategic Hamlets in South Vietnam*, 40.

90. In addition to the agroville example mentioned earlier in the chapter, there are numerous other instances of this grievance in the American and Vietnamese documentary record. John Heble, the American Consul in Hue, reported that the "villagers in Central Vietnam can see no advantage in the strategic hamlet program and they complain because work on the hamlets takes them away from their fields." Memorandum from Robert H. Johnson of the Policy Planning Staff to the Counselor of the Department of State (Rostow), October 16, 1962, *FRUS 1961-1963,* vol. 2, *Vietnam* (Washington, D.C.: United States Government Printing Office, 1990), 704. Prior to this, the civic action cadres encountered similar resistance when they were attempting to mobilize villagers to participate in community development-type tasks designed to improve their welfare. Tinh Tuong Baria Kinh goi Ngai Bo Truong tai Phu Tong Thong [Memorandum from the Province Chief of Baria to the Secretary of State for the President in the Office of the President], August 29, 1956, Folder 16065; and To Trinh ve Dai Hoi Cong Dan Vu [Report on the Civic Action Conference], January 11, 1958, Folder 16297, PTTDICH, TTLTQ2.

Beyond the Peace Accords

Legacies of America's Secret War in Laos

Nengher N. Vang

In early September 2016, Barack Obama became the first American president to visit Laos for a summit of Southeast Asian nations. The president's four-day visit brought attention to one of the dark legacies of the Vietnam War: the vast quantities of unexploded ordnance left by American bombing raids in Laos during the war, which have killed or injured at least 20,000 Laotian people since 1975. According to Legacies of War, an organization based in Washington, D.C., which raises awareness and advocates for the clean-up of the bombs in Laos, the United States dropped more than two million tons of ordnance on the country from 1964 to 1973.[1] By the time the bombing had stopped, as President Obama acknowledged, the United States dropped more bombs on Laos than it did on Germany and Japan combined during all of World War II, making "Laos, per person, the most heavily bombed country in history."[2] About

30 percent of those bombs did not explode, leaving an estimated eighty million unexploded, baseball-sized cluster bombs across the countryside. To help Laotians heal, the president pledged a dramatic increase in funding for bomb-clearing from the $20 million total over the past twenty years to $90 million for the next three years ($19.5 million alone for 2017, a significant increase from the $2.5 million allotment a decade ago).[3]

This dark chapter of America's secret war in Laos has been widely documented by scholars and non-scholars alike. Another legacy of this war that scholars often highlight is the emigration of more than 250,000 refugees from Laos to the United States after the Vietnam War.[4] Scant attention, however, has been given to any of the other legacies. Indeed, most accounts of this war have focused mainly on the origins of American involvement and events leading up to the communist takeover of Laos in 1975.[5] Until recently, only a few studies have begun to explore the meaning, impact, and consequences of this war for those involved, including the Hmong, the United States, and Laos.[6] As such, we are left with the impression that the Vietnam War and, thus, America's secret war in Laos, ended more than forty years ago. For the United States, its involvement ended officially with the peace agreements in 1973 and, practically, when the last American departed the country in 1975.

America's secret war in Laos, however, did not end in 1975. Instead, it eclipsed into another secret war in Laos between the Lao PDR government and remnants of America's Hmong secret army from the 1960s. It also set in motion more than forty years of Hmong diasporic involvement in this new secret war. Lastly, it led to a long, persistent, but ultimately contradictory relationship between the United States and the Hmong throughout the last half-century. In the end, America's secret war in Laos transformed not only the Hmong, their community, and their relationships with Laos, but also the United States, Thailand, and to a certain extent, Vietnam, China, and others; it shows that wars do not end with the signing of peace accords. Their effects continue to be felt long after they are officially declared to be "over."

America's Secret War in Laos

Until the end of World War II, American interest in Indochina was minimal. For American diplomats and entrepreneurs alike, the region held little promise.[7] President Franklin D. Roosevelt did not feel the Vietnamese were ready for self-governance at the end of World War II. Rather than support Vietnam's independence, FDR recommended that the Vietnamese come under the tutelage of an international trusteeship.[8] The rise of global communism and its infiltration of Southeast Asia, however, changed the mindset of the Americans about the region. France's defeat only hastened their desire to do something about it. Unable to send troops to Laos because of the 1954 Geneva Accords, the United States created a Program Evaluation Office (PEO) in the country in 1955. On the surface, the PEO was a humanitarian mission; in reality, it was a military operation. The United States had staffed the PEO entirely with retired military officers and officers temporarily placed on reserve status. These officers, shortly after the PEO was established, began secretly training men from the Lao police and the Royal Lao Army, including the Hmong, to promote a strong anti-communist government in the country.[9]

Things backfired in August 1960 when Captain Kong Le, a young paratrooper from southern Laos who acted largely in response to American interference in Laotian politics, launched a successful coup d'état of Vientiane and installed the neutralist Souvanna Phouma as Prime Minister. In late 1960, backed by the United States and Thailand, right-wing forces loyal to Prince Boun Oum Na Champassak and General Phoumi Nosavan successfully regained control, driving Kong Le's forces to northern Laos, where they later joined the communist Pathet Lao.[10] By early 1961, both outgoing President Dwight D. Eisenhower and incoming President John F. Kennedy were convinced that Laos was the key to Southeast Asia, and that if it were lost to the communists, the whole region would be lost.[11] However, not only would direct American military interventions in Laos be "logistically difficult and extremely expensive," it would also be an overt violation of the 1954 Geneva Accords. More importantly, Kennedy worried that such interventions might also "provoke the Chinese, as it had in Korea, or worse, unleash war with the Soviet Union."[12] In order to circumvent the 1954 agreement, avoid potential collision with China and the Soviet Union in Indochina, and still promote a strong anticommunist agenda in Laos with the least possible expenditure, Kennedy ordered American personnel in Laos and Thailand to seek out the Hmong.

Other Americans had met the Hmong before, but in January of 1961, an encounter in the mountains of Xieng Khouang Province between Colonel Vang Pao of the RLA and a soft-spoken, thirty-five-year-old Central Intelligence Agency (CIA) agent from Texas named James William Lair solidified the relationship between the two factions.[13] For over a decade following this historic meeting, the CIA worked closely with large numbers of Hmong as well as other ethnic groups who served as America's front-line force in Laos. Hmong served in both the regular RLA and the Special Guerilla Units (SGUs), the paramilitary units authorized by the RLA but directly supported by the CIA. Some Hmong became pilots and flew on air strike missions. Others were spies and radio operators gathering critical intelligence on the movement of Pathet Lao and North Vietnamese troops. As America's foot soldiers, countless Hmong lost their lives trying to rescue downed American pilots.[14] As the war in Laos dragged on and American involvement in the wider war in Southeast Asia escalated, the SGU forces grew, many of which were organized along ethnic lines.[15] In 1964, 30,000 men, mostly Hmong, were under Vang Pao's command.[16] By 1969, Vang Pao's troop strength had grown to 40,000 men.[17] Overall, over 60 percent of the Hmong in Laos had family members fighting for the Americans.

For their alliance with the United States, the Hmong suffered incredible losses. In March 1963, Edgar "Pop" Buell, a former farmer from Indiana in charge of United States Agency for International Development (USAID) operations in Hmong areas in northern Laos, reported:

> Vang Pao has lost at least a thousand men since January 1, killed alone, and I don't know how many more wounded. He's lost all

> but one of his commanders... A short time ago we rounded up three hundred fresh recruits. Thirty percent were fourteen years old or less, and ten of them were only ten years old. Another 30 percent were fifteen or sixteen. The remaining 40 percent were thirty-five or over. Where were the ones between? I'll tell you – they're all dead... and in a few weeks 90 percent of (the new recruits) will be dead.[18]

Image 1. Vang Pao and his CIA-backed secret army in Laos

Source: Special Collections, Center for Hmong Studies, Concordia University, St. Paul, Minnesota.

By one account, 25 percent of the Hmong who enlisted were killed.[19] By the time the Communists took over Laos, 30,000, representing 10 percent of the entire Hmong population of approximately 300,000 in Laos, were dead.[20] In his 1974 *National Geographic* article, W.E. Garrett, who arrived in Laos in 1973 to gather information for his story, compared the decimation of Hmong in the war to a "holocaust that wiped out 18,000,000 [Americans] and forced the remainder of the population to flee to Mexico."[21]

Despite their sacrifice, however, throughout much of the war, the American public knew very little about the Hmong and their role in American efforts in Laos. Senior officials in Washington had kept the U.S. militarization of the Hmong and other ethnic groups in Laos secret, which Secretary of State Henry Kissinger believed had helped to prevent North Vietnam from overpowering Laos.[22] America's clandestine operation in Laos became public knowledge only after *Time* and *Life* correspondent Timothy Allman and a French reporter made an authorized visit to Long Cheng, where Vang Pao's military headquarters was located, and exposed it in early March 1970.[23]

In the end, despite the heavy bombings and secret operations by the Americans, Laos was lost to communism. By the time President Richard M. Nixon took office in January 1969, many Americans had become weary with the war in Vietnam and questioned the morality, purpose, and prospect of American presence in the region, especially after the Tet Offensive in early 1968. Determined to end the war but convinced that a precipitous withdrawal of American troops would harm South Vietnam's prospect for survival as well as American global prestige and credibility, Nixon opted for Vietnamization. Meanwhile, Nixon's special assistant for national security affairs, Henry A. Kissinger, had been secretly negotiating with Le Duc Tho, his North Vietnamese counterpart. Their negotiations later led to the peace agreement that the United States, North Vietnam, South Vietnam, and the Viet Cong signed in Paris on January 27, 1973, which ended American involvement. A month later, the communist Pathet Lao and the Laotian government, which the United States had been supporting, also reached an agreement to end the war in Laos.[24] Shortly after the Vientiane agreement was signed on February 21, 1973, the United States withdrew all funding to the Royal Lao Government and its army, of which the SGU was a subset, and left the region, leaving its allies, both Hmong and those from other ethnic groups, entirely on their own to defend themselves. Without the aid of the Americans, the Hmong were ultimately defeated despite the gallant effort of officers, such as General Vang Pao and other soldiers, to hold off the communists.[25] On May 14, 1975, one day before the communists gained full control of Laos, the United States made its final evacuation of its military personnel from Laos. Only a few planes were flown in, and they were there largely to rescue the Americans, Vang Pao, his top military advisors and officers, and their families.[26] Of the tens of thousands of Hmong who flooded Long Cheng airbase in fear of communist retaliation, only 2,500 were airlifted out. Many Hmong in nearby areas did not even know their leaders were being evacuated out of Long Cheng until the operation was over. As Capt. Jack Knotts, the Bird Air and former Air America helicopter pilot who flew Vang Pao and Jerry Daniels, a key CIA military advisor to Vang Pao during the war, out of Long Cheng, testified: "The evacuation was solely as a cover to get Vang Pao and Jerry safely out of Long Tieng [Cheng], and there was no intention of taking thousands and thousands of Hmong out of Laos."[27] The remaining Hmong had to return to their home villages and try to make peace with the communists.

The Second Secret War in Laos

For Americans, the Vietnam War was over in 1975. So was America's secret war in Laos. Conflict in Laos, however, did not end with the Paris Peace Accords in January 1973. Nor did it end with the Vientiane Agreement in February 1973 or the communist takeover of Laos on May 15, 1975. Instead, America's secret war became the precursor to a second secret war in Laos. Like its predecessor, this new war involved multiple parties, including Hmong, the United States, and Laos, among others like Vietnam, Thailand, and China.[28]

Many factors contributed to the outbreak of this new war, but the underlying reason centered on the policies and actions of the Pathet

Lao. Once in power, it could have promoted the full integration of the Lao people into the new Lao state and society. Instead, the Pathet Lao was determined to purify Laos of all vestiges of Western imperialism and eliminate all potential threats to the new regime. Accordingly, not only did it force all foreigners to leave Laos immediately, the Pathet Lao also pursued "American collaborators" for elimination. Because America's secret army of Hmong guerillas was the greatest obstacle to communist victory during the war, Vang Pao supporters became the Pathet Lao's primary target for retaliation. Indeed, on May 9, 1975, six days before it took full control of Laos, the Pathet Lao declared in the *Khaosan Pathet Lao* newspaper: "We must eradicate the Meo [the pejorative name for Hmong] minority completely."[29] Hmong fears of retaliation against their people were confirmed when Pathet Lao soldiers opened fire on a crowd of 40,000 Hmong men, women, and children as they marched peacefully toward Vientiane to seek protection from Prince Souvan Phouma, President of the National Coalition Government formed by the 1973 peace treaty. Hmong scholar Yang Dao estimated that the massacre killed between 120 and 140 people. Speaking of the fate of the Hmong, Prince Souvana Phouma said, "The Meo have served me well. It is unfortunate that the price of peace in Laos is their disappearance."[30]

After this massacre, thousands of Hmong found life under communist rule too risky and decided to follow Vang Pao to Thailand. As one Hmong later told Thai photographer Anant Chompeun, who witnessed Pathet Lao soldiers herding the surviving Hmong at gunpoint back to the hills, "I want to stay with my father Vang Pao."[31] By the end of May 1975, some 25,000 Hmong had fled to Thailand.[32] From Thailand, Hmong refugees were then dispersed across the globe. The majority chose to go to America, where Vang Pao had gone, but many Hmong refugees were also accepted and resettled in other countries, including France, French Guiana, Australia, Canada, Germany, and Argentina. More than 130,000 Hmong immigrated to America alone between 1975 and 1996.[33] Meanwhile, nearly 60,000 Hmong loyal to Vang Pao took refuge in Phou

Bia, the highest mountain in Laos. There they waited and hoped for the political situation in the war-torn nation to stabilize.[34]

That hope, however, was wrecked by the Pathet Lao. According to Yang Dao, in October 1975, to pacify anti-communist Hmong and bring them under communist control, the Pathet Lao sent a cadre of soldiers to round up the Hmong in Pha Ngou, a village located in the mountain range of Phou Bia. Upon seeing the Pathet Lao soldiers, a group of startled Hmong farmers ran in different directions. The soldiers opened fire, killing several individuals and wounding several others. Exasperated by this shooting, several hundred Hmong came down from Phou Bia and retaliated against Pathet Lao soldiers by attacking them in their posts in Mouang Cha.[35] This attack, thus, became the start of what I contend is the Second Secret War in Laos: one that continued to mobilize Hmong in the diaspora for intervention and forever transformed the relationship among the Hmong, Laos, and the United States.

Forty Years of Resistance and Hmong-U.S. Relations after 1975

Between 1975 and 1979, the second secret war in Laos was chiefly an intrastate conflict. It was fought primarily between the Lao People's Army (LPA), the armed forces of the Lao PDR government, and remnants of the CIA and Vang Pao's secret army in Phou Bia and adjacent areas. Those Hmong fighting the LPA during this period were divided into two groups. One group, called *Chao Fa*,[36] was led by Pa Kao Her and Zong Zoua Her. Sai Soua Yang, a former Hmong *tasseng* from Xieng Khouang province, led the other group. Initially, these groups used leftover arms from the previous war to temporarily take control of Hmong-populated areas, especially areas near the Phou Bia massif south of the Plain of Jars. Though a noble effort, they were no match for what lay ahead. In the summer of 1977, Laos signed a twenty-five-year special friendship treaty with the Socialist Republic of Vietnam. This agreement introduced tens of thousands of Vietnamese troops to Laos to help quell the resistance.

According to Hmong who later escaped to Thailand, following this agreement, Laos also used lethal Soviet-engineered chemical weapons against those Hmong resisting government control in the country.[37] Survivors dubiously referred to the weapon as "Yellow Rain" because it resembled "an oily yellow liquid with a relatively large droplet size that made a sound like rain when it struck the ground, vegetation, and the roofs of houses."[38]

By late 1978, the Hmong resistance in Laos was in disarray, forcing some 8,000, mostly from Phou Bia, to flee to Thailand that year. In 1979, 24,000 Hmong, including Pa Kao Her, crossed the border to Thailand, followed by an additional 15,000 in 1980.[39] In May 1980, Sai Soua Yang also gave up and fled to Thailand. "We tried our best, but there was nothing we could do without outside help," Yang later told journalist and historian Stanley Karnow in Thailand's Ban Vinai refugee camp.[40] In October 1980, Quan Doin Nhan Dan, an official of the People's Army of Vietnam, proudly pronounced the victory of the communists: "After three years of struggle to crush the Hmong pirates, the soldiers of the Lao Liberation Army have penetrated the last strongholds of the Phou Bia pirates. Fifteen thousand inhabitants of the region have been liberated."[41]

Despite Dan's announcement, however, the second secret war in Laos had not ended. In fact, by this point, it had ballooned into an international and transnational conflict. Anti-communist Hmong inside Laos and the LPA were no longer the only participants. By the early 1980s, both General Vang Pao and Pa Kao Her had reorganized the Hmong in the United States and Thailand, respectively, to provide support for the anti-communist resistance in Laos. Other countries, including Thailand, Vietnam, China, the United States, and, to a certain extent, the Soviet Union, also became direct or indirect participants in the war because of the Cold War scramble for control over the region that occurred after the end of the Vietnam War.

In 1980, after escaping to Thailand, Pa Kao Her founded the Ethnic Liberation of Laos (ELOL) near the Thai-Lao border in northeast Thailand.

Documents that Pa Kao Her prepared for the Democratic Chao Fa Party of Laos, which replaced the ELOL in the 1990s, indicate that Pa Kao Her's *Chao Fa* group wanted "a free and democratic nation" in Laos. They sought "a democratic, multi-party" government fashioned after the United States in which "power will be shared by the legislative, the executive, and the judicial branches" of government.[42] Some supporters of Pa Kao Her, however, contended that the *Chao Fa* envisioned Laos to be a federation of autonomous regions, including one governed by the Hmong. Yang Thao, chief ELOL military strategist, for example, spoke of a united Laos, in which the north was governed by the Khmu, the center by the Hmong, and the south by the Lao.[43] Younger activists inspired by Pa Kao Her, however, insisted that what the *Chao Fa* always wanted was a separate and sovereign Hmong state.[44]

To organize Lao and Hmong refugees against the Lao PDR government, Vang Pao also formed his own organization— the United Lao National Liberation Front (ULNLF)— with other exiled Lao leaders, including Lao Prince Chao Sisouk na Champassak, Inpeng Surignadhay, Ngon Sananikhone, Khamphanh Panya, General Kouprasith Abhay, Houmphanh Saignasith, and General Phoumi Nosavan. More widely known as *Neo Hom Pot Poi Xat* (or simply *Neo Hom*), the ULNLF set out to expel the Vietnamese from Laos, overthrow the Lao PDR government, and, following the liberation, install a monarchy with a democratically elected government in Laos.[45]

The formation of the ULNLF in June 1981 was by no means accidental. It was formed after President Ronald Reagan made it his goal not only to contain but also roll back Soviet-style communism throughout the world. Under Reagan's new policy, which later became known as the Reagan Doctrine, the United States indirectly challenged Soviet expansionism by assisting guerrilla "freedom fighters" to destabilize or topple pro-Soviet governments in the Third World, including Laos and Vietnam, even if they were unable to directly confront the Soviet Union.[46] Accordingly, while the continuing strong anti-Vietnam War sentiment among the American public kept the Reagan administration from directly, or at least openly, re-engaging in Indochina and from providing direct military aid or other support to anti-Lao PDR resistance organizations, it did not stop private individuals and institutions from supporting groups, both in the United States and overseas, who were opposed to the communist governments in Laos and Vietnam. In fact, the Reagan administration deliberately overlooked and secretly encouraged actions by private individuals and organizations opposed to the Lao PDR and Vietnamese governments, including the ELOL and the ULNLF.

Because of the Reagan Doctrine, throughout what Fred Halliday has called the Second Cold War, the ULNLF was able to actively raise funds from Hmong families in America to aid Hmong and Lao anti-resistance forces in Southeast Asia.[47] In a series of reports throughout the 1980s, journalist Ruth Hammond documented that ULNLF members paid $100 down and $10 a month thereafter for their membership. Those who paid $500 or more received certificates that they believed entitled them to a free trip to Laos after the "liberation." In the mid-1980s, the ULNLF also sold offices in Vang Pao's future government to its members, with some paying $1,000 or more to secure a position and up to $1,000 a month to hold it.[48] It is difficult to know how much the ULNLF was actually able to collect from its members because, as political scientist Gabriel Sheffer had observed with other diasporic communities, most of the ULNLF's fundraising activities were done in secret and with very few, if any, written records.[49] Hmong political scientist Shoua Yang, however, estimated that, by the late 1980s, the ULNLF sold 17,139 civilian positions and 1,200 military positions, generating an estimated $6.7 million for the organization.[50] Keith Quincy similarly estimated that, by the end of 1988, Neo Hom earned nearly $9 million from selling "fictitious offices" to its supporters.[51] Vang Pao himself conceded that not all of the money raised went to resistance fighters in Laos for weapons, food, and medicine. He did, however, insist that a substantial amount of it was spent on activities in support of the resistance, including travels by Vang Pao and other *Neo*

Hom officers to visit resistance fighters in Asia and to lobby the American government as well as private American individuals and groups.[52]

Furthermore, the Reagan Doctrine provided Vang Pao a platform to garner support from key figures and interest groups in the United States, including American war veterans who wanted to find missing comrades in arms in Southeast Asia, and the constituents of the conservative, right wing-influenced Heritage Foundation in Washington, D.C. In February 1987, for example, Vang Pao convinced the Heritage Foundation, which had identified Laos as one of the nine communist nations to be overthrown in 1984, to bring him to the nation's capital as a special guest speaker. In his speech, he called the Socialist Republic of Vietnam a "devious and wily" imperialist bent on exterminating the Laotian people, described the Lao PDR government as a "puppet regime" for Vietnam, and outlined the primary objective of the ULNLF as the mobilization of the Laotian people, inside and outside Laos, to overthrow the Lao PDR government.[53]

The Reagan Doctrine also allowed Pa Kao Her to garner similar support from conservative right wing groups in the U.S. for his resistance. Pa Kao Her's principal supporters in the United States were Lewis Lehrman, a Republican millionaire who served as chairman of the Citizens for America, a pro-Reagan foreign policy entity, and retired U.S. Major General John Singlaub, chairman of the United States Council for World Freedom (USCWF), the American arm of an anti-communist organization known as the World Anti-Communist League (WACL). In June 1985, Lehrman, an associate of Singlaub, flew Pa Kao Her and Yang Teng from Thailand, and Bee Moua, ELOL's U.S. representative at the time, to Jamba, Angola. There in the Angolan jungle, Pa Kao met Jonas Malheiro Savimbi, President of the National Union for the Total Independence of Angola (UNITA), Adolfo Calero, Director of the Nicaraguan Unity of Opposition, and Ghulam Wardak, a colonel in the Islamic Unity of Afghanistan Mujahideen.[54] Honored as the leader of the freedom fighters in Laos, Pa Kao formed a unity pact called the Democratic International with Savimbi, Calero, and Wardak. The four leaders vowed to cooperate to liberate their nations from the Soviet Union, which they, echoing the language of the Reagan Doctrine, called "an empire more vicious and oppressive than all others that passed before" and the "common enemy of mankind."[55] At the conclusion of the meeting, Lehrman presented each delegate with a framed copy of the Declaration of Independence and read aloud portions of a letter from Reagan.[56]

Image 2. Pa Kao Her (third from the left) with other anti-Soviet leaders at the Democratic International meeting in Angola, 1985

Source: Bee Moua Collection, Hmong Archives, St. Paul, Minnesota.

Three months after Lehrman's sponsored Democratic International meeting in Angola, Major General Singlaub flew Pa Kao Her, Yang Teng, and Bee Moua to Dallas, Texas, to participate in the 18th Conference of the WACL. In letters to Pa Kao Her, Singlaub wrote that his presence at the Dallas conference would help "generate increased financial and moral support" for the "eight active anti-communist movements in the world" at the time, including efforts in Afghanistan, Angola, Cambodia, Ethiopia, Laos, Mozambique, Nicaragua, and Vietnam.[57] Following the conference, Singlaub donated "an unspecified amount of money" to the ELOL for the purchase of arms. In October 1985, the ELOL reported having received 1,050,000 (currency not indicated, presumably dollars) from the United States government for its operating costs.[58]

Throughout the 1980s, the Reagan administration also provided moral support for Hmong diasporic intervention in Laos. Using largely the testimonies and evidence Vang Pao and his supporters gathered from Hmong refugees in Laos and Thailand, top government officials and agencies repeatedly confirmed the use of "Yellow Rain" by the Soviet-backed Lao PDR government against Hmong resistance fighters in Laos to condemn the Soviet Union for violating international treaties banning the production, stockpile, and use of chemical weapons. In 1979, the CIA, for example, declared that "chemical warfare (CW) agents have been used in Laos by the Laotian and Vietnamese forces against dissident Meo tribesmen."[59] In his report to Congress in March 1982, Secretary of State Alexander Haig stated:

> [S]elected Lao and Vietnamese forces, under direct Soviet supervisions, have employed lethal trichothecene toxins and other combinations of chemical agents against H'Mong resisting government control and their villages since at least 1976. Thousands have been killed or severely injured. Thousands also have been driven from their homeland by the use of these agents.[60]

In November 1982, the new Secretary of State, George Schultz, in an update of the Haig report, again concluded: "Vietnamese and Lao troops, under direct Soviet supervision, have continued to use lethal and incapacitating chemical agents and toxins against the H'Mong resistance in Laos throughout at least June 1982."[61] That same year, James Phillips, a policy analyst at the Heritage Foundation also published a report claiming communist forces in Laos and Cambodia were using chemical weapons against Hmong and Cambodians in those countries, respectively.[62]

In 1983 book *The Yellow Rainmakers*, Grant Evans contended that stories of Yellow Rain were "largely a product of uncontrolled rumors among a tribal people, the Hmong, whose recent history and worldview predispose them to believe and recount gassing that have no basis in fact."[63] The Hmong's evidence was also challenged by Harvard University geneticist and microbiologist Matthew Meselson, who, with the help of his colleagues, concluded that what Hmong refugees claimed were chemical toxins were nothing more than bee feces falling from the sky when bee colonies took mass defecation flights.[64]

Hmong and the Americans, however, were unimpressed. Hmong advocates like Vang Pao, Pa Kao Her, and their followers continued to insist that what their coethnics described as "Yellow Rain" was, in fact, the product of a chemical weapon. Similarly, after Evans, Meselson, and others challenged the Hmong evidence, the United States still maintained that Yellow Rain could not have been a natural occurrence. If it were organic, the alleged attacks would not be limited to certain times and places and would instead be more broadly distributed throughout the region. Yet, Yellow Rain incidents were reported only in areas where the Soviet-backed Pathet Lao forces were engaged in brutal attacks on resistance forces. It was therefore illogical to insist that honeybees would defecate selectively on rebel villages in Laos and Cambodia.[65]

Despite earlier American support, direct and indirect, for the ELOL and ULNLF, however, the United States ended its support for anti-communist Hmong as soon as the political winds in Washington and around the world changed at the end of the 1980s. With the denouement of the Cold War, the United States no longer needed the aid of those President Reagan had called "freedom fighters" to end the global expansion of Soviet imperialism. The Hmong knew they had lost American support once they attended the first ever U.S.-based conference discussing the human rights crisis in Laos.[66] Over 200 Hmong refugees and activists from across America gathered at Yale University's Schell Center for International Human Rights in early December 1990 to testify to the use of lethal chemical agents by the Soviet-backed governments in Laos and Vietnam against the Hmong in Laos. Yet, Dr. Vang Pobzeb, founder and director of the Lao Human Rights Council in Wisconsin, an organization connected to the ULNLF, was the only Hmong person allowed to speak.[67] Insisting that thousands of Hmong had died from Soviet-engineered "Yellow Rain" in Laos, Vang Pobzeb said:

> From 1975 to 1990, the Soviet Union and Vietnam provided chemical weapons to the Pathet Lao government to kill more than 75,000 citizens in Laos. The Soviet fighter planes carried "yellow rain" from Moscow and Hanoi to drop in Laos... Between January and May 1990, the Soviet fighter planes and MiG-21s dropped many chemical bombs on civilians, domestic animals and farming areas in the Xieng Khoung, Borikhan and Vang Vieng provinces and many other areas in the countryside. The bombings killed 5,000 people, women, men, children and civilians and thousands of domestic animals.[68]

Activists brought a video of Hmong victims of chemical warfare to play at the conference, but the video was never shown. When they tried to play it, Drew Days III, Schell Center Director, told them to turn off the T.V. When they showed it to Scott Marciel, the State Department official at the conference, he refused to watch it, declaring that the State Department had a copy and that he had already seen it. The video, journalist/activist Jane Hamilton-Merritt told Marciel in anger, was "brand new information." In response, Marciel explained the State Department was no longer interested in "Yellow Rain" in Laos. At the top of the State Department's priorities were, he explained, programs "to achieve the fullest possible accounting of Americans missing in the Vietnam War and to decrease drug trafficking."[69]

In exchange for its assistance in locating missing American service personnel, Laos insisted the State Department work with Laos and Thailand to close all the refugee camps in Thailand, including those occupied by the Hmong. Until the end of the Cold War, the camps, especially Ban Vinai in Loei Province, served as centers for recruiting and mobilizing fighters, both Hmong and non-Hmong, opposed to the Lao PDR.[70]

To obtain the cooperation of the Lao PDR, the George H.W. Bush administration severed official and unofficial ties with all Lao and Hmong resistance groups and began negotiations with Thailand and Laos to shut down the camps. In 1989, Thailand, Laos, and the United States came together with sixty-seven other governments at the Second Conference on Indochinese Refugees in Geneva and adopted a new regional approach known as the Comprehensive Plan of Action (CPA). The CPA proposed repatriating all Hmong determined not to be political refugees to Laos and resettling all those classified as genuine political refugees in "third countries" by the end of 1995.[71] In June 1991, Thailand, Laos, and the United Nations High Commissioner for Refugees (UNHCR) finally signed the Luang Phrabang Tripartite Agreement, which the State Department helped to broker, to act on the CPA.[72] For its part, "the Bush administration contributed $15 million to subsidize the cost of closing the camps and transporting Laotians and Hmong back to Laos."[73]

To strengthen its relationship with Laos, Washington also called directly on Hmong resistance groups to end their resistance against the Lao PDR government. In mid-October 1992, the State Department issued an official warning to all Laotian resistance groups, particularly those associated with Vang Pao and his colleagues, that supporting armed insurgents overseas was a violation of the U.S. Neutrality Act. Furthermore, any resident who violated U.S. neutrality laws could face up to three years of imprisonment, a $3,000 fine, or both.[74] By the mid-1990s, Hmong anti-communist resistance groups in America and overseas, once considered foot soldiers in America's secret war against communism, had become nothing more than armed insurgents in the eyes of many in Washington.

After taking office in 1993, President William J. "Bill" Clinton continued the Bush policy of appeasement with Laos. To further strengthen U.S.-Laos relations, Clinton not only donated $3 million between 1993 and

1994 to help defray the costs of the repatriation of Hmong refugees to Laos, he also, in 1997, initiated bilateral trade agreements with Laos and Vietnam.[75] The Hmong American community was divided over the issue from the outset.[76] Staunch anti-communist individuals and organizations, including the Lao Human Rights Council, the United Lao Movement for Democracy, and Veterans of America, all of whom were linked to the ULNLF, and the newly developed Hmong International Human Rights Watch vehemently opposed the United States extension of Normalized Trade Relations (NTR) status to Laos. They argued that the Lao PDR government must improve its poor human rights record, particularly its intolerable treatment of Hmong people in Laos, before NTR is provided. Granting NTR status to Laos would not improve the livelihood of most people there. On the contrary, they said, granting NTR would strengthen the communist regime, enabling it to massacre more Hmong and Lao people. Continued pressure on the Lao PDR government for economic restructuring and democratic reform was presented as the only way to "save lives that have not yet been lost."[77] Furthermore, NTR with Laos would, they maintained, work against American interests. Laos had professed friendship with North Korea and denounced the American war in Iraq.[78]

In contrast, Lao and Hmong proponents of NTR, including Chao Lee of Minnesota, Congresswoman Betty McCollum's office, and Dr. Yang Dao, a former member of the ULNLF, and his associates, contended that NTR would help raise exports and job creation and provide social uplift for many Laotians, including the Hmong minority, out of poverty. Opposing NTR would further prevent the path of reconciliation between the Laotian and Hmong diaspora communities and the Lao PDR government and bring more suffering to the ethnic Hmong people in the country. Ultimately, NTR would bolster U.S. leverage with Laos, including pressure on human rights issues, and help reformers within the Lao PDR government push for political and economic reform.[79]

In the early 2000s, Vang Pao and his supporters, including Dr. Vang Pobzeb, Wangyee Vang of Lao Veterans of America, and Phillip Smith of the Washington-based Center for Public Policy Analysis, found some sympathetic allies in Congress. These alliances helped delay the United States's extension of NTR status to Laos. The arrest of two Bangkok-based European journalists, Belgian Thierry Falise and Frenchman Vincent Reynaud, and their interpreter, Rev. Naw Karl Mua, a Hmong-American pastor of the Light of Life Lutheran Church in St. Paul, on June 4, 2003, further interrupted the passage of NTR.[80] The men were arrested as they tried to document human rights abuse and religious persecution in Laos and write a follow-up report to Andrew Perrin's heart-wrenching story on the plight of the Hmong in the Lao jungle in *Time Asia* magazine in May 2003.[81] Pressures from the Hmong community and their Congressional supporters, including Minnesota Republican Senator Norm Coleman, eventually forced the Lao PDR government to release the pastor and journalists in July after having sentenced them to fifteen years in prison for the killing of a village security officer, obstruction of police work, and illegal possession of a gun and an explosive device.[82] By July 10, Naw Karl Mua was back in St. Paul.[83]

Nevertheless, Congress, driven by a policy to establish trade relations with Laos as a means to offset China's rising economic influence in the region, overwhelmingly passed the Miscellaneous Trade and Technical Corrections Act of 2004 (P.L. 108-429) to extend NTR treatment to Laos in mid-November of 2004, and did so despite continued opposition from anti-communist Hmong in the United States, those who once made up the bulk of the CIA secret army in the country and later served as freedom fighters during the Reagan era, and despite the available evidence of human rights violations in Laos.[84] On November 19, the same day it granted NTR status to Laos, the U.S. Senate also agreed to S. Res. 475, "A Resolution to Condemn Human Rights Abuses in Laos," a bill introduced by Republican Senator Norm Coleman of Minnesota.[85] On December 3, 2004, U.S. President George W. Bush signed the bill into law.

In the aftermath of the terrorist attacks on September 11, 2001, Washington's main foreign policy in Laos was not political reform, greater respect for human rights, or self-determination for ethnic Hmong in the country. Instead, it was to encourage the Lao PDR government to cooperate with the U.S. in its War on Terror. For this reason, Americans could no longer allow domestic private individuals and organizations to work against Laos, particularly those continuing to aid anti-Lao PDR resistance forces in the Laotian jungle. Cognizant of the continued support of many die-hard anticommunist Hmong residing within the United States, Washington brought fifty Hmong and Lao leaders from Minnesota and elsewhere to the nation's capital in February 2004. The State Department issued a stern warning to both. The message of Deputy Assistant Secretary for East Asia and Pacific Affairs, Matthew Daley, to the gathered leaders was, in essence, that the Vietnam War was over. The Cold War was over. The United States no longer supported, and, in fact, they recognized it as a crime for anyone to support "armed insurgents" fighting governments with which the United States is at peace, including the Lao PDR government. Any Hmong or Lao private resident or citizen in the United States who aided such insurgents would be considered a "terrorist."[86] Six months earlier, to end the continued Hmong-American opposition to Laos, the United States negotiated with Thailand to shut down the unofficial camp at Wat Tham Krabok, which Hmong refugees had called home since the closing of the Ban Vinai and Chiang Kham refugee camps in the early 1990s. By this point, the camp at Wat Tham Krabok had allegedly become a haven for illegal drug activity. Allowing such activities to continue would defeat the purpose of the monastery, which was known internationally for its drug rehabilitation program. More importantly, like the Ban Vinai refugee camp before it, Wat Tham Krabok had become a conduit for the Hmong in the diaspora to recruit fighters and transfer funds to supply fighters to fight against the Lao military.[87] From 2004 to 2005, just over 15,000 Hmong resettled mainly in the United States.[88]

Because of the continued support of some Hmong Americans for Hmong resistance groups in Laos, the Hmong became characterized as "terrorists" under the broad provision of the Real ID Act of 2005, which President Bush signed into law as an attachment to the USA Patriot Act of 2001. The act barred Hmong in America from obtaining green cards and full citizenship and prevented Hmong refugees in Thailand from gaining entry or resettlement in the United States.[89] It took three years of advocacy and pressure by the Hmong American community, with the aid of some sympathetic allies in Congress, to convince the United States government to insert an amendment in the Consolidated Appropriations Act of 2008, which Bush signed into law on December 26, to remove the terrorist label for the Hmong.[90]

In the meantime, agents of the U.S. Federal Bureau of Alcohol, Tobacco, Firearms, and Explosives (ATF) had been conducting their own investigation of anti-communist Hmong leaders in America. The investigation was dubbed "Operation Tarnished Eagle," and it involved an undercover agent posing as an arms dealer and meeting secretly with former U.S. Army Lt. Col. Harrison Ulrich Jack and his Hmong colleagues, including Vang Pao, on multiple occasions over six months. During that time, they purportedly discussed plans to purchase and transfer military weapons worth several millions of dollars to Thailand and Laos with the intention of equipping Hmong resistance fighters in their fight against the Lao PDR government and military. The sting operation subsequently led to the arrest of Vang Pao, Jack, and eleven other alleged Hmong co-conspirators in June 2007.[91] The federal criminal complaint, known as *USA v. Harrison U. Jack, et al.*, alleged these men were planning to purchase weapons, including Stinger anti-aircraft missiles, AK-47 machine guns, C-4 explosives, Claymore land mines, night vision goggles, as well as other arms and munitions to equip insurgents in the highlands of Laos who planned to attack Vientiane, the capital of the Lao People's Democratic Republic (Lao PDR or Laos), reduce government targets to rubble, and make them look like the results of the attack upon the World Trade Center in New

York on September 11, 2001. For this alleged plot, Vang Pao and his co-defendants faced possible life prison sentences if convicted.[92]

On September 19, 2009, after two years of legal maneuvering in and outside of court and sustained protests by Vang Pao supporters outside the Sacramento district court, federal prosecutors, however, dropped all charges against Vang Pao, declaring they did not have sufficient reliable evidence to prosecute the Hmong leader.[93] "In our measured judgment, and based on the totality of evidence in the case and the circumstances regarding defendant Vang Pao, we believe that continued prosecution of this defendant is no longer warranted," stated U.S. Attorney Lawrence Brown, Special Agent in Charge of the San Francisco Field Division of the Bureau of ATF.[94] On January 10, 2011, just four days after Vang Pao passed away in a hospital in Clovis, California, at the age of eighty-one, the charges against the rest of Vang Pao's twelve co-defendants were also dropped.[95]

From court documents, press releases, and media reports, it is still unclear whether the sting on Vang Pao and his colleagues was orchestrated with the knowledge and sanction of the highest level of the U.S. government or whether it was done based largely on a tip in September 2006 that the ATF office in Arizona received from a friend of Harrison Jack about Jack's effort to locate and purchase five hundred AK-47 automatic weapons for the Hmong in the Lao forests, ostensibly for them to use for their protection.[96] There is no doubt, however, that the sting operation was connected to the American War on Terror. The political environment after the 9/11 attacks was such that ATF agents believed they were stopping a terrorist plot in the making, as these federal agents bragged about after the arrests. U.S. Attorney McGregor Scott, for example, stated:

> These defendants flagrantly violated numerous federal laws, including the Neutrality Act, in planning to topple the government of Laos. The ATF, and in particular a very brave and dedicated agent of the ATF, as well as the FBI and its Joint Terrorism Task

> Force members, deserve enormous credit for their extraordinary investigation.[97]

Assistant Attorney General for National Security Kenneth Wainstein added, "Thanks to an exceptional investigation effort by the ATF, FBI, and U.S. Attorney's office for the Eastern District of California, the plotters have been arrested and the threat neutralized."[98] ATF Acting Director Michael Sullivan, too, boasted, "These defendants posed a substantial threat to public safety abroad. Fortunately, we were able to disrupt their activities before their plot evolved into a coup against a country with which the United States is at peace [Laos]."[99] In addition, after the arrests, federal prosecutors painted Vang Pao as a "Laotian bin Laden" and charged that he was a terrorist who plotted to "murder thousands and thousands of people." In open court, they called the case a conspiracy as immense as the attacks of 9/11.[100]

There is also indication that the arrest of Vang Pao and his co-defendants, whether directly or intentionally orchestrated by the federal government or not, had helped to strengthen U.S.-Laos relations while causing collateral damage to all those connected to Vang Pao internationally. As Mary Grace McGeehan, who was then the U.S. Charge d'Affaires in Laos, wrote in a classified State Department cable obtained by WikiLeaks: "Since the arrests, we have made a surprising amount of progress in areas of our relationship with the Lao government where we had previously experienced difficulty."[101] On the other hand, Laos and Thailand forcibly deported thousands of legitimate Hmong war refugees from Thailand to Laos immediately after Vang Pao's arrest, calling it the perfect opportunity to do so.[102]

CONCLUSION

America's secret war in Laos fundamentally transformed the identity of the Hmong from a largely agrarian, nonliterate, and localized people in the Lao highlands into a thriving globalized and transnational diaspora.

During the war, a record number of Hmong received education or formal training, and many assumed prominent roles in both civil society and the military, including teachers, school principal, nurses, military officers, and pilots.[103] Forty years later, and after their global diaspora, hundreds of them have received advanced, terminal, or professional degrees, many of them from top universities in the United States. Many have been elected to public offices in America while several others have been appointed to positions in the Lao PDR government. The Hmong in the West, particularly those in America, as Hmong specialists Gary Yia Lee and Nicholas Tapp have observed, have become "an example to watch and follow and... the voice for the Hmong in other parts of the world."[104]

America's secret war in Laos also forever changed the Hmong's relationship with Laos, the United States, and to a certain extent, Thailand. Instead of ending with the peace agreements in 1973 or the communist takeover in 1975, America's secret war in Laos has left not only a dark legacy of millions of unexploded bombs that continue to kill and maim people in the Laotian countryside but also another secret war. Tens of thousands of people, on both sides of this new conflict, have died since 1975. Those Hmong resisting government control in the Laotian jungle continued to be "hunted like animals" by government forces, resulting in egregious human rights violations, including the rape and torture of countless women and girls.[105] Meanwhile, those Hmong who migrated to America as part of the diaspora created by the first secret war have continued to aid and abet those who remained in Laos and Thailand during the second one. At times, to keep the resistance going, they even encouraged those in Thailand to remain in the refugee camps rather than accept resettlement to a third country. Because of this, Hmong refugees now hold the dubious honor of being the longest standing refugees in Thailand's history. Indeed, the last legitimately recognized group of Hmong refugees did not leave Thailand until 2005, some thirty years after the first Hmong arrived in the country.

Furthermore, because of the secret wars in Laos, the United States and their Hmong allies developed a long and persistent, but ultimately contradictory relationship. At times, the United States used the Hmong, both those overseas and those in America, to promote American policy interests overseas; yet, when the political winds in Washington and around the world changed, the U.S. quickly severed ties with the Hmong and, at times, penalized them for actions they previously supported or condoned. In the 1960s, when the United States needed the Hmong to fight the communists in Laos, it considered them America's most important force on the ground. As America's foot soldiers in Laos, the Hmong were, as some would say, America's most loyal allies. When Laos fell to the communists in 1975, however, the United States left, with little apparent concern for most of its secret Hmong allies. Thousands were killed, and even more were displaced and experienced intense suffering after the communists took power and retaliated against pro-American Hmong guerrillas and their families. During the Reagan era, when the United States needed them to cripple Soviet influence in the world, it regarded Hmong guerrillas as "America's freedom fighters." Once the Cold War ended, though, Hmong guerrillas became "insurgents" in the minds of their former American allies. Worse, their cries for help to end the Lao PDR government's alleged campaign to gas the Hmong in the Lao highlands with "Yellow Rain" were silenced. In the post-9/11 era, for Laos' cooperation with the U.S. War on Terror as well as American economic influence in the region, the Hmong were transformed into "terrorists" and, in the bizarre terrorism case against Vang Pao and his co-defendants, "criminals." But then, in yet another ironic turn of events, when Vang Pao died in 2011, the charges against his colleagues were almost immediately dropped, and many American military figures and politicians came out and praised Vang Pao in ways that would have been hardly imaginable shortly after his arrest.[106] In February 2012, a school in Fresno, California, for example, was named after Vang Pao.[107] Ten months later, a six-foot granite statue of Vang Pao was installed in Chico, California, in his honor in front of the Chico Municipal Center.[108] In short, only by taking seriously the history of the secret wars in Laos, both before and after the communist takeover in 1975, and especially the U.S.-Hmong relationship in the past half-century can we achieve not only a more complete and dynamic understanding of America's involvement in the Vietnam conflict but also the lasting impact and consequences of a war on groups, such as the Hmong, long after peace accords were signed as well as the often convoluted and contradictory character of American foreign policy.

NOTES

1. Legacies of War, "Secret War in Laos," accessed September 3, 2017,http://legaciesofwar.org/about-laos/secret-war-laos/.
2. "Remarks of President Obama to the People of Laos," accessed September 3, 2017, https://obamawhitehouse.archives.gov/the-press-office/2016/09/06/remarks-president-obama-people-laos.
3. Thomas Maresca, "Obama becomes the first sitting president to visit Laos," *USA Today*, September 6, 2016; "Obama, in Laos, pledges $90 million to clear unexploded ordnance," *Associated Press*, September 6, 2016.
4. Robinson, W. Courtland, *Terms of Refuge United Nations High Commissioner for Refugees* (London: Zed Books, 1998), 270-76.
5. See, for example, Timothy Castle, *At War in the Shadow of Vietnam: The United States' Military Aids to the Royal Lao Government, 1955-1975* (New York: Columbia Univ. Press, 1993); Victor Anthony and Richard Sexton, *The War in Northern Laos, 1954-1973* (Washington, DC: US Air Force, 1993); Kenneth J. Conboy, *Shadow War: The CIA's Secret War in Laos* (Boulder, CO: Squandron/Signal,1995); Roger Warner, *Shooting at the Moon: the Story of America's Clandestine War in Laos* (South Royalton, VT: Steerforth Press, 1996); Thomas L. Ahern, *Undercover Armies: CIA and Surrogate Warfare in Laos* (Washington, DC: Center for the Study of Intelligence, 2006); Christopher Robbins, *The Ravens. The Men Who Flew in America's Secret War in Laos* (New York: Crown Publishers, 1987); Thomas L. Briggs, *Cash on Delivery: CIA Operations During the Secret War in Laos* (Rockville, MD: Rosebank Press, 2009); and Billy G. Webb, *The Secret War in Laos and General Vang Pao, 1958-1975* (Bloomington, IN: Xlibris, 2016).
6. Jane Hamilton-Merritt, *Tragic Mountains: The Hmong, the Americans, and the Secret Wars for Laos, 1942-1992* (Bloomington, IN: Indiana Univ. Press, 1994); Keith Quincy, *Harvesting Pa Chay's Wheat: The Hmong and America's Secret War in Laos* (Spokane, WA: Eastern Washington Univ. Press, 2000); John Prados, *Safe for Democracy: The Secret Wars of the CIA* (Chicago: Ivan R. Dee, 2006).
7. Len E. Ackland, "No Place for Neutralism: The Eisenhower Administration and Laos," in *Laos: War andRevolution*, eds. Nina S. Adams and Alfred W. McCoy (New York: Harper & Row, 1970), 139; Charles A.

Stevenson, *The End of Nowhere: American Policy toward Laos since 1954* (Boston, MA: Beacon Press, 1972), 28.

8. Mark P. Bradley, "Franklin Roosevelt, Trusteeship, and US Exceptionalism," in *A Companion to the Vietnam*, eds. Marilyn B. Young and Robert Buzzanco (Oxford: Blackwell Publishers, 2002), 130-45.
9. Sucheng Chan, *Hmong Means Free: Life in Laos and America* (Philadelphia, PA: Temple Univ. Press, 1994), 23-24.
10. Ahern, *Undercover Armies*, 29-30; Anthony and Sexton, *The War in Northern Laos*, 44.
11. Castle, *At War in the Shadow of Vietnam*, 10 and 20-27.
12. Tim Pfaff, *Hmong in America: Journey from a Secret War* (Eau Claire, WI: Chippewa Valley Museum, 1995), 38-39.
13. Hamilton-Merritt, *Tragic Mountains*, 88-91; William M. Leary, "CIA Air Operations in Laos, 1955-1974," *Intelligence Studies* 42, no. 2 (1998): 71-86.
14. Fred Branfman, "Presidential War in Laos," in *Laos: War and Revolution*, 252-253; Stevenson, *End of Nowhere*, 198.
15. Ian G. Baird 2010, "The US Central Intelligence Agency and the Brao: The story of Kong My, a non-Communist space in Attapeu Province, southern Laos," *Aséanie* 25 (2010): 23-51; Hjorleifur Jonsson, "War's ontogeny: Militias and ethnic boundaries in Laos and exile," *Southeast Asian Studies* 47, no. 2 (2009): 125-49.
16. Pfaff, *Hmong in America*, 29.
17. Chan, *Hmong Means Free*, 32.
18. Fred Branfman, "Presidential War in Laos," 253.
19. Charles Stevenson, *End of Nowhere* (Boston, MA, 1972), 198.
20. Sue Murphy Mote, *Hmong and American: Stories of Transition to a Strange Land* (Jefferson, NC: McFarland & CO., 2004), 110; John Duffy, et al., *The Hmong: An Introduction to their History and* Culture (Washington, DC: Center for Applied Linguistics, 2004), 4; Tou Fu Vang, "The Hmong of Laos," in *Introduction to Indochinese History, Culture, Language and Life*, ed. John K. Whitmore (Ann Arbor: Center for South and Southeast Asian Studies, Univ. of Michigan, 1979), 93-192.
21. W.E. Garrett, "The Hmong of Laos: No Place to Run," *National* Geographic, January 1974, 83.
22. Linda McFarland, *Cold War Strategist: Stuart Symington and the Search for National Security* (Westport, CT, 2001), 153-54.
23. "Laos: Deeper into the Other War," *Time*, March 9, 1970.
24. "Text of the Text of Cease-Fire Agreement Signed by Laotian Government and the Pathet Lao," Special To the New York Times, February 22, 1973,

accessed July 3, 2018, https://www.nytimes.com/1973/02/22/archives/text-of-ceasefire-agreement-signed-by-laotian-government-and-the.html.

25. William E. Colby, "The Hmong and the CIA: A Friendship, Not A Scandal," *Hmong Forum* 2 (1991): 25-34.
26. Hamilton-Merritt, *Tragic Mountains*, 341-345; Gayle L. Morrison, *Sky is Falling: An Oral History of the CIA's Evacuation of the Hmong from Laos* (Jefferson, NC: McFarland & Co., 1999), 26-28.
27. Paul Hillmer, *A People's History of the Hmong* (St. Paul: MN Historical Society, 2009),158.
28. The ELOL and other resistance groups operating in Laos also received training and arms in southern China from the communist government in the late 1970s and early 1980s to destabilize the Lao PDR government and its closest ally, Vietnam, which China attacked in February 1979 not long after Vietnam invaded Cambodia and ousted China's close ally, the Khmer Rouge. Throughout the 1980s, with permission from the Royal Thai government, the ELOL and other groups also received training from the Thai army at the military camps they set up in northeast Thailand. Following the collapse of the Soviet Union, however, the People's Democratic Republic of China and the Royal Thai government ended their support for Hmong fighters opposed to the Lao PDR government. See Nengher N. Vang, "Peace-makers or Peace-wreckers: the Hmong in the Conflicts in Laos during and after the Cold War," *Journal of North Carolina Association of Historians* 22 (2014): 57-82; Gary Y. Lee, "Bandits or Rebels: Hmong Resistance in the New Lao State," *Indigenous Affairs* 4 (2007): 6-15; and Gary Y. Lee, "Hmong Rebellion in Laos: Victims or Terrorists" in A Handbook in Terrorism and Insurgency in Southeast Asia, ed. Andrew T.H. Tan (Northampton, MA: Edward Elgar Pub., 2007), 352-73.
29. Yang Dao, "Why did the Hmong Leave Laos?" in *The Hmong in the West*, ed. Bruce T. Downing and Douglas P. Olney (Minneapolis: Center for Urban & Regional Affairs, 1982), 13.
30. Ibid.
31. Grant Evans, "Laos: Situation Analysis and Trend Assessment," A Writenet Report commissioned by United Nations High Commissioner for Refugees, Protection Information Section (DIP), (May 2004): 5.
32. Gary Yia Lee, "Minority Policies and the Hmong," in *Contemporary Laos: Studies in the Politics and Societies of the Lao People's Democratic Republic*, ed. Martin Stuart-Fox (London: Univ. of Queensland Press, 1982), 215.

33. Stacey Lee, *Up Against Whiteness: Race, School, and Immigrant Youth* (New York: Teachers College Press, 2002), 12.
34. Duffy, *The Hmong*, 8.
35. Yang Dao, "Why did the Hmong Leave Laos?", 4.
36. Chao Fa is a Lao language phrase that has been translated as "Lord of the sky." The term is widely used to refer to all the Hmong in the Lao forests.
37. Carlyle A. Thayer, "Laos and Vietnam: The Anatomy of A 'Special Relation'," in *Contemporary Laos,* 255; Martin Stuart-Fox, "National Defense and Internal Security in Laos," in *Contemporary Laos,* 230.
38. Jonathan B. Tucker, "The 'Yellow Rain' Controversy: Lessons for Arms Control Compliance," *The Nonproliferation Review* (Spring 2001): 26.
39. Quincy, *Harvesting Pa Chay's Wheat*, 418, 425.
40. Stanley Karnow, "U.S. Giving Little Attention to Meos, Once Allies, Now Genocide Target," *Washington Post,* August 20, 1979.
41. Quincy, *Harvesting Pa Chay's Wheat*, 419.
42. Pa Kao Her, "Goals and Policies of the Democratic Chao Fa Party of Laos," Special Collections, Hmong Archives, St. Paul, Minnesota.
43. Yang Thao, interview with author, St. Paul, Minnesota, August 13, 2009.
44. Xue Her, interview with author, St. Paul, Minnesota, November 10, 2009; Gymbay Moua, interview with author, Minneapolis, Minnesota, March 9, 2009.
45. United Lao National Liberation Front, "Statement on the United Lao National Liberation Front," 1981; United Lao National Liberation Front, "Manifesto of the United Lao National Liberation Front," 7 September1981. Special Collections, Hmong Archives, St. Paul, Minnesota.
46. Charles Krauthammer, "Essay: The Reagan Doctrine," *Time,* 1 April 1, 1985; Ronald Reagan, "Address before a Joint Session of Congress of the State of the Union, February 6, 1985," *Public Papers of the Presidents: Ronald Reagan 1985* (Washington, DC, 1988), 135.
47. Fred Halliday, *The Making of the Second Cold War* (London: Verso, 1983).
48. Ruth Hammond, "Rumors of War," *Twin Cities Reader,* Oct. 25-31, 1989.
49. Gabriel Sheffer, *Diaspora Politics: At Home Abroad,* (Cambridge: Cambridge Univ. Press, 2003), 87.
50. Shoua Yang, "Hmong Social and Political Capital: Formation and Maintenance of Hmong American Organizations" (PhD diss., Northern Illinois University, 2006), 184-92.
51. Quincy, *Harvesting Pa Chay's Wheat,* 454.
52. Vang Pao, interview with author, Santa Ana, California, July 28, 2010.

53. Vang Pao, *Against All Odds: the Laotian Freedom Fighters* (Washington, D.C: Heritage Foundation, 1987).
54. Alan Cowell, "Four Rebels Units Sign Anti-Soviet Pact," *New York Times*, June 6, 1985; "A Fledging Alliance," *Time*, June 17, 1985; Michael Sullivan, "Rebels Opposing Marxist Regimes in 4 Nations Unite," *Washington Times*, June 6, 1985.
55. Jonas M. Savimbi, et.al., "The Democratic International, June 2, 1985," Bee Moua Special Collections, Hmong Archives; Nina J. Easton, *Gang of Five: Leaders at the Center of the Conservative Crusade* (New York: Simon & Schuster, 2000), 165-67.
56. Walter Shapiro and Peter Younghusband, "Lehrman's Contra Conclave," *Newsweek*, June 17, 1986;President Ronald Reagan, letter to Mr. Lewis E. Lehrman, May 30, 1985, Bee Moua Special Collections, Hmong Archives.
57. John K. Singlaub, letter to Bee Moua, August 14, 1985; John K. Singlaub, letter to Pa Kao Her,August 14, 1985, Bee Moua Special Collections, Hmong Archives.
58. Hamilton-Merritt, *Tragic Mountains*, 482.
59. U.S. Congress, Subcommittee on Asian and Pacific Affairs, Committee on Foreign Affairs, *Use of Chemical Agents in Southeast Asia Since the Vietnam War*, Hearing, December 12, 1979, 96th Congress, 5th Session, Washington, DC: Government Printing Office.
60. U.S. Department of State, *Chemical Warfare in Southeast Asia and Afghanistan*, Report to the Congress fromSecretary of State Alexander M. Haig, Jr., March 22, 1982, Pub. 98, Washington, DC: Government Printing Office.
61. U.S. Department of State, *Chemical Warfare in Southeast Asia and Afghanistan: An Update*, Report fromSecretary of State George P. Shultz, November 1982, Pub. 104, Washington, DC: Government Printing Office.
62. James A. Phillips, *Moscow's Poison War: Mounting Evidence of Battlefield Atrocities* (Washington, DC: Heritage Foundation, 1982).
63. Grant Evans, *The Yellow Rainmakers: Are Chemical Weapons being used in Southeast Asia?* (London: Thetford Press, 1983), 172.
64. Julian Robinson, Jeanne Guillemin, and Matthew Meselson, "Yellow Rain in Southeast Asia: The Story Collapses," *Foreign Policy* 68, (Autumn, 1987): 100-117.
65. William Kucewicz, "Bee-Feces Theory Still Has No Sting," *Wall Street Journal*, September 17, 1987.
66. Yale Law School, *Laos: Human Rights in a Forgotten Country*, December 8, 1990, Special Collections, HmongArchives.

67. Jean Falbo, "Laos Human Rights Conference Sponsored by Yale, Southern," *Southern News,* December 13, 1990; Paul Boudreau, "Human Rights: Issue of Real People," *Southern News,* December 13, 1990.
68. Vang Pobzeb, "Address to the Conference on Human Rights in Laos, Yale Law School, Yale University, NewHaven, Connecticut, December 8, 1990." This address was included as Appendix 1 in Vang Pobzeb, "White Paper on Human Rights Violations in Laos Since 1975," *Paper Presented to the First Conference on Human Rights inLaos, Yale Law School,* December 8, 1990, 55-65.
69. Susana Martins, "Conference A Mixture of Truth, Lies," *Southern News,* December 13, 1990.
70. Lynellyn D. Long, *Ban Vinai: the Refugee Camp* (New York: Columbia Univ. Press, 1993).
71. W. Courtland Robinson, "The Comprehensive Plan of Action for Indochinese Refugees, 1989-1997: Sharing the Burden and Passing the Buck," *Journal of Refugee Studies* 17, no. 3 (2004): 320; Sara Davies, *Legitimizing Rejection: International Refugee Law in Southeast Asia* (Boston: Martinus Nijhoff Pub., 2008), 198; S.A. Bronee, "The History of the Comprehensive Plan of Action," *International Journal of Refugee Law* 5, no. 4 (1993): 540; Refugee Policy Group (RPG), *The Second International Conference on Indochinese Refugees: A New Humanitarian Consensus?* (Washington, DC: RPG, 1989), 30.
72. Thana Poopat, "Laos Urged to Relocate 60,000 Refugees," *The Nation,* June 28, 1991.
73. Tim Bartle and Phillip Smith. *Report to the Congress of the United States: Fact Finding Mission to ThailandRegarding the Status of Hmong/Lao Refugees and Asylum Seekers, 28 December 1994 to 2 January 1995.*(Washington, DC: House of Representatives, 1995), 13.
74. Quincy, *Harvesting Pa Chay's Wheat,* 469.
75. Bartle and Smith, *Report to the Congress of the United State,* 13.
76. Vaudine England, "Laotians Are Divided Over U.S. Trade," *Wall Street Journal,* September 1, 2004;Frederic J. Frommer, "Free Trade Deal for Laos Splits Hmong Community," *Associated Press,* May 6, 2003.
77. U.S. Congress, House of Representative, Subcommittee on Trade of the Committee on Ways and Means, *Written Comments on the Extension of Normal Trade Relations to the Lao People's Democratic Republic,* November 4, 1999, 106th Congress, 1st Session, Washington: Government Office Printing, accessed September 1, 2017, https://www.gpo.gov/fdsys/pkg/CPRT-106WPRT60250/html/CPRT-106WPRT60250.htm.

78. Rep. Mark Green and Rep. George Randovich, Letter to Philip Crane, Chairman, Subcommittee on TradeCommittee on Ways and Means, April 12, 2003; Senator Russell Feingold, Floor Statement, *Congressional Record*, 10 July 2003, S9236; "Congressmen Call on Bus to Block Laos Trade Drive," *Agence France-Presse*, April 26, 2003.
79. Thomas Lum, "Laos: Background and U.S. Relations," *CRS Report for Congress*, April 22, 2004; Thomas Lum, "Laos: Background and U.S. Relations," *CRS Report for Congress*, November 22, 2004; and "US-Lao NTR Coalition urging Congress and Senate to support Normal Trade Relations (NTR) with Laos," *accessed on August 8, 2017, ffrd.org/indochina/laos/laopacket.doc.*
80. Todd Nelson, "St. Paul Pastor Arrested in Laos," *Pioneer Press*, June 12, 2003; Martha Sawyer Allen, "St. Paul Pastor, 2 Journalists Detained in Laos," *Star Tribune*, 12 June 2003; Ron Corben, "Lao Arrests European Journalists, American in Battle with Rebels," *Bangkok Post*, June 11, 2003.
81. Andrew Perrin, "Welcome to the Jungle," *Time Asia Magazine*, May 5, 2003.
82. Frederic J. Frommer, "Minnesota: Coleman Urges Slow Approach to Laos Trade," *Associated Press/Pioneer Press*, June 21, 2003; Vijay Joshi, "St. Paul Pastor, 2 Others Sentenced to 15 Years in Laotian Jail," *Associated Press*, June 30, 2003; Tom Webb, "Washington, D.C.: Ambassador Urges Resolution for Pastor," *Pioneer Press*, June 26, 2003; Tom Webb and Todd Nelson, "Scenario Outlined to Free Pastor," *Pioneer Press*, June 28, 2004.
83. Tom LaVenture, "Minnesota Minister Freed From Laos Prison Said He Did Not Admit Guilt," *Associated Press*, 12 July 2003 and Tom LaVenture, "Welcome Home: Rev. Mua Relieved but Grieves for Hmong Laos," *Asian American Press*, July 18, 2003.
84. Kevin Diaz, "Senate Approves Measure to Normalize Trade with Laos," *Star Tribune*, November 20, 2004; Thomas Lum, "Laos: Background and U.S. Relations," *CRS Report for Congress*, February 5, 2007; Thomas Lum, "Laos: Background and U.S. Relations," *CRS Report for Congress*, October 19, 2005; Thomas Lum, "Laos: Background and U.S. Relations," *CRS Report for Congress*, January 22, 2007.
85. U.S. Congress, Senate, *Resolution to Condemn Human Rights Abuses in Laos*, November 19, 2004, 108th Congress, 2nd Session, Washington: Government Printing Office, accessed Sept. 1, 2017, https://www.congress.gov/bill/108th-congress/senate-resolution/475/text.
86. Tom Webb, "U.S. Spells Out Advice to Hmong—Aid to Lao Rebels Violates Foreign Policy," *St. Paul PioneerPress*, February 27, 2004; Tom Webb,

"Hmong, U.S. Officials Set for Historic Meeting," *Pioneer Press*, February 26, 2004.

87. Grit Grigoleit, "Coming Home? The Integration of Hmong Refugees from Wat Tham Krabok, Thailand, into American Society," *Hmong Studies Journal* 7 (2006): 1–22; Tunya Sukpanich, "Home at Last?" *Bangkok Post*, January 11, 2004.
88. Embassy of the U.S.A., "The U.S. to Open a Refugee Resettlement Program for Lao/Hmong at WatTham Krabok," December 18, 2003; Maisee Yang, "Special Report from Wat Thamkrabok, Thailand: A Firsthand Perspective from Inside, (Part 1)" *Hmong Today*, February 26, 2004; Maisee Yang, "Special Report From Wat Thamkrabok, (Part 2)," *Hmong Today*, March 11, 2004; Maisee Yang, "Special Report From Wat Thamkrabok, (Part 3)," *Hmong Today*, March 25, 2003.
89. Jennie Pasquarella, "Blaming Terror's Victims," *Legal Times*, May 29, 2006; Anna Husarska, "Old Allies, Tagged Terrorists," *Washington Post*, December 16, 2006.
90. Jean Hopfensperger, "Senate Act is Good News for the Hmong Community," *Star Tribune*, September 13, 2007; Frederic J. Frommer, "Some Hmong to Get Waiver on 'Terrorist' Designation," *Star Tribune*, October 27, 2007.
91. "Defense keys on federal agent's behavior in Laos plot case," *Sacramento Bee*, September 26, 2009; Roger Warner, "On Exaggeration, Context and the Wages of A Covert War," *Pioneer Press*, June 20, 2007; Roger Warner, "The Weirdest Terrorism Court Case in America," *Huffington Post*, March 11, 2009.
92. *USA vs. Harrison Ulrich Jack*, 207-MJ-0178 (June 4, 2007); and *USA vs. Harrison Ulrich Jack*, 207-CR-0266 (September 20, 2010).
93. Stephen Magagnini, "Hmong Express Relief Over End of Case for Vang," *Sacramento Bee*, September 18, 2009; Eric Bailey and My-Thuan Tran, "Charges Against Californian Hmong Leader Accused of Plotting to Overthrow Lao Government Are Dropped," *Los Angeles Times*, September 18, 2009; Jesse McKinley, "U.S. Drops Case Against Exiled Hmong Leader," *New York Times*, September 18, 2009.
94. U.S. Department of Justice, "Superseding Indictment Handed Down in Plot to Overthrow the Government of Lao," *Press Release*, September 18, 2009.
95. Bob Egelko, "U.S. drops charges in alleged Laotian coup plot," *San Francisco Chronicle*, January 11, 2011.

96. "Defense keys on federal agent's behavior in Laos plot case," *Sacramento Bee*, September 26, 2009.
97. Nina Delgadill, Tom Mangan, and Rosemary Shaul, "'Operation Tarnished Eagle' Thwarts Plot to Overthrow the Government of Laos," *Interagency Press Release*, June 4, 2007.
98. Ibid.
99. Ibid.
100. Tim Weiner, "General Vang Pao's Last War," *New York Times Magazine*, May 11, 2008.
101. Michael Doyle, "Wikileaks Cable Bares Secrets of U.S.-Laotian Relations." *McClatchy Newspapers*, April 22, 2011.
102. "Indictments Hurt Hmong Worldwide, Advocate Says," *Orange County Register*, July 18, 2007; "Deportations' Link to Pao Denied," *Orange County Register*, June 10, 2007; Roger Warner, "On Exaggeration, Context and the Wages of A Covert War," *Pioneer Press*, June 20, 2007.
103. Chia Youyee Vang, "Rethinking Hmong Women," Claiming Place: on the Agency of Hmong Women (Minneapolis: Univ. of MN Press, 2016), 56-84; and Chia Youyee Vang, *Fly Until You Die: Hmong Pilots in the Vietnam War* (Oxford: Oxford Univ. Press, 2017).
104. Gary Yia Lee and Nicholas Tapp, *Culture and Customs of the Hmong* (Santa Barbara, CA: ABC-CLIO, 2010), xiv.
105. Perrin, "Welcome to the Jungle," Thomas Fuller, "Old U.S. Allies, Still Hiding in Laos," *New York Times*, December 17, 2007; William Lloyd George, "Secret Army still Fighting Vietnam War," *The Independent*, February 17, 2010; Rebecca Sommer, "Report on the Situation in the Xaysomboun Special Zone and 1100 Hmong-Lao Refugees Who Escaped to Petchabun, Thailand, 2004-2005," May 2006; Rebecca Sommer, "Hunted Like Animals," DVD, 2006; and Amnesty International, "Lao People's Democratic Republic: Hiding in the Jungle, Hmong Under Threat," March 23, 2007.
106. John Boyle, "The amazing life of Vang Pao," *Chico News and Review*, February 16, 2012.
107. Heather Somerville, "Fresno school named after Hmong Gen. Vang Pao," *Fresno Bee*, February 8, 2012.
108. Christina Rafael, "Statue of General Vang Pao Unveiled at Hmong Festival in Chico," *ChicoEr*, December 8, 2012.

Leopard Spots, Patchworks, and Crazy Quilts

A Geography of Nixon's Vietnam War

Martin G. Clemis

When Lyndon Johnson sent American combat forces to the Republic of Vietnam (RVN) in the spring of 1965, he was committing America's foreign policy and national defense establishment to a war unlike any the nation had ever experienced. Politically, the Second Indochina War was a revolutionary struggle for power and the right to determine Vietnam's social, political, and economic future. The end of French rule and national partition in 1954 gave rise to two competing Vietnamese regimes, one communist and the other anticommunist. Both governments were driven by an ideological vision for postcolonial Vietnam, and both were determined to actualize through war, their own blueprint for an autonomous nation. Militarily, the war in South Vietnam was a "hybrid" war that included a complex and continuously-mutating blend of conventional large-scale combat, guerrilla warfare, and political subversion at the local level. By the time U.S. combat forces arrived, an armed insurgency directed by the Democratic Republic of Vietnam (DRV) and carried out by the National Front for the Liberation of South Vietnam (NLF), had already metastasized and embedded itself within the social fabric of rural South Vietnam. The military and political wings of the NLF – the People's Liberation Armed Forces (PLAF), or Viet Cong as they were called, and the clandestine political apparatus known as the Viet Cong Infrastructure (VCI)– operated to varying degrees in every province and in nearly every district of South Vietnam. Furthermore, large numbers of People's Army of Vietnam (PAVN) regulars had crossed into South Vietnam and were conducting offensive operations against RVN military outposts, government installations, and the Army of the Republic of Vietnam (ARVN) main-force units. This doctrinal and operational mélange prompted some observers to characterize the conflict as a "mosaic" war. Simultaneously, the war in one area could have involved conventional warfare between communist and allied main-forces; in another, mid-level guerrilla warfare; and in yet another, low-level insurgency and political struggle.[1] "There were forty-four provinces in South Vietnam," Maxwell Taylor wrote in 1972, "and the situation in one province was quite different from its neighbors."[2]

At its heart, the Second Indochina War was a competition to control contested political spaces– a "control war" in which the competing factions vied for supremacy over the people, territory, and resources of South Vietnam. In 1969, the Vietnam Special Studies Group, an ad hoc assessment body assembled during the Nixon administration, made the following observation: "Control of the people and resources of the countryside is vital to both contestants in the war... The struggle for control of the countryside is the 'control war.' This is what gives the Vietnam conflict its insurgency character and distinguishes it from more conventional types of warfare."[3] Former ARVN officers, Nguyen Duy Hinh and Tran Dinh Tho agreed. "The rural areas were the warehouse of manpower and material resources," they recollected. "Our opponents regarded the rural areas as a strategic objective to be captured, which was the reason why the RVN and its allies defended them at all costs."[4] Although the war in South Vietnam has been largely cast as a contest to garner political legitimacy and win the "hearts and minds" of the population, the reality is that efforts to gain popular support were subordinate to a violent struggle to seize and maintain military and administrative control over land and people. Establishing dominion over rural areas was critically important to both the Vietnamese communists and the RVN. Physical and human geography not only provided the material requirements necessary for waging a protracted civil war in the countryside, including manpower, foodstuffs, supply, lines of communication, combat support, and intelligence, they also fulfilled critical psychological and political needs by legitimating ontological claims to sovereignty, authority, and power. This material and ideational significance made rural areas the locus and medium of the Second Indochina War. Much like a traditional battlefield, where the site of combat is part of the territory contending armies fight to possess, the South Vietnamese countryside was both a *place* and an *object* of military and political struggle.

Efforts to control contested political spaces had been a critical component of the Second Indochina War from its beginning. They assumed unprecedented urgency, however, in the years following the 1968 Tet Offensive, when the political shockwaves generated by this seminal event profoundly impacted its conduct, its character, and the strategy pursued by Washington and Saigon.[5] The sequence of offensives, called *Tet Mau Than* (Tet, year of the monkey) by the Vietnamese, was a watershed moment because it exposed the failure of American policy and provoked a new set of politico-military variables, which redefined the war. The shock of the attacks along with a growing frustration and increased pessimism among American policymakers and the public prompted key changes. These included Johnson's refusal to run for re-election, the removal of General William Westmoreland as head of the Military

Assistance Command, Vietnam (MACV), termination of the strategic bombing campaign against the DRV, the commencement of formal peace negotiations, a greater emphasis on rural pacification, and the decision to de-escalate and return political and military stewardship back to RVN. The timely arrival of U.S. combat forces three years earlier may have stemmed the surging tide of communist insurgency, saved the RVN from certain collapse, and helped the Saigon regime regain its footing and live to fight another day. Nonetheless, Westmoreland failed to gain the upper hand or bring the war closer to conclusion by 1968, this despite three years of intense fighting and the infusion of nearly a half million troops. Lyndon Johnson and the defense establishment failed to solve the intractable political and military problems in South Vietnam. Consequently, the president halted American military escalation, opened the door to peace talks and the possibility of a negotiated settlement, and declined to run for another term. Thus, *Tet Mau Than* and the political fallout it generated transformed the war in Vietnam, and effectively destroyed Johnson's presidency. When Johnson left office, the war he handed off was more complex and more intractable than the one he took on in the spring of 1965.

NIXON'S INHERITANCE

In January 1969, Richard Nixon and his administration inherited a war that was at once familiar and new. On the one hand, *Tet Mau Than* changed the conflict's dynamics and affected significant policy revisions. Although the communist offensive failed to break the military stalemate or present a clear-cut advantage for either the communists or the RVN and its American ally, the attacks shaped the succeeding course of action taken by both sides. For Hanoi, Tet laid bare the reality that the combined military strength of the RVN and the U.S. was too much to overcome, and that the PLAF/PAVN simply could not sustain the high casualties and materiel losses they suffered over the previous three years. The only way the revolution could survive, the Vietnam Workers' Party

(VWP) reasoned, was to shift from a predominantly military approach, built around main-force combat and the General Offensive and General Uprising strategy, to a method that merged protracted war and diplomacy. For Washington, the attacks underscored the fact that the war could not be settled on the battlefield and that the United States had to revise its current course of action. The realization that American military power alone could not bring the war to conclusion or solve the fundamental social and political issues that fueled civil war in Vietnam prompted the United States to initiate a new agenda built on de-escalation, strengthening the RVN's political and military institutions, and working toward a negotiated peace. Vietnamization, a revitalized pacification program, and the Paris Peace Talks became the centerpiece of this new approach.

On the other hand, the war retained its nationalist and ideological contours as well as its sophisticated blend of conventional military operations, irregular warfare, and grass roots political struggle. It also maintained the unique spatiality created by this complex operational matrix. The war's hybrid character along with its mercurial and exceedingly fluid nature produced a highly irregular and fragmented collage of political and military control throughout South Vietnam. Unlike conventional wars, which produce relatively defined front lines, the war created an ever-shifting kaleidoscope of intermingled occupation zones and nebulous territorial boundaries, which defied easy generalization. Political and military control varied widely throughout South Vietnam, producing a contested and ever-shifting patchwork of friendly areas directly adjacent to or intermingled with enemy areas. "It was almost impossible to determine what area was under whose control," one South Vietnamese general lamented. "This was especially true of contested areas to which both laid claim but in which neither side had a permanent military presence."[6] American journalist Arnold Isaacs argued that attempts to identify combatant zones of control was like asking someone to distinguish "the whites and yolks in a dish of scrambled eggs."[7] Another observer claimed the landscape did not look "so much like Viet Cong islands in a Saigon lake, nor like Saigon islands in a communist lake but rather like marshland— with land and water pretty much indistinguishable and fluctuating with the tides and storms."[8] To the Vietnamese, the unique mixture of RVN and NLF enclaves resembled the spots on a leopard. Thus, the spatial formation created by interspersed pockets of communist and allied control was called a "leopard spot" configuration. Although the Second Indochina War is frequently called a "war without fronts," it was in fact a war of innumerable fronts; as communist revolutionaries, and the RVN and its American ally vied for supremacy over an atomized conflict environment that spanned four military regions, forty-four provinces, 236 districts, and more than 11,000 hamlets. The struggle for South Vietnam was not one geographical war, but many.

The Second Indochina War's unique spatiality had a profound impact on the conflict. Although rarely touched upon in the literature, geography played a central role in the Nixon administration's Vietnam policies. Nearly every major decision and platform, including the conditions set forth in the Paris Peace Talks, the ceasefire and negotiated settlement that ended the American war in Southeast Asia, the Vietnamization-pacification strategy, the military incursions into Cambodia and Laos, and the drawdown of U.S. combat forces, was rooted in geographical considerations and the territorial disposition of opposing forces inside South Vietnam. The political, military, and diplomatic policies of the Nixon administration were a direct response to the chaotic spatial configuration generated by this highly irregular and multifaceted "area war."[9]

Image 3. South Vietnam: Vietnam Special Studies Group Control Map, September 1972

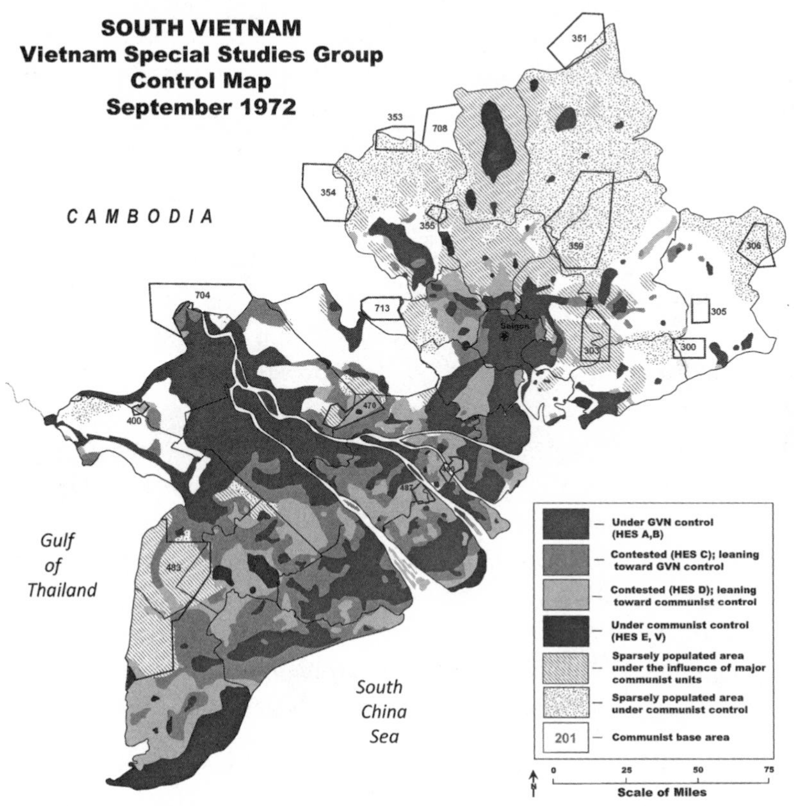

Source: Provided by the author.

The Paris Peace Talks, In-Place Ceasefire, and Territorial Accommodation

When delegates from the United States convened in Paris in May 1968 to begin formal peace talks, no one imagined it would take almost five years to reach a negotiated settlement. The reason deliberations were so protracted lies in the stubborn refusal by both sides to acquiesce on several key issues.

For Hanoi and the NLF, the overall purpose of peace talks was not to achieve a compromised solution, but to win the war. Despite their willingness to negotiate, the communists refused to renounce the revolution's fundamental purpose: the overthrow of the Saigon regime and unification of the country under communist rule.[10] Winning the war, however, first meant securing a favorable set of circumstances that would improve their chances of toppling the RVN after the United States had withdrawn. The communists' central negotiating plank, therefore, rested on three key conditions: the complete, unilateral withdrawal of American forces; the removal of the RVN's heads of state, president Nguyen Van Thieu and vice president Nguyen Cao Ky; and the formation of a coalition government— one that would be dominated by the NLF and other entities handpicked by the VWP.[11] The first demand would improve Hanoi's chances of conquering a peace through military force during the postwar period by providing a territorial platform for launching a major offensive; the second and third conditions would facilitate an overthrow of the Saigon regime through political means by decapitating the staunchly anticommunist South Vietnamese government and reestablishing the revolution's political infrastructure in the villages.

The opening of Hanoi and the NLF's diplomatic front was accompanied by an amendment in the military front. After years of main-force combat and hopes of delivering a rapid knockout blow against the RVN via the General Offensive and General Uprising, Hanoi and the NLF shifted back to a protracted war strategy, which combined low-level economy-of-force tactics with conventional operations and occasional large-scale offensives. This change in approach was intended to preserve communist forces, maintain constant military pressure on allied forces, defeat the Vietnamization and pacification programs, and gain control of rural areas. It was also meant to inflame anti-war sentiment in the U.S. and pressure the Nixon administration to concede to communist demands in

Paris.[12] The decision to implement a protracted war strategy after 1968 was prudent as it allowed communist forces to maintain a geographical patchwork of influence and control throughout the South Vietnamese countryside.

For Nixon and his top advisor, Henry Kissinger, the objective of peace talks was to bring the war in Southeast Asia to conclusion and preserve the national sovereignty of the RVN. Another goal was to create conditions that would allow the United States to "honorably" extricate itself from an exceedingly unpopular and divisive war— this is known as "Peace with Honor." The overall aim was to end armed hostilities and create a postwar environment that would allow the people of South Vietnam to choose their own government peacefully, democratically, and without "outside" interference.[13] Thus, Nixon and Kissinger set out to win two primary concessions: the mutual withdrawal of North Vietnamese and American forces from South Vietnam, and the preservation of Thieu and Ky as heads of state.[14] Both conditions were considered essential if a brokered and lasting peace was to be achieved. Should only American and other allied military forces withdraw while PAVN forces remain, they reasoned, Hanoi would likely use the territory it occupied inside South Vietnam to launch a major military offensive and conquer the RVN by force. Should Thieu and Ky be replaced by a coalition government dominated by the NLF, they maintained, the communists would use the extensive network of "liberated areas" under their control to reconstitute the VWP's political infrastructure, outmaneuver the RVN at the grass roots in the run-up to national elections, and overrun the Saigon regime through political rather than military means.

The territorial-centric conditions presented at the Paris Peace Talks were considered essential preconditions for any ceasefire agreement that would precede a negotiated settlement. Ceasefires have normally been looked upon as welcome developments during times of war. In Vietnam, however, a coordinated cessation of hostilities was problematic. The difficulty lay with the war's "mosaic" nature and the patchwork state of control that existed throughout South Vietnam. Because the conflict was a civil war wherein a partially homegrown insurgency had metastasized and established enclaves throughout the host nation, the type of ceasefire where the opposing armies would disperse and regroup within carefully proscribed zones was unlikely. The possibility of a ceasefire in Vietnam raised several practical concerns regarding territorial apportionment and the designation of respective zones of control south of the 17th parallel. It was obvious that should a ceasefire be declared, the NLF and the RVN would claim authority over the territory and hamlets they controlled. Moreover, they would seek to rapidly expand their control over land and people just prior to a ceasefire and make every effort to "fly the flag" over areas they occupied and in as many contested areas as possible.

The prospect of a ceasefire was concerning given the interspersed zones of control in South Vietnam and the politico-military "checkerboard" they created.[15] "When two armies oppose each other on either side of a clearly defined front line, a ceasefire is much easier to arrange," noted one observer. "Each side continues to hold its ground while the shooting dies away. In Vietnam, however... there is no front line, no clearly demarcated area belonging to each of the combatants. Rather than a well-defined zone across the country, a depiction of government-held areas and those controlled by the Viet Cong would, on a map, appear to be a series of intermixed blotches."[16] Most observers understood that a ceasefire would more than likely perpetuate hostilities, albeit in a different form, rather than reduce them. "A ceasefire in South Vietnam," noted one American official, "does not imply a shift from war to peace. It means instead a shift from military to political conflict."[17] "If there existed a front line with unchallenged control behind it, as in Korea, the solution would be traditional and relatively simple," Kissinger argued. Furthermore, he contended:

> ...the two sides could stop shooting at each other and the ceasefire line could follow the front line. But there are no front lines in Vietnam; control... depends on who has forces in a given area and on the time of day. If a ceasefire permits the government to

> move without challenge, day or night, it will amount to a Saigon victory. If Saigon is prevented from entering certain areas, its means in effect partition which... tends towards permanency... the pattern would be a crazy quilt, with enclaves of conflicting loyalties all over the country.

Aside from partition and sustained conflict, the Nixon administration also feared an in-place ceasefire would make it virtually impossible to verify the withdrawal of PAVN forces from South Vietnam should Hanoi agree to this demand.[18]

The modalities of a ceasefire in a war of innumerable fronts proved highly problematic. For the United States, then, the only alternative was an in-place or "standstill" ceasefire accompanied by territorial accommodation— a political solution that would allow the RVN and the NLF to remain in place once hostilities had ended. Introduced by Harvard professor Samuel P. Huntington in 1968 and later embraced by the Nixon administration, territorial accommodation proposed partitioning South Vietnam into respective zones of control and allowing the NLF to administer the areas they currently occupied in exchange for its recognition that the RVN was the sole, legitimate national authority. It was hoped such an arrangement would integrate the NLF into the RVN's political structure and allow for an interim distribution of power at the local level.[19] Many believed this would expedite an agreement by assuaging communist concerns about elections and convincing Hanoi and the NLF that Saigon was willing to share power in South Vietnam.[20]

Thieu and other Saigon officials vehemently opposed any plan that would partition South Vietnam and grant the NLF jurisdiction over the scattered areas it occupied. While the Saigon regime repeatedly claimed they were amenable to a supervised, in-place ceasefire as a *temporary* measure, they would never accept such a plan as a permanent solution. Such an arrangement would not only allow the communists to rebuild their political and military strength in rural areas and resume the struggle, it would gradually dissolve the Saigon government through the steady growth of an insurgent anti-state within the national territory. "To accept a leopard-spot solution," Thieu informed the press in July 1970, "is to go from step to step toward a coalition government, from rear to high echelons, from local areas to the entire nation. I confirm that I will never accept it." Saigon also feared interspersed zones of control would undermine national sovereignty and Saigon's claims to political legitimacy by establishing a *de facto* communist state within the geographical borders of South Vietnam. "A leopard-skin solution," he lamented, "would mean the communists control certain areas by themselves, including political organization, with their own flags, their own military organization, their own government— tiny communist nations situated in [South] Vietnam."[21] Many in Saigon likened communist leopard spots to a "cancer" that would grow and metastasize through sustained guerrilla activity, political struggle, and accommodation between the population and insurgents at the local level.[22] They also feared the acceptance of NLF enclaves would create a "third Vietnam"— i.e. a situation where zones of communist control were not only delineated but legitimated through the establishment of a communist capital and international recognition of the Provisional Revolutionary Government (PRG) as the legitimate political authority in areas under communist control. [23] "A third Vietnam... is more than we can afford to give," roared one Saigon official. "We dread it."[24]

The Vietnamization- Pacification Strategy

The new era that emerged from *Tet Mau Than* had a profound impact on Nixon's Vietnam War. Beginning in the fall of 1968, efforts to help the RVN attain political and military proficiency and expand its hold on the countryside had assumed unprecedented urgency. Once Nixon took office, rapidly expanding government control over rural areas and preparing the RVN to assume the burden of its own defense without American combat support had become a top priority thanks to the advent of the Paris Peace Talks and the possibility of a negotiated settlement, which would freeze opposing political and military forces in place and grant each contender authority over the population and territory they occupied. Over the next four years, these efforts would dominate the war in South Vietnam and serve as a touchstone for the ongoing diplomatic efforts in Paris.

Nixon's strategy for ending the war was to gradually withdraw U.S. forces while simultaneously strengthening the RVN's political and military institutions so the Saigon government could reinforce its hold on rural areas, solidify ties with the rural population, revive the rural economy, and build a fighting force that could effectively meet the hybrid threat posed by the PLAF/PAVN. Vietnamization and pacification became the centerpiece of allied efforts during the Nixon administration.[25] The Vietnamization-pacification strategy was designed to help the RVN strengthen its political and economic infrastructure and provide for its own defense by improving and modernizing the Republic of Vietnam Armed Forces (RVNAF) and expanding Saigon's control over the countryside. "Vietnamization has two principal components," Nixon informed Congress in February 1970. "The first is the strengthening of the armed forces of the South Vietnamese in numbers, equipment, leadership and combat skills, and overall capability. The second component is the extension of the pacification program in South Vietnam."[26]

By the time Nixon took office, the decision to reduce America's combat role had already been made. The RVN, it was argued, had to assume responsibility for its own defense. However, its political and military institutions had to be strengthened if the Saigon government was to have a fair chance of survival once American forces had departed. A central feature of Vietnamization, then, was the phased drawdown of American combat forces paired with accelerated advisory, training, and military aid programs. The plan was that as American troops withdrew, the RVNAF— which included ARVN main-forces and territorial forces known as Regional Forces and Popular Forces (RF/PF also known as "Ruff-Puffs")— would take their place.[27] Vietnamization and the American drawdown, however, placed tremendous pressure on the RVNAF and

MACV, demanding the former achieve combat proficiency and the latter get them there within a limited timeframe. Although the extraction of American forces was gradual, South Vietnamese security forces had to be expanded and brought up to fighting trim so that the transition was seamless and there were no gaps in allied combat capabilities. "The process of withdrawal was likely to become irreversible," Kissinger wrote after the war. "Henceforth, we would be in a race between the decline in our combat capability and the improvement of South Vietnamese forces – a race whose outcome was at best uncertain."[28]

Pacification and its emphasis on expanding Saigon's presence and control in rural areas was critical given the ongoing negotiations in Paris and the possibility of an in-place ceasefire and territorial accommodation. The level of control each side held over the territory and population was a central factor in the deliberations: the ability of Washington and Saigon to win concessions and secure those conditions that would help safeguard South Vietnam's future were directly linked to the allies' capacity to shrink the insurgency and grow RVN presence in rural areas. "Relative control in the countryside is going to be one of the things that will largely determine the shape of any settlement reached between the North and South Vietnamese," Robert Komer declared in his final press conference as the civilian head of Civil Operations and Revolutionary Development Support (CORDS).[29] U.S. ambassador Ellsworth Bunker agreed. "Success in the pacification and military sphere will have a direct effect on the negotiations," Bunker informed the White House in December 1968. "By extending territorial control and driving enemy forces across the border into Laos and Cambodia," he continued, "the South Vietnamese greatly strengthen their position at Paris. This is obviously a strong incentive, and Thieu is pushing his people to get on with the war effort and pacification faster and with better effect than at any other time since I arrived."[30] Thieu himself was more succinct. "At the conference table in Paris," he stated in December 1968, "there will be long discussion as to who controls the land and the people... as to who has governments in the villages and hamlets."[31] One American journalist placed the resurgence of pacification at the center of allied efforts in the wake of *Tet Mau Than* and the commencement of formal peace talks in Paris. "No one speaks of conventional 'military victory' over the 110,000-man North Vietnamese army, with its secure Laotian and Cambodian rear base areas. Such talk died among working-level folk here long before it vanished from U.S. official rhetoric in the wake of the communist Tet Offensive last January," he wrote. "The goal... is more modest: rapid consolidation of South Vietnamese government authority over as many of Vietnam's 17.5 million people as possible in 1969, before any ceasefire agreement is reached in Paris."[32]

Determined to gain the upper hand in Paris and buy time for the South Vietnamese armed forces to develop, the Nixon administration and the Saigon regime worked feverishly to maximize the RVN's social, political, and military footprint and establish some degree of physical presence over as much of the rural geography as possible. Instead of applying the slower, more methodical tasks of nation building, which addressed socioeconomic development as well as security, the allies implemented a method that privileged the rapid (although tenuous) extension of government control over population and territory through military force. Much like efforts to improve and modernize South Vietnam's armed forces, pacification and the extension of government control over rural areas had to be done quickly. Looking back, Nixon concluded: "Our defeat of the Tet Offensive had produced a political vacuum in the countryside. Areas that the National Liberation Front had controlled for years were now up for grabs. We knew that whichever side won the race to take control of the hamlets would have won half the battle."[33] American withdrawal elicited a need for speed not only on the military side of Vietnamization but also on the nonmilitary side (pacification and the expansion of government control). In short, Saigon had to rapidly "pacify" the countryside and create an environment that was both safe and productive if the nation was to, on its own, manage the ongoing insurgency and survive.[34]

The push to gain control of rural areas began shortly after the communists launched the first leg of *Tet Mau Than* and continued throughout 1968. In November, U.S. and RVN military forces launched the Accelerated Pacification Campaign (APC), a three-month nationwide blitz meant to rapidly expand government control in the countryside and improve the security ratings of nearly 1,000 hamlets that were either contested or controlled by the NLF.[35] The campaign was followed over the next three years by several pacification programs that applied the same principles.[36] The decision to pursue politico-military control rather than politico-economic development lay at the heart of the Accelerated Pacification Campaign and subsequent operations. The objective was not to thoroughly develop rural areas but to rapidly establish government presence throughout the countryside. Thus, nation-building and its emphasis on social, economic, and political development took a back seat to expanding RVN control and eliminating communist military forces and political infrastructure.[37] "The accelerated pacification program," noted one journalist, "has wisely shed some overambitious attempts at rural reform... It is now purely and simply an effort to wrest control of hamlets and villages from the Viet Cong."[38]

The APC and subsequent campaigns meshed pacification and military operations in accordance with the allied "one war" strategy— an approach that unified military operations and nation-building efforts. According to MACV, the plan did not recognize "a separate war of big battalions, war of pacification, or war of territorial security." Rather, friendly forces were to "carry the battle to the enemy simultaneously, in all areas of conflict."[39] Beginning in 1969, the "one war" strategy was applied to a geographically-based defense framework designed specifically to address South Vietnam's "mosaic" character and the shifting patchwork of government and insurgent control. Known as the Area Security Concept (ASC), the strategy made upgrading population security and consolidating Saigon's hold over its land and its people the primary goal of allied operations. "The ultimate objective is security up to the borders of South Vietnam, which is not dependent on the continued presence of

US combat forces. This is a 'win' strategy: The enemy will not be able to exercise political control in South Vietnam; his intervention forces will not be supported locally, and therefore will be more vulnerable." The ASC divided areas of the countryside into designated zones according to security levels. It then prescribed an appropriate military force and combat action within each zone. Conceptually, the boundaries that divided the zones were to be treated as "phase lines," and the objective was to keep them moving forward and to expand security until it encompassed the RVN's territory and population in their entirety. Although controversial, the ASC was central to the Vietnamization-pacification strategy during the years of American withdrawal.[40]

Image 4. South Vietnam: 41st Division Tactical Area, September 1968

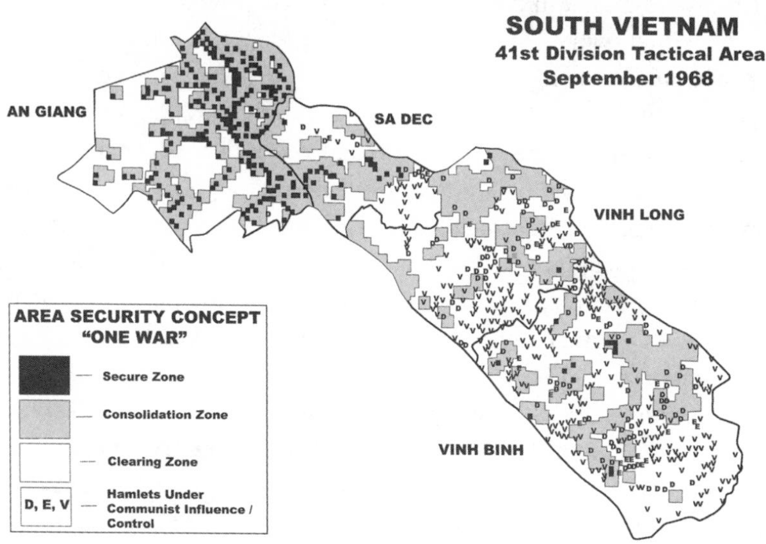

Source: Provided by the author.

Pacification and the "one war" strategy brought unprecedented levels of government control over South Vietnam's territory and population.

By November 1968, one month into the APC, MACV had reported that 73.3 percent of South Vietnam's total population was living in "relatively secure" areas. The percentage living in "contested" and "Viet Cong-controlled" areas, meanwhile, dropped to 13.3 percent and 13.4 percent respectively. The largest increase was among the rural population living "relatively secure" areas, which increased to 60.7 percent.[41] Twelve months later, the percentage of the total population living in "relatively secure" areas had climbed to 93 percent. This roughly translated into 15.8 million people out of a total population of 17 million. The year of 1969 turned out to be a banner year for pacification and allied progress in the countryside. While forward momentum began to slow in November and would continue to stagnate into the early part of 1970, the year had still witnessed the largest and most rapid pacification gains of the war.[42]

The progress made in 1968 and 1969 continued through 1970 despite the gradual withdrawal of American combat forces. By December 1970, the overall population living in "relatively secure" areas had jumped to nearly 95 percent. In the countryside, RVN control of the rural population was equally impressive, increasing more than twenty-five percentage points since August 1969. End-of-year estimates showed Saigon in full control of more than 66 percent of rural inhabitants. "The war in South Vietnam has wound down to a point well below the levels of previous years and has entered a period of relative quiescence," the office of the Deputy Assistant Secretary of Defense (ODASD) declared in its end-of-year report. "Pacification progress and activity has exceeded expectations, despite reduced U.S. forces and activity," the report continued. "Experienced observers returning to Vietnam after long periods out of the country unanimously agree that security conditions in the countryside are better than ever before."[43] Much of these gains were a product of the devastating losses suffered by PLAF units during Tet, a significant decline in communist main-force activity beginning in 1968, and a large demographic shift from rural to urban areas. Nonetheless, the sharp increase in RVN control was made possible principally through conventional combat actions by American and RVNAF forces. "Gains in territorial security and population control are due in part to the slackening of enemy opposition," Bunker informed the White House, "but that slack is in turn due in considerable degree to the fact that we continue to push him relentlessly."[44]

MACV concluded that the overall progress in security was largely the result of the allies' increasingly effective use of military resources to clear target areas and a strong emphasis on developing local government and local defense.[45] Several key American officials agreed that the improved conditions in the countryside were the product of conventional combat actions. In 1969, Westmoreland's successor, General Creighton Abrams, made the following statement: "The accelerated pacification program, which we feel is progressing quite favorably, is made possible largely by friendly military initiative which keeps the enemy from concentrating his forces against our pacification program."[46] Abrams' predecessor agreed. "At the time we entered, the government held only a few enclaves," Westmoreland informed the House of Representatives Committee on Appropriations in February 1970. He further noted:

> It took a great deal of effort, sweat and blood to expand the enclaves to the point that the countryside opened up. In the process of that, we have had to grind down the guerrilla force, which has been done. Pacification has been extended bringing more people and area under government control. The indigenous enemy in the south has been reduced. The enemy now has been required to take refuge in remote areas of South Vietnam, in Cambodia, in Laos, and in the DMZ area.[47]

Besides military operations inside South Vietnam, the record levels of RVN control over its national territory and population during this period were made possible by the Nixon administration's decision to expand the war into Laos and Cambodia. For years, Hanoi and the NLF used the difficult terrain in these countries to establish base areas for launching attacks against the RVN and safe havens to provide shelter for battered PLAF/PAVN main-force units. Despite such provocations, however, these regions had been untouched by invasion. Laos and Cambodia's terrestrial sanctuaries were immune from allied ground attack due to the neutrality of these two countries and the political turmoil it would have provoked, both in the United States and abroad. From the perspective of American and South Vietnamese officials, the situation was akin to, in the words of one former officer, "a loaded and cocked pistol... being held to the head of South Vietnam."[48] In the spring of 1969, just as the APC was beginning to yield substantial security gains in the countryside, RVNAF and U.S. forces initiated the first of several cross-border attacks against Cambodia and Laos. The purpose was to buy time for the Vietnamization-pacification strategy to take hold by attacking formerly inviolable communist sanctuaries and disrupting communist capabilities for launching attacks into South Vietnam. In March, the Nixon administration ordered covert bombing raids against communist base areas in eastern Cambodia. Known as Operation Menu, the air campaign was the first of a series of offensive cross-border operations against communist sanctuaries. In May 1970, the Nixon administration upped the ante by approving a joint U.S./RVNAF ground attack into Cambodia. The following year, the allies launched another cross-border invasion against PLAF/PAVN sanctuaries, this time into Laos. The invasion was dubbed Operation Lam Son 719, and it was conducted by ARVN units without the assistance of U.S. ground forces; MACV provided logistical, artillery, and aerial support. Overall, Operation Menu, the Cambodian incursion, and Lam Son 719 did little to alter the strategic balance of forces in Indochina. They did, however, provide the RVN an opportunity to consolidate its gains in the countryside and continue to prepare the RVNAF for a future without American combat assistance. In Cambodia, joint U.S./RVNAF operations cut a vital North Vietnamese supply line and preoccupied PLAF/PAVN main-force units, which otherwise would have threatened Saigon and the Mekong Delta. In Laos, Lam Son 719 reduced the flow of men and materiel down the Ho Chi Minh Trail and delayed a possible North Vietnamese invasion for a year— this despite a poor combat performance by ARVN main-forces. "From the viewpoint of the Military Assistance Command, Vietnam," historian Graham Cosmas contends, "three years of cross-border operations kept the enemy at bay and won time in South Vietnam for Vietnamization and pacification to run their course."[49]

Military force was a cornerstone of Nixon's strategy to end the war in Vietnam. Although the administration maintained Johnson's bombing moratorium against the DRV, it made no corresponding limitations in the use of force south of the 17th parallel, or in the cross-border operations in Cambodia and Laos. Much like Hanoi, the White House pursued a "talk-fight" strategy (*danh vu dan*) and used U.S. combat operations to exert pressure on Hanoi to negotiate, advance the Vietnamization-pacification strategy, buy time to strengthen the RVN's military forces and political infrastructure, and expand Saigon's hold over the national territory and its population.

A "New Optimism" in Washington

The improved security situation and high levels of government control in rural areas had given rise to a new sense of optimism in Saigon and Washington by 1970. According to some observers, the Vietnamization-pacification strategy had "carved out a new set of realities on the ground in Vietnam."[50] These new realities along with the allies' ascendant position in the countryside had given a number of officials cause to celebrate. In the fall of 1969, General Abrams declared, "The pacification program is no longer a laughing matter from his [the communists'] viewpoint... I must say when you take the whole thing... the progress in pacification... no one has to buy the 90 percent or 86 percent, but the fact that security of the people is improving every month, I think is clear... the march of events seems to me to be inexorable."[51] Robert Thompson, a onetime critic of the American war and informal advisor to the Nixon administration, was equally optimistic. "I was very impressed by the improvement in the military and political situation in Vietnam, as compared with all previous visits, and especially in the security situation both in Saigon and the rural areas," Thompson wrote. "The position of the

RVN is undoubtedly more stable and its performance increasingly effective. This has best been demonstrated in the 1969 pacification program which has resulted in greatly increased government control in rural areas."[52] The positivity surrounding pacification and the control war in 1969 and 1970 was so strong that it persisted long after the war had been lost. "Pacification worked wonders in South Vietnam," Nixon declared years later. "We were in control of areas that we had previously not dared to enter... our pacification program had extended Saigon's control throughout the country down to the hamlet level."[53]

The feeling of progress that emanated from the Vietnamization and pacification programs deeply affected the Nixon administration. This was particularly true regarding the withdrawal of U.S. military forces. The White House was convinced that improvements in the RVNAF's combat capabilities and the extension of government control into rural areas made the American drawdown possible. "These two things, together," undersecretary Johnson informed Congress, "mean a lessening need for a U.S. role and are thus what enable us to bring about a reduction of our forces without endangering the existence of this program."[54] Other officials agreed with this assessment. "This withdrawal program, at least in the areas of ground combat, could and should be accelerated," Congressman Howard W. Robinson informed the Select Committee on United States Involvement in Southeast Asia in July 1970. "The military situation in South Vietnam today," he continued, "is better for both the U.S. and the South Vietnamese than at any time since American units first entered the war in the summer of 1965. In addition, the South Vietnamese fighting units have undoubtedly gained new self-confidence as a result of their role in the Cambodian sanctuary operation."[55] The steady withdrawal of U.S. forces between 1969 and 1971 was, in part, a product of increasing confidence over the Vietnamization-pacification strategy.[56] The expansion of RVN control over territory and population and general improvements in the RVNAF convinced the Nixon administration that U.S. forces could redeploy without serious consequences.

The Vietnamization-pacification strategy instilled enough confidence that it also shaped Nixon's stance on an in-place ceasefire. Despite some initial reservations, the administration proposed such an arrangement in October 1970. After convincing a reluctant Thieu to agree to a standstill ceasefire and some type of accommodation with the NLF at the local level, Nixon announced the United States and the RVN were ready to negotiate an internationally supervised ceasefire followed by an Indochina Peace Conference. "I do not minimize the difficulty of maintaining a ceasefire in a guerrilla war where there are no front lines," Nixon declared. "But an unconventional war may require an unconventional truce; our side is ready to stand still and cease firing." Nixon's offer for an in-place ceasefire reflected a growing confidence in Washington that the dual strategy of pacification and Vietnamization was working, and that progress in these areas, along with the recent allied incursion into Cambodia, had made the allied position strong enough to make an offer for territorial concessions possible. During his October 7 speech, Nixon stated his new peace initiative had "been made possible in large part by the success of the Vietnamization policy."[57] Several days later, a White House spokesman informed the *New York Times* Nixon had made the decision "because of the improved military and pacification picture." That same week, pacification officials reported that 92.8 percent of the population was living in "relatively secure" areas.[58] American newspapers were quick to pick up on Washington's newfound optimism. "White House officials acknowledged... that as recently as last year U.S. military leaders opposed a ceasefire in Vietnam on grounds it would then be extremely disadvantageous to allied forces. Now the tables are turned enough for the United States and South Vietnam to propose what they once feared would be thrust at them," noted the *Washington Post*.[59] "It was a sense of military and political weakness that had hitherto caused both the Johnson and Nixon Administrations to shy away from the idea of a ceasefire," the *New York Times* declared. "These fears," it continued, "have been dispelled in recent months. Even officials who continue to doubt the ability of Saigon to withstand a long guerrilla war believe that its position for the time being... has been made reasonably secure."[60]

The Nixon administration's shifting stance on an in-place ceasefire and territorial accommodation was not the only policy revision undertaken by the president. In what many would argue was the White House's most significant and tragic decision on the war in Vietnam, Nixon and Kissinger abandoned the condition set forth in the Paris negotiations for the mutual withdrawal of all U.S. and North Vietnamese forces. This change in policy occurred in the spring of 1971, when the administration quietly dropped its demand for the mutual extraction of all "outside" military forces from South Vietnam. In May, Nixon authorized Kissinger to concede this point at a secret meeting with the North Vietnamese delegation and retract the demand for mutual withdrawal.[61] On May 31, 1971, the seven-point "final" proposal for a settlement presented by the American delegation in Paris made no mention of the removal of communist forces. The long-standing American demand for mutual withdrawal, a cornerstone of America's diplomatic strategy for ending the war in Vietnam, had been abandoned.[62]

Nixon's concession to allow PAVN units to remain in South Vietnam rested partly on the conclusion that it was the only way to break the diplomatic stalemate in Paris and advance the negotiations.[63] The decision also stemmed from the administration's recognition that its bargaining power would wane over time given the ongoing extraction of U.S. forces.[64] Kissinger recognized by late 1970 that Congress would never allow American forces to remain in Vietnam, even if Hanoi refused to extricate its troops following an armistice. Moreover, Hanoi and the NLF would likely never surrender at the negotiating table what they had not lost on the battlefield. Thus, the administration had no choice but to proffer a deal that gave the communists discretion in removing their military forces from Southern soil. "The decision to propose a standstill ceasefire in 1970 thus implied the solution of 1972," Kissinger recalled. "That North Vietnamese forces would remain in the South was implicit in the standstill proposal; no negotiation would be able to remove them if we had not been able to expel them by force of arms."[65] Finally, the concession that allowed NVA main-forces to remain in South Vietnam likely sprung from the allies' ascendant position in the control war and Saigon's unprecedented hold on territory and population. Although no explicit evidence linking the two has been found, it is reasonable to assume that the decision to drop the demand for mutual withdrawal was tied to the RVN's relatively strong position in the countryside.

On one hand, the Nixon administration was confident that the Vietnamization-pacification strategy had progressed to the point that such a decision was possible. To begin, the ODASD reported in May 1971 that 94 percent of South Vietnam's population were living in "relatively secure areas."[66] A national intelligence estimate released just prior to Kissinger's secret meeting with Hanoi that month provided an equally optimistic assessment of allied prospects: "The outlook in South Vietnam for the remainder of 1971 is reasonably good," it stated. "The past three years have produced a more stable political situation, a marked improvement in security conditions, and considerable progress in Vietnamizaton. Meanwhile, communist problems in supporting the insurgency have mounted." Although the report warned the communists maintained the capacity and desire to continue a protracted war against the RVN, Hanoi's ability to engage in large-scale military activity would be limited.[67] High-level meetings that spring between Kissinger, the Joint Chiefs of Staff, the Central Intelligence Agency, and the National Security Council revealed equally confident assessments. According to the meeting's minutes, senior officials believed Saigon could maintain its dominant position in the countryside and handle the communist threat.[68]

On the other hand, concerns over the durability of the RVN's ninety-plus percent security ratings may have prompted the Nixon administration to drop its demand for the removal of PAVN units from South Vietnam. Determined to achieve an "honorable peace" while under intense domestic political pressure to end the war, Nixon likely proffered the deal to elicit a negotiated settlement at a time when Washington and Saigon held the upper hand. Pacification had achieved notable gains between November 1968 and December 1971, bringing a reasonable degree of security to most of the South Vietnamese population. Despite the unprecedented level of RVN control over territory and population and historically low levels of communist insurgent activity in the countryside, however, there was cause for concern. Security levels in many provinces were extremely fragile and susceptible to regression should the communists step up anti-pacification activities or launch another large-scale offensive.[69] In fact, security ratings had declined somewhat during the first quarter of 1971.[70] While everything may have appeared relatively quiet on the surface by May 1971, there existed putrefaction underneath that belied the RVN's quiescent façade. Not only had the communist insurgent state survived, leaving pockets of rebellion and sustained politico-military conflict throughout South Vietnam, but the pacification and Vietnamization programs were beset by a host of debilitating problems that grossly undermined Saigon's ability to maintain control over the national territory and its population with diminishing assistance from the United States.

Regardless of the impetus, Nixon's decision to allow PAVN units to remain in South Vietnam bore bitter fruit in the years that followed. In March 1972, Hanoi launched what was at the time the largest communist offensive of the war. Known as the Nguyen Hue or "Easter Offensive" as the Americans and South Vietnamese called it, the operation involved four separate thrusts against key strategic regions throughout the RVN. Although beaten back, the PAVN offensive created a permanent communist foothold inside South Vietnam. In April 1975, Hanoi used the enlarged footprint it secured during the Nguyen Hue Offensive along with the Nixon administrations' abandonment of mutual withdrawal in May 1971 to launch the conventional coup de main that toppled the Saigon regime. The ability of Hanoi and the NLF to control contested political spaces and build a "third Vietnam" inside South Vietnam, as Thieu and others had feared, proved a Trojan horse. When coupled with the withdrawal of American combat forces, diminished economic and military aid from

Washington, and the need to maintain a high level of military preparedness via a conventional military invasion by an increasingly muscular and modern PAVN, the RVN's inability to expel communist forces from South Vietnam along with Thieu's stubborn refusal to surrender any of the national territory before finally abandoning the Central Highlands and northern coastal provinces in the final weeks of the war, proved disastrous. In the end, the Saigon regime was simply overwhelmed by insurmountable geostrategic obligations and an enemy who successfully applied a geospatial strategy that not only maintained an insurgent anti-state within the host nation, but that stretched out and ultimately exhausted the RVN through incessant attack across a broad, multifaceted geographic front. As one observer noted just prior to the fall of Saigon: "Few people ever really believed that the South Vietnamese alone would be able to do what the Americans and South Vietnamese together had never completely managed, namely to defend the entire geographical border of South Vietnam."[71]

Conclusion

Geography and territory were intrinsic to every major issue and policy decision made by the Nixon administration to end the war in Vietnam. The diplomatic demands made in Paris, particularly the issue of unilateral or bilateral withdrawal of American and North Vietnamese combat forces and the retention or deposition of the Thieu and Ky regime; the modalities of an in-place ceasefire and territorial accommodation; the pace of the American drawdown; the improvement and modernization of South Vietnam's armed forces; and the push to expand the rural pacification and Saigon's hold on rural areas, were all rooted in geography and the disposition of opposing forces in a hybrid war without fronts. Although largely unspoken, South Vietnam's national territory and the population it sustained were the foundation upon which the survival of the RVN and the outcome of the war depended. Efforts to expand and maintain allied control over land and people was an integral part of the Nixon administration's military and diplomatic policies. Thus, geography was an overarching consideration that shaped and, in many ways, defined Nixon's Vietnam War.

Notes

1. Phillip B. Davidson, *Secrets of the Vietnam War* (Novato, CA: Presidio, 1990), 20.
2. Maxwell D. Taylor, *Swords and Plowshares* (New York: W.W. Norton, 1972), 405.
3. Vietnam Special Studies Group, "The Situation in the Countryside," May 13, 1970; 3-5. RG 472 / A1 462 / Box 17 / Folder: 1601-04 VSSG Final Study #55/Folder 1/1970, National Archives and Records Administration (Hereafter NARA II).
4. Nguyen Duy Hinh and Tran Dinh Tho, *The South Vietnamese Society* (Washington D.C.: U.S. Army Center of Military History, 1980), 109-10.
5. See Martin G. Clemis, *The Control War: The Struggle for South Vietnam, 1968-1975* (Norman: University of Oklahoma Press, 2018).
6. Cao Van Vien and Dong Van Khuyen, *Reflections on the Vietnam War* (Washington: U.S. Army Center of Military History, 1980), 118.
7. Arnold R. Isaacs, *Without Honor: Defeat in Vietnam and Cambodia* (Baltimore: Johns Hopkins University Press, 1983), 89.
8. Peter R. Kahn, "Shape of Peace: Vietnam Accords Seem Likely but May Lead To a New Kind of War," *Wall Street Journal*, November 14, 1972.
9. William Westmoreland used this term to describe the Vietnam War's lack of front lines. William C. Westmoreland, *A Soldier Reports* (New York: Doubleday & Company, 1976), 68.
10. Vietnam Documents and Research Notes (Hereafter VNDRN), Document No. 39, "Indoctrination Notes on Peace Talks: A Call for 'Violent Revolution' to the End," 3.
11. The essential elements of the communist negotiating platform can be seen in the National Liberation Front's "Principles and Main Content of an Overall Solution to the South Vietnam Problem— The Ten Point Plan." See Murrey Marder, "VC Offer New Plan at Paris," *Washington Post*, May 9, 1969. Also see Memo, Kissinger to Nixon, 3 July 1969, Foreign Relations of the United States (Hereafter FRUS), 1969-1976, 6: 1108-1111.
12. "Campaign X and the Mini-War;" Undated, RG 472 / A1 456 / Box 6 / Folder: Viet Cong 1969-70; Pacification Studies Group, "Study of Effects of COSVN 9," Undated, RG 472 / A1 462 / Box 16 / Folder: PSG Studies 1970/Book II/Folder II/1970, NARA II.

13. "Transcript of President Nixon's Address to the Nation on the War in Vietnam," *New York Times*, May 15, 1969.
14. Jeffrey Kimball, *The Vietnam War Files: Uncovering the Secret History of Nixon-Era Strategy* (Lawrence: University Press of Kansas, 2004), 24.
15. Allan E. Goodman, "South Vietnam: Neither War nor Peace," *Asian Survey* 10 (February 1970): 110.
16. William Tuohy, "Vietnam Cease Fire Could Cause Enormous Problems," *Los Angeles Times*, November 1, 1968.
17. Memo, Formation of the Office of Civil Operations, No Date, RG 472 / A1 462 / Box 89 / Folder: 1601-11A/Ceasefire Planning/CD&LD/Folder I/1973.
18. Henry A. Kissinger, "The Vietnam Negotiations," *Foreign Affairs* 47 (January 1969): 226-27.
19. See: Samuel P. Huntington, "The Bases of Accommodation," *Foreign Affairs* 46, no. 4 (July 1968): 642-56; Henry A. Kissinger, "The Vietnam Negotiations," *Foreign Affairs* 47, no. 2 (January 1969): 211-34; and Samuel P. Huntington, "Getting Ready for Political Competition in South Vietnam," Southeast Asia Development Advisory Group Discussion Paper, 29 March 1969, Folder 06, Box 07, John Donnell Collection, Texas Tech University Vietnam Center and Archive.
20. Memo, Kissinger to Nixon, 11 September 1969, *FRUS, 1969-1976,* 6: 385-86.
21. "Thieu Ends Rumors of Ceasefire," *The Baltimore Sun*, August 1, 1970.
22. Peter R. Kann, "Shape of Peace: Vietnam Accord Seems Likely but May Lead to a New Kind of War," *Wall Street Journal*, November 14, 1972.
23. On June 10, 1969, the NLF announced the formation of the Provisional Revolutionary Government (PRG), an organization that assumed the mantle of "national" leadership and was immediately recognized as such by a number of communist nations. The PRG was meant to establish a formal governmental structure at the regional and local levels and to create a "central political entity" that could compete with Saigon from a formal, legal standing. See Truong Nhu Tang, *A Viet Cong Memoir* (San Diego: Harcourt Brace Janovich, 1985), 146-47.
24. Peter R. Kann, "Two Views in Vietnam," *The Wall Street Journal*, January 31, 1975.
25. For a full exploration of these programs and their impact, see James H. Willbanks, Abandoning Vietnam: How America Left and South Vietnam Lost Its War (Lawrence: University Press of Kansas, 2004); and Kevin M.

Boylan, *Losing Binh Dinh: The Failure of Pacification and Vietnamization, 1969-1971* (Lawrence: University Press of Kansas, 2016).

26. "Nixon's Report to Congress on Foreign Policy," *New York Times*, February 19, 1970.
27. In the three years that followed *Tet Mau Than* the RVNAF grew by more than 400,000 troops, swelling their ranks to 1,045,000 personnel by 1971. The following year, overall enrollment peaked at 1,090,000 men under arms. RF / PF, meanwhile, jumped from 392,000 to 532,000 members during the same period. In 1972, South Vietnam's territorial forces had a membership of 520,000 personnel. Source: Thomas C. Thayer, *War Without Fronts: The American Experience in Vietnam* (Boulder and London: Westview Press, 1985), 34-35.
28. Henry Kissinger, *White House Years* (Boston & Toronto: Little, Brown, and Company, 1979), 272.
29. Memo, "Ambassador Komer's Final Press Conference," 3 November 1968, DepCORDS Files, U.S. Army Center of Military History (Hereafter CMH).
30. Ellsworth Bunker, "Seventy-Fourth Weekly Telegram, December 19, 1968" in Douglas Pike, ed. *The Bunker Papers: Reports to the President from Vietnam, 1967-1973* (Berkeley: Institute of East Asian Studies University of California, 1990), II: 629.
31. Memo, "Remarks by President Thieu," 22 December 1968, DepCORDS Files, CMH.
32. Peter Braestrup, "Viet Pressure Keeps Up," *Washington Post*, January 5, 1969.
33. Richard Nixon, *No More Vietnams* (New York: Arbor House, 1985), 105.
34. House of Representatives Select Committee on United States Involvement in Southeast Asia, Report, *United States Involvement in Southeast Asia*, 91st Congress, Second Session, July 6, 1970, 11.
35. Military Assistance Command, Vietnam (MACV) *1968 Command History Vol. 1*, 521-22.
36. See: Republic of Vietnam Central Pacification and Development Council, *1969 Pacification Campaign Guidelines*, MACV Command Historian's Collection, Series II: MACV Staff Sections, MACV J-3, CORDS, MHI; Republic of Vietnam Central Pacification and Development Council, 1970 *Plan for Pacification and Development*; and Republic of Vietnam Central Pacification and Development Council, 1971 *Community Defense and Local Development Plan*, Republic of Vietnam Central Pacification and Development Council, MHI.

37. *Bunker Papers*, II: 386-87; Memo, "Forsythe to Bunker," 4 April 1968, DepCORDS Files, CMH.
38. "The War Starts Up Again," *The Guardian*, January 14, 1969.
39. MACV, "Commanders Summary of the MACV Objectives Plan," 22-23, RG 472 / A1 455 / Box 4 / Folder: Readings Files/Misc./Folder II, NARA II.
40. Report, "The Principles and Application of Area Security," 10, RG 472 / A1 455 / Box 4 / Folder: Area Security, NARA II. The Area Security Concept was a central feature of the 1970 Combined Campaign Plan, the 1970 Pacification and Development Plan, and the 1971 Community Defense and Local Development.
41. Memo, "Pacification," 16 December 1968, 2-3, DepCORDS Files, CMH.
42. Southeast Asia (SEA) Analysis Report February 1970, 9, RG 472 / A1 472 / Box 6 / Folder: Southeast Asia Analysis Reports Oct 1969-Feb 1970; Vietnam Special Studies Group, "The Situation in the Countryside," May 13, 1970; 1-9, RG 472, A1 462, Box 17, Folder: 1601-04 VSSG Final Study #55/ Folder 1 1970, NARA II.
43. Southeast Asia (SEA) Analysis Report November/December 1970, p.1, RG 472 / A1 472 / Box 6 / Folder: Southeast Asia Analysis Reports Mar 1970-Dec 1970, NARA II.
44. *Bunker Papers*, II: 631.
45. Report, "Status of Pacification – 31 December 1969 – Final," RG 472 / A1 474 / Box 86 / Folder: #102238 Status of Pacification Report for 1969, NARA II.
46. Quoted in: Graham A. Cosmas, *MACV: The Joint Command in the Years of Withdrawal, 1968-1973* (Washington D.C.: Center of Military History, 1984), 245.
47. House Committee on Appropriations, *Department of Defense Appropriations for 1971*, 91st Cong., 2nd sess., 1970, 95.
48. Dave Richard Palmer, *Summons of the Trumpet: U.S.-Vietnam in Perspective* (Novato, CA: Presidio, 1978), 229.
49. Cosmas, *The Joint Command in the Years of* Withdrawal, 343.
50. Maynard Parker, "Vietnam: The War that Won't End," *Foreign Affairs* (January 1975): 360-61.
51. Lewis Sorley, ed. *Vietnam Chronicles: The Abrams Tapes, 1968-1972* (Lubbock, Texas: Texas Tech University Press, 2004), 280.
52. Memo, "Sir Robert Thompson's Report," 1; RG 472 / A1 474 / Box 71 / Folder: #101991 Sir Robert Thompson's Views in Vietnam, January 1970, NARA II.
53. Nixon, *No More Vietnams*, 133, 140-41.

54. House of Representatives, *Supplemental Appropriation Bill, 1971*, 1249.
55. House of Representatives, *United States Involvement in Southeast Asia*, 71.
56. The first round of American withdrawals, which included 25,000 troops, was announced on June 8, 1969, and completed by the end of August. Another 35,000 were removed by December. A third increment of 50,000 was withdrawn by the end of April 1970. On April 20, Nixon announced plans to withdraw an additional 150,000 troops over the next year. By that point, American troops had been leaving Vietnam at a rate of about 12,000 men a month. As of May 1, 1971, nearly half of all U.S. forces had returned home from Southeast Asia. Of the remaining 284,000, another 257,000 were sent back to the United States over the next 18 months. By the end of 1972, there were only 27,000 American military personnel left in South Vietnam, most of them advisors. Source: Nguyen Duy Hinh, *Vietnamization and the Cease-Fire* (Mclean, Virginia: General Research Corporation, 1976), 22.
57. "Text of President Nixon's Talk," *Boston Globe*, October 8, 1970.
58. "Challenge to Hanoi," *New York Times*, October 11, 1970.
59. Murrey Marder, "Proposal Unlikely to Stir Foe," *Washington Post*, October 8, 1970.
60. "Nixon Seeks New Path," *New York Times*, October 11, 1970.
61. Lein-Hang T. Nguyen, *Hanoi's War: An International History of the War for Peace in Vietnam* (Chapel Hill, NC: The University of North Carolina Press, 2012), 194.
62. Memorandum of Conversation, 31 May 1971, *FRUS, 1969-1976*, 7: 653.
63. Memo, Kissinger to Nixon, 20 July 1970, *FRUS, 1969-1976*, 7:1134.
64. Ibid.
65. Kissinger, *White House Years*, 974.
66. Thayer, Thomas, ed. *A Systems Analysis View of the Vietnam War, 19651972*, vol. 9: 247, Washington D.C.: Office of the Assistance Secretary of Defense (Systems Analysis), 1975.
67. National Intelligence Estimate, "South Vietnam: Problems and Prospects," 29 Apr 1971, in John K. Allen, John Carver, and Tom Elmore, eds., *Estimative Products on Vietnam, 1948-1975* (Pittsburg: U.S. Government Printing Office, 2005), 577.
68. Minutes of a Meeting of the Senior Review Group, 9 Jun 1971, *FRUS, 1969-1976*, 7: 701-715.
69. US MACV / RVNAF JGS, "Combined Strategic Objectives Plan, 1971," Folder 01, Box 19, Douglas Pike Collection: Unit 01 - Assessment and

Strategy, TTUVA; Michael Parks, "Erosion of Saigon Control Feared as Pacification Lags," *Baltimore Sun*, May 27, 1971.

70. Thayer, *A Systems Analysis View of the Vietnam War*, 9: 240.
71. Maynard Parker, "Vietnam: The War That Won't End," *Foreign Affairs* 53 (Jan 1975): 362.

Vietnam, the Student Movement, and the South

The War and Regional Identity

Jeffrey A. Turner

In 1967, Vanderbilt student and activist Bill Fugate showed up at a Nashville television station to be interviewed for a segment on the university's political left. One of the leaders of Vanderbilt's small band of Liberal-Left activists, Fugate was accustomed to feeling like an outsider on the conservative campus where, according to one of his colleagues, students who wore their hair too long or did not wear Gant shirts were judged to be outsiders. Fugate had not had time to shave before the interview and, perhaps conscious of these standards of personal appearance, apologized to the program director. "That's all right," the director replied. "That's just the way we want you."[1] Like an actor out of central casting, Fugate, at least to the TV news producer, was there to play a role.

By late 1965, as American involvement in Vietnam deepened, an image of an archetypal student activist seemed to loom over the South and its college campuses. The 1964 Free Speech Movement and the subsequent anti-war demonstrations at the University of California at Berkeley proved a powerful image for students penning pieces for their respective campus newspapers; in particular, they hoped that their own universities could foster the kind of intellectual spirit and engagement evident at Berkeley. Others, perhaps drawing on the very same images from television coverage, warned of the negative influence of self-indulgent, even dangerous student activists and hoped their university could be insulated from the effects. Either way, some version of the prototypical anti-war activist— the bearded, engaged, passionate, draft card-burning radical— seemed to influence those who endorsed and opposed the movement. "Bearded Radical Hits Suppression," declared a 1965 headline in the Emory University *Wheel* for a story about a campus visit by a veteran of the Berkeley Free Speech Movement. "I am against the fanatics who are burning the draft cards," a University of Georgia student wrote to the campus paper in 1965. "I believe they are a disgrace to the students in the colleges and universities of our GREAT UNITED STATES. At this time the University of Georgia is not in disgrace and let's keep it that way."[2] The language southern students used to describe "activists" reveals that southern students responded to Vietnam with some preconceived notions about the meaning of activism and what it might look like in the South.

The irony of this dynamic— this sense among many southern college students that "activism" represented either a potential import or a possible invasion from other parts of the nation— is that the South had already played a crucial role in the development of the decade's student movement. Black students in the South created the sit-in movement of the early 1960s, and that massive mobilization against segregation led to the creation of the Student Nonviolent Coordinating Committee and inspired the incipient New Left of the Students for a Democratic Society. Organizers attempted to fan these flames as institutional desegregation unfolded at varying rates throughout the region. Nevertheless, by mid-decade, students on the South's predominantly black and white campuses frequently complained in their campus newspapers that their colleagues were apathetic, complacent, disengaged from the controversies engulfing other parts of the country. It was in this environment that the issue of American involvement in Vietnam emerged on southern university campuses.

Vietnam loomed large for southern college students in the second half of the 1960s. It breathed new life into the region's sputtering student movement, providing a mobilizing issue that rivaled race as the touchstone for activists who were continuing to open southern campuses to dissent, promoting a sort of southern *glasnost.* At the same time, Vietnam helped widen the gap between a nascent southern New Left and conservative students. By the end of the decade, many if not most of the South's campuses were politically divided in ways that would have seemed strange and foreign at the outset of the decade. The political spectrum, and the corresponding range of political identities available to southern students, was broader than it had ever been. But campuses were polarized.

Given how insular southern institutions were as the 1960s dawned, the mere existence of an anti-war movement on southern campuses, limited as it was, is remarkable. Yet despite the region's deeply embedded hawkishness, which engendered a level of support for the war that exceeded that of other parts of the country, some student activists in the South organized in opposition to American policy in Vietnam. A growing body of scholarship has emerged to challenge the perception that anti-war activism only happened at places like Berkeley and Columbia.[3] And yet sorting out the meaning and significance of the southern anti-war movement, and, more generally, the southern student movement, has remained elusive and debatable. As Robert Cohen notes in a recent volume on southern student activism, "Beyond revisionism, we need a deeper, more nuanced history, showing that in spite of some similarities, southern student activism often differed markedly from its northern counterpart."[4]

What did Vietnam mean to southern students? And what did the mobilization of a minority of southern students in opposition to American policy in Vietnam mean to the region and the campuses that those students inhabited? Untangling the war from the other issues that dominated the late 1960s can be difficult. And determining what constitutes "the anti-war movement" can be a challenge. American policy in Southeast Asia competed with a host of other concerns: Black Power, women's rights, attitudes about sex and drug use, and the meaning of education in an explosive time, to name a few. And all of this played against the backdrop of a rapidly changing South: a conservative region where previously dominant ideas, chief among them white supremacy, were under assault.

Origins of the Anti-war Movement

"Led by the organized structure of the fraternities and sororities, the great hotbed of philistinism in the 1950s, this campus, as others surely did, reached unprecedented heights of carefully planned frivolity— parades with homemade floats, sing-songs, carnivals— anything, in fact, to do something meaningless with all that energy," wrote Willie Morris of the University of Texas in the 1950s. His description of Texas would reveal much about campus life throughout the South on the eve of the 1960s. Heavily influenced by political and social conservatism, tempered, perhaps, by a heavy dose of apathy, southern campus newspapers revealed campuses where blood drives, dances, beauty pageants, and football games often took center stage. When students wrote of international events and issues in the pages of their school paper, they often used the language of Cold War orthodoxy. And though student government elections often featured intense competition, the campaigns usually avoided the most controversial issues of the day. In 1955, United States

National Student Association (NSA) President Harry Lunn traveled throughout the South, visiting colleges and universities in the hopes of increasing membership in his organization. In a report filed after his tour, he noted that though the southern political scene was vibrant, "issues in elections are virtually unknown." Instead, southern student politics was usually organized around competition between "independents" and "fraternity men," who sought to gain office as a stepping stone to a political career in the real world. It was, he argued, the worst sort of political training. "The motivation is bad," he argued, "and the training points them into the same thought patterns as their elders— certainly not a very hopeful sign for Southern leadership."[5]

Looming in the background of Lunn's analysis was the reality of race. In the early postwar period, race more than any other issue distinguished southern higher education from the rest of the nation. A history of racism and legalized segregation had created dual systems of higher education: one for black people, the other for white people. The threat posed to that system by United States Supreme Court rulings had the effect of intensifying opposition to desegregation among white southerners. In fact, as an organization that welcomed members regardless of race, the NSA was at times a lightning rod for white segregationists who, at the same time, were being shaped by the rise of massive resistance to integration. The placid surface of southern campuses belied another reality. Despite the beauty pageants and football games, southern higher education sat at the epicenter of forces that would reshape the South in the late 1950s and 1960s.

In the following years, institutional desegregation would put southern universities on the front pages of the nation's newspapers during the attempted desegregation of the University of Alabama in 1956 and the eventually successful effort in 1963. They also received national attention during the riots in response to the admission of two black students to the University of Georgia in 1961 and the violent clashes surrounding the entrance of James Meredith to the University of Mississippi in 1962.

These and other conflicts revealed that southern college campuses were never insulated from political conflict.

Even more significantly, beginning in 1960, students from historically black colleges and universities in the South provided the foot soldiers for a nonviolent assault on segregated public establishments. The first high-profile sit-ins occurred in Greensboro, North Carolina, in February 1960. Thanks to news coverage as well as word-of-mouth communication, students in other parts of the South initiated their own local movements in the spring of 1960, and nonviolent assaults on segregation continued in parts of the region throughout the early 1960s. The student-generated sit-in movement breathed new life into the civil rights movement in the early 1960s, which led to the creation of the Student Nonviolent Coordinating Committee and inspired early members of the New Left.

The outlines of the narrative of the New Left and its role in the anti-war movement are familiar. From Port Huron to the Berkeley Free Speech Movement to the teach-ins and early demonstrations of 1965, college students were drawn first into a critical view of Cold War orthodoxy and, with the advent of the escalation of American involvement in Vietnam, a debate about the conflict itself. Southern students are often missing from that narrative, and there is a reason for that omission. Even at the height of the student anti-war movement with demonstrations following the Kent State shootings in May 1970, southern campuses were notably less affected by the protests than those in other parts of the country. According to a survey conducted after the spring 1970 conflicts, 76 percent of institutions in the Northeast experienced a "significant impact," compared to only 41 percent of southern institutions.[6]

It is not my goal to argue that southern campuses were just as active as campuses in other parts of the country. They were not. But the South's role in the origins of the student movement of the 1960s, as well as the reality that, though less active, southern students nevertheless engaged the war in a way that was regionally distinctive, make the story of the southern anti-war movement significant. So how did the anti-war movement emerge in the South? More generally, what did southern students talk about when they talked about the war?

By 1965, the energy and ferment created by the sit-in movement had subsided. The crusade-like environment that had developed, especially on many historically black campuses, had waned. Nevertheless, efforts to desegregate restaurants and other establishments created a cadre of activists who, at mid-decade, often served as bridges connecting the race-focused activism of the early 1960s with the multi-issue, campus-based movement of the late 1960s. Some of those activists had begun as student participants in the sit-in movement and then joined movement organizations such as the Southern Student Organizing Committee (SSOC). Others, and this category might be broadened to include not only students but also faculty, were still on their campuses or in southern communities. The combined ranks of these veterans of early-sixties activism might be considered the core of the southern New Left. Vietnam emerged at a crucial time. Though the continuing power of Cold War orthodoxy, intensified by its tendency in the South to connect the communist threat with civil rights activism, presented a challenge for students who wanted to engage the war, Vietnam eventually served as a galvanizing issue for the late-sixties southern student movement.

1965-1967: The Halting Emergence of Anti-war Activism

Vietnam emerged as a mobilizing issue in 1965, as American escalation in Southeast Asia and anti-war teach-ins both became lead stories in the national news. That news coverage was reflected in the pages of southern student newspapers, where student columnists wrestled not only with the role of the U.S. in Vietnam but, more frequently, with the propriety of student protest against it. Thus, while the University of Michigan gained fame and notoriety as the host of the first teach-in in March of 1965, and the University of California's Berkeley campus hosted a series of high-profile demonstrations in the spring of the same year, southern campuses proved slow to respond.

The first teach-in in the South occurred at Emory University in October 1965 and attracted an impressive turnout of about 1,200 people. Initially proposed by an Emory theologian who had attended the first known Vietnam teach-in at the University of Michigan the previous March, the event was organized by activists who had cut their teeth in the civil rights movement. Dubbed "Conversation: Viet Nam," the event gave equal time to pro- and anti-war points of view. It was a decidedly moderate event. And yet it prompted a conservative backlash: an event titled "Affirmation: Viet Nam," led by students at Emory and the University of Georgia but involving institutions throughout the state. The initiative began with a "poll" of college and university students, which was actually an overt attempt to generate support for American policy; organizers noted that, though "an affirmative reply is desired, negatives will be accepted." It culminated in a rally at the open-air Atlanta Stadium in February 1966, which attracted 20,000 people despite the rain. Speakers included Secretary of State Dean Rusk and both of Georgia's U.S. senators, but the centerpiece of the rally was the presentation of the poll, which found that 96.6 percent of respondents from forty-seven Georgia colleges and universities supported the nation's commitment to Vietnam.[7]

The whole episode revealed the challenges faced by southern students who, even at this early date, were opposed to the war. A moderate event that produced an impressive turnout— more than a thousand people— could be met with a more conservative initiative that turned out twenty times as many people. It reflected not only the inherent conservatism of the region but also the weaknesses of the incipient movement.

By mid-decade, the southern New Left was limited. Activism on black campuses had waned after the intense activity of the early 1960s while a white student movement was only beginning to emerge. In 1965, the Field Foundation received four applications for $100,000 that would go toward developing progressive student programs in the South. Surveying the region as he exchanged letters with representatives of the organizations, Executive Director Leslie Dunbar saw the potential for an awakening on southern campuses but still expressed reservations about "the student movement, if that can be the correct word, in the South. It is weak."[8]

Regional and national organizations such as the National Student Association, Students for a Democratic Society (SDS), and the Southern Student Organizing Committee attempted to tease out a progressive southern movement, while local activists tried to find like-minded people in their own communities and campuses. For these activists, Vietnam could be a perplexing issue. The question was this: How does one open up space for a New Left that is critical of anti-communist American foreign policy without alienating the masses of conservative southern students under the way of Cold War orthodoxy? As Gregg Michel has noted in his study of SSOC, when Vietnam began to emerge as a controversial issue, leaders in the organization debated whether they ought to engage it and how that should be done. A few SSOC activists supported American policy. Others believed SSOC should stick to local issues, specifically race and the Civil Rights movement. [9]

To the degree that organizers were reluctant to engage Vietnam, their hesitancy could have been related to an understanding that opposition to military action aimed at containing communism might not play well in a region where opponents of the movement were already accustomed to link activism with communist influence. The anti-communist crusade of the postwar period was a national phenomenon, one that had a significant impact on higher education. Loyalty oaths and political attacks on radical faculty members threatened the independence of universities throughout the nation. That threat was not necessarily greater in the South than elsewhere. But in the South, race frequently became associated with anticommunism, opening civil rights activists to charges of disloyalty. For example, in North Carolina, legislators in 1963 banned communist speakers from appearing at state institutions in response to civil rights activities in Chapel Hill. The fight against the North Carolina Speaker

Ban became the central issue for University of North Carolina activists in 1966. In other parts of the South, such "speaker bans" highlighted the limits on discourse that existed in southern colleges and universities.[10]

One might consider this hostility to unorthodox ideas a lingering effect of an older phenomenon, what journalist W. J. Cash called the "savage ideal... where under dissent and variety are completely suppressed and men become, in all their attitudes, professions, and actions, virtual replicas of one another."[11] In such an environment, it is not surprising to see a University of Georgia student journalist describe the attitudes of her fellow students toward anti-war demonstrations of 1965 with these words: "Most agreed that the demonstrations were communist inspired."[12]

In this environment, some students in 1965 began to venture, cautiously, into a consideration of American involvement in Vietnam and some of the ways in which it connected to their lives. The process unfolded slowly. In some places, such as Deep South campuses located in more rural locations, 1965 and 1966 passed with little to no sign of anti-war sentiment. An example of this can be seen at the University of Georgia. Located in Athens, about seventy miles east of Atlanta, UGA gained national attention in 1961 when two black students, Charlayne Hunter and Hamilton Holmes, desegregated the institution despite the rioting of segregationist students on campus. The riots failed to prevent Hunter and Holmes from matriculating, but they provided a revealing indication of the campus political climate. Athens was a city that did not experience a mass sit-in movement, and nonviolent direct action was not introduced at the local level in the early 1960s. Indeed, the chaotic, poorly organized demonstrations against integration constituted the only mass mobilization of UGA students before 1968.[13]

In the pages of *The Red and Black*, the University's student newspaper, a Cold War orthodoxy, one that conflated criticism of the United States with disloyalty, often held sway. When the paper conducted a poll measuring opinions on anti-war demonstrations in October 1965, the responses were, as the reporter described them, "generally opposed" to the protesters. The question itself was revealing. Rather than asking students for their opinions on American policy in Vietnam, the reporter polled students about their opinions on opponents of that policy, as well as a provocative statement made by one of Georgia's senators about how to punish activists: "What do you think of the recent demonstrations protesting U.S. involvement in Viet Nam and Sen. Herman Talmadge's suggestion to draft the demonstrators?" The article did not purport to measure student opinion scientifically, but the quoted responses suggest something about the range of student opinion. "Demonstrators are playing into the hands of the Communists by giving a wrong impression of popular support for U.S. policy and thereby tending to prolong the war," said senior political science major Rick Wingo, who added that demonstrators should have their draft deferment revoked. Editor-in-Chief Carlton Brown Jr. echoed those comments: "If students in our institutions of higher learning haven't got anything better to do than conjure up demonstrations, they might as well leave. But then they'd get drafted."[14] In the following months, the pro-war "Affirmation: Viet Nam" would receive significant coverage in *The Red and Black.*

Pro-war sentiment turned up in notable ways on other southern campuses, even those where early-sixties demonstrations had occurred. A student-fueled sit-in movement had developed in New Orleans in the early 1960s. When it did, it attracted a handful of student participants from Tulane University. In 1962, some students and faculty had led a nonviolent demonstration against the university's still-segregated dining hall, one of the earliest episodes of nonviolent direct action on a predominantly white southern campus. Others published an underground newspaper of sorts, *The Reed,* which featured criticism of American involvement in Latin America. Nevertheless, when Vietnam emerged into the public consciousness at Tulane in the fall of 1965, it was the pro-war students who seized the initiative. In November 1965, more than 3,500 students, faculty, and staff signed a petition supporting U.S. policy in Vietnam. Significantly, one of the organizers of the petition was political science professor Henry L. Mason, who earlier in the decade had been an advisor to *The Reed.* An early-sixties liberal, Mason would represent the side favoring the war in debates on Vietnam in following years. In 1967, Mason would lead the opposition to granting a local chapter of SDS status as an official student organization. Mason argued that SDS was interested in action, not discussion of the issues or academic interests, and that the group was becoming "the fascists of the left."[15]

Located in Nashville, Vanderbilt University sat at the epicenter of the early 1960s sit-in movement. James Lawson, who played as large a role as anyone in laying the intellectual and moral foundation for the movement, was a divinity student at Vanderbilt before his expulsion. And in the early 1960s, a coterie of activist students emerged. Connected to activists associated with the Southern Student Organizing Committee, which had been founded in Nashville in 1964, their taproot was race.[16] In the early 1960s, a small number of Vanderbilt students and faculty participated in sit-ins and the picketing of local restaurants that still refused service to black people. But members of this group felt themselves to be a besieged minority. Meanwhile, the pages of *The Vanderbilt Hustler*, the student newspaper, featured concerned articles about the apathy of most students.

This was the milieu as activists first began to engage Vietnam. A campus chapter of Students for a Democratic Society provided the first organizational engine. Members set up a booth on campus and attempted to generate debate. According to an article in *The Vanderbilt Hustler*, SDS leader Lee Frissell, "stressed that the purpose of the Vanderbilt chapter is 'more to create a dialogue on campus than to maintain a doctrinaire position... We were very pleased with the response to our last booth. Many people stopped to exchange ideas with the people at the booth. This is exactly what we are aiming for." But within months, it became apparent these efforts to generate discussion were not translating into a movement, and by October 1965 the local SDS chapter disbanded; in part, it seems, because of a sense that the national organization did not understand southern students.[17] In the following months, other organizations would follow but struggle with the same combination of apathy and opposition.

By early 1967, *The Vanderbilt Hustler* would devote an entire issue to the problem of apathy. Titled "The Dead Issue," student reporters scrutinized the Vanderbilt campus, seeking to explain why debate, not just about Vietnam, but also about other political and social issues, was so rare. "The problem with controversy on the Vanderbilt campus is that there isn't any," wrote one reporter. The proposed explanations ran the gamut: Vanderbilt students were from provincial, wealthy, and conservative families who tended to be intolerant of new ideas while Vanderbilt offered little that would challenge students to consider new ideas. "The liberals," *The Vanderbilt Hustler* reported, "compare the Vanderbilt intellectual atmosphere to that of southern finishing school, or a southern Bible college." Another writer complained of dry, lecture-style classes that rarely challenged students to think, instead encouraging them to digest and regurgitate ideas: the result of which was described as the university's "mother-hen" suffocation of students.[18]

The same criticisms might have been directed— indeed, *were* often directed— at institutions throughout the South. Such forces kept the student anti-war movement small. Even the University of North Carolina, an institution with a storied history of liberalism and a national academic reputation, saw its anti-war movement struggle to gain traction. To be sure, UNC activists had a stronger foundation on which to build. Students chartered a chapter of the Student Peace Union in 1961, and the group focused its early activities on segregation, suggesting in a 1963 resolution that the "problems of world peace and the problems of civil rights and human freedom are not separate." But local racism, not international politics, was the main emphasis on UNC's SPU chapter. Moreover, by 1965, when Vietnam began to emerge, the anti-communist Speaker Ban was the dominant issue on campus. An SDS chapter was the most prominent campus activist organization at this point, but its energies were focused on combating the Speaker Ban. Though SDS and other campus organizations engaged issues surrounding the war in 1965 and 1966, they received little attention.[19]

The issue began to get mainstream traction in 1966 when the UNC student body president, Robert Powell, signed a letter to President Lyndon Johnson expressing doubts about the war. Signed by student leaders from more than one hundred colleges and universities (and representing, according to the *New York Times*, "a far more moderate university group than members of the student New Left"), the letter generated some controversy on the UNC campus. Powell insisted he was acting on his own, but critics complained he represented the university's students as student body president. Shortly thereafter, a visit by Vice President Hubert Humphrey to the UNC campus prompted demonstrations, which seemed to give the campus anti-war movement momentum.[20]

1968-1970 – A Movement Emerges and Recedes

In its most visible phase, the student anti-war movement in the South was capable of turning out significant crowds. It mobilized thousands of students on campuses and in the streets of surrounding communities. Campus newspapers featured passionate debates. For many schools, where evidence of the movement was apparent, the last two years of the 1960s constituted "The Sixties," a compressed period of demonstrations and manifestations of the counterculture and other challenges to mainstream culture. The narrative that unfolded on each campus had its own cast of characters and its own trajectory, which intersected at times with the national trajectory. It would be impossible in this space to chronicle each one with sufficient attention to the nuances. It mattered that Stephen Abbott and not someone else was the student body president at Emory University during the 1968-69 academic year; that David Mathews was president of the University of Alabama during post-Kent State demonstrations; that individual students chose to attend, or not attend, protests on their campuses. Nevertheless, regional trends and tendencies are apparent.

Movement organizations, chiefly the Southern Student Organizing Committee and Students for a Democratic Society, attempted to fan the local flames into a regional or national conflagration. SSOC organizers moved throughout the South on a Peace Tour in 1967 and 1968. Sometimes, they met with opposition in some locales, but moreover, their efforts stirred up opposition to the war.[21] Other campuses gravitated to SDS, though, at times, the connection between a local chapter and the national organization were tenuous at best. But by 1968, as many southern campuses were beginning to exhibit signs of anti-war activism, those two organizations, at odds with each other over the nature of the South and whether it constituted a distinctive region that required a separate analysis and organizing strategy, were both headed toward dissolution.[22]

The deaths of SSOC and SDS occurred as the movement was peaking on many southern campuses. In their own way, those organizations had played a central role in the development of southern student activism. SDS and SSOC pamphlets circulated through southern campuses, and organizers from each affected the dynamic of student politics at many institutions. But the southern student movement was simultaneously local and regional/national. Even though each campus movement grew from a unique cast of characters, similar issues emerged on campuses throughout the region.

On many campuses, the presence of the Reserve Officers Training Corps (ROTC) was a flashpoint, and anti-war students focused their opposition to the war on ROTC requirements, and at times the existence of the program itself. At the University of Georgia, for example, a graduate student in history named Paul W. McBride waged a campaign against mandatory ROTC during the 1967-68 academic year. An Army veteran who had served for two years in Vietnam, McBride did not fit the mold of the archetypal anti-war activist, a fact that, perhaps, added to his influence on campus. He argued in articles in *The Red and Black* that the ROTC's military values, which emphasized obedience, were antithetical to the values of an academic community. He also took aim at what he argued was an antiquated curriculum taught by unqualified instructors. The fact that the program was compulsory made the matter even worse.

"The manual 145-45 used now at the University of Georgia still refers to the danger of the 'Sino-Soviet conspiracy,'" he complained in one article. "It is pardonable to be wrong, but when error is forced upon the civilian college system, and when the military instructors are forbidden to vary from doctrine, then the situation is intolerable in an educational context."[23] McBride was a member of SDS and publicly defended the organization in the student newspaper. When SDS championed a bill in the student senate that made participation in the ROTC voluntary, the bill passed overwhelmingly. Voluntary participation was implemented during the 1969-70 academic year, and enrollment dropped in the program precipitously.[24] Elsewhere in the South, opposition to ROTC programs received significant attention at Tulane, the University of Alabama, Emory, and the University of North Carolina.[25]

The draft was another issue that emerged throughout the region. In 1967, Michael Smedburg, a veteran of the Berkeley Free Speech Movement, moved to North Carolina as a full-time organizer. He joined two UNC students in creating a chapter of the Resistance with the goal of bringing draft resistance and, more generally, a stance of "personal confrontation" to the North Carolina anti-war movement. But local Resistance leaders "found an unwillingness on the part of students to take the same steps taken by activists at Berkeley in opposing or non-cooperating."[26] Nevertheless, the South saw high-profile examples of draft resistance. In Atlanta, eleven men were indicted for draft evasion in March 1967. In early 1968, the city's alternative newspaper, *The Great Speckled Bird*, often known just as "The Bird," chronicled the stories of three of these resisters. Two of them were connected to Emory University. Each had followed a different path to opposing the war and the draft – one emanating from the South, the other from outside the region. Gene Guerrero's activism had begun when, as an Emory undergraduate student, he had gotten involved in the civil rights movement. The first chairman of SSOC, Guerrero was a full-time organizer in 1968. "He was raised a good Baptist," *The Great Speckled Bird* noted, and attended high school and college in Atlanta. Guerrero's views on civil rights seemed intimately connected to his views on the draft and Vietnam: "The draft is a sign of the society's sickness," he told the newspaper. "It is sick when a Negro looks to being drafted and serving in the army as a way out of the ghetto." [27]

The other resister was Stephen Abbott, a graduate student from Nebraska who was elected as the student body president for the 1968-69 academic year. "Steve is a good expression of the Yankee who comes to the South— and concealed in his intellectual luggage are strong convictions about killing and injustice," the article noted. Abbott, a self-described Christian pacifist, had spent two years studying in a Benedictine seminary in Nebraska. Abbott published a series of columns in the *Emory Wheel* examining the anti-war and student movements in 1968 and 1969. And as he developed a more radical stance in the student newspaper's editorial pages, he was becoming a figure in Atlanta's burgeoning counterculture. Abbott married a fellow graduate student in February 1969, while still serving as student body president. Later that year, in the wake of the Stonewall riot of June 1969, a signal event in the development of the gay rights movement, Abbott came out as bisexual. He would go on to play a role in Atlanta's Gay Liberation Front and serve as the gay liberation editor for *The Great Speckled Bird*, the city's alternative newspaper and chronicler of all manner of activities on the left.[28]

Before his stint as student body president, Abbott had been involved in a November 1967 demonstration against the Dow Chemical Company, the manufacturer of napalm. Such protests constituted another common feature of anti-war activism on southern campuses, as students mobilized against the presence of Dow and the complicity of the university in allowing the company to recruit on campus. Activists at Duke University developed one of the most sophisticated analyses of the problem, and their mobilizing efforts were provocative. Played out against the backdrop of a new "pickets and protest" policy that sought to maintain order on campus by prohibiting "illegitimate" demonstrations, the February protests against Dow developed over several days. At one point, demonstrators blocked the door to a booth where the Dow recruiter was interviewing, violating the new policy. Warned that they had five minutes to move, the activists waited until the last second before disbanding. Following the demonstrations, which played out over several days, four Duke students drove to New York City to present a statement to the investment committee of the university's board of trustees. When the committee refused to meet with the students, they picketed the meeting outside, on Sixth Avenue. Eventually, one of the students did win a meeting with Thomas Perkins, the chairman of the investment committee. The ensuing discussion revolved around the morality of Duke's investments in Dow, which produced napalm, and eventually landed on the question of whether a citizen had a responsibility to disobey immoral orders. Writing in the aftermath of the Duke-Dow demonstrations, one anti-war activist at nearby UNC declared that the events represented "a new stage in the development of a radical student movement in N.C."[29]

Indeed, in the following months, the multi-issue student movement would assume a central role on both the Duke and UNC campuses. At Duke, a four-day "silent vigil" in April 1968 brought out hundreds of students to the main quadrangle after the assassination of Martin Luther King, Jr. The following year, in February 1969, about sixty black students seized the first floor of the Duke administration building and issued a list of eleven demands, all related to racial issues on campus. After Duke President Douglas Knight called in police, the episode escalated, eventually resulting in dozens of injuries. At UNC, a food workers' strike in 1969 dovetailed with the emergence of a vocal Black Student Movement that applied a black-power analysis to the university. Meanwhile, anti-war demonstrations widened with the national Vietnam Moratorium in October 1969 and reached a high point, in terms of participation, in May 1970 following the American incursion into Cambodia and the Kent State shootings.[30]

As the foregoing summary suggests, Vietnam was not the only story that was unfolding on southern campuses in the late 1960s. Race still profoundly influenced student activism, as students debated the meaning of desegregation on formerly segregated campuses. The rise of Black Power at times intensified conflicts. Nevertheless, at a profound level, evidence of the influence of Vietnam could be seen in other issues that were not directly related to the war. There was Vietnam, and then there was *Vietnam*, the symbolic issue that opened the door to a host of other controversial issues. Lists of demands that might ostensibly have been prompted by the war could include issues such as the rights of black students, the continued existence of restrictive curfews, and the role of the student in the university's decision-making process. It was, truly, a "movement of movements." Skeptics viewed the multi-issue orientation warily. "I thought it was very amusing— and pointed this out to students that came in with a rally over Vietnam— and what their demands consisted of was to eliminate visitation restrictions to dormitories, something related to the food in the cafeteria, a series of parietal rules, and these kinds of things, totally unrelated to the war," recalled Joab Thomas, who served as vice president for student affairs at the University of Alabama in the late 1960s and, later, as president of the university in the 1980s.[31]

Thomas's comments reflect a cynical view of this multi-issue orientation. But the rapid evolution of student activism at Alabama in the late 1960s demonstrates the power that anti-war activism, built on a foundation of racial conflict and progress, could have.[32] Before 1965, student activism, outside of the mobilization of students in opposition to integration in 1956 and 1963, was practically nonexistent. Only after the Selma-to-Montgomery march of 1965 was any left-of-center student mobilization evident. The slow pace of developing activism began to pick up speed in late 1967, with the formation of the Democratic Students Organization (DSO). Led by several traditional student leaders, including a former student government president and his 1966 campaign opponent, its members declared the DSO would be a force for "progressive action," which they defined to include support for Eugene McCarthy's presidential campaign, backing for the university's fledgling Experimental College, and opposition to the war in Vietnam. Three months later, the DSO began weekly peace vigils on the steps of the University Union. The first vigil, which lasted only fifteen minutes, attracted ninety-five protesters and 150 spectators. One leader declared that the organization would continue to "hold these vigils continuously each Friday noon until the war in Vietnam is stopped."[33]

In the following two years, the student culture of the University of Alabama would undergo a significant metamorphosis. The emergence of a small but notable anti-war movement coincided with the rise of a critical mass of black students who began to assert their presence, as well as a nascent feminist consciousness, apparent in the pages of the *Crimson White* and in student government. Rebelling against curfews and visitation rules that treated women differently from men, they also called for a louder voice and a place for students in the university's decision-making process. At the same time, a pocket of the counterculture, students and members of the community who experimented with drugs and listened to rock music while defying the cultural standards regarding sexuality and appearance, manifested itself in such ways as a regular festival, a sort of Woodstock-in-'Bama, at a place called Woods Quad.

Vietnam was an important part of a larger transformation at the University of Alabama. A young president, an alumnus of the university named David Mathews, attempted to channel the revolutionary impulses while quelling the concerns of other alums and politicians who were appalled by these developments. "Appeasement of any militant group is kind of like feeding peanuts to a lion," Mathews declared at a June 1969 luncheon speech in Anniston, Alabama. "It works fine until you run out of peanuts, and then you're in trouble."[34] Meanwhile, activist students, nurtured by faculty members in the law school and other pockets of dissent, pushed not only for a full engagement of the issues of the day but against limitations against student mobilization and speech. In March 1970, Mathews nixed an invitation to Abbie Hoffman to be part of an Emphasis '70 program with George Wallace because the Chicago Seven defendant represented a "clear and present danger" of unrest. In response, the Emphasis chairman for the year, along with several other students and faculty, filed suit to prevent the ban, and about 250 students staged a sit-in outside Mathews' office. Mathews argued he was a supporter of the presentation of diverse viewpoints on the campus. He cited his previous opposition to a proposed speaker-ban bill, but he suggested to the students that the public "feels we want to hear what is sensational rather than sound."[35]

Students were less concerned with who the particular speaker was than with the fact that they were being denied the right to hear a speaker. To many students, a visit from someone as renowned as Hoffman would have been an indication that the university was finally arriving on the national scene— for a reason other than opposition to integration. One activist later recalled when another Chicago defendant, Jerry Rubin, came to campus on May 4 of the same year in an unauthorized visit, students were elated. "Just his presence meant something," said Mike O'Bannon, who was an undergraduate psychology major at the time. "To a lot of people it meant that we had, in a lot of ways, arrived... it did say to a lot of people, 'Look, the University of Alabama is part of this whole thing.'"[36]

By the time Rubin spoke, student unrest had reached a fever pitch throughout the country. On April 30, Richard Nixon announced that U. S. and South Vietnamese troops had crossed the border into Cambodia. Thousands took to the streets. In Kent, Ohio, national guardsmen fired more than sixty times into a crowd of about 200 students, killing four and wounding nine. With the ferment of the preceding months in the background, the clashes between students and administration, the increasing boldness of activist students, a circus of activity erupted on the Alabama campus. From May 6 to the end of the semester, the campus was the scene of meetings, demonstrations, and counter-demonstrations. The administration attempted to keep things under control by instituting a curfew each night and prohibiting demonstrations during the day.

For support, Mathews called in the state police. Students responded by demonstrating against the restrictions.

For several days, the activities had little order. Some complained that, to too many participants, activism was a fad. One activist later suggested, though a small number of people "were very into the whole political thing, into changing themselves, into a whole different view of what the world could be like," for most people "it was as much a fad as streaking or goldfish swallowing was in the '50s."[37] To be sure, many students participated even though they may have sympathized for some time with the causes of "the movement," they had not yet participated in demonstrations. Eventually, a list of demands emerged from the chaos, authored by a coalition of faculty and students. The list drew on issues that had emerged in the previous months and years, including restrictions on women at the university, the concerns of black students, and free speech. In a profound sense, Vietnam was the leverage point for all the students' concerns. Nevertheless, despite the importance of the war as a mobilizing issue, none of the demands eventually released by the coalition pertained either to the war or, more narrowly, to ROTC or university complicity in the war through defense research.[38]

A similar dynamic played out on other southern campuses. Anti-war activism peaked with responses to Cambodia and Kent State in the spring of 1970. On many campuses, that peak manifested itself in large demonstrations in which all the issues that had animated the previous two years of activism, race and gender relations, student power on campus, the rights to speak and dissent, and manifestations of the war on campus, were aired. Because the peak occurred as the academic year was concluding, on some campuses the rallying issue was whether students should be required to sit for exams. And then the academic year ended, and most students went home.

The war continued. But the levels of activism declined when class resumed in the fall of 1970. By this time, a growing number of southern anti-war students had added their voices to those in other parts of the country who opposed the war. Whether that rising chorus had changed the minds of the nation's "masters of war" is still debated.[39] In the South, anti-war activists remained in the minority at the dawn of the 1970s. Perhaps, as Joseph Fry suggests in a recent examination of the American South and Vietnam, this reality indicates the influence of southern anti-war activists had "a primarily national, rather than southern application," as the South remained the region that supported the war most ardently.[40]

Viewed more broadly, the impact of the Vietnam era on southern student life and politics was significant. Some victories took the form of university reforms: more student representation in the campus decision-making machinery, reduced oversight of students' nonacademic lives, revisions to curricula designed to focus more on the African American experience, and other changes that demonstrated the southern student movement had its most immediate impact on the relationships that immediately surrounded students. In a broader sense, the student movement opened the campus up to dissent. While never in the majority, progressive student activists now had more free space from which to engage controversial issues with fewer repercussions. Given the reality at the outset of the decade, the continuing manifestations of W. J. Cash's "savage idea," this victory was perhaps the most significant of the southern student movement. Vietnam had played a significant role in that process, which had the effect of lessening the differences between southern campuses and those of other parts of the nation. Indeed, the war in Vietnam made southern student culture less *southern.*

NOTES

1. *The Vanderbilt Hustler*, 28 February 1967, 1.
2. Emory *Wheel*, 30 April 1965, 2; *The Red and* Black, 11 November 1965, 4.
3. Works on southern student activism include Doug Rossinow, *The Politics of Authenticity: Liberalism, Christianity, and the New Left in America* (New York: Columbia University Press, 1998); Williams J. Billingsley, *Communists on Campus: Race, Politics, and the Public University in North Carolina* (Athens: University of Georgia Press, 1999); Gregg L. Michel, *Struggle for a Better South: The Southern Student Organizing Committee, 1964-1969* (New York: Palgrave, 2004); and Joy Ann Williamson, *Radicalizing the Ebony Tower: Black Colleges and the Black Freedom Struggle in Mississippi* (New York: Teachers College Press, 2008); Jeffrey A. Turner, *Sitting In and Speaking Out: Student Movements in the American South, 1960-1970* (Athens: University of Georgia Press, 2010); and Robert Cohen and David J. Snyder, eds., *Rebellion in Black and White: Southern Student Activism in the 1960s* (Baltimore: Johns Hopkins Press, 2013).
4. Robert Cohen, "Prophetic Minority versus Recalcitrant Majority," in Cohen and Snyder, eds., *Rebellion in Black and White: Southern Student Activism in the* 1960s, 15.
5. Harry H. Lunn Jr. to Constance Curry, 8 March 1955, U.S. Student Association Records, Box 68, Wisconsin Historical Society. For a fuller description, see Jeffrey Turner, *Sitting In and Speaking Out: Student Movements in the American South, 1960-1970* (Athens: University of Georgia Press, 2010), 34-36.
6. Richard E. Peterson and John A. Bilorusky, *May 1970: The Campus Aftermath of Cambodia and Kent State* (Berkeley: Carnegie Commission on Higher Education, 1971), 15, 59-60.
7. Turner, 231-32.
8. Leslie Dunbar to Philip Sherburne, 24 November 1965, Papers of the U.S. Student Association, Box 2, Wisconsin Historical Society. Turner, 135.
9. Michel, *Struggle for a Better South*,103-14.
10. On the impact of anti-communism on American colleges and universities, see Ellen Schrecker, *No Ivory Tower: McCarthyism and the Universities* (New York: Oxford University Press, 1986). See also M.J. Heale, *McCarthy's Americans: Red Scare Politics in State and Nation* (Athens: University of Georgia Press, 1998) and Jeff Woods, *Red Scare: Segregation*

and Anti-Communism in the South, 1948-1968 (Baton Rouge: Louisiana State University Press, 2004). On the North Carolina Speaker Ban, see Billinsgley, *Communists on Campus.*

11. W. J. Cash, *The Mind of the South* (1941; repr., New York: Vintage, 1991), 90-91.
12. *The Red and Black*, 26 October 1965, 2.
13. On desegregation at the University of Georgia, see Robert A. Pratt, *We Shall Not Be Moved: The Desegregation of the University of Georgia* (Athens: University of Georgia Press, 2002). On student attitudes at Georgia toward race and desegregation, see Robert Cohen, "'Two, Four, Six, Eight, We Don't Want to Integrate': White Student Attitudes Toward the University of Georgia's Desegregation," *Georgia Historical Quarterly* vol. 80, no. 3 (Fall 1996): 616-645.
14. *The Red and Black*, 26 October 1965, 1, 4.
15. Tulane *Hullabaloo*, 11 November 1965, 15 December 1967.
16. On the founding of SSOC, see Michel, *Struggle for a Better South*, chapter 2.
17. *Vanderbilt Hustler*, 23 April 1965, 1; 22 October 1965, 1.
18. *Vanderbilt Hustler*, 28 February 1967, 1, 3.
19. Turner, 240.
20. Ibid., 241.
21. Michel, 143-152.
22. For an examination of SSOC's emphasis on southern distinctiveness and SDS's role in the dissolution of SSOC, see Michel, 190-214.
23. *The Red and Black*, 24 October 1967, 5.
24. Ibid., 16 January 1968, 4; 11 April 1968, 1; 7 October 1969, 5. See Turner, *Sitting In and Speaking Out*, 237-238.
25. Turner, 254-55, 258, 260-62.
26. *Duke Chronicle*, 13 November 1967, 1.
27. *Great Speckled Bird*, 15-28 March, 1968, 2.
28. Alysia Abbott, *Fairyland: A Memoir of My Father* (New York: W.W. Norton, 2014), 4-5.
29. For a fuller treatment of the development of the anti-war movement at Duke, see Turner, 242-49.
30. Ibid., 205-15, 261-62.
31. Author's telephone interview with Joab Thomas, 16 May 1998.
32. On the development of the student movement at the University of Alabama in the late 1960s, see Gary S. Sprayberry, "Student Radicalism and the Antiwar Movement at the University of Alabama," in Cohen and

Snyder, eds., *Rebellion in Black and White*, 148-70; Earl H. Tilford, *Turning the Tide: The University of Alabama in the 1960s*, especially chapter 7; and Turner, 253, 257-59.

33. *Crimson-White,* 14 December 1967, 1; 18 March 1968, 1.
34. Anniston *Star*, 16 June 1969, in Bound (Oversized) Newspaper Clippings, Hoole Library, University of Alabama.
35. University of Alabama *Crimson-White*, 5 March, 9 March 1970, 1.
36. Interview with Mike O'Bannon, 1977, from collection of papers from an oral history class, transcript in possession of E. Culpepper Clark.
37. Ibid.
38. The Student-Faculty Coalition demands were the repeal of special rules for women; repeal of mandatory food contracts; acceptance of the new student-approved SGA Constitution; student control of student funds; an end to speaker bans; student representation; the implementation of the demands of black students, previously issued by the AAA; guaranteed federal minimum wage for university-associated employees, right to collectively bargain for university employees, the end to the use of outside police forces on campus; a monthly meeting with President Mathews; and amnesty from any disciplinary action for participants in Student-Faculty Coalition activities. "Demands of Student-Faculty Coalition," undated, in Box 20, Mathews papers.
39. Tom Wells argues the movement shortened the war in *The War Within: America's Battle Over Vietnam* (Berkeley: University of California Press, 1994). Adam Garfinkle takes the opposite position in *Telltale Hearts: The Origins and Impact of the Vietnam Antiwar Movement* (New York: St. Martin's Press, 1995). And although it is not a central point in his argument, Kenneth Heineman also suggests in passing that the anti-war movement did not end the war in *Campus Wars: The Peace Movement at American State Universities in the Vietnam Era* (New York and London: New York University Press, 1993), 1-2.
40. Joseph Fry, *The American South and the Vietnam War: Belligerence, Protest, and Agony in Dixie* (Lexington: The University Press of Kentucky, 2015), 320-22.

Part II

The Combatants and Their War

A Parable of Persisting Failure

Project 100,000

Geoffrey W. Jensen

Born during the zenith of the Great Society, Project 100,000 strove to rectify the manpower shortage the American Armed Forces faced during the Cold War, while also playing a role in the War on Poverty by accepting into the ranks those who had failed to pass the Armed Forces Qualification Test (AFQT).[1] This "Guns and Butter" approach designed to protect the republic and ward off poverty was met with stiff resistance from two very different groups for two very different reasons: the American military, which viewed it as a waste of time, resources, and objected to its use of substandard manpower; and segments of the Civil Rights movement that believed it was a calculated genocidal endeavor designed to send poor black men to their deaths. They both agreed, however, that it was a failure before it even began.[2]

This deleterious image of the program seeped into the historiography of the Vietnam War. Those who criticized it, and those who still do, often do so by parroting the criticisms that emanated in the 1960s and 1970s. When they do so, they overlook the counter-scholarship that suggests aspects of the program worked. In short, Project 100,000's critics have focused on its shortcomings and perpetuated a historical motif that casts the program as a failure that manipulated the poor of America. In particular, they focus on how it exploited African American males by drafting them and sending them off to fight in an unpopular war. At best this view cheapens, at worst ignores, why the Johnson Administration attempted to launch the program to begin with; it fails to recognize that the genesis of the program occured *before* the Americanization of the war; and that similar uses of manpower of this educational and physical ilk had happened in past wars, and according to a study of Project 100,000 in the Marine Corps, was likely to happen during the conflict in Vietnam regardless. This essay does not seek to white wash the history of Project 100,000, but to understand it as it was, warts and all. It serves as a corrective to the prevailing historical notion of it as a calculated and nefarious endeavor against the poor, specifically impoverished African American men, which was doomed to fail from the start.[3]

Daniel P. Moynihan, who served as the Assistant Secretary of Labor for Policy Planning and Research for both President John F. Kennedy and Lyndon B. Johnson, was a member of "the social scientist-politicos." The group coupled their social science education with their familiarity of the inner political workings of Washington to achieve change. It was Kennedy, though, who first tasked Moynihan and other members of an assembled Task Force to rectify the military's manpower woes. In 1963, Moynihan dutefully penned *One Third of a Nation: A Report on Young Men Found Unqualified for Military Service*, a work that ultimately became the ideological foundation for Project 100,000. The report focused on the rising number of young men who failed to pass the armed forces induction examination. It gloomily declared: "if the entire male population of draft age were examined, about one-third would be disqualified." Moynihan believed poverty was the culprit behind this dilemma. While an issue that engulfed all Americans, *One Third of a Nation* focused specifically on the plight of young black males. It noted that of all the men interviewed, 31 percent were out of work; of these, 29 percent were minorities. African-American males who held a job fared little better as the majority (75 percent) worked as unskilled laborers and made less on average ($1,563) per year than that of the national average ($2,656). This fostered a multi-generational cycle of poverty that forced young black men to leave school early so they could help support their families economically.[4]

Image 5. National Security meeting on Vietnam, 7/21/1965

Source: (A886-8). White House Photo Office Collection. LBJ Library photo by Yoichi Okamoto.

Johnson and McNamara became joined at the hip when it came to casting blame for the war in Vietnam. Their involvement with Project 100,0000 was no different.

Moynihan's report landed on President Lyndon Johnson's desk. Suffering from an acute case of "messiah complex," Johnson believed that his "Great Society," offered the best chance at a better way of life for all Americans. A program like Moynihan's that hinted at the possibility of uplifting the poor, most notably African-American males, through a stint in the military, and therefore, "on the cheap," intrigued the president. It also seemed to marry well with his goals for the War on Poverty. So, Johnson recruited Secretary of Defense Robert McNamara to the cause.[5] "I've seen these kids all my life," Johnson mused during a cabinet meeting, "I've been with these poor children everywhere." But who would save them? The president had an answer: McNamara's Department of Defense. "I know that you can do better by them than the NYA [National Youth Administration] or the Job Corps can. The Defense Department," the Texan concluded, "can do the job best."[6]

In August 1964, the *Journal of the Armed Forces* leaked information about the administration's bid to use the military as a social uplift apparatus. This forced McNamara to introduce his program, the Special Training and Enlistment Program (STEP), earlier than anticipated. STEP proposed to accept 60,000 recruits previously rejected from military service by providing them with remedial educational training and, when necessary, corrective medical treatment that would bring them up to induction standards. Some within the military's leadership immediately balked at the prospective program and unceremoniously dubbed it the "Moron Corps," a title that carried over to its successor, Project 100,000. Undaunted by the criticism, Johnson buoyed up McNamara by reminding him that the armed forces offered the nation's impoverished youth something that no other organization could: character and discipline. To make his point, the president recalled a story about a White House staffer who had purloined a few items from his secretary's desk. The difficulties facing this young man were not insurmountable, Johnson felt, but rectifiable by way of the discipline of the military:

> I think you've got to take boys like that and give them some discipline. I just don't believe that all the vocational training... I never really seen a kid that came out of any of those vocational schools that is equipped to be a carpenter or mechanic or anything else, he learns a little basic stuff, but I don't think he is really prepared for it... but I think, your people, you have the discipline built in there, you have the camps built in there, you have the cooks

> built in there, and if they don't do a damn thing but count trucks for you or something, you can keep them, you have the teachers...

McNamara heartily agreed: "We can teach them work discipline. When you're supposed to be at a place at eight o'clock in the morning, by god they get there or they get disciplined."[7]

Regardless of its potential to instill character and discipline into the downtrodden, certain members of Congress vehemently refused to pass STEP. Southern Democratic segregationists, who opposed the use of the federal government to uplift blacks, and fiscally minded and socially conservative Republicans, who opposed the price tag of $135 million, both balked at the program. Georgia Senator Richard Russell, who was a segregationist and head of the Senate Armed Services Committee, spearheaded this resistance. Despite this early setback, Johnson remained confident that he could get Russell, a friend, confidant, and sometimes adversary, on board. During a March 1965 telephone call, Johnson and the Georgian discussed several matters with the conversation ultimately turning to the lowering of the Navy's induction requirements leading Johnson to float to his longtime colleague the idea of lowering the requirements across the board for all the armed forces— the goal, it appears, was to wind the conversation back to STEP. That did not move the needle much with Russell, however; so, Johnson tried a different tact: the senator's racism. "It seems to me that you're paying a mighty big price on an Anglo-Saxon white man to make his boy go and fight Vietnam," Johnson said, "but none of the others can because... they don't have the exact IQ...." The president's cajoling worked. "I held up the whole thing for years, when they tried to cut it back.... Smart boys, black and white— you're killing them, and the damn dumb bunnies [low IQ inductees] escape!" Russell admitted. Sensing the senator's regret, Johnson made his pitch:

> Well... I think we can improve them [low IQ inductees]... The Navy has said that all this talk about the draft— [Barry] Goldwater is going to repeal it and all that kind of stuff— has ruined their

> program. They can't get people for it now. So, they're going to have to lower their physical and mental standards to get them... If they do that then we'll have to lower them for the others [armed services]... But just the borderline. In other words, if you say I can't come in to your committee and testify unless I've got a B average, I would modify it to B-minus, that's all. I wouldn't drop it to D or F. I wouldn't take a second-grader, but I would just gradually do a little. And you don't have to move it much to pick up ten thousand.

With Russell seeming to reconsider STEP, Democratic Senator Gaylord Nelson of Wisconsin backed a new proposal attempting to fund the program. There it met sharp opposition from two of Russell's most powerful segregationist allies, Strom Thurmond of South Carolina and John Stennis of Mississippi. They argued it was not the armed forces' responsibility to get personnel up to snuff for military service nor should it serve as a sociological laboratory to uplift the impoverished. Both men missed the point, Nelson believed. Metaphorically clutching the flag, he reasoned that the point of STEP was to provide a chance to serve for those disqualified from military service. A more logical move, he believed, then relying on the allegiance of draftees who were forced to serve for two years and were likely to leave following their initial enlistment. Though his argument downplayed the social reform aspect of the program, even he conceded, "There can be little question that STEP, like any program of education, will help to reduce poverty; but that is not its main purpose." Indeed, Nelson made clear that "the main purpose of STEP is to reduce the Army's training costs, and to secure a higher caliber of manpower for the Army." The southern segregationist trio of Thurmond, Stennis, and Russell, who had decided to remain firm in their stance, were not buying what Nelson was selling, however, as all voted against it once again.[8]

Amidst the battle over STEP, Moynihan applied his efforts to a more controversial project called "The Negro Family: The Case for National Action"— a document once referred to as "nine pages of dynamite" within the Johnson Administration. Better known as the "Moynihan Report," it made the bold claim that young African-American males suffered, and, in turn, their community and the nation suffered when denied the potential of a traditional family upbringing based on the principles of deference and discipline. As Moynihan put it, "the breakdown of the Negro family is the principal cause of all the problems of delinquency, crime, school dropouts, unemployment, and poverty which are bankrupting our cities, and could very easily lead to a kind of political anarchy unlike anything we have known." He outlined his solution in seven steps, one of which included the increased induction of black men into the armed forces. Service in the military would provide young black men with a social sanctuary from the distractions of the urban ghetto. In particular, they could break away from the influence of a female driven household, and Jim Crow segregation, a place where modicum of white and black equality existed; a place "run by strong men of unquestionable authority, where discipline, if harsh, is nonetheless orderly and predictable, and where rewards, if limited, are granted on the basis of performance."[9]

Moynihan's report met with a mixed response. There were those in the Department of Labor for instance who believed it to be flawed. In the Civil Rights community, some, like the NAACP's Robert Carter, viewed it as a reminder of that which was already known; others viewed it as "anti-negro" and claimed that Moynihan was a "subtle racist," a charge that longtime civil rights crusader, Bayard Rustin, found "silly." Though Rustin came to Moynihan's defense, he questioned the juxtaposition of the state of black families to that of white ones, observing that what may seem unhealthy to one (whites), might in fact, not be considered as such by the other (blacks). Meanwhile, James Farmer, the founder and leader of the Congress of Racial Equality (CORE), appreciated the sentiment and sincerity of the report, but wondered if it had not opened the door for "a new racism" to come rampaging in.[10]

Despite the mixed response about the "Moynihan Report" and STEP's failure to pass, Moynihan continued to bang the drum of reform. In a 1965 memo to Harry McPherson, Special Assistant and Counsel to the President, he claimed that "the biggest opportunity to do something about Negro youth has been right under our noses all the time." That opportunity was embodied by the American military. According to his data, blacks made up 11.8 percent of the nation, but only 8 percent of the armed forces.[11] The underrepresentation of African Americans in the military was an obstacle to blacks escaping poverty. Recognizing that the unemployment rate for African American men from the ages of seventeen to thirty-four was 11.5 percent, he proposed a ledger swap: "If 100,000 nonwhite men were added to the Armed Forces, and resulted in a decrease of 100,000 in the unemployed, that unemployment rate would drop from 11.5 percent to 6.4 percent." Excited about this potential solution, Moynihan buoyantly declared:

> If there was a proportionate racial balance in the Armed Forces, the unemployment rate from young Negro men would be lower than that for whites! That has not occurred for two generations. In truth, if you exclude agriculture, it has never happened in American history.

He also understood that his idea would agitate southern segregationists in Congress. Instead of making the same mistake as they made with STEP, Moynihan suggested the Johnson Administration, with as little fanfare as possible, should alter the AFQT in a manner that allowed more low-scoring inductees into the military. For that matter, they should "say nothing" to Congress or anyone else about what they were doing.[12]

In a speech to the Veterans of Foreign Wars (VFW) a year later, McNamara embraced Moynihan's suggestion to ignore Congress, but he failed to heed the latter warning by publicly unveiling STEP's successor, Project 100,000. Behind the scenes, Johnson wanted the program to succeed because of the Vietnam War's growing economic toll on the Great Society. To do so, the president needed the acquiescense of Russell. During a conversation with the senator regarding the war's manpower needs, Johnson baited Russell into a discussion of Project 100,000 by proposing to call the reserves to active duty:

> Let me make a deal with you. I'll work on the reserve thing, follow your suggestions on that, if you follow mine on letting me call up everybody, letting me draft all of them, give me a little STEP program like you promised me one time; you made me a firm commitment and ran out on me... but you just let me call up these damn folks, get them off the marijuana and out of the jungles, and out of the rats eating on them, and let me put them out in these damn camps.

"You can work the hell out of them if you want to," Russell retorted. "Work the hell out of them and feed them, I'm going to do it... but I don't want you cussing at me," the president responded. "I won't say a critical word, not one," the senator pledged. The Georgian then quipped: "I think you're going to waste a lot of money on them, though..." Was the senator evolving on the issue of race? Perhaps, but it is far more plausible that Russell, as biographer Jeff Woods has noted, was a hawkish Cold Warrior who acquiesced to Johnson solely to put more boots, regardless of race or socioeconomic background, on the ground in Vietnam.[13]

With Russell neutralized, McNamara informed the nation that the military had a new enemy: poverty. What that meant was the armed forces would now admit those men whose scores placed them amongst Category Four recruits, which typically prevented them from induction.[14] By serving in the military and taking part in its vast educational network, McNamara believed they would "return to civilian life with skills and aptitudes which for them and their families will reverse the downward spiral of human decay." Although mainstream American society had failed them, McNamara hoped, the most powerful military in the world would not. This last point was important to the Secretary of Defense as he admonished those teachers who shortchanged or gave up on the impoverished. "Too many instructors look at a reticent, or apathetic, or even hostile student and conclude: He is a low-aptitude learner... In most cases," he argued, "it would be more realistic for the instructor to take a hard honest look in the mirror and conclude: 'He is a low-aptitude teacher.'"[15]

Image 6. President Lyndon B. Johnson reads wire service ticker and talks on phone as Marvin Watson holds phone console, 05/04/1965

Source: (A397-6). White House Photo Office Collection. LBJ Library photo by Yoichi Okamoto.
Johnson often worked the phones seeking advice, counsel, and to cut a deal on a pending program or piece of legislation.

McNamara's harsh critique of America's education system was not merely lip service. Throughout his tenure, he remained committed to the social aspects of the program. For instance, McNamara and program administrator Thomas Morris were concerned that inductees' poor educational backgrounds might funnel them right into combat units. To protect New Standards Men, the official designation for Project 100,000 personnel, from combat, McNamara required the Navy and Air Force to absorb some of them. His idea was that these two branches, both more technically oriented than Army or Marine infantry, provided a sanctuary from ground warfare and an opportunity for these men to acquire a technical skill.[16]

According to the research of historians Sherie Mershon and Steve Schlossman, the philosophical concept of "Military efficiency" had been deployed as a bulwark against liberal attempts to racially reform aspects of the American Armed Forces— this concept made its twentieth century debut during the debate over the racial integration of the military. Indeed, reform programs such as the racial desegregation of the military were considered counterintuitive to the maintaining of a cohesive military as it introduced social issues into its confines that had the potential to divide. And though racial integration proved a success, the concept of "military efficiency" as a defense against further social reform within the ranks, continued to be used. Such rhetoric appears throughout the commentary of those in the military against Project 100,000. For example, *The Army Times* openly wondered: "Is this any time to require the services to take on a large scale 'poverty-war' training mission? We would think not." While the newspaper politely deliberated the issue, New Standards Men received various belittling nicknames from their comrades: "McNamara's Morons," "McNamara's Moron Corps," "Stupid and Super-Stupid," and "McNamara's Million." Even an architect of the war, Gen. William Westmoreland, bitterly lambasted the program and its personnel. At best, he declared, "Category four is a dummy. You can probably make a soldier out of ten percent of him." For Westmoreland, not only were they stupid, but he argued they were nothing more than criminals responsible for discipline problems and the festering drug culture of Vietnam. It was their presence, he believed, that undercut the war effort. While serving as a battalion commander in Vietnam, Charles Cooper supported Westmoreland's scapegoating of the program when he bemoaned, "Thanks to Project 100,000 they were just flooding us with morons and imbeciles. It doesn't mean they couldn't eat and talk and move around, but they couldn't learn well and they'd get frustrated and become aggressive."[17]

Other veterans viewed it as an abomination and a moral outrage.[18] "I think McNamara should be shot," exclaimed Herb DeBose, an African American lieutenant who had served in Vietnam and commanded Project 100,000 men. McNamara and the military, in his mind, had erred by sending men to fight who were not capable to do so, and they were morally corrupt because they shirked on their promises of additional training once the fighting concluded:

> Many weren't even on a fifth grade-level. And the Army was supposed to teach them a trade in something— only they didn't. Some were incorrigible, always fighting, and *did not belong there.* They brought their mentality with them. I had people who could only do things by rote. I found out they could not read. No skills before. No skills *after.* Disciplinary problems while in the military. Like any other guy in that war, they began to ask *why,* and when *they* asked *why,* it was often viewed as a discipline problem.

Gary Roberts, who served as infantry platoon leader in Vietnam, concurred. "They took 100,000 basically not very smart kids, eighteen, put them through basic training, gave them a rifle and sent them to Vietnam." From there, the men made their way out in units operating out in the field, where their lackluster intellects did them little good. "That's just criminal," Roberts felt. In *My Lai 4,* Seymour Hersh attempted to draw a connection between the massacre of innocents at My Lai and the under-educated soldiers of Project 100,000. Hersh implied the presence of thirteen undereducated New Standards Men along with their equally inept and undereducated lieutenant, William L. Calley, created an infantry unit willing "to take orders, not question them." Though the Peers Commission, which investigated the unit's actions at the time, and historian Michal Belknap's later research, debunks this idea, the question of the mental capacity of the New Standards Men lived on in the trial that followed the incident.[19]

Like Westmoreland, others worried less about the morality of sending the undereducated to war compared to the criminal element they believed underscored the program, an idea that runs counter to the evidence. Veteran Richard Bowen recalled two individuals with nefarious backgrounds. One was a car thief, the other a lockpicker. Bowen believed them both to be New Standards Men, and that they were in the military largely because they chose that fate over incarceration. While Bowen understood the logic behind the recruitment of such men, he remained convinced that the majority were criminals:

> So I think in this group, there was a high percentage of people who had had some type of background with the law, and they were in our unit. For the most part, they had skills (laughs) that the rest of society wished they didn't have, and they were not afraid to use them. It turns out that we had other people who were arsonists, who had burned or tried to set people's houses on fire, so they got caught doing stuff like that. We had a lot of those kinds of people who were in the military during this time period.[20]

Serving as a company commander of an engineer unit in Vietnam, Lloyd Brown recalled that part of his command included a small naval component, which he believed to be a "dumping ground for people..." Within its ranks were "27 Project 100 Thousand people...[which] included 2 people who had been convicted of voluntary manslaughter..." He specifically remembered an incident where he almost lost his life at the hands of a substandard soldier. According to Brown, this soldier worked in supply and faced continuous slandering from his colleagues. One night, he finally lost his temper when he apprehended and threatened his belittling comrades with a loaded M-14. When Brown tried to talk him down, the soldier responded: "Don't you get near me, Sir, I will blow you away, along with all these other 'Sons of Bitches...'" Eventually, Brown diffused the situation and sent the man to the psychiatrist for counseling instead of the stockade. After the psychiatrist cleared him and returned him to duty, Brown, out of an effort to keep an eye on the soldier, made him his driver— a capacity, the commander recalled, that he excelled in.[21]

Nowhere was the criticism greater than in the Marine Corps. During the Vietnam War, the Marines contributed proportionately more men to the fight than any other branch. According to its records, 30 percent of the Marine Corps was committed to Vietnam; and indeed, from 1967-1970, 58.5 percent of all New Standards Men in the branch served in combat roles. In a situation where the need for manpower never subsided, it seemed that the Marines would have readily accepted the help. The exclusive and conservative nature of the branch combined with its combat burden in Vietnam, as historian David Dawson observed, led its leadership instead to conduct a war of resistance against Project 100,000. First, Marine leadership complained they should not have to accept New Standards Men, while rejecting applicants who scored higher on the AFQT. When this failed, the Assistant Chief of Staff (G-1) of the Marines suggested they manipulate the system in their favor. Project 100,000 consisted of two pools of participants: mental and medical rejectees. With the stigma surrounding mental rejectees, the Marines opted for accepting more men from the medical pool. Medical rejectees— with the clear majority being either over or under weight— were those individuals with a correctable medical condition. The problem, though, was that very few (less than 1 percent) came from this group, and the plan was quickly abandoned.[22] They then turned to internal performance evaluations, which they hoped would illuminate the program's shortcomings. According to these reports, New Standards Men were inferior to Marines who achieved higher AFQT scores. As overall performers, 35 percent of them received lower quality ratings from their commanders; in comparison, only 20 percent of Marines from a control group received similar ratings. A little over 20 percent of New Standards Men proved unable to complete their contracts as many washed out after eighteen months of service. And, one-third of New Standards Men recycled, which meant they had to redo a portion of their initial training. Most alarming, New Standards Men in the Marine Corps perished at twice the rate of their counterparts. While ignoring the fact that most of these men met expectations, Marine leadership believed these findings proved Project 100,000 men could not mentally cut it.

Dawson, however, disagreed. Certainly, New Standards Men struggled because of their lack of education to net technically oriented positions in the Marine Corps, but that was not entirely their fault. The Spartan-like nature of the institution, he observed, offered few opportunities to escape combat. Taking that into account, it was likely that they perished at such a high rate because there was nowhere else in the branch for them to serve.[23]

The political desires of the Johnson administration along with the bitter reality of waging an unpopular war betrayed their efforts to halt Project 100,000. Initially, Marine recruiters were instructed to maintain their quota of New Standards Men for fear that a failure to do so would lead to the Department of Defense drafting such men into the branch. Better, it seems, for the Marine Corps to pick and choose which New Standards Men they would accept. Interestingly, Marine recruiters ultimately inducted more New Standards Men than the Department of Defense had required. The reason was necessity. For Dawson, it highlights a reality the Marines were unlikely to admit at the time: "To fill its ranks, the Marine Corps would have been forced to lower enlistment standards and accept large numbers of recruits scoring in Mental group IV with or without Project 100,000."[24]

Thwarted by their own recruiters, commanding officers throughout the Marines decided to remove New Standards Men from leadership roles. To do this, they had to decipher the code system that protected their identities. Some commanders even claimed they had successfully done so. No one can confirm the accuracy of their guesswork, let alone the amount of false identifications made. More concerning and a reflection of the racial turmoil of the era, some used race in their determination of who was a participant in the program. Though Vietnam was the first truly integrated war for the American military, the armed forces still struggled with issues of racial prejudice. In *Semper Fidelis*, historian Alan Millett observed that while the policy of the Marines was one of nondiscrimination, the real-world reality of the situation was the contrary. During off-duty hours, often taking place at bars, brothels, or any place where alcohol, drugs, and prostitues were present, racial violence between Marines occurred and African American Marines, whether Project 100,000 men or not, often shouldered the blame. Perhaps this explains why the majority of white Marines polled by Dawson believed most New Standards Men in the branch were black (the actual amount was 40.3 percent), when in fact the majority were white (58 percent).[25] Though less than 10 percent of New Standards Men had a criminal conviction on their record, those polled by Dawson believed that not only had the majority been black, but that they were nothing more than criminals. One white Marine veteran bitterly complained: "They were a crime wave in themselves."[26]

Criticism of Project 100,000 emerged also from within the black community, a community struggling with the number of sons, brothers, and fathers serving in Vietnam. During the war, the proportion of African Americans living in the nation hovered around 12 percent. From 1965 to 1970, however, 14.3 percent of new inductees into the military were black. Several reasons for this emerge. As historian James Westheider noted, this was the result of the military's desire to curb the amount of personnel accepted into service based on the guidelines of the Selective Service Act of 1948. After the Korean War, the Pentagon incorporated a system of deferments that placed an emphasis on drafting men from the ages of eighteen to twenty-five. To acquire higher quality personnel, the military's leadership also raised the physical and mental entrance requirements of the armed forces. Under "manpower channeling," these deferments "exempted students, professionals, and skilled workers." Though these changes were meant to benefit society, such deferments ended up largely protecting middle and upper-class whites from Vietnam. Adding to the problem was the lily-white racial composition of local draft boards. Indeed, only 1.3 percent of draft board members were African American, which meant the possibility existed for using the draft as a weapon against blacks. Lastly, African American men found it difficult to join the National Guard and Reserves in the South as the region maintained a defacto state of segregation that allowed white college students entrance, but largely prohibited black recruits from following suit.[27]

Beyond numbers, it also mattered where they served; in Vietnam, black recruits overwhelmingly served in combat units. The reasons for this vary, Westheider explains. Their poor education, lack of technical skills, and the "Euro-cultural bias in the AFQ tests" all contributed to the problem. There were also those African-American personnel who sought to serve in these units for their own reasons. For some, the prestige of being an Army Ranger or Airborne trooper proved too difficult to pass up; for others, the monetary benefits of serving in combat and special operations units trumped risks; and of course, others served out of patriotic pride.[28] Lastly, though questions and concerns had arisen within their community, the military was still viewed during the war as a viable option. In a 1966 *Newsweek* poll, 47 percent of black Americans believed the military provided a better way of life for their children than one in the predominately segregated civilian world.[29] As Ethyl Payne, the First Lady of African American Journalism, surmised: "Denied the rights and opportunities to advance at home, they flock to the Armed Forces in search of a "better shake" than they can get in civilian life."[30]

While statistics can be a cause for consternation and controversy for historians of today, and perhaps inaccurately display the reality of how soldiers perished in a theater of war, they became a cause for alarm in the eyes of the untrained and concerned citizen during their era. According to a 1966 *The New York Times* piece, black deaths in the Army "from 1961-1965 was 18.3 percent," while the amount in the Marine Corps was 11.3 percent.[31] They were not just serving disproportionately, but they were also dying disproportionately. [32] Things had gotten so out of hand by 1968 because of the rising "death rate" that the Department of Defense instituted "a cutback in front-line participation by Negroes."[33]

It was at this critical juncture in the loss of life of black men that segments of the civil rights community condemned the newly launched Project 100,000 and did so even though African American men made up only 36.7 percent of the project.[34] Though they were not the majority, they disproportionately represented their race in the project, which, of course, was the intended result of the Johnson Administration all along. What the administration failed to foresee was that the program would be perceived as a system of racial genocide tied directly to the draft. But that is exactly how many African-American leaders viewed it. Longtime civil rights champion and New York Congressman Adam Clayton Powell, Jr., deemed it: "genocide." "It's brutal," he reasoned. "It's nothing more than killing off human beings that are not members of the elite." While Powell condemned it, others met in New York to speak out against it. The Chairman of the New York City Human Rights Commission, William Booth argued that Project 100,000 was "another attempt to get more Negroes into conflict." "They should," he added, "escalate the war on poverty instead of the draft." Stokely Carmichael, the leader of the Student Nonviolent Coordinating Committee (SNCC), viewed the program as an insidious attempt by "the [white] man to get rid of black people in the ghettoes." Project 100,000 was nothing more than "a cynical method to punish black youths for the social ills imposed on them by the major society," added Black Power advocate and leader of the Congress of Racial Equality (CORE), Floyd McKissick. Equally damning for the critics, and in many ways reinforcing their negative opinions about it, they learned in the fall of 1966 that the remedial education portion of Project 100,000 would be voluntary.[35]

Throughout the program, the National Association for the Advancement of Colored People (NAACP) and the leadership of the Southern Christian Leadership Conference (SCLC) offered no comment. In 1967, though, Dr. Martin Luther King, Jr., the leader of the SCLC, rebuked not only the federal government's actions in Vietnam but lamented the great casualty of that effort: the War on Poverty. The "demonic, destructive suction tube" of Vietnam was not only purloining money, men, and talent, but it was robbing those who needed help the most. Though he never publicly castigated Project 100,000, it was likely that King viewed it not as a cure for poverty, but another example of "a society gone mad on war."[36]

Although a slight majority (54 percent) of Project 100,000 personnel volunteered to serve, the program found itself inexplicably intertwined with the unpopular draft. Frustrations throughout the war regarding the number of African Americans fighting and dying in Vietnam help to partially explain this misunderstanding. But a greater culprit seems to be the actions of the nation's outspoken and opinionated head of the Selective Service, General Lewis B. Hershey. Hershey was a conservative Republican from Indiana whose views on race evolved over time, but he was no Moynihan. As the nation's longstanding Selective Service chief, racial reform in the armed forces mattered to him because he recognized the damage racism had on the military. He also felt it could provide the necessary discipline the downtrodden of America needed to improve their lot. Hershey had been a member of the Task Force that researched the nation's growing manpower problems in the early 1960s, which led to the creation of *One Third of a Nation.*[37]

Nonetheless, using the armed forces as a social reform instrument always took a back seat to the more important matter of fielding a strong army. Nowhere was this more evident than his controversial stance against war protesters. Though he begrudgingly accepted in 1965 a bill to prosecute those who burned their draft cards, Hershey repeatedly emphasized that it was better to draft them than jail them. In the fall of 1967, he unleashed a political firestorm when he informed the branches of the Selective Service that they should reexamine all war protestor's draft status. While the Supreme Court reversed this action a year later, such maneuvers made him an enemy of the anti-war and civil rights communities. This negative public image led to a more cynical belief about Hershey, namely that he controlled Project 100,000. This became an idea so potent that it influenced historian Kimberly Phillips to suggest he used Project 100,000 to target black power civil rights advocates. The idea that he did so, or ordered draft boards to do this, however, is entirely unfounded. Enough evidence exists to show some local draft boards did target various blacks for military service, from those seeking Conscientious Objector (CO) status, such as boxing great, Muhammad

Ali, to those who were civil rights leaders. It is possible that *some* of these boards, especially those in the South, viewed Project 100,000 as a tool against black social ascendancy, but this certainly was not the point of the program nor does it mean that all those involved in the Selective Service viewed it that way.[38]

Johnson grew increasingly incensed as criticism poured in against Project 100,000 and the larger poverty program. "I'm ready to kill [the poverty program] quietly through George Mahon [chair of the House Appropriations Committee]" the president angrily informed Bill Moyers, "...and get the damn thing out of the way if the niggers are just going to be that mean to me and [Sargent] Shriver's group is going to be disloyal." Frustrations aside, the administration did not abandon the program. Especially when they thought it was working. Alfred Fitt, the Assistant Secretary of Defense for Manpower, praised Project 100,000: "by applying to these men the Defense Department's experience in educational innovation and on-the-job training, we are transforming them into competent military personnel, serving in such diverse occupational areas as electronic equipment repairmen, medical and dental specialists, as well as in combat arms." According to a 1968 study, 96 percent of New Standards Men graduated from basic training. A year later, a progress report showed that the program, now in its third year, was still graduating New Standards Men at a high rate (94.6 percent). These statistics also applied to the Marine Corps, where 88.9 percent of New Standards Men became Marines. In addition, 92 percent of them, often considered mentally unfit and the general bane of the branch, received ratings of either: Good, Excellent, or Outstanding.[39]

Praise did not solely come from those behind the project. While most of the military disagreed with with the program, some felt it had merit. One commander believed the armed forces had a duty to act if it could on social issues: "If the country is faced with formidable problems such as poverty and lack of education, and the armed forces can help, they should." An Air Force commander observed:

> I've heard no complaints about the Air Force's accepting rejects. In fact, many people think it's a hell of a good idea... There are two categories of the guys who don't make it in the service: those who could but won't, and those would but can't. We may be getting a group of people who can, but who never have had the chance to prove it.[40]

Though he believed New Standards Men required a little more training, infantry officer Ralph Hagler concurred: "I must honestly say that for being a grunt in Vietnam during that time frame, 1966-1967, they were more than adequately equipped from the duty-honor-country standpoint to carry the mission out very well." Some even relished working with individuals with lower educations. An Army commander, who had served in Korea, believed that lower standards men proved to be better soldiers: "These men make the best infantrymen, mortar men and mechanics... Practically all will do their best to do a good job. I'd prefer a company of riflemen with fifth-grade educations over a company of college men anytime." This commander's comments are especially telling as researcher Thomas Sticht noted the military had dipped into this classification for manpower prior to Vietnam. During World War II and the Korean War, the military accepted similar recruits; for that matter, more Category Four men fought in Korea than in Vietnam under Project 100,000. Others became converts only after they saw these men in action. Colonel Walter Olson, an artillery commander in Vietnam, recalled his initial apprehension of New Standards Men; a concern, he admits, that was quickly alleviated after working with them:

> My fears were unwarranted because they came around brilliantly, were probably the best soldiers that I've ever had to lead, although I went to Vietnam with some great fears that they were going to disintegrate and crumble and would not be able to do the job. I was absolutely astounded when I gave up my command in Vietnam how well they actually did. They were outstanding. They weren't

> the smartest people in the world, but they did their job and they did it very well.[41]

Regardless of its supporters' opinions, a movement emerged in the late 1960s to back away from a volunteer system supplemented by a draft to an all-volunteer force. For these advocates, change could not come fast enough, as many believed it would end the discipline problems and racial strife plaguing the military, which, some contended, had been partly caused by Project 100,000.[42]

In 1968, Fitt confessed, "We don't pretend that we turn them into supermen, but they all meet minimum standards for graduation." But what did this mean for the military and the men of the program? Did Project 100,000 turn them into cannon fodder? Did it impair the military? Worse yet, did it leave these men high and dry after the fact as some claimed? The answer to those questions depend on the researchers involved. Janice Laurence and Peter Ramsberger for example did not believe Project 100,000 was an unmitigated "disaster" as many did, nor did they find it an overwhelming success. They certainly did not believe these men were cannon fodder. While a large portion of those in the Army (34.5 percent), Marine Corps (56.5 percent), and the Navy (34.9 percent) served in combat professions, this represented only one-third of the over 350,000 individuals involved in the program. According to their findings, the majority had not been combat soldiers, but instead clerks, technicians, cooks, and mechanics. That said, they questioned the legitimacy of the data coming from the Department of Defense on other aspects of the program. Specifically, they wondered whether these were truly substandard men or not. Did unscrupulous recruiters desperate to find substandard inductees turn to more intelligent recruits and coach them to score lower on the AFQT?[43] They also accused some base commanders of graduating basic training classes, whether ready or not. No evidence, however, has emerged to support either claim. As for the discipline of the men, they observed that New Standards Men were "1.5 to nearly 3 times more likely" to quit their initial training and were "1.3 to 3 times more likely" to face punishments than those of a control group. When these men returned to civilian life, they did little better. Laurence and Ramsberger noted that civilians made more money, had the discipline to seek out further educational training past High School, and were more likely to be married and not have children out of wedlock as compared to New Standards Men. If Project 100,000's goal was to aid the military and improve these men's lives, they believed that it failed to do so.[44]

From their findings, and the work of other scholars, the failure motif of Project 100,000 continued into more recent studies. In *The Vietnam Wars*, historian Marilyn Young ascertained that Project 100,000 provided a painless solution to the manpower crisis facing the Johnson Administration without having to rely on the politically unsavory option of calling up the reserves or nabbing college students from campuses across the country. It consisted of undereducated black males plucked from poverty and dumped into the killing fields of Vietnam. Those who survived the horrors of war were court-martialed at twice the rate of their counterparts. Instead of uplifting these men, Young felt, Project 100,000 made "civilian life far more difficult than if they had never served at all." Noted journalist Myra MacPherson agreed. Her article, "McNamara's *Other* Crimes," served as a counter to Robert McNamara's apologia on the war, *In Retrospect* (1996).[45] On the list of McNamara's crimes was Project 100,000, a program that MacPherson believed swept up the marginal at best, at worst the "legally retarded," from the ranks of the downtrodden and sacrificed them before the alter of the Cold War.[46]

Thomas Sticht disagreed. He believed Project 100,000 was not a failure, that these men were not a drag on the military, or that their time in the service failed to help them ascend socio-economically. Both Sticht, and later, Dawson, noted that less than 10 percent of New Standards Men who entered the armed forces had a criminal record. Nor did they wash out easily as 84 percent completed their enlistments as compared to 92 percent percent of a control group. Though 3.2 percent were court-martialed, 95 percent were not. As for rules infractions or other indiscretions resulting in disciplinary punishments, the majority never received any: "The percentages without such punishment were 96 percent in the Air Force, 93 percent in the Navy, 82 percent in the Army, and 76 percent in the Marine Corps (comparable rates for controls were 99, 97, 90, and 82 percent, respectively)." Did they inhibit the combat ability of the armed forces? In his study of Project 100,000 in the Marine Corps, Dawson did not believe so: "Any failure on the battlefield cannot be ascribed to the presence of New Standards men. Any blame to be placed must be placed elsewhere." Historian Gregory Daddis agreed: "evidence suggests, however, little disparity in the capacity for New Standards Men to function as capable soldiers, compared to those serving in the army before the inception of Project 100,000." As for the program's lasting impact, over eight thousand New Standards Men remained in the military, and by 1974, 68 percent of them used their G.I. Bill benefits. Sticht concluded: "the findings presented... for Project 100,000 personnel indicate that far and away the majority of these men did perform satisfactorily, they did not cause excessive disciplinary problems, and they did benefit from the training and educational offerings of the military."[47]

So, what should we make of Project 100,000? Generally speaking, and contrary to popular belief, it was not the absolute failure or moral atrocity that it has been made out to be.[48] For that matter, it was not an absolute success, either. And that may be the problem in a nutshell. It was at best, a draw, at worst ineffective. What has damned Project 100,000 historically was the same thing that damned the war in which it was conducted: It failed to achieve what it sought to do; and that failure came with a terrible cost for those involved with it. Considering that many of the groups involved in Project 100,000, regardless of race, who suffered with poverty then still do so today, it is easy to understand the venom that some have for the program. But often, their backlash against it has unfairly ignored the compelling counterargument presented by Sticht and others about the areas where it succeed.[49]

On the other hand, the best way to answer the question is to understand the motives of those behind the program. Understanding what we now know about it, those motives seemed to be pure. But that does not mean there were no flaws in the philosophy of discipline, deference, and masculinity that ideologically fueled it. As Christian Appy observed: "Graham Greene might have said about Project 100,000 what he said about the well-intentioned Alden Pyle in his novel *The Quiet American*: "I never knew a man who had better motives for all the trouble he caused." Poverty is, was, and always will be a serious dilemma for the republic. It is both a moral and national security issue that demands our attention. Solutions "on the cheap," such as what Moynihan, Johnson, and McNamara proposed by way of a stint in the military, however, do not adequately provide a panacea for it; especially, considering it had a controversial social/racial engineering aspect to it, which sought to save the black community from itself. Though well-meaning, this latter notion, in particular, was paternalistic, racist, and out of touch with the larger problems facing black America. To be fair, the men behind the program seemed to recognize generally that sending the poor and undereducated, though it had been done before, to war was a dangerous proposition— recall McNamara's efforts to squirrel some of these men away from the treacherousness of ground combat. But racially, all saw this program as an elixir for what ailed black society. That never changed.[50]

For some scholars, Moynihan, Johnson, and McNamara's intransient belief in the program, whether right or wrong, has become the justification for the fabrication of a more insidious rationale for it that revolves around the ideas of political manipulation— specifically, that Project 100,000 prevented Johnson from having to call up the reserves or opening up the draft to thousands of college age white males— and racial prejudice— namely that African American men were being systematically targeted for either being black, poor, or members of the Civil Rights movement, or all of the above. And though it is incorrect, and does not truly wrestle with what Project 100,000 was, this latter explanation has become the bedrock of our historial understanding of the program. Thus, the historical story of Project 100,000 that we remember was not the tale of a trio of determined, but philosophically flawed, reformers who attempted to save the downtrodden, and, in particular, a race from social degradation, and did so largely through a plan cooked up *before* the war; but instead, we remember Project 100,000 as a parable of persisting failure with insidious intentions behind it from the start.

Notes

1. This essay is dedicated to the research and work of my mentor in this profession, Professor Randall Woods, John A. Cooper Distinguished Professor of History, University of Arkansas, Fayetteville. That said, many folks have looked over versions of this work over the years and have provided tremendous insight. My thanks goes out to them all. Perhaps most familiar with it, though, is my friend and co-editor, Matt Stith, who has read over several iterations of this essay. I owe a great debt to him for his patience and insightful suggestions. Segments of this chapter first appeared in my doctoral dissertation, see Geoffrey W. Jensen, "It Cut Both Ways: The Cold War and Civil Rights Reform Within the Military, 1945-1968" (Ph.D dissertation, University of Arkansas, 2009).
2. Many earlier examples exist of the military serving as a tool for social uplift. For example, during the Civil War, historian Dudley Taylor Cornish demonstrated how the Union Army had aided in the education of black soldiers. For more see, Dudley Taylor Cornish, "The Union Army as a School for Negroes," *The Journal of Negro History* 37, no. 4 (Oct 1952): 368-82.
3. Those seeking to understand the emergence of social scientific and historical criticisms of the program should examine the following: Seymour Hersh, *My Lai 4: A Report on the Massacre and Its Aftermath* (New York: Random House, 1970); Peter Barnes, *Pawns: The Plight of The Citizen-Soldier* (New York: Alfred A. Knopf, 1972); Paul Starr, *The Discarded Army: Veterans After Vietnam* (New York: Charterhouse, 1973); Lawrence M. Baskir and William A. Strauss, *Chance and Circumstance: The Draft, The War, and The Vietnam Generation* (New York: Alfred A. Knopf, 1978); Lisa Hsiao, "Project 100,000: The Great Society's Answer to Military Manpower Needs in Vietnam", *Vietnam Generation Journal* 1, no.2, (Summer 1989): 14-37; Janice Laurence and Peter F. Ramsberger, *Low-Aptitude Men in the Military: Who Profits, Who Pays?* (New York: Praeger, 1991); Marilyn Young, *The Vietnam Wars: 1945-1990* (New York: Harper Collins, 1991); Myra MacPherson, "McNamara's *Other* Crimes: The Stories You Haven't Heard", *The Washington Monthly*, June 1995, 28-29 and *Long Time Passing: Vietnam and the Haunted Generation, New Edition* (Bloomington, Indiana: Indiana University Press, 2001); Kimberly Phillips, *War! What Is It Good For?: Black Freedom Struggles and the U.S.*

Military from World War II to Iraq (Chapel Hill: University of North Carolina Press, 2012).

4. Lee Rainwater and William L. Yancey, *The Moynihan Report and the Politics of Controversy* (Cambridge, Massachusetts: The M.I.T. Press, 1967), 18, 19-20; The President's Task Force on Manpower Conservation, *One Third of a Nation: A Report on Young Men Found Unqualified for Military Service*, January 1, 1964, 11, 15; Daniel Patrick Moynihan, *Miles to Go: A Personal History of Social Policy* (Cambridge, Massachusetts: Harvard University Press, 1996), 216; three decades later, Moynihan openly questioned his rationale in the early 1960s on the issue; specifically, the influence social behavior had on the issue of poverty within the United States. For more, see *Miles to Go*, 218-20.
5. Though Johnson had the utmost confidence in McNamara, he was an unlikely accomplice in the president's mission to make Moynihan's plan to save the poor a reality. Early in his tenure, McNamara had relied heavily on his special assistant, Adam Yarmolinsky, a Harvard and Yale trained lawyer known for his passion on the issue, to spearhead the department's civil rights efforts. Throughout his time in office, though, that seemed to change. In his memoir, *The Essence of Security*, published after his exodus from the Department of Defense, he counted among the "new missions" of the United States military the need to recognize that poverty was not only a national security issue for the United States during the Cold War, but also a social malady that withered away the creative genius and ambition of human beings. For more see, Morris J. MacGregor, Jr., *Integration of the Armed Forces, 1940-1965* (Washington, D.C.: Center of Military History, United States Army, 1981), 530; Robert S. McNamara, *The Essence of Security: Reflections in Office* (New York: Harper & Row, 1968), 122-23,128-31.
6. Randall Woods, *Prisoners of Hope: Lyndon B. Johnson, The Great Society, and the Limits of Liberalism* New York: Basic Books, 2016), 244; see also Randall Woods, *LBJ: Architect of American Ambition* (New York: Free Press, 2006), 20, 62-65, 670- 71; For more on Johnson's desires as a social reformer, a good place to begin is by exploring his experiences as a school teacher; see Doris Kearns Goodwin, *Lyndon Johnson and the American Dream* (New York: St. Martin's Press, 1991), 66.
7. TeleCon,"Lyndon Johnson and Robert McNamara on 13 August 1964," Conversation WH6408-19-4913, *Presidential Recordings Digital Edition*, ed. David G. Coleman, Kent B. Germany, Ken Hughes, Guian A. McKee, and Marc J. Selverstone (Charlottesville: University of Virginia Press, 2014).

URL: http://prde.upress.virginia.edu/conversations/4000757, Accessed on November 29, 2017; Frank M. Best, "'Sub-Standard' Men May Join the Ranks," *Journal of the Armed Forces,* 15 (August 1964): 1, 25; Edward J. Drea, *McNamara, Clifford and the Burdens of Vietnam: 1965-1969* (Washington, D.C.: Historical Office, Office of the Secretary of Defense, 2011), 266; TeleCon, "LBJ and McNamara on November 14, 1964," WH6411.20, LBJ Library.

8. Michael R. Beschloss, *Reaching for Glory: Lyndon Johnson's Secret White House Tapes, 1964-1965* (New York: Touchstone, 2001), 210-13; Drea, 266; MacGregor, *Integration of the Armed Forces,* 568; Representative Glenard Paul Lipscomb, *Congressional Record* 111:11 (June 23, 1965), 14475-76; For the debate between Senators Thurmond, Stennis, and Nelson, see *Congressional Record* 111:16 (August 25, 1965), 21719-21722.
9. Steven Weismen, ed., *Daniel Patrick Moynihan: A Portrait in Letters of An American Visionary* (New York: Public Affairs, 2010), 90-96; Daniel Patrick Moynihan, "The Negro Family: The Case For National Action" (Washington D.C.: Office of Policy Planning and Research, United States Department of Labor, 1965), 42; see also, David Sanford, "McNamara's Salvation Army", *The New Republic,* Sept 10, 1966, 13-14.
10. Rainwater and Yancey, *The Moynihan Report,* 172-73, 201, 410, 421-22; "Moynihan Report Racist Tract, Says James Farmer," *The Chicago Defender,* Dec 20, 1965, 6.
11. At this time, 2,709,000 men were in the armed forces. See Memo, Daniel Patrick Moynihan to Harry McPherson, July 16, 1965, LBJ Library, Office Files of Harry McPherson, Box 21, McPherson: Civil Rights-1965 (2).
12. Memo, Daniel Patrick Moynihan to Harry McPherson, July 16, 1965, LBJ Library, Office Files of Harry McPherson, Box 21, McPherson: Civil Rights-1965 (2).
13. TeleCon, "Lyndon B. Johnson and Richard Russell on June 6, 1966, 8:05 PM," Citation #10204, Recordings and Transcripts of Conversations and Meetings, LBJ Library. For more on Russell's promise to LBJ, see TeleCon, "Lyndon B. Johnson and Robert McNamara on November 24, 1964, 7:20AM," Citation #6471, Recordings and Transcripts of Conversations and Meetings, LBJ Library; Jeff Woods, *Richard B. Russell: Southern Nationalism and American Foreign Policy* (New York: Rowman & Littlefield, 2006), 149; R. Woods, *LBJ,* 669-71.
14. Divided into five classifications based on their performance on the AFQT, recruits either scored above-average (Categories One and Two),

average (Category Three), or fell within the ranks of those that scored below average (Categories Four and Five).

15. "Armed Forces to 'Salvage' Draft Rejects," *The Chicago Defender*, Aug 24, 1966, 2; Homar Bigart, "McNamara Plans to 'Salvage' 40,000 Rejected in Draft", *The New York Times*, Aug 24, 1966, 1-2; Deborah Shapley, *Promise and Power: The Life and Times of Robert McNamara* (Boston: Little, Brown and Company, 1993), 385.
16. Shapley, 386.
17. Thomas G. Sticht, William Armstrong, Daniel Hickey, and John Caylor, eds., *Cast-off Youth: Policy and Training Methods From the Military Experience* (New York: Praeger, 1987), 15, 22-23 190; Sherie Mershon and Steven Schlossman, *Foxholes and Color Lines: Desegregating the U.S. Armed Forces* (Baltimore: The Johns Hopkins University Press, 1998), 20-22; Janice Laurence and Peter F. Ramsberger, *Low-Aptitude Men in the Military: Who Profits, Who Pays?* (New York: Praeger, 1991), 60; Laura Palmer, "The General, at Ease: An Interview with Westmoreland," *MHQ: The Quarterly Journal of Military History* (Autumn 1988): 34; David Anthony Dawson, "The Impact of Project 100,000 on the Marine Corps" (M.A. Thesis, Kansas State University, 1994), 115; Gregory A. Daddis, *No Sure Victory: Measuring U.S. Army Effectiveness and Progress in the Vietnam War* (New York: Oxford University Press), 185-86; Christian G. Appy, *Patriots: The Vietnam War Remembered From All Sides* (New York: Penguin Books, 2003), 445.
18. Perhaps the most light-hearted tale, but one that still questioned the mental prowess of substandard manpower, comes from Barney Cole, an Air Force veteran, who recalled an incident involving three alleged New Standards Men who were painting a shed. At one point, he noticed the men had stopped painting and were throwing rocks at an object. Cole investigated the situation. "I said "aren't you boys supposed to be painting?" Well [they responded] "there's a monster out there" and I go out there and there's this poor frightened little horny toad that's had rocks fall all around it." For more see, Transcript, Interview with Barney Cole, The Vietnam Center and Archive at Texas Tech University, The Vietnam Archive Oral History Project, 2008-8-14, OH0626, 20-21.
19. MacPherson, *Long Time Passing,* 561; Transcript, Interviews with Gary B. Roberts, 2005-01-31 and 2005-02-02, Kennesaw State University oral history series, Kennesaw State University Oral History Project, 1973- , KSU/45/05/001, Kennesaw State University Archives, 19; Seymour Hersh, *My Lai 4: A Report on the Massacre and Its Aftermath* (New

York: Random House, 1970), 17-19, 20-43; Rick Perlstein, *Nixonland: The Rise of a President and the Fracturing of America* (New York: Scribner, 2008), 481. The lack of education dialog carries on into a couple of studies involving My Lai 4 and the subsequent trial. See Louise Barnett, *Atrocity and American Military Justice in Southeast Asia: Trial by Army* (New York, Routledge press, 2010), 222; Michal Belknap, *The Vietnam War on Trial: The My Lai Massacre and the Court-Martial of Lieutenant Calley* (Lawrence, University Press of Kansas, 2002), 40; Michael Bilton and Kevin Sim, *Four Hours in My Lai* (New York: Penguin Books, 1992), 51.

20. Transcript, Interviews with Richard Bowen, 2010-03-03 and 2010-03-11, by Mark DePue, Abraham Lincoln Presidential Library *Veterans Remember* Oral History project, VRC-A-L-2010-009.1, Abraham Lincoln Presidential Library, 29, 32.
21. Ibid.; Transcript, Interview with LTC Lloyd K. Brown, 1983-4-13, US Army War College and US Army Military History Institute, Company Command in Vietnam oral history project, 21, 23.
22. According to Dawson, only 9.5 percent of New Standards Marines throughout the entirety of Project 100,000 were from the medical pool, see Dawson, 90.
23. Dawson, 88-93, 92, 99-100; Office of the Assistant Secretary of Defense (Manpower and Reserve Affairs), Project One Hundred Thousand: Characteristics and Performance of New Standards Men: Final Report, June 1971, (unpublished), Table A-7 and E-5, HumRRO collection. Here after, Project One Hundred Thousand: Final Report, (unpublished).
24. Dawson, 88-89-91, 102. For more on the Marines manpower struggles see 102-108.
25. In comparison, African American Marines that were not part of Project 100,000 made up 11 percent (10.7 percent) of the Marine Corps. See Dawson, 144 and Project One Hundred Thousand: Final Report, (unpublished), Table B-2.
26. Researcher Janice Laurence notes "In the early stages of the program, in fact, NSM were given service identification numbers beginning with 67, and they became widely known as the "sixes and sevens." Laurence, 59-60; Shapley, 387 Dawson, 142, 144-47; Project One Hundred Thousand: Final Report, (unpublished),Table B-11; Allan Millett, *Semper Fidelis: The History of the United States Marine Corps*, 598-600; Project One Hundred Thousand: Characteristics and Performance of "New Standards" Men, Office Secretary of Defense— Assistant Secretary of Defense Manpower and Reserve Affairs, December 1969, xx.

27. James E. Westheider, *The African American Experience in Vietnam: Brothers in Arms* (Lanham, Maryland: Rowman& Littlefield, 2008), 22-23, 27, 34-36.
28. Westheider also included the Draft and Project 100,000 as part of this matrix. See James E. Westheider, *Fighting on Two Fronts: African Americans and the Vietnam War* (New York: New York University Press, 1997), 14.
29. Along similar lines, the disproportionate number of black combat soldiers who fought in the jungles of Southeast Asia was also an intended consequence of the Civil Rights movement. African American civil rights leaders, throughout the twentieth century, used the armed forces as an apparatus through which members of their community could ascend above the social and economic limitations placed upon them by Jim Crow segregation. Past leaders such as W.E.B. DuBois, though he would later question his logic, had especially wanted black men to take part in combat to prove themselves and their race to their white counterparts.
30. Westheider, *Fighting on Two* Fronts, 14-15; Rodger Streitmatter, *Raising Her Voice: African-American Women Journalists Who Changed History* (Lexington: University Press of Kentucky, 1994) 125-26; Ethel L. Payne, "GIs Tell How They Stand On the Viet War", *The Chicago Defender*, April 11, 1967, pg.2; "The Great Society—In Uniform", *Newsweek*, Aug 22, 1966, pg. 46.
31. Black service in the Army was 14.8 percent, while it was 8.9 percent in the Marine Corps. See Jack Raymond, "Negro Death Ratio in Vietnam Exceeds Whites'", *The New York Times* , March 10, 1966, 4.
32. According to Westheider's later findings: "Between 1961 and the end of 1967, African Americans accounted for more than 14 percent of American fatalities in Southeast Asia." See Westheider, *Fighting on Two Fronts*, 13.
33. Jack Raymond, "Negro Death Ratio in Vietnam Exceeds Whites'", 4; Thomas A. Johnson, "The U.S. Negro in Vietnam", *The New York Times*, April 29, 1968, 16.
34. According to the final report of the program, 61.8 percent were Caucasian, 36.7 percent were African American, and 1.5 percent were other. The "other" hail largely from Spanish American or Puerto Rican descent, Project One Hundred Thousand: Final Report, (unpublished), Table B-2. Consequently, very little has been written on the experiences of Spanish American or Puerto Rican New Standards Men.

35. "Rights Leaders Deplore Plan to 'Salvage' Military Rejects", *The New York Times*, Aug 26, 1966, 3; Benjamin Welles, "Negroes Expected to Make up 30% of Draft 'Salvage", *The New York Times*, Aug 25, 1966, 6; Laurence and Peter F. Ramsberger, *Low-Aptitude Men in the Military*, 37; Neil Sheehan, "Military Ready to Absorb Influx of Former 'Rejects'", *The New York Times*, Oct 16, 1966, 9; Shapley, 386; Baskir and Strauss observed that as the war progressed, the "rehabilitation programs became a shadow of what McNamara originally had in mind." But this does not seem to be an example of a "bait and switch", but the unfortunate reality of a taxing war. See Baskir and Strauss, 127.
36. "Rights Leaders Deplore Plan to 'Salvage' Military Rejects"; Marvin E. Gettleman, et.al., eds, *Vietnam and America: The Most Comprehensive Documented History of the Vietnam* War (New York: Grove Press, 1995), 311.
37. Project One Hundred Thousand: Final Report, (unpublished), Table A-5; George Q. Flynn, *Lewis B. Hersey, Mr. Selective Service* (Chapel Hill: University of North Carolina Press, 1985), 16, 118-21, 228-31, 255-57.
38. Ibid., 235-37, 260, 267; Woods, *LBJ*, 676-77; Kimberly Phillips, *War! What Is It Good For?: Black Freedom Struggles and the U.S. Military from World War II to Iraq* (Chapel Hill: University of North Carolina Press, 2012), 204-5; Westheider, *Fighting on Two Fronts*, 27-29; indeed, racist congressmen, such as Louisiana Representative Edward Hebert, viewed it as a tool against outspoken blacks. After hearing about Project 100,000, he quipped: "Maybe now they'll get Cassius Clay (Muhammad Ali)." See Paul Starr, *The Discarded Army: Veterans After Vietnam* (New York: Charterhouse, 1973), 191.
39. Remarks by Alfred B. Fitt before the Rotary Club of Wichita, Kansas and the Kansas Chamber of Commerce, April 15, 1968, 4, LBJ Library, Alfred Fitt Papers, Box 5, Personal Files: Speeches; For statistical information on Project 100,000 see Memo, Clark Clifford to Lyndon B. Johnson, July 31, 1968, LBJ Library, Alfred Fitt Papers, Box 2, Correspondence: General 7/1/68-9/13/68; Project One Hundred Thousand: Characteristics and Performance of "New Standards" Men, Office Secretary of Defense—Assistant Secretary of Defense Manpower and Reserve Affairs, December 1969, xv, xix; Dawson, 92, 99-100, 136-37, 189; Woods, 671.
40. "Military Hopes to Help Rejects", *The New York Times*, Sept 4, 1966.
41. Transcript, Interview with Col. Walter E. Olson, 1984-4-24, US Army War College and US Army Military History Institute, Company Command in Vietnam oral history project, 2-3.

42. "Military Hopes to Help Rejects", *The New York Times,* Sept 4, 1966; Transcript, Interview with Col. Ralph L. Hagler, 1985-4-24, US Army War College and US Army Military History Institute, Company Command in Vietnam oral history project, 3-4; Sticht, 13-16.
43. The assertion that it was difficult to find lower level inductees clashes with the views of Peter Barnes. Barnes observed that recruiting numbers were increased in low income areas and "were filled quite easily." Furthermore, his discussion on the subject leads back to the central theme of race and racism through the targeting of poor black males for military service. David Dawson later questions the racial charges of Barnes and offers alternatives that toe the line established by Johnson and McNamara about Project 100,000's War on Poverty mission. For more see, Barnes, 44-45 and John C. Worsencroft, "Salvageable Manhood: Project 100,000 and the Gendered Politics of The Vietnam War" (M.A. Thesis, University of Utah, 2011), 4; Dawson, 202-3.
44. Transcript, Alfred B. Fitt Oral History Interview, 10/25/68, by Dorothy Pierce, 16-19, LBJ Library; Laurence and Ramsberger, 21, 37, 40-41, 56-61, 118, 120-22 . A great deal of Laurence and Ramsberger's research on the program became the basis for their Congressional testimony on Project 100,000. For more: U.S. Congressional Record, *Readjustment of Project 100,000 Veterans. Hearing before the Subcommitee on Oversight and Investigations of the Committee on Veteran's Affairs, House of Representatives, One Hundred First Congress, First Session, Serial No. 101-38* (Washington, D.C.: U.S. Government Printing Office, 1990).
45. The criticism of the Johnson era program did not end with MacPherson. Within the last decade, the specter of Project 100,000 haunted another manpower dilemma facing the American military. As the United States military groped for a manpower solution during the wars in Afghanistan and Iraq, political scientist Kelly M. Greenhill warned against the idea of accepting low standard men stating that "Project 100,000 was a failed experiment... Forty years later, amid new conflicts and a renewed manpower shortfall, we would do well not to make the same mistake again."; for more see, Kelly M. Greenhill, "Don't Dumb Down the Army," *The New York Times,* Feb 17, 2006, 23.
46. Young, *The Vietnam Wars,* 319-20; MacPherson, *Long Time Passing,* 30, 558-62; and "McNamara's *Other* Crimes: The Stories You Haven't Heard", 28-29.
47. Sticht 45-46, 52-53, 62, 64; Sticht challenged the credibility of Laurence and Ramsberger's congressional testimony in "Project 100,000 in the

Vietnam War and Afterward" in *Scraping the Bottom of the Barrel: The Military Use of Substandard Manpower, 1860-1960*, ed. Marble Sanders (New York: Fordham University Press, 2012), 254-269; Dawson, 136-37, 189; Project One Hundred Thousand: Final Report, (unpublished),Table B-11; Daddis, 187, 189, 193-95.

48. The military in fact will use substandard manpower again after Project 100,000. See both Sticht and Laurence and Ramsberger for more.
49. Robert K. Griffith, Jr., *The U.S. Army's Transition to the All-Volunteer Force, 1968-1974* (Washington, D.C.: Center of Military History, 1997), 158-60; Sanders, 254, 269; Laurence and Ramsberger, 57; Additionally, most studies that have commented on Project 100,000 ignore or overlook a companion program known as Project Transition designed to aid those, including New Standards Men, returning from the war. For more on it, see Sticht and Laurence and Ramsberger.
50. Christian G. Appy, *Working-Class War: American Combat Soldiers and Vietnam* (Chapel Hill, The University of North Carolina Press, 1993), 32.

Women, Gender, and the War

Heather Marie Stur

It was sunrise on a June morning in 1969, and First Lieutenant Sharon Lane's shift at the 312th Evacuation Hospital in Chu Lai was coming to an end. Just before 6:00 a.m., a rocket hit the hospital, landing directly on the Vietnamese ward, where Lane, a U.S. Army nurse, was working. Other nurses tried to avoid the ward, in part because it held Viet Cong prisoners of war, the enemy. Lane saw them simply as patients, even those who kicked and spat at her as they writhed in their restraints while she treated them. The ward became her usual assignment, and she dedicated herself to the work.[1] When the rocket struck, a piece of shrapnel hit Lane below the collarbone and sliced her aorta. Jay Maloney, a medic who worked with Lane at the 312th Evac, remembered the nightmare that ensued. "Ward 4 was awash with smoke and screams," Maloney wrote years later. "But my strongest image from that morning is the ocean of bright red, rust-scented, still-warm blood that seconds earlier had filled her small body. Sharon Lane was a gentle, sweet-souled girl. And this one death, this one among the vast crowd, this one was so particularly purposeless, so cruel, that my light went out that morning. I was as empty as she was, extinguished and spent."[2]

Lane's death was equally traumatic for nurse Sylvia Lutz Holland, whom Lane replaced in the Vietnamese ward when it was time for Holland to move on to a rotation in the emergency room. A group of corpsmen rushed Lane into the emergency room after the attack, but Holland took one look at her and knew she was gone. "She had a big hole in her neck," Holland remembered, "She was pale and her pupils were fixed... The surgeon came in and tried to start an IV but there weren't any veins. Then he was gonna open her chest and massage her heart. I said there was no reason to do it, she's dead. He kept saying, 'No she isn't.' Then he started crying." It was as though nurses, the caregivers some wounded soldiers considered angels, should be immune to combat injuries and death. When the realities of war pierced through that gendered ideal, it sometimes was more than a GI could handle. Holland struggled with survivor's guilt for a long time after Lane's death, knowing that she would have been the one in the line of fire had Lane not arrived in-country to replace her.[3] As Jeanne Holm has written, the dangers nurses faced "were generally greater than those experienced by the clerks, personnel specialists, intelligence officers, stenographers, and others," both men and women, who were assigned to rear posts in Vietnam.[4] Nine Army nurses died in Vietnam, one of whom was Sharon Lane.

There is another Vietnam War experience, a kind of lawless escapism aided by men like William Crum. During the war, Crum was in the business of entertainment, running companies that distributed liquor, dry goods, and games such as slot machines. The son of an American Yangtze River pilot, Crum was born in Shanghai in 1915 and lived there until 1935, when his family moved to California. The military fascinated him, and he tried to enlist in the Navy when the U.S. entered World War II, but poor health kept him out of the service. By the time of the Korean War, though, Crum had figured out a way to get close to the military and almost feel a part of it. He pitched his business to post exchanges, officers' clubs, and enlisted men's clubs in hopes of getting distribution contracts for military installations. When the U.S. escalated its role in the war in 1965, Crum saw an opportunity to expand his business ventures.[5]

In bidding to win military contracts, Crum did more than submit proposals; he offered bribes. The practice had almost caught up with him in Korea, where a sergeant in charge of the PX system there was court-martialed for allegedly accepting bribes from Crum. Crum fled Korea in 1960 and made his way to Vietnam, where he found other military officers willing to accept his kickbacks. In late 1965, the Army and the Air Force ran the post exchange (PX) system in Vietnam, and five American men—one military officer and four civilians— oversaw the operations there. As a 1971 Senate inquiry into corruption in the club and PX systems stated, "when these men arrived in Vietnam, William Crum and his associates were ready to make their stay more comfortable."[6]

Upon the arrival of Lieutenant Colonel John G. Goodlett Jr. and his civilian assistants, Peter B. Mason, Richard Llewellyn, and Clarence Swafford in the fall of 1965, Crum provided them accommodations in a villa in Saigon. The two-story home featured five bedrooms, living room, dining room, three bathrooms, two maids, and a cook. According to Senate investigations, it appeared the men did not pay Crum for lodging. In a letter to Mel Peterson, vice president of Jim Beam, Crum wrote that he and the men were "getting along like peas in a pod" and that he "showed them the brand-new house I am decorating for them and they are absolutely delighted." The men lived together and partied together, with Crum sparing no expense to "cultivate the good will of PX personnel in Saigon." He entertained "lavishly" and always provided "good food, plenty of liquor, and female companionship."[7] Theirs was a bachelor pad for grown men living in a city known for its "outlaw spirit" and "all-or-nothing mentality."[8]

In the quagmire version of the Vietnam War story, American male soldiers grapple with survivor's guilt after seeing a comrade blown away in battle. Women are on the margins of the quagmire story; margins that, as the story goes, were fairly safe, such as offices in Saigon or someplace back home. But if we look beyond the quagmire narrative's conventional wisdom, we find that American women saw combat while some American men enjoyed freedom and leisure in Saigon. Understanding the complex nature of the Vietnam War and its far-reaching consequences for the U.S. requires a new examination of American wartime experiences. American women served in various roles, from the Women's Army Corps and military nursing positions to civilian roles with the Red Cross and other organizations. Just as the war deeply affected men who served, it influenced the lives of American women long after the conflict. In Vietnam, their experiences were shaped by dominant gender ideas about men, women, sexuality, and who should be in a war zone. According to mainstream attitudes, men were in harm's way, and women arrived only to provide entertainment and comfort. Mostly, American women in Vietnam were interlopers in an all-male world. Those ideas also shaped men's experiences and Americans' perceptions of the Vietnamese. Looking beyond the conventional story reveals a muddier, and more complete, picture of the American experience in the Vietnam War.

Marion Williams, an African-American journalist and nurse who went to Vietnam in 1967, wrote that there were two sides to the American war in Vietnam: the "non-combat luxury war" and the "field hardship war." "The bitching war is hell for the frontline internment along the DMZ and the Mekong Delta," she wrote, "while in Saigon, Cam Ranh Bay, and many other places, the luxury men live high on the 'roof.' They have nice living quarters, maid service, enlisted men's clubs, cold beer, T-bone steaks, J&B scotch, not to mention many other fine scotches and bourbons. Some even had automatic washers and dryers. Just like state-side living. If war could be like this for all men, it would become a pleasure to go to war."[9] Williams' observations illustrate that not all American men experienced the Vietnam War from the battlefields. Yet the story is even more complex than Williams describes because the two sides she described included both men and women.

From the 1950s to the fall of Saigon on April 30, 1975, female American military personnel deployed to Vietnam with the Women's Army Corps (WAC), the Navy, and the Marines, as well as the Army Nurse Corps.

Civilian women traveled to Vietnam with the American Red Cross, U.S. government agencies, nongovernmental humanitarian organizations, and as civilian employees of the military. Women were not subject to the Vietnam-era draft, and for some, the war offered an opportunity to travel and postpone marriage and motherhood, which were still the expected roles for young women in the 1960s. Some military women volunteered to go to Vietnam because they wanted to support the war effort or to see for themselves what was really happening on the ground. Others enlisted in the military for college and employment benefits after recruiters promised they would not be sent to Vietnam.

Due to deficiencies in government recordkeeping, we can only estimate how many American women served with the U.S. military in Vietnam. While the Defense Department did not keep accurate records on women, it has estimated that approximately 7,500 women served in Vietnam. The Veterans' Administration has set the number at 11,000. The majority were nurses, mostly from the Army Nurse Corps (ANC). Among those who were not nurses, about 700 women were members of the Women's Army Corps (WAC), while much smaller numbers served in the Navy, Air Force, and Marines.[10] Pinning down the numbers of civilian women who worked in Vietnam is even more difficult; estimates have gone as high as 55,000.[11] Although a few women went to Vietnam before the U.S. committed combat troops and remained in country until 1975, the majority who served in either military or civilian capacities arrived between 1965, the year of the first deployment of ground troops, and 1973, when the last American combat troops departed.

Military Nurses

Of the military women who served in the war, the majority, about 5,000, did so through the Army Nurse Corps. As historian Kara Dixon Vuic explained, the Army began deploying nurses to Saigon in 1956 to train Vietnamese nurses. Nurses had the double duty of treating the physical wounds of servicemen, and sometimes Vietnamese civilians, and offering an emotional salve to injured and dying troops. Some nurses held men as they cried out for their parents and took their last breaths. They broke the news that a man would never walk or see again. Literally and figuratively, nurses carried wounded servicemen across the threshold from combat to the aftermath, which could be a drastically altered life, or death.

The number of ANC nurses in-country increased to a peak of 906 in June 1968 before declining as U.S. troops withdrew from Vietnam, and in total, approximately 5,000 Army nurses served in the conflict between 1956 and 1973. Nurses served one-year tours, held various medical specializations, and worked in hospitals of all sizes, in Saigon and out in the field.[12] Nurses had a variety of reasons for joining the corps, including the wish to avoid, at least temporarily, becoming wives and mothers. Even as they viewed the Army as an escape from the assumed social roles, nurses faced some servicemen who viewed them as angelic caregivers who were stand-ins for women back home, and others who resisted their authority and sexually harassed them, expressing either an unwillingness or an inability to accept female nurses as legitimate military personnel. Although male nurses served in the ANC, men comprised less than 30 percent of Army nurses in Vietnam, illustrating the staying power of the idea that nursing was women's work.[13]

Linda Pugsley was a twenty-two-year-old registered nurse working at Boston City Hospital when she joined the Air Force in 1967. She went through basic training and flight school and was commissioned a second lieutenant. At the time, she had no political feelings about the Vietnam War, but she wanted to help take care of American servicemen who were injured there. She figured she could handle it. A weekend shift at Boston City Hospital usually included gunshot and stab wounds, car wrecks, and other sorts of bloody trauma. Nothing could have prepared her for Vietnam, though.[14]

Pugsley soon realized she was not just tending to physical wounds. She and other nurses spoke of how injured troops saw them as angels. There was something about seeing a woman, a woman taking care of them, that brought them comfort. Some nurses wore perfume because it reminded their patients of home. In a military hospital in a war zone, it was at once utterly incongruous and a desperately needed bit of normalcy. Like donut dolly Emily Strange, Pugsley eventually stopped learning the names of her patients as a coping mechanism. Lynda Van Devanter, a nurse whose memoir, *Home Before Morning*, was the inspiration for the television drama *China Beach*, wore ribbons in her hair to uphold the feminine image her patients expected and needed. At the same time, she suppressed her emotions and steeled herself to cope with the mental burden of being soothing and pretty to broken and dying men.[15]

Women's Army Corps

After nurses, the next largest number of servicewomen who went to Vietnam deployed with the Women's Army Corps. Throughout the course of the Vietnam War, about 700 WACs worked in-country as stenographers, intelligence analysts, typists, clerks, air traffic controllers, cartographers, reporters, and photographers. In general, they worked in offices, and none were armed for combat. The WAC detachment was stationed at Tan Son Nhut Air Base until the end of 1968, when it moved to new barracks at Long Binh. Like nurses, the first WACs went to Vietnam to train personnel in South Vietnam's Women's Armed Forces Corps (WAFC).[16]

Major Kathleen I. Wilkes and Sergeant 1st Class Betty L. Adams arrived in Saigon in January 1965 and worked with Major Tran Cam Huong, director of the WAFC. Corps personnel worked primarily in secretarial roles to assist the Army of the Republic of Vietnam (ARVN) in its various clerical needs. Some WAFCs also worked as nurses and in "welfare service," taking care of dependents who traveled with ARVN soldiers. WAFCs, like WACs, were not trained in combat, but those employed in the welfare service stayed near combat zones with troops, thus performing "the most dangerous assignments in the corps."[17] In order to be eligible for officer training, WAFC recruits had to pass a test demonstrating that they had the equivalent of a U.S. eleventh grade education. All other recruits needed the equivalent of a U.S. junior high school diploma.[18]

By the end of 1967, membership in WAFC had risen to about 2,700, and by 1969, the number had jumped to 4,000. At the WAFC school, which was completed in March 1965, recruits took an eight-week basic training course during which they participated in physical training, first aid, sanitation, and the use of weapons. An officer training program was created in October 1966, which required officer candidates to take an additional twenty-week course after completing the eight-week basic training. In addition to the skills learned in basic training, officer candidates studied military tactics, public speaking, leadership, and military justice.[19] As part of the officer training program, fifty-one Vietnamese female officers completed advanced training with the Women's Army Corps at the WAC headquarters at Fort McClellan, Alabama.[20]

Linda McClenahan grew up in Berkeley, California, and joined the WAC after her high school bus was rerouted one day due to an anti-war protest. She worked in the USARV Communications Center from 1969 through 1970, and one of her jobs was to process casualty reports. She was often one of the first to read the names of men who were killed in action. Lieutenant Colonel Janie Miller, a career WAC who served in Korea and Vietnam, managed a U.S. Army mortuary in Saigon. She rotated her staff through every three months because of the work's emotional toll. When Pinkie Houser, a WAC who volunteered for Vietnam in 1968, lost her commanding officer in battle, she processed his records and sent his personal effects to his family. It was one of the hardest things she had to do during the war.[21]

DONUT DOLLIES

The Red Cross had sent teams of women overseas to work with troops since World War II. They served coffee and donuts, which earned them the nickname "donut dollies." The Red Cross initiated the Supplemental

Recreational Activities Overseas (SRAO) program in 1953 when it sent teams of women to South Korea to work with U.S. troops fighting in the Korean War. In 1965, fearing the impact of what was already looking to be a long war on troop morale, Defense Department officials asked the Red Cross to establish an SRAO program in Vietnam. From 1965 through 1972, nearly 630 women served in Vietnam through the program. Defense officials also requested donut dollies work at recreation centers wherever Defense Department authorities noted that it was possible U.S. troops could be in for a "long duration" with infrequent combat moments and thus considerable idle time. Boredom coupled with isolation could make it "difficult to maintain the morale of trained, combat ready troops."[22]

Some donut dollies staffed recreation centers established by the Army's Special Services division and the United Service Organizations (USO) where servicemen could shoot pool, listen to music, read, play games, write letters, or sit and talk.[23] Others traveled, usually by helicopter, to fire support bases in remote areas where troops waited to go into battle. SRAO women traveled in pairs and brought with them games, snacks, soda, and juice. In the pre-departure training session, Red Cross instructors told the women that they were meant to be a "touch of home" for the troops, a reminder of wives, girlfriends, mothers, and sisters back home. The teams of donut dollies were known as "clubmobile" units, and they were meant to provide a pleasant diversion from the monotony of waiting for combat. They should be the girl next door— cute, friendly, and caring. Not sexual. Their powder blue dresses projected a perky innocence but were impractical in Vietnam's heat, dust, and mud.

Some SRAO workers lived on bases, others in small houses or apartments in the village adjacent to the U.S. military installation where they worked. On-base billets ranged from Quonset or wood huts with detached bathrooms and showers to air-conditioned trailers with indoor plumbing.[24] The program was open only to women who were college graduates between the ages of twenty-one and twenty-four, so the women tended to be a few years older and more educated than the average U.S.

GI in Vietnam. From 1967 to 1968, the program's peak year in Vietnam, an average of 280,500 servicemen participated in SRAO activities monthly at twenty major bases. Clubmobile units traversed an average of more than 27,000 miles each month to remote fire bases isolated from larger military installations. The Red Cross estimated that clubmobile teams traveled more than two million miles during the seven years the SRAO program operated in the Vietnam War.[25]

Smiling was a job requirement for donut dollies, so they had to compartmentalize their own fear and sadness about the war. After her friend, Michael Stacy, died in a helicopter crash in March 1969, donut dolly Emily Strange stopped learning the names of the servicemen she met in Vietnam. She was stationed in the Mekong Delta with the 9th Infantry Division and Mobile Riverine Force beginning in 1968. She had become close with Stacy because they both played guitar, and they often strummed folk tunes together. After Stacy died, Strange realized she needed to put distance between herself and the guys she worked with. It was scary to think about herself dying, but it was worse to worry about her friends dying. So, she stopped learning names. Long after the war, she believed there were probably guys she knew on the Vietnam Wall, but she would not have to face the pain of knowing for sure. It was her job to make lonely, frightened soldiers feel better, and she had to show up and do her job despite the fear and isolation she herself felt. She called it putting on her "Eleanor Rigby" face she kept in a jar by the door.[26]

Like so many veterans, Emily Strange struggled to settle back into "the World." When her girlfriends called her up and invited her to go shopping, she wondered how anyone could possibly care about something so frivolous. She knew it was not that her friends were shallow, that it was her. What she had experienced in Vietnam made it difficult for her to enjoy everyday life back home. She found solace writing poetry, and she connected with other donut dollies as well as military veterans. She attended and spoke at vets' reunions, and she built a website where veterans could publish their stories and find one another. Strange remained connected with fellow donut dollies and Vietnam veterans until she passed away in July 2016.[27]

American Men and Women in Saigon

Saigon, the capital of South Vietnam, was not a primary site of combat in the way surrounding villages were. The Viet Cong carried out a strategy of urban terrorism aimed at perpetuating political instability and instilling fear in urban elites and students, but other than the 1968 Tet Offensive, the bulk of sustained fighting took place in the countryside. Rural war sent refugees to the cities, and South Vietnam's urban populations, especially Saigon's, surged. At the same time, the U.S. presence created a demand for employees in services catering to Americans. U.S. military headquarters was in the city, at Tan Son Nhut air base, and the large number of American servicemen swarming Saigon had encouraged the growth of a vice trade. Women comprised a large portion of the urban labor force because able-bodied men were conscripted into the Army of the Republic of Vietnam, and the combination of American men and Vietnamese women facilitated the development of a heterosexual male-focused atmosphere, which caused concern among American and Vietnamese authorities. U.S. Senators J. William Fulbright of Arkansas and Daniel Inouye of Hawaii spoke out against the sex trade, and Fulbright called Saigon an "American brothel."[28]

South Vietnamese President Nguyen Van Thieu tried repeatedly to close down the bar scene in Saigon, and in August 1966, U.S. President Lyndon Johnson ordered the military to reduce its presence in the city. The plan, known as "Operation MOOSE" for "Move Out of Saigon Expeditiously," relocated the majority of U.S. Army personnel from Tan Son Nhut air base in Saigon to the base at Long Binh, twenty miles north of Saigon.[29] By 1967, the move was complete. According to a *Time* magazine report, Operation MOOSE cut the number of American soldiers in Saigon from about 71,000 to about 36,000 by the end of 1967.[30] Operation MOOSE also made Saigon off-limits to combat GIs on R&R and to all incoming troops.

Yet American journalists, government workers, civilian employees of the military, and independent contractors lived and worked in Saigon throughout the entirety of the war, some remaining in the city long after the last U.S. combat troops had departed Vietnam.

Shifting the focus from nature's jungle to the air-conditioned jungle of Saigon reveals the contours of the war outside the combat moment. Ordinary encounters between Americans and Vietnamese took on meanings that signified the power relationship between the U.S. and South Vietnam. For many Americans, Saigon was a place of adventure and leisure built on the labor of Vietnamese workers who had migrated to the city from rural villages because the war made farming difficult, if not impossible. Businesses such as restaurants, bars, beauty shops, tailors, and massage parlors catered to American patrons, and the employees who served them were almost always Vietnamese, particularly women, because most able-bodied Vietnamese men served in the ARVN. Specific "women's work" performed by restaurant hostesses, bar girls, and maids was in demand by both American men and women, and the intertwined forces of race and gender defined the economic structure, which developed in Saigon as a result of U.S. intervention. Surveyed from the battlefields, the Vietnam War was the purview of American male soldiers and an unseen enemy, but examined from Saigon, the U.S. presence in South Vietnam involved women and men, Americans and Vietnamese, in an intricate dance that signified the push-and-pull of power relations. As Ann Laura Stoler wrote, one way to trace power and power relations is to examine the "intimate" moments of daily life— instances when ordinary encounters among people define social hierarchies and categorize individuals for the sake of creating or maintaining power.[31]

Saigon challenges the conventional wisdom by revealing a wider cast of characters who experienced the war. American civilians, including women, lived and worked in Saigon for the entirety of U.S. intervention: before combat troops arrived and after they had departed. Viewing the Vietnam War from Saigon disrupts the gendered assumptions about who participated in the conflict, and, by extension, illustrates the disconnect between the image of American military engagements and the reality of how U.S. influence bled into multiple layers of Vietnamese society. The concentration of Americans and Vietnamese in a city that was not a primary site of battle facilitated the development of a social and economic hierarchy, which reflected U.S. dominance and control over Vietnam.

Marital status often determined the course of an American's experience in Vietnam. In the case of dependents, President Lyndon Johnson and his advisers believed wives and children were a distraction in Vietnam. On February 7, 1965, Johnson announced all American dependents of U.S. personnel in Vietnam were to be evacuated immediately from the country. The directive came in the wake of growing anti-American sentiment, violence against Americans, and sneak attacks in Saigon. Most dependents were wives and children of American diplomats and advisors, and the vast majority lived in Saigon, the heart of U.S. operations in the early 1960s.[32]

Members of the Johnson administration had been in talks about evacuating American dependents since January of 1964 "in light of recent terrorism against Americans in Saigon." By February 20, 1964, Americans had reported fifteen attacks, including the bombing of a theater for U.S. personnel and a softball game in which five Americans died and more than fifty, including dependents, were wounded.[33] But despite the attacks on Americans, some officials opposed the evacuation of dependents from Saigon because they feared it would cause panic among Vietnamese who might consider the evacuation a sign the U.S. was preparing to abandon them.[34] Others, such as General William Westmoreland, worried that sending wives and children home would harm the recruiting efforts of some agencies and prevent personnel from staying in Vietnam beyond a one-year tour of duty.[35] From the perspectives of some of Johnson's advisors, evacuating dependents held serious consequences for the U.S. mission in Vietnam.

Attacks on Saigon had continued through 1964 as did discussions of what to do with American dependents. In November, a group of Vietnamese students seized a school in Saigon and held an American woman teacher hostage in protest of the draft.[36] On Christmas Eve, 1964, Viet Cong guerrillas drove a car loaded with explosives into a parking lot behind the Brinks Hotel Bachelor Officers Quarters in central Saigon. The blast from the explosives tore through the hotel, killing two U.S. servicemen and wounding more than sixty American military personnel and Vietnamese civilians. In light of the conversation about evacuating American women from Vietnam, it is ironic that among the wounded were four Navy nurses who were injured while caring for U.S. servicemen hurt in the attack. On January 9, 1965, the nurses, Lieutenant Barbara Wooster, Lieutenant Ruth Mason, Lieutenant (junior grade) Ann Darby Reynolds, and Lieutenant Frances L. Crumpton, received the Purple Heart for their service.[37]

By the end of December 1964, Johnson told his staff that he was prepared to set plans in motion for a full-scale war in Vietnam. Regarding dependents, Johnson told Ambassador Maxwell Taylor that "I simply do not understand why it is helpful to have women and children in the battle zone." Johnson proceeded to tell Taylor, "my own readiness to authorize larger actions will be very much greater if we can remove the dependents and get ourselves into real fighting trim." He argued the U.S. military had been training Special Forces, Marines, and other military units to fight a ground war in Vietnam "since 1961, and I myself am ready to substantially increase the number of Americans in Vietnam if it is necessary to provide this kind of fighting force against the Viet Cong."[38] As Joint Chiefs of Staff Chairman General Earl Wheeler maintained, the presence of American dependents in Saigon "is a hurdle which trips decisions."[39] In short, wives and children stood in the way of war. In the final analysis, one of the points Johnson administration officials used to make the decision to evacuate dependents was the "desirability of freeing family heads of any concern for their dependents and of all domestic distractions."[40] In an ominous moment of foreshadowing, Taylor, Deputy

Ambassador U. Alexis Johnson, national security assistant McGeorge Bundy, and Assistant Secretary of Defense John McNaughton mused over lunch that the school that had educated American children in Saigon might be converted into a hospital.[41]

Despite the evacuation of dependents, Saigon did not become a city of men. American men were not the only ones who enjoyed, as Marion Williams described it, the "non-combat luxury war." For some women, the war brought them job opportunities that might not have been available to them otherwise. Sometimes, the jobs they held in Vietnam were gendered based on attitudes about who belonged in war zones and what their duties in those spaces should be. But the jobs brought them to Saigon, and they became part of the world created by the U.S. presence there. Although American men lived and worked in Saigon, studying women's experiences breaks the link between men and war and broadens the view of what the Vietnam War was, who participated in it, and what its widespread consequences were. Their daily lives in Saigon show the ways in which militarization extended well beyond combat and relied on women as well as men, civilians as well as soldiers. Saigon symbolized how deeply embedded the U.S. had become in the culture, politics, and society of South Vietnam beyond the sites of combat. Together, American women and men shaped the U.S. relationship with Vietnam and the culture surrounding it.[42]

American women continued to come to the city as journalists, government workers, and civilian employees of the military. Some Red Cross and military women lived in Saigon during their tours of duty. By and large, though, American women and men living in the city were single, and some of their experiences seem marked by a sense of adventure and abandon. The rules were different in Saigon, a place so near yet so far from "the Vietnam War." Because of the war, American women and men in Saigon lived and worked in ways they might not have back home.

One of the main careers that sent American civilian women to Vietnam was journalism. American women journalists often worked with editors, by and large men, who believed women reporters did not belong in war zones covering battles. Sometimes, the sentiment stemmed from a paternalistic desire to protect women journalists, but in other instances, it reflected the attitude that women were not tough enough to report on war. Denby Fawcett, a twenty-four-year-old white American woman, went to Vietnam in 1966 as a reporter on assignment from the *Honolulu Advertiser.* Her editor gave her the task of writing "color stories on Saigon and its environs" and "articles on men and women who are lending their teaching, building, and medical skills to winning the peace." She wrote feature stories, the kind that might work nicely on the "women's pages" of the newspaper.[43]

Fawcett eventually got to go out into the field and report on combat, but she noted that newspaper editors and military commanders believed men should cover combat. Her *Advertiser* colleague and boyfriend, Bob Jones, went to Vietnam during the same time as Fawcett, but his job was "to take care of the dangerous war coverage." Fawcett also believed that while military leaders feared men journalists might die covering combat, "they were even more horrified at the thought of a woman reporter getting shot." She remembered an officer denying her permission to enter a combat area because she "reminded him of his daughter."[44] In 1966, General William Westmoreland, commander of U.S. forces in Vietnam from 1964 through 1968, tried to pass an order forbidding female reporters from spending the night in the field with troops. He argued that soldiers might put themselves in danger trying to save the women in the event of an attack. The order would have made it difficult for women reporters to cover combat because of lack of regular transportation out of battle areas in the evenings. However, a group of female journalists petitioned the Defense Department against Westmoreland and succeeded in retaining access to combat sites.[45] Therefore, some American women journalists did go out into the field, cover battles, and get wounded in the line of duty. Their reports undoubtedly contributed to Americans' knowledge of the combat side of the war, but accounts of their lives in Saigon provide a glimpse of another side of the Vietnam War.

Based in Saigon, Fawcett lived in a small apartment above a souvenir shop. In the bedroom, a ceiling fan hung above a king-sized bed to stir a breeze in the thick Saigon heat. A balcony looked out over the busy bar and entertainment district on Tu Do Street ("tu do" translates to "freedom" in English), where Americans threw back whiskey and beer, ate continental cuisine prepared by Chinese chefs, and played in nightclubs, which beckoned them with neon signs and, often, Vietnamese women. Fawcett hung out at the French café Brodard's, where she listened to "California Dreamin'" and other American tunes on the jukebox. At night, she dined on pepper steak and fresh vegetables shipped in from the resort city of Da Lat and prepared by a French-trained cook at a restaurant called Aterbea. Sometimes, she went to Caruso's, which featured candlelight dinners, French and Italian cuisine, and imported French wine. After a meal, she liked to join friends at Jo Marcel's, a nightclub where rich Vietnamese young women danced in miniskirts and drank Coca-Cola. When Ann Landers came to Vietnam to visit wounded soldiers, she invited Fawcett to have dinner with her at the posh Caravelle Hotel's rooftop restaurant. They ate frog legs, rice, and chocolate éclairs, and they sipped espresso high above Saigon, seemingly far off from a war they could see in the distance.[46]

Fawcett also experienced the kind of sexual abandon that might have seemed out of the ordinary in her life back in Honolulu, where her mother played tennis with Westmoreland's wife.[47] Reflecting back on her time in Vietnam, Fawcett said sex was her way of "blocking out the war." She had public, sexual encounters she likened to "breathing good air, a stamp of gratitude for being alive. I was in love with my life and too selfish to be interested in a permanent relationship with anyone."[48] In Vietnam, it seemed, that was okay. Vietnam was not a place for dependents, as Johnson decreed in 1965, and thus for some young, single Americans, it became a place where the opportunities found in free time were the rewards for working there. Just as some American men who stayed at William Crum's bachelor pad partook of the female companionship Crum provided, some American women enjoyed the sexual side of their time in Vietnam.

Americans in Saigon had other leisure activities outside the explicitly sexual variety. When a day's work was done, there was time for golf in Saigon, according to Ann Morrisy Merick, a white American journalist with ABC news stationed in Vietnam in 1967. The Golf Club of Saigon, near Tan Son Nhut Airport, offered eighteen holes on a relatively flat, easy course. The most challenging parts of the course were not sand traps or lagoons, but rather the occasional outpost where ARVN soldiers stood on guard, watching for Viet Cong infiltrators. Barbed wire, land mines, and armed guards protected the outposts, so landing a golf ball near one was akin to landing a ball in a pond. The caddies were "sturdy Vietnamese women not much bigger than the bags they carried," Merick observed.[49]

For those who did not care to play golf, there was the Cercle Sportif, a sprawling athletic club in downtown Saigon left behind by the French. Restless diplomats and tired embassy employees could pick up a tennis match or relax by the pool with a gin and tonic. Merick remarked that American men especially enjoyed the scenery, including "the lithe figures of the young Vietnamese ladies in their brief bikinis." Adventuresome Americans and wealthy Vietnamese went waterskiing on the Saigon River, skimming past U.S. Navy river boat patrols. Nearby was a ritzy yacht club called Cercle Nautique.[50] On weekends, some Americans hopped a plane or helicopter and retreated to Nha Trang, a coastal village turned resort town where lobster dinners, coconut trees, and glass-bottom boats awaited them.[51] Evenings meant cocktails and dinner parties. Merick noted that U.S. Ambassador Ellsworth Bunker threw some of the best parties, featuring brandy, cigars, and imported Russian vodka. His soirees were for the "A-list" of Saigon, but for those without an invitation, there usually was a party going on somewhere, in the apartment of an American embassy worker or perhaps at the Rex Hotel. "It was a welcome break from being in the field, and we all got gussied up and partied," Merick said.[52]

Leisure activities, hotels, and imported goods were available for the foreigners occupying Saigon during the war. Vietnamese workers provided much of the labor that built the society in which Americans lived, worked, and played. Largely because most able-bodied Vietnamese men were drafted during the war, Vietnamese women were the primary employees in Saigon's wartime economy.[53] On Merick's ride from Tan Son Nhut Airport into downtown Saigon, she noticed a crew working on the road. It consisted of "six women all dressed in white Vietnamese blouses, loose-fitting black pants, and conical straw hats that were tied under their chin to protect them from the sun."[54] Merick hired a French-trained Vietnamese cook and knew that "many correspondents had a houseboy or a woman who cooked for them. We all had seamstresses and tailors who could create a dressy outfit from the elegant silks and cottons that were available from our R&R shopping trips to Hong Kong and Bangkok."[55] A brochure for civilian employees of the U.S. Air Force boasted, "one of the many pleasant aspects of duty in the Republic of Vietnam is the fact that one can afford servants." It listed the average costs per month in U.S. dollars for hired help— cooks charged about $40 to $80, while maid service ran $35 to $60.[56] Vietnamese workers made clothes, kept house, and provided entertainment for Americans in Saigon.

In addition to providing housekeeping and cooking services to Americans, the Vietnamese, and even Saigon itself, provided for the needs of Americans stationed in the country during the war. Not all of Saigon's amenities developed as a result of the arrival of Americans. Some hotels, restaurants, and shops dated back to the days of French colonialism. Americans recognized this, and some U.S. policymakers feared the republic's involvement in Vietnam would appear colonial. In 1964, as the Johnson administration discussed sending more personnel to Vietnam, Ambassador Henry Cabot Lodge expressed concern that more Americans, particularly civilians, in Vietnam would give a "colonial coloration" to the U.S. presence there.[57] Discussions about sending combat troops to Vietnam included fears that the conflict would look like "a white man's war against the brown."[58] General Maxwell Taylor wondered what the

U.S. should do about the "growing 'colonialist' image of the white man."[59] Throughout the course of the relationship between the U.S. and Vietnam, some American government officials worried the U.S. would appear to have imperial aspirations for Vietnam, but all the while, American women and men lived in a world in Saigon marked by a colonial character. Vietnamese workers labored in a service industry aimed at providing for the needs of Americans, many of whom were in Vietnam to aid the U.S. effort to prevent communist rule from taking South Vietnam.

Advertisements in the English-language magazine *Life in Vietnam*, a publication distributed to U.S. military installations in Vietnam and Vietnamese embassies throughout the world, showcased Saigon's amenities and painted a picture of what Saigon looked like during the U.S. occupation of Vietnam. By the mid-1960s, the Saigon skyline was made of seven and eight-story hotels that lifted guests high above the city and offered them sweeping, city-wide views which allowed them to gaze down at the lives below. The Mai Loan Hotel featured air-conditioned rooms with balconies, a snack bar with a panoramic view of Saigon, and a restaurant offering Chinese and American foods. While the Majestic Hotel also provided air-conditioned rooms and panoramic views, it also boasted "refined French cuisine" and the "attractive and talented Ngoc Nhi" performing every night in the bar on the fifth floor. Not to be outdone, the Manhattan Hotel and Restaurant stood in "the heart of Saigon's shopping area" and presented guests with a penthouse, seventh-floor restaurant and "delicious French and Chinese dishes by an excellent cook from Hong Kong." After settling into their accommodations, visitors might have strolled down one of the city's commercial boulevards to find a tailor and ensure they had proper party attire. Waloc and Ashoka tailors both offered ready-to-wear and custom-made men's and women's clothing, and ads for the shops featured a drawing of a white man in a business suit. One stop at Beautex, a "fully air-conditioned salon," and a visitor could walk out with the latest French hairdo courtesy of a Paris-certified stylist.[60] Snippets of life in Saigon add another layer to the complex set of experiences American men and women had in

Vietnam, and the subtle and overt ways in which ideas about gender shaped their time in-country.

Conclusion

More than forty years later, Americans continue to tell a Vietnam War story centered on a quagmire involving male troops in jungle combat and politicians in the United States. Beyond the quagmire narrative are stories of American women in combat zones, and men and women high on the adrenaline of life in Saigon, which, while still part of the war, offered escapism via rowdy bars, fine restaurants, and skyscraper hotels. In both the countryside and the city, the experiences of American women enforced and challenged the dominant gender roles of the time. Military women saw combat up close, but only because they were nurses, an acceptable specialty for female personnel. Donut dollies rode helicopters out to remote fire support bases while wearing dresses and smiles. WACs processed Army intelligence reports, but received no arms training to defend themselves in case of an attack. In Saigon, women journalists enjoyed the same excitement of a dangerous wartime city as their male counterparts did.

There are larger lessons in looking beyond the quagmire, too, in addition to offering a fuller accounting of who served and how. Because combat infantrymen are central to the quagmire narrative, those male troops who walked, ran, fought, and sometimes slept in the literal quagmire of rice paddies and jungle terrain, Americans have invested in a myth of the Vietnam War as a unique experience of male hardship. Historian Meredith Lair has argued that, depending on the year, most American servicemen in Vietnam were not on the front lines of combat. Most served in the rear echelon, where boredom and disillusionment about going to war posed the most dangerous threat to morale.[61] To be sure, combat— that traumatic, life-shattering, experience of war— destroyed the families of those who perished and devastated the men who survived.

What Americans have not known or acknowledged is that servicemen in combat was not the only or even the primary Vietnam War experience.

Focusing closely on the combat experience and telling the dramatic story of broken young men, lives lost too soon, and a lack of support and comfort upon return makes it easier to blame the war and its outcome on selfish, misguided politicians and a faceless anti-war movement. Had the U.S. and South Vietnam won the war, perhaps Americans might have worked to hide the trauma of combat under a cloak of victory parades and efforts to push "normalcy" on returning veterans as they did after World War II. In light of the failure of Vietnam, the combat narrative has allowed Americans to see themselves as victims, too, not just perpetrators of a lost war, an immoral war, even an illegal war. Tales of American women and men having adventures and living a good life in Saigon challenges that victim narrative. If some Americans used Saigon in a colonial way, enjoying restaurants, bars, and hotels built for them by their French predecessors, served by Vietnamese maids, houseboys, drivers, and prostitutes, then the victimization of combat troops becomes a less compelling method for generating sympathy for American involvement in Vietnam. If American experiences in Vietnam were not exceptional, were not uniquely distressing relative to other wars, then perhaps U.S. policies toward and behaviors in Vietnam were not anomalies, either. Perhaps the Vietnam War was just one example of what America does in the world.

Considering American women's experiences in and with combat also challenges the victimhood narrative by revealing that the archetypal American soldier was not the only one harmed in the war. Women saw the disastrous aftermath of combat in their daily jobs, from bandaging the stumps of amputated limbs to holding a serviceman's hand while he cried because he lost half his platoon in an ambush. Their jobs were to care for servicemen emotionally and physically, and they had to figure out how to do their jobs while managing their own mental trauma. American women who served in Vietnam were small in number compared to the men who served, but because of that, their exposure to combat and its consequences was concentrated. If women also experience stress and trauma in war, then war is not exclusive to the male realm. Put another way, while Americans remember the Vietnam War experience as uniquely traumatic for male troops compared to other U.S. wars, females do not factor prominently in the narrative of Vietnam War exceptionalism because women have always cared for wounded soldiers during war. Women have always been there, and women's war work has always been bloody and traumatic, whether they cared for men's bodies or their spirits.

NOTES

1. Dave Kang, "Friends Recall Only Nurse Killed by Hostile Fire in Vietnam," *U.S. News and World Report*, May 28, 2017; also available online at: https://www.usnews.com/news/us/articles/2017-05-28/friends-recall-only-nurse-killed-by-hostile-fire-in-vietnam.
2. Kara Dixon Vuic, *Officer, Nurse, Woman: The Army Nurse Corps in the Vietnam War* (Baltimore: Johns Hopkins Univerity Press, 2010), 2; Heather Stur, *Beyond Combat: Women and Gender in the Vietnam War Era* (New York: Cambridge University Press, 2011), 132.
3. Christian Appy, *Working-Class War: American Combat Soldiers and Vietnam* (Chapel Hill, NC: University of North Carolina Press, 1993) 173.
4. Jeanne Holm, *Women in the Military: An Unfinished Revolution* (Novato, CA: Presidio Press, 1982) 207.
5. "Fraud and Corruption in Management of Military Club Systems: Illegal Currency Manipulations Affecting South Vietnam." Report of the Committee on Government Operations, United States Senate, Permanent Subcommittee on Investigations (Washington, DC: U.S. Government Printing Office, 1971), 9-11, 13, 93.
6. Ibid., 97.
7. Ibid., 98, 102, 104.
8. Tad Bartimus et al., *War Torn: Stories of War from the Women Reporters Who Covered Vietnam* (New York: Random House, 2002) 253-54.
9. Marion L. Williams, *My Tour in Vietnam: A Burlesque Shocker* (New York: Vantage Press, 1970), 36.
10. Another 500 women served in the Air Force during the Vietnam War, but most of them were stationed in the Pacific and other parts of Southeast Asia, not in Vietnam. Fewer than thirty women Marines served in Vietnam. In addition to nurses, nine women Navy officers served tours of duty in Vietnam. See Kathryn Marshall, *In the Combat Zone: An Oral History of American Women in Vietnam* (Boston: Little, Brown and Co., 1987), 4; Ron Steinman, *Women in Vietnam* (New York: TV Books, 2000), 18-20; Susan H. Godson, *Serving Proudly: A History of Women in the U.S. Navy* (Annapolis, MD: Naval Institute Press, 2001), 213; Col. Mary V. Stremlow, *A History of the Women Marines, 1946-1977* (Washington, DC: History and Museums Division Headquarters, U.S. Marine Corps, 1986), 87.

11. Marshall, 4; Milton J. Bates, *The Wars We Took to Vietnam: Cultural Conflict and Storytelling* (Berkeley, CA: University of California Press, 1996), 163.
12. Vuic, 2. See also, Elizabeth Norman, *Women at War: The Story of Fifty Military Nurses Who Served in Vietnam* (Philadelphia: University of Pennsylvania Press, 1990); Lynda Van Devanter, *Home Before Morning: The Story of an Army Nurse in Vietnam* (Amherst, MA: University of Massachusetts Press, 2001); Winnie Smith, *American Daughter Gone to War* (New York: Pocket Books, 1994).
13. Vuic, 2-12.
14. Author's telephone interview with Linda Pugsley, November 2009, Hattiesburg, MS.
15. Author's telephone interview with Linda Pugsley, November 2009, Hattiesburg, MS.
16. A precedent for WAC service in Asia was set during World War II, when WACs served in India, China, Burma, and Ceylon. However, the Army did not deploy WACs to the Korean War. See Holm, 207-9.
17. Memo, "Women's Armed Forces Corps," Office of Information, U.S. Military Assistance Command Vietnam, November 12, 1966, NARA RG 319.
18. Harvey H. Smith, et al., *Area Handbook for South Vietnam* (Washington, DC: U.S. Government Printing Office, 1967), 138.
19. Phung Thi Hanh, "South Vietnam's Women in Uniform."
20. Bettie J. Morden, *The Women's Army Corps, 1945-1978* (Washington, DC: U.S. Government Printing Office, 1990), 217.
21. Stur, *Beyond Combat,* 105-41.
22. Ibid.
23. "Department of Defense Request for SRAO in Vietnam," June 4, 1965, NARA RG 200.
24. "How the SRAO Staff Live in Vietnam." National Archives, Record Group 200 – Records of the American National Red Cross, 1965-1979 [hereafter NARA RG 200].
25. "Red Cross Clubmobile Girls Coming Home from Vietnam," American Red Cross News Service, May 26, 1972. Jeanne Christie Collection, University of Denver Penrose Library, Special Collections, Denver, CO.
26. Author's interview with Emily Strange, May 2002, Johnson Creek, WI.
27. Heather Stur, "I Stopped Learning Names..." *The Year of the Cat,* July 24, 2016, URL: https://hmstur.wordpress.com/2016/07/24/i-stopped-learning-names/, Accessed on Dec 1, 2017.
28. Stur, *Beyond Combat,* 17-63.

29. Memo, Department of the Army, 28 Headquarters, USA Regional Communications Group Vietnam, "Report of MOOSE Action, FY69," October 31, 1968, National Archives, Records of the United States Forces in Southeast Asia. Record Group 472, Box 116, Folder 1378 – "Project Moose Reports." See also, Memo, "United States Army, Vietnam MOOSE Plan, FY 70," April 1, 1969. National Archives, Records of the United States Forces in Southeast Asia. Record Group 472, Box 116, Folder 1378 – "Project Moose Reports."
30. "Cleaning Up Saigon," *Time*, December 1, 1967; also available online at: http://www.time.com/time/magazine/article/0,9171,712011,00.html.
31. Ann Laura Stoler, "Intimidations of Empire: Predicaments of the Tactile and Unseen," in *Haunted By Empire: Geographies of Intimacy in North American History*, ed. Stoler, (Durham, NC: Duke University Press, 2006).
32. Stur, *Beyond Combat*, 48.
33. Message from the Ambassador in Vietnam (Lodge) to the President, Saigon, February 20, 1964, *Foreign Relations of the United States, 1964-1968,* (Washington, DC: U.S. Government Printing Office, 1992), 1:94-95. [Hereafter *FRUS*, followed by year and volume].
34. Memorandum from the Secretary of Defense (McNamara) to the President, Washington, March 16, 1964, *FRUS, 1964-1968,* 1:153-67.
35. Summary Record of a Meeting, Honolulu, June 1, 1964, *FRUS, 1964-1968,* 1:422-33.
36. "Students seize school in Saigon," *New York Times*, November 24, 1964, 1.
37. Telegram from the Department of State to the Embassy in Vietnam, Washington, December 24, 1964. *FRUS, 1964-1968,* 1:1038.
38. Telegram from the President to the Ambassador in Vietnam (Taylor), Washington, December 30, 1964. *FRUS 1964-1968,* 1:1057-8.
39. Telegram from the Chairman of the Joint Chiefs of Staff (Wheeler) to the Commander, Military Assistance Command, Vietnam (Westmoreland), Washington, December 31, 1964, *FRUS 1964-1968,* 1:1063-5.
40. Telegram from the Embassy in Vietnam to the Department of State, Saigon, February 1, 1965. *FRUS, 1964-1968,* 2:116.
41. Memorandum of Conversation, Saigon, February 4, 1965, *FRUS, 1964-1968,* 2:139.
42. Marion L. Williams, *My Tour in Vietnam: A Burlesque Shocker* (New York: Vantage Press, 1970), pp. 35-53.
43. Heather Stur, "Dragon Ladies, Gentle Warriors, and Girls Next Door: Gender and the Vietnam War," Ph.D. Dissertation, University of Wisconsin, 2008, 10.

44. Stur, "Dragon Ladies, Gentle Warriors, and Girls Next Door,", 6-7.
45. Stur, "Dragon Ladies, Gentle Warriors, and Girls Next Door,", 12-15.
46. Ibid., 6, 22-24.
47. Ibid., 13.
48. Ibid., 19.
49. Ibid., 13.
50. Ibid., 118, 133.
51. "Nha Trang," *Life in Vietnam,* No. 143, December 16, 1967, 39, Glenn Helm Collection, Vietnam Archive, Texas Tech University, Lubbock, TX.
52. Bartimus et al., 117.
53. "The Women," *Time*, November 8, 1968; also available online at: http://www.time.com/time/magazine/article/0,9171,902501,00.html.
54. Bartimus, et al., 94.
55. Ibid.
56. Pacific Air Forces Pamphlet, U.S. Air Force Civilian Employment, Republic of Vietnam, Area Information Pamphlet, November 3, 1969, Sally Vineyard Collection, University of Denver Penrose Library, Special Collections, Denver, CO.
57. Draft Memorandum by the Secretary of State's Special Assistant for Vietnam (Sullivan), Washington, June 13, 1964, *FRUS, 1964-1968,* 1:503.
58. Telegram from the Embassy in Vietnam to the Department of State, Saigon, January 6, 1965, *FRUS, 1964-1968,* 2:26.
59. Paper Prepared by the President's Special Consultant (Taylor), Washington, January 1, 1967, *FRUS, 1964-1968,* 5:2.
60. *Life in Vietnam,* various issues, Glenn Helm Collection.
61. Meredith Lair, *Armed with Abundance: Consumerism and Soldiering in the Vietnam War* (Chapel Hill, NC: University of North Carolina Press, 2011).

China's Intervention and the End of the Communist Alliance in Vietnam

Xiaobing Li

The Democratic Republic of Vietnam's (DRV) communist neighbor, China, was wary of President Lyndon Johnson's decision to escalate the American war effort throughout the southern region of the Republic of Vietnam (RVN). Chinese authorities feared western encroachment could lead to the perpetuation of the South along non-communist lines in addition to the eventual collapse of the North. In June 1965, the People's Republic of China (PRC) became directly involved in the war by sending the People's Liberation Army (PLA) to Vietnam.[1] By March 1966, China had dispatched 180,000 troops.[2] Mao Zedong (Mao Tse-tung), Chairman of the Chinese Communist Party (CCP), launched a nationwide movement to "assist Vietnam and resist America." Between 1965 and 1970, China sent 320,000 troops, totaling twenty-three divisions, to Vietnam to support North Vietnam's war against America.[3] On September 18, 1968, the first PLA troops, roughly 26,000 men including anti-aircraft artillery (AAA) and engineering troops, entered Laos. From 1969 to 1973, the PLA sent five more divisions, totaling 110,000 troops, to Laos to provide air defense, construct and repair highways, and maintain transportation and communication along the Ho Chi Minh Trail.[4]

Even though a few Western historians speculated about China's involvement in the Vietnam War, no primary source or personal accounts had been available to support their claims. And yet, a new international perspective may help students and the public in the West to gain a better understanding of the Vietnam War. Vietnam War historiography is incomplete without a careful examination of the level of Chinese communist involvement in the conflict. This chapter aspires to tell the story from the "other side of the hill."

Chinese involvement in the war did not come without costs. In 1970, the PLA began withdrawing its troops from Vietnam; three years later, all of its troops were gone. By the time the last Chinese officer left in August 1973, 1,715 Chinese soldiers had been killed and 6,400 more were wounded. An additional 269 were killed and 1,200 were wounded in Laos. The soldiers and officers killed during the war were buried in the region: a reality which continues to trouble the families of the deceased.[5]

In retrospect, international communist support to North Vietnam, including troops, logistics, and technology, proved to be the decisive edge that enabled the North Vietnamese Army (NVA or PAVN) to survive the American bombing campaign (Operation Rolling Thunder), and helped the National Liberation Front (NLF, also known by the derogative designation, "Viet Cong" or "VC") prevail in the war of attrition and eventually defeat South Vietnam.[6] Chinese and the Union of Soviet Socialist Republics (USSR or Soviet Union) support prolonged the war, making it impossible for the United States to win. As two historians point out, "It was having China as a secure rear and supply depot that made it possible for the Vietnamese to fight twenty-five years and beat first the French and then the Americans."[7]

Nevertheless, the Vietnam War seriously tested the limits of the Communist international alliance. Chinese and Soviet military assistance to North Vietnam between 1965 and 1973 did not improve Sino-Soviet relations, but rather created new competition as each attempted to gain leadership of the Southeast Asian Communist movements after the Sino-

Soviet split. The Vietnamese, by bringing both Russian and PLA troops into North Vietnam, increased competition between Chinese and Soviet Communists. The Chinese-Russian rivalry in Vietnam from 1965 to 1968 worsened the Sino-Soviet relationship. From 1969 to 1971, China gradually shifted its defense focus and national security concerns from the United States to the Soviet Union. Eventually, the hostility between Beijing and Moscow led to Sino-Soviet border clashes during that same three-year period.[8] In retrospect, the Vietnam War, seemingly becoming a "double-edged sword," undermined the international communist alliance and transformed the Cold War from a bipolar standoff to a confrontation on multiple fronts. This conflict seeded a triangular relationship between the nations during the 1980s. Indeed, the Americans and the Soviet Union each proved willing to play the proverbial "China card" against the other.

To obtain the maximum material support against America, North Vietnam remained neutral in the Sino-Soviet rivalry from 1965 to 1970. The triangular relationship, however, changed in favor of the soviets after Ho Chi Minh died in 1969. Thus, Hanoi began moving closer to Moscow in 1970-1972, while the traditional alliance between the PRC and DRV fell apart. After the Paris Peace Treaty was signed and American troops withdrew from Vietnam in early 1973, the Chinese Navy occupied the Paracels Islands in the South China Sea in 1974. In 1979, the Chinese Army launched a large-scale invasion, sending more than 220,000 troops into Vietnam. Some divisions returned to Vietnam not as allies, but as invaders. In less than six years, former Cold War allies had become bitter enemies.[9]

Mao's Concerns and the PLA Intervention

After the founding of the PRC in 1949, the Chinese government was involved in the First Indochina War (1946-1954) and also joined North Vietnam against South Vietnam in their civil struggle (1955-1963). The Chinese military's involvement in the First Indochina War, known in China as the "Fight to Assist Vietnam and Resist France" (*Yuanyue kangfa douzheng*), became a historical precursor for later intervention in the Vietnam War against America. Chinese security considerations and policy decisions to aid Ho Chi Minh's wars against France first and then America reflected a strategic culture that advocated concepts of an active defense to protect the Communist state from both a possible foreign invasion and a potential Western threat. Chen Jian points out, "for the purpose of promoting the PRC's international reputation and enhancing its southern border security, the CCP leadership was willing to play an outstanding role in supporting the cause of their Communist comrades in Vietnam."[10]

In the early 1960s, Mao warned CCP leaders of a U.S. military encirclement of China. The party chairman believed the United States was building military bases and establishing its influence in Asian countries along China's eastern and southern borders in order to surround the PRC. Mao's concerns were reinforced by Johnson's decision to escalate America's war efforts in South Vietnam. In order to break the encirclement, China increased material support to North Vietnam and began considering the possibility of dispatching troops to the war in 1965.[11]

After Rolling Thunder started on March 2, 1965, Chinese leaders made a quick decision on April 8-9 to secretly send tens of thousands of PLA troops as "volunteer forces" to Vietnam to secure transportation lines, provide air defense of key points, build and repair major railways and roads, and construct air fields and coastal defense works. The "Chinese Volunteer Forces to Assist Vietnam" were simply regular PLA troops who had been assigned to the Vietnam War. The North Vietnamese also pushed China into action. Ho Chi Minh sent a VWP delegation led by Le Duan and General Vo Nguyen Giap to Beijing in April, and Vietnamese leaders formally requested China to send troops to Vietnam.[12] In mid-May, Ho Chi Minh visited Mao in China asking about Mao's plan to send Chinese anti-aircraft artillery and railroad engineering troops to Vietnam. Mao told Ho the decision had been made and added: "[we] obey Chairman Ho's orders; China will take care [of these], no problem."[13]

On the night of June 9, 1965, the first Chinese troops entered North Vietnam disguised as the vanguard of the First Division from the PLA Railway Engineering Corps and wore NVA gray uniforms with no Chinese insignias or names; all of their vehicles bore NVA license plates.[14] By July, all of the First Division's 30,000 troops had entered Vietnam.[15] In June, General Van Tian Dung, Chief of the NVA Staff, met with Grand General Luo Ruiqing (Luo Rui-ching), Chief of the PLA General Staff, to discuss operations of the Chinese AAA troops in North Vietnam. Dung specifically requested China send two anti-aircraft artillery divisions to defend Hanoi and areas north of it against intensified bombing. Luo agreed.[16] On July 24, the Vietnamese General Staff telegraphed the PLA General Staff, formally requesting China send "the two anti-aircraft artillery divisions that have long completed their preparations for operations in Vietnam. The earlier the PLA sent its AAA troops, the better for the NVA. If possible, they may enter Vietnam on August 1."[17] The next day, the Chinese cabled Hanoi, stating China would immediately send two AAA divisions and one regiment to Vietnam.[18]

On August 1, 1965, the 61st AAA Division entered Vietnam from China's Yunnan province to provide air defense northwest of Hanoi. On August 9, the 61st moved into action against Rolling Thunder and shot down an American F-4 fighter/bomber near the Yen Bai area. It was the first American plane to be downed by Chinese AAA units.[19] In the meantime, the 63rd Division crossed the border from Guangxi in the northeast to protect the critical Hanoi-Youyiguan [Friendship Pass] railway between China and North Vietnam. The 63rd engaged in its first battle with the Americans in the Kep area on August 23.[20] The two Chinese divisions, totaling 21,000 AAA troops, were part of North Vietnam's air defense under the NVA Air Defense-Air Force Command (AD-AFC), which was established in October 1963 with Senior Colonel Phung The Tai as its commander and Dang Tinh Duc as political commissar. In early 1965, the command had twenty-one Vietnamese AAA regiments and forty-one battalions, about 36,000 regular troops.[21] By the fall of 1965, 35 percent of the 59,500 air defense troops stationed in North Vietnam were Chinese.

A year later, the PLA began rotating its AAA divisions. From 1965 to 1967, the PLA rotated nine AAA divisions or nearly 100,000 troops.

In late 1966, the PLAAF sent an additional AAA division to the central region of North Vietnam. By December of that year, the 62nd Division was assigned to protect Thai Nguyen, a steel-manufacturing city in the north-central region of the country. Eight months later, the 32nd Division replaced it in August 1967. By that fall, the number of Chinese AAA troops in Vietnam had increased to 32,000 men, over 44 percent of all 72,500 air defense troops in North Vietnam.[22] The NVA AD-AFC reorganized its air defense units into five AAA divisions in June 1966, totaling 38,000 Vietnamese regulars.[23]

In retrospect, from 1965 to 1967, the nine Chinese AAA divisions had provided effective coverage over their defense areas. Their operational experience reveals the challenges the Chinese faced, and it provides new and penetrating insights into the key differences between the Chinese army and other armed forces in the Vietnam War. Spencer Tucker states, "Despite [Russian] SAMs and MiG interceptors, guns remained the deadliest threat to attacking American aircraft. Of the 3,000 American aircraft lost during the Vietnam War, 85 percent were downed by guns. Missiles accounted for only 8 percent; indeed, less than 2 percent of 9,000 SAMs fired at U.S. aircraft reached their targets."[24] Although U.S. Intelligence followed Chinese troop involvement closely, it underestimated the scale of the Chinese intervention from 1965 to 1967. In his August 4, 1967, special intelligence estimate, the CIA director reported, "For some time Chinese military personnel have been present in North Vietnam; current strength is estimated at 25,000 to 45,000. They included AAA troops, engineers, construction crews, and various other logistical support groups."[25] By August 1967, the PLA had 181,000 men in Vietnam, including 44,000 in air defense, 30,000 in railway construction and repair, 27,000 in combat engineering, and 80,000 in highway construction.

Beijing's Military Aid to the NVA and NLF

In 1964-1965, the Central Committee of the CCP reached an agreement that China would continue its military and economic aid to North Vietnam, even though the country faced bankruptcy. Premier Zhou Enlai (Chou En-lai) explained the foreign aid policy to his ministers at a State Council executive meeting on July 18, 1964. "We must seize the moment and take a firm grasp of the central issue [of our economic foreign policy]," because the current international situation offered "a great opportunity" for the PRC to increase its influence among the Southeast Asian nations.[26] Shuguang Zhang states, "In the early 1960s, China joined the big-power league in the field of economic diplomacy. The use of economic and military aid in pursuit of foreign policy objectives did not seem alien to the CCP leaders." Also, "China's aid policy toward the Vietnam conflict happened to become a major part of the CCP's new diplomatic thrust." To guarantee foreign aid, Zhou directed many domestic economic projects to prioritize overseas assistance efforts.[27]

Beijing increased its military aid to Hanoi with an all-out, nationwide effort.[28] For example, China provided 80,500 automatic rifles in 1964, 141,531 in 1966, 219,899 in 1968, and 233,600 in 1973, almost three times more than the total aid of 1964. The heavy artillery totaled 1,205 pieces in 1964, 3,362 in 1966, 7,087 in 1968, and 9,912 in 1973. Artillery amounts increased by nine times between 1964 and 1973. The PRC provided 335,000 artillery shells in 1964, 1.06 million in 1966, 2.08 million in 1968, and 2.2 million in 1973. The increase in tanks and vehicles was dramatic: forty-one in 1964, ninety-six in 1966, 462 in 1968, and 8,978 in 1972. The deliveries of tanks and vehicles increased 200 times from 1964 to 1972.[29]

By 1974, China had sent Vietnam 2.14 million rifles and automatic guns, 1.2 billion rounds of small arms ammunition, 70,000 artillery pieces, 18.1 million artillery shells, 170 airplanes, 176 gunboats, 552 tanks, 320 armored vehicles, 16,000 trucks, 18,240 tons of dynamite, 11.2 million set of uniforms, as well as other war supplies. Between 1971 and 1972, China also shipped into Vietnam 180 Chinese-made Hongqi-02 anti-aircraft missiles and all the control equipment, radar, and communication facilities for a surface-to-air missile regiment.[30] From 1966 to 1973, China provided military aid totaling 42.6 billion *yuan* (about $14 billion), including guns, ammunition, tanks, naval vessels, armored vehicles, trucks, airplanes, medicine, medical instruments, and other war materials. Thus, during the Vietnam War, China had provided North Vietnam with a total of $20 billion in aid.[31]

In the summer of 1966, Le Duan headed an NLF delegation to visit Beijing. Zhou met the Southern Communist leaders and briefed Mao about their urgent needs from China.[32] Mao instructed the premier that "Whatever materials the South request, so long as we are capable of giving these, should be provided by us unconditionally; some materials, including mosquito nets, umbrellas, and raincoats, medicines, first-aid dressings and kits, or even ship's biscuit which the Vietnamese delegation has not requested but we are able to provide should also be offered by us."[33] Mao had also previously directed the high command that the PLA "should send in more supplies... in large quantity" to the NLF in the South. Among the items on Mao's list were dried meat, canned pork, salt fish, and egg flour[34].

On June 11, 1967, China signed another military aid agreement with the NLF logistics representatives. Beijing agreed to provide NLF troops with more than 650 categories of weapons, ammunition, and daily needs via the Ho Chi Minh Trail.[35] In August 1968, Li Qiang (Li Chiang), vice minister of China's Foreign Trade Ministry, reported to Zhou regarding China's financial aid to the NLF in South Vietnam. Li briefed the premier that China provided the NLF with $49 million of hard currency in 1968, and that the total would increase to $57.5 million in 1969.[36]

To supply the NLF in the South directly, Beijing maintained and expanded the land and sea transportation routes linked to China. Beginning in early 1966, Chinese forces participated in operations along the Ho Chi Minh Trail. The PLA General Staff sent its officers to the HQ of Group 559 (NVA Military Transportation) under the command of

Major General Phan Trong Tue. The Chinese officers also worked at the key transport depots such as Thanh Hoa, Vinh, Tchepong (Laos), and Lomphat (Cambodia) to supervise PLA transportation and road engineering operations, track Chinese aid to the South, and report troop casualties, vehicle damage, and shipment losses along the Ho Chi Minh Trail as a result of American bombing.[37] Some of the trucks reached the South Vietnamese border at the Thua Thien region. The others traveled farther south into Cambodia and reached South Vietnam around the Plei Mok Den area. The annual ground delivery of the Chinese military aid from the border along the Ho Chi Minh Trail to the NLF in South Vietnam totaled 28,000 to 30,000 tons in 1966-1968.[38] Nonetheless, the PLA staff reported to Beijing that about 55-68 percent of Chinese supplies were destroyed or interdicted along the Ho Chi Minh Trail, a result of American warplanes flying 3,000 combat missions per month against targets in Laos.[39]

In 1967, China helped the NVA and NLF improve transportation along the Ho Chi Minh Trail by adding two more truck regiments, the 48th and 49th Transit Regiments with 1,000 trucks, to speed up direct delivery of military aid from China to South Vietnam. From 1967 to 1969, the additional regiments delivered 17,500 tons of food, weapons, and ammunition.[40] The annual delivery of Chinese military aid to the NLF in South Vietnam increased to 40,000 tons in 1969-1970, which was more than a 40 percent increase of the annual shipment in 1966-1968.[41]

To supply some of the NLF battalions deep in the south, Chinese naval transit vessels first shipped weapons, ammunition, and food to the high sea off the coast of South Vietnam. There, Chinese ships unloaded the supplies on to smaller Vietnamese fishing junks, which could penetrate the southeastern coast. In some cases, the fishermen threw the supplies packed in inflated waterproof plastic bags into the water, allowing them to float to shore and reach the NLF guerrillas.[42]

In the meantime, Mao approved the construction of China's sea route addition to the Ho Chi Minh Trail, or a southern counterpart of the Ho

Chi Minh Trail, through Cambodia to the southwestern border of South Vietnam. China shipped its military aid south through the South China Sea, first to the Sihanouk Harbor in Cambodia, where Beijing had spent huge amounts to build a new port. The Chinese supply line then crossed Cambodia northward by road and reached Svay Rieng and Chiphu, two Cambodian border towns close to the Viet Cong bases in southwest Vietnam. NLF guerrilla troops could easily cross the border and receive Chinese supplies there.[43] U.S. Army General Creighton Abrams estimated at the time that, while the majority of supplies entering the north end of the Ho Chi Minh Trail were destroyed, "virtually all supplies entering through Sihanoukville reached destination until Cambodia incursion of May 1970."[44]

Chinese support, particularly their transportation of war materials directly to the South, largely guaranteed the NLF's battle initiatives in the region. Zhang concluded that "Without China's aid, the Vietnamese could not have sustained the burden of fighting a guerrilla war that was, in some sense, a war of attrition with the United States."[45] All these efforts for the South, however, did not slow nor reduce China's aid to North Vietnam, despite Hanoi's complaints in 1968-1970. From 1960-1977, China also provided large-scale, free military aid to Laos, including 115,000 automatic rifles, 2,780 artillery pieces, thirty-four tanks, 170 million rounds of ammunition, 2.7 million artillery shells, 920,000 hand grenades, 254,000 land mines, 2,530 wireless radios, 2,654 telephones, 773 military vehicles, 958 tons of explosives, 2,570,000 uniforms, and 7,710 tons of food. The Chinese military aid helped the Laotian Communist forces to win their war against a pro-American government.[46]

Soviet Aid and Technology Gap

In the meantime, the North Vietnamese also received military and economic aid from the Soviet Union. They knew the Soviet Union and China, though both communist, were rivals, and as such, each claimed itself *the* key supporter of the Vietnamese Communist struggle against the west. This rivalry motivated the Soviet Union to use all means possible to win Vietnam over as a political ally. After the Moscow-Hanoi agreement in February 1965, the Soviets began sending forces to Vietnam, including SAM missile regiments, air-defense radar units, security battalions, technology training instructors, and logistics officers. This initial aid agreement requested the Soviets send a brigade of combat troops and other armored vehicle personnel, totaling 4,000 troops, to Vietnam in the spring of 1965.[47] By April, the Soviet Union began to deliver economic and military aid to North Vietnam.[48] During the second half of 1965, the Soviet Union, along with its Eastern European allies, shipped a total of 592,000 tons of non-military and military aid to Vietnam by sea or railroads by the end of the year.[49]

The Soviet Union increased military aid to Vietnam in 1966-1967 and exceeded China in terms of military and economic aid to the North. Moscow's military aid increased to 357 million rubles (about $350 million), 70 percent of its total aid of 500 million rubles (about $500 million) in 1968. Moscow's aid was more than 50 percent of annual aid from all Communist states— thus, exceeding the Chinese.[50] From 1968 to 1972, the Soviets provided a total of $3 billion in aid to Vietnam, including $2 billion in military aid.[51] A CIA memo on August 26, 1966, pointed out the significance of increasing Soviet military aid to Vietnam. The "Soviet backing has the effect of buttressing the Vietnamese Communist will to persist in the conflict. The Vietnamese probably judge that they can continue to count indefinitely on Moscow's assistance along recent lines so long as the war continues in its present context. They probably believe, in fact, that the Soviets now are locked into a struggle in view of Moscow's desire to retain leadership of the Communist camp."[52]

The Soviet Union also increased its intelligence activities drastically in Vietnam. A former KGB agent recalled that after 1965, the Vietnam War became the KGB's first priority.[53] In 1966, the KGB doubled the number of its agents at the embassy and by 1970 the number increased again.[54] One of the agents, who was assigned to collect political and military information on China and Beijing-Hanoi relations, told the author that "At that time, the KGB worked hard against China, an immediate threat to Soviet security and international relations."[55] The agents worked inside of the Chinese news corps, recruited Chinese informants, translated important information from Vietnamese to Russian, and wrote reports. For instance, the agent told the author that he spent a lot of time writing reports, about ten pages each day. These reports were then coded into telegrams and sent to Moscow. The agents did not share any information with each other, and they did not know what other agents were doing, as it was prohibited to do so in the interest of maintaining KGB security. Colonel Konstantin Preobrazhensky told the author that it had been part of its culture and tradition that the KGB did not trust its own people. All the Russian agents in the embassy kept an eye on each other and reported any suspicion of any possible collaboration with foreign intelligence. The KGB headquarters had internal control to protect itself as an institution at home and abroad. It aimed to discover traitors and potential defectors. The extent of the distrust and peer spying "hurt many honest agents and officers." Preobrazhensky called it "a professional disease inside the KGB. Sometimes it just drove you crazy."[56]

To provide an effective air defense in North Vietnam against Rolling Thunder, the Soviet high command established a special Vietnam unit of the Soviet missile troops, or so-called military detachment #31920, under the command of Major General Alexander Stuchilov. General Stuchilov was also the chief commander of the Soviet anti-aircraft defense forces in Vietnam in 1967-1969. Even though the total number of Soviets in Vietnam is still inconclusive, U.S. intelligence believed that 1,500 to 2,500 Soviet missile troops engaged in the air defense in North Vietnam in September 1965.[57] The unit HQ was in Moscow and it provided missile transportation and training for the missile officers and soldiers before leaving for Vietnam. From 1965 to 1972, the Soviet Union shipped ninety-five sets of launchers, along with control systems, N-12 radar systems, and 7,658 SAM missiles to North Vietnam.[58] Among the most effective Soviet SAM missiles were the CA-75M (or C-75) high-altitude guided surface-to-air missiles, known as the SAM-2 and their improved SAM-3 systems. The Soviet SAM air defense system became operational in North Vietnam in April 1965. The Russian missile regiments' first engagement was on July 25, shooting down three U.S. warplanes that day. The NVA and the Soviets claim that their SAMs shot down "1,300 American warplanes," and that they had the best air defense system for North Vietnam through the war.[59]

In the spring of 1965, Soviet SAM officers began training Vietnamese missile troops that had joined the Soviet SAM operations in late 1965. One of the former Russian missile instructors told the author that he worked at a training center in a mountain north of Hanoi. Established in the spring of 1965, the center had sophisticated Russian-made training facilities, including an indoor (actually in-cave) missile launcher model, operation demo equipment, underground classrooms, and comfortable living quarters. The Russian training program focused on the operation and routine maintenance of the CA-75M (or C-75) high-altitude guided SAM-2 model and later the improved SAM-3 system. More than forty Russian instructors and officers had been teaching and working at this center for more than a year. They had about three hundred Vietnamese students, including commanding officers, HQ staff, missile operators, radar operators, technicians, and logistics officers. These NVA officers studied missile technology and operation in different programs for a period of between one and six months. Most of them did not speak Russian. The Russian instructors totally depended on the Vietnamese translators. Most of the Russian instructors served in the center for two or three years.[60]

The Russian instructors followed General Stuchilov's principle in training, as he said, "do as I am doing." His principle guided the missile training, and it worked well. The Russian instructors emphasized basic knowledge, practical skills, and hands-on learning. The Vietnamese officers could understand Russian missile operations quickly by following the moves and memorizing the procedures with a little instruction or missile technology background. Following the translated operation manuals, the Russians demonstrated missile operation step by step, and showed the Vietnamese officers how missile operations worked. All the Vietnamese officer students worked hard and learned fast. Their evaluations and assessments showed that they had mastered the technology and were capable of operating Russian radar/missile systems as the major element of their air defense in North Vietnam by 1967.[61]

By early 1968, North Vietnam had established one of the most effective air defense systems in the world. Clodfelter concludes that "the Tet Offensive provided the most graphic illustration of Rolling Thunder's failure to affect the Southern war."[62] The U.S. tried to develop new technology to improve the bombing result in Vietnam. For example, the USAF employed the new F-111 fighter/bomber during Rolling Thunder in early 1968 after the Tet Offensive Campaign. Its cutting-edge technology included "internal radar and a bombing computer in poor weather conditions to maneuver to their targets, where the ordnance was automatically released."[63] On March 17, six F-111s arrived at a U.S. air force base in Thailand. A week later, the F-111s began their bombing missions. The Vietnamese, however, almost immediately learned how to deal with the U.S. high-tech aircraft. On March 28 and 30, the NVA missile troops shot down two F-111s in Ha Tinh province.[64] By the end of the war, more than thirty Soviets and Vietnamese missile regiments had launched 6,806 missiles and lost fifty-six sets of launchers and radar systems in their air defense against American bombing.[65] By 1973, the Vietnamese had sixteen SAM-6 missile regiments and six radar regiments. In addition, it had seven air defense divisions, totaling 50,000 troops.[66]

Compared to superior Soviet missile technology, Chinese air defense offerings, from 1965-1968, were largely inadequate.[67] Though, American intelligence gave a measure of credit to the Chinese AAA divisions for their air defense of the LOCs in North Vietnam,[68] Vietnamese officers, however, believed the Chinese did not shoot down enough airplanes.[69] They complained incessantly about the deficiencies of the Chinese radar technology and air defense, while they praised the Soviet-made SAMs, which shot down many American warplanes, including B-52 bombers.

In the end, no matter how hard the Chinese tried, Soviet military technology won over the Vietnamese while also effectively cutting the ideological bond between the two east Asian nations. Moreover, after Ho's death in 1969, Hanoi relied more on Moscow for better military technology and more economic aid. This pivot point aided in the erosion of the Sino-Soviet relationship, which by the late 1960s had moved from rivalry to outright hostility and confrontation. For the Soviets, China's increasing influence in Southeast Asia was a challenge to Russian ascendency in that region.[70] Li Danhui points out that "Faced with the prospect of increasing closeness between Vietnam and the Soviet Union, China became increasingly anxious and wary of Vietnam even as it sent its neighbor massive amount of aid and a rift began to develop between the two countries."[71] Meanwhile, Chinese leaders realized their experience of the "people's war" did not help the Vietnamese much in their war against American forces. Mao admitted this difference to DRV leaders in Beijing, "you are meeting new situations at present, so a lot of your ways of dealing with them are and ought to be different from ours in the past. We learned how to fight step by step and frequently suffered defeat in the beginning; it was not as smooth as for you."[72]

Image 7. Sino-Soviet Border War map

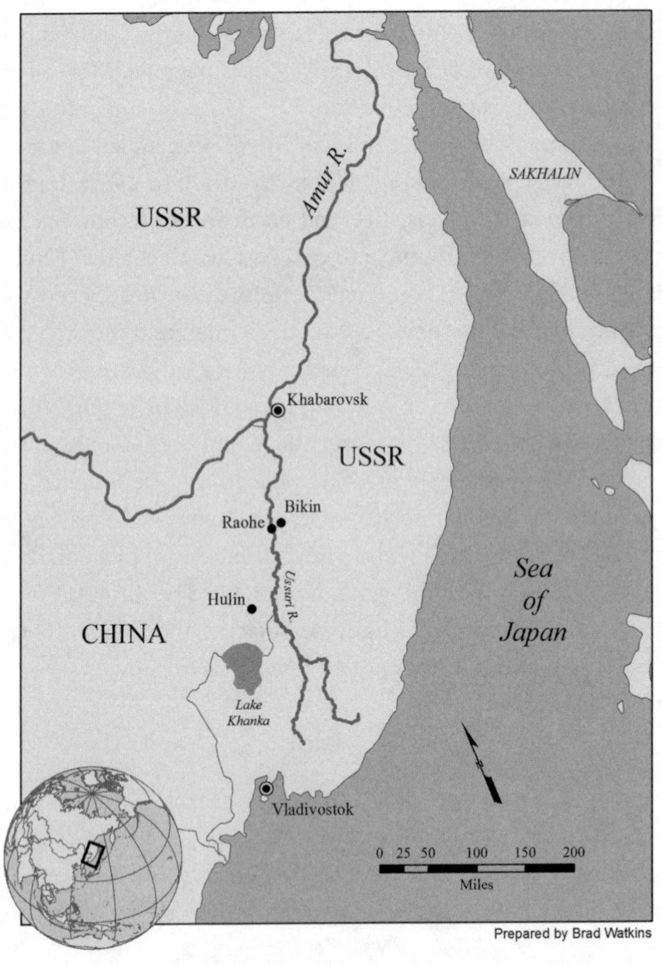

Source: Created for the author by Brad Watkins.

THE SINO-SOVIET BORDER WAR

On March 31, 1968, Johnson announced a bombing halt over North Vietnam. Intended as a new peace gesture, the announcement evoked a positive response from Hanoi, which declared on April 3 its readiness to negotiate with the Americans. China, however, knew nothing about the U.S.-DRV peace talks until much later. In April-May, Beijing began to criticize Hanoi for following the Soviet Union and compromising with the U.S. After the Paris negotiations began on May 13, Beijing continued to berate Hanoi for conducting negotiations with Washington.[73] Eventually, on October 31, Johnson suspended all American air raids, bombing, shelling, and coastal harassment against North Vietnam. Moscow was enthusiastic about the negotiations, while Beijing refrained from intervening and participating in the Paris Peace Talks.

At this point in the war, Marshal Lin Biao, China's defense minister, considered the Soviet Union to be more of an immediate threat to China. After the Soviet Army invaded Czechoslovakia in 1968, its troops broke into the Chinese Embassy and "savagely" beat Chinese diplomats.[74] While the tension mounted, the Soviet Union deployed a large number of Red Army troops along the Soviet-Chinese borders.[75] Zhou told Vietnamese Prime Minister Pham Van Dong on April 29 that "Now the Soviet Union is also encircling China. The circle is getting complete, except [the part of] Vietnam."[76] By the end of that year, Moscow increased its troops from seventeen divisions to twenty-seven divisions along the borders. In 1968-1969, the PLA was apparently under tremendous pressure and felt directly threatened by the Soviet Union.[77] In October 1968, Lin warned the army and the country that Soviet forces would soon invade China.[78] Nicholas Khoo claims that the increasing Sino-Soviet conflict had a major impact on Soviet-Vietnamese relations, and "because the new Soviet leadership to take a more nuanced and effective approach to undermining Chinese influence in North Vietnam."[79] As the Vietnamese became more friendly with the Soviet Union, China distanced itself further from Vietnam: "Hanoi continued to send delegations to Beijing, but there was no reciprocity."[80]

Niu Jun points out that a major change took place in China's strategic thinking in 1968. The Soviet Union replaced the United States as Beijing's leading security concern, promoting China's withdrawal of its troops from Vietnam.[81] The Communist coalition in Southeast Asia collapsed. Beijing began to prepare for an expected war against the Soviet Union and to repel a Soviet invasion in north China. Nicholas Khoo also argues that "the threat represented by the Soviet Union was the central and overriding concern of Chinese foreign policy-makers, a fact that was strongly reflected in Sino-Vietnamese relations."[82]

Beginning in March 1969, border skirmishes erupted along the Sino-Soviet borders at the Zhen Bao (Damansky) and Bacha Islands in Heilongjiang, Northeast China; at Taskti and Tieliekti in Xinjiang, Northwest China.[83] In the first clash, more than forty Chinese soldiers were killed. The Soviets lost eight men and one T-62 tank that sank in the river when artillery fire shattered the two-meter thick ice cover.[84] For the rest of the year, sporadic fighting continued along their borders, and both nations stood on the brink of war, with the Soviets threatening nuclear retaliation. Among the border incidents, on June 10, fifty Soviet soldiers attacked the Chinese in Taskti, Xinjiang. On July 8, the fighting in Heilongjiang extended to the Bacha Island along the Amur River. On August 13, more than 300 Soviet troops supported by twenty tanks and two helicopters engaged in Tieliekti, Xinjiang, and annihilated all the Chinese troops in the battle, but the border conflicts did not escalate into open warfare between the two Communist countries.[85] Chinese Premier Zhou Enlai met Soviet President of the Ministers Council Aleksei Kosygin in Beijing on September 11, 1969, despite continued border clashes along the Chinese-Russian borders until the late 1970s. Beijing demanded a reduction in the number of Soviet troops on the Sino-Soviet and Sino-Mongolian borders as one of the three conditions for a normalization of relations with Moscow.[86]

IMAGE 8. Map of the Sino-Vietnam War

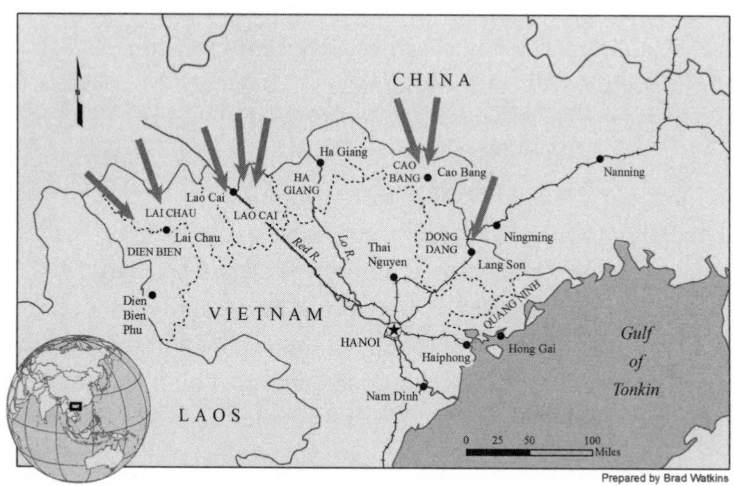

Source: Created for the author by Brad Watkins.

By the early 1970s, the Soviet Union had deployed up to forty-eight divisions, constituting nearly one million troops along the Russian-Chinese border. Reportedly, Moscow's leaders considered using a "preemptive nuclear strike" against China.[87] To prepare for a total war, the PLA high command reinforced more troops from the south to the northern border. As a result of its frequent engagements against the Soviet Red Army, the PLA increased to more than six million men, its highest point in Chinese military history. A CIA National Intelligence Estimate (NIE) predicted on August 12, 1969 that "It is almost certain that there will be no significant easing of tensions [between China and the Soviet Union] during the next two or three years. Conflicting national interests, competition for leadership of the Communist movement, and genuine fear of each other's intentions will prevent a rapprochement. Even the border problems are not likely to be resolved."[88]

The increasing conflict between Moscow and Beijing had a major impact on Soviet-Vietnamese relations. Khoo points out that the Sino-Russian border war "caused the new Soviet leadership to take a more nuanced and effective approach to undermining Chinese influence in North Vietnam."[89] As the Vietnamese continued to increase their cooperation with the Soviets, Beijing distanced itself further and further from Hanoi after 1969. China's military and material support to Vietnam continued, but the quantity began to drop in 1970 after it peaked in 1969. In Beijing's and Hanoi's open propaganda, the assertion that China and Vietnam were "brotherly comrades" could still be heard from time to time, but the enthusiasm disappeared. Chinese influence over North Vietnam diminished as that of the Soviet Union grew.[90] Hanoi considered the marked improvement of relations between China and the United States in the wake of Nixon's visit as tantamount to betrayal on China's part. Leaders in Beijing, from geopolitical considerations, had decided that they could not stand by while Vietnam was engaged in a war that might endanger Chinese security.[91]

From Honeymoon to Divorce

As China's strategic focus shifted from the south to the north and the Soviet Union replaced the United States as its immediate threat, Beijing decided to pull its troops out of Vietnam. On November 17, 1968, Mao suggested to Premier Pham in Beijing that some of the Chinese troops withdraw back to China. The CCP chairman said that "As for some of our personnel who are at present not required in your country, they may withdraw to China... We can send them back to you if the Americans return."[92] Mao had to accept that China would not win a war of ideology with shells and bodies in the air defense of North Vietnam. Mao developed a fresh scheme to reignite China's cause by "exploring a Soviet conspiracy" in Vietnam. [93] Hanoi, however, refused to join Beijing's propaganda and political campaign against Moscow. Beijing became isolated and upset by Hanoi's non-involvement in China's anti-Soviet campaign within the Communist and Socialist camp.[94]

In March 1969, Chinese troops began withdrawing from Vietnam and returned to China.[95] By July 1970, all Chinese AAA troops withdrew back to China. Khoo concludes that "the Chinese viewed their relationship with the Vietnamese communists primarily through the prism of a deteriorating Sino-Soviet relationship. When Hanoi and Moscow consolidated relations after the Soviet intervention in Czechoslovakia in August 1968, Sino-Vietnamese relations declined."[96] After China withdrew its troops and reduced its aid to Hanoi, Moscow filled the gap and continued its military and economic assistance. From 1969 to 1971, Moscow signed seven economic and military aid agreements with Hanoi.[97] Hanoi considered the marked improvement of relations between China and the United States in the wake of Nixon's visit as tantamount to betrayal on China's part.

After 1969, the Soviet Union replaced the United States as Beijing's leading security concern, prompting changes in China's strategic thought. Thereafter, the high command prepared for an expected war against the Soviet Union and to repel a Russian invasion. The Soviet threat and conflicts pushed Chinese leaders to improve their relationship with the United States. The Vietnam War, therefore, created an opportunity for Sino-American rapprochement, which could provide some solutions to their immediate security and political concerns. Strategic need, therefore, eventually led to the normalization of the Sino-American relations when President Richard Nixon visited Beijing in February 1972 and the United States established diplomatic relations with China on January 1, 1979.[98]

In terms of the impact it had upon East Asia and the global Cold War, Sino-American rapprochement dramatically shifted the balance of power between the two super powers in the Cold War. While policymakers in Washington found it possible to concentrate more of America's resources and strategic attention on dealing with the Soviet Union, Moscow's leaders, having to confront the West and China simultaneously, caused the Soviet Union's strength and power to become seriously overextended.[99]

Chinese-Vietnamese relations became worse and worse after the signing of the Paris Peace Agreement in 1973, and the two countries immediately fell into a series of disputes after the Vietnamese Communist won their country's unification in 1975. Among other issues, border disputes caused a rapid deterioration in the Vietnam-China relationship. And Hanoi claimed the Paracels and Spratly Islands in the South China Sea, occupied by the Chinese navy since 1974. In the Chinese view, North Vietnam was an ingrate challenging China under Soviet protection. China lamented the loss of its soldiers' lives and the expenditure of so many resources for so little in return. For the Vietnamese, the Chinese "Northern threat," replaced America as the enemy. Since Vietnam aligned with China's principal enemy, now Hanoi became Beijing's "secondary enemy."[100] In this sense, the Vietnam War became a "lost war" for China.

On December 20, 1977, Vietnam sent troops into Cambodia. Joining the international community and the United States, Beijing denounced the invasion and asked for an immediate and full withdrawal of the Vietnamese troops. Since the Vietnam War ended in 1975, the tension over the border had mounted between the countries. In 1978, Chinese sources reported 1,100 border incidents, in which about three hundred Chinese troops and civilians were killed or wounded. That same year, the PLA reinforced the border with twenty infantry divisions.[101] Both international and internal factors played an important role in the changes of China's security concerns.

Deng Xiaoping, the head of the second generation of the CCP leadership after Mao died in 1976, decided to punish Vietnam as a warning to some neighboring countries, while pleasing others like Thailand, which was worried about Vietnam's aggressive foreign policy. Other matters with Vietnam emerged for China as well. These included the expulsion of 200,000 Chinese-Vietnamese refugees into China and the challenging of Chinese claims over the South China Sea islands.[102] On December 25, 1978, China closed the border. The next day, the PLA began to deploy 220,000 troops along the Vietnamese border.

On January 28, 1979, Deng paid a state visit to America. He told President Jimmy Carter in Washington that Asia "is very unstable." At the meeting with the Senate Foreign Affairs Committee on January 30, a senator asked if China would attack Vietnam since the Beijing-supported government in Cambodia was overthrown and the country was in a serious crisis. Deng answered that "We will not allow Vietnam to make so many troubles [in Asia]."[103] In early February, on his way back to China, Deng told the Japanese prime minister in Tokyo that "To deal with the Vietnamese, it seems no effect by any other means than a necessary lesson." Deng wanted to teach Vietnam "a lesson."[104]

On February 17, the CMC ordered the 220,000 PLA troops to attack Vietnam. The PLA crossed the border and took over Lao Cai on February 20 and Cam Duong in the northwest on February 25. The Chinese occupied Cao Bang on the same day in the northeast. By March 4, the PLA took over Lang Son and threatened Hanoi, only eighty miles away. The Chinese invaders, however, did not press on but stopped at Lang Son because of heavy casualties. During the nineteen days of the offensive, the PLA suffered 26,000 casualties, about 1,350 per day. From March 6 to 16, the Chinese began to withdraw from Vietnam. By the end of the Sino-Vietnamese border war, about 23,000 Chinese were killed and 61,000 were wounded. About 37,300 Vietnamese troops were killed and 2,300 were captured.[105]

The brief 1979 war was a grievous misfortune for both China and Vietnam, not only because of the material and human losses suffered by both nations, but also because it brought years of earlier cooperation to such a dispiriting conclusion. The war showed that American concerns about the domino theory were misplaced, since two Communist countries, one of which had just attained national liberation, were now in conflict with each other. Each valued its own national interests much more than the common communist ideology.

In the meantime, the Soviet threat and conflicts pushed Chinese leaders to improve their relations with the United States. Their strategic needs eventually led to President Nixon's visit to Beijing and the normalization of the Sino-American relationship. Sino-American rapprochement dramatically shifted the balance of power between the two superpowers in the Cold War. While policymakers in Washington found it possible to concentrate more of America's resources and strategic attention on dealing with the Soviet Union, Moscow's leaders, having to confront the West (America) and East (China) simultaneously, saw their strength and power become seriously overextended, signaling the beginning of the end of the Cold War.[106]

Notes

1. General Zhang Aiping (defense minister, 1982-1988), *Zhongguo renmin jiefangjun* [The Chinese People's Liberation Army] (Beijing: Dangdai zhongguo chubanshe [Contemporary China Press], 1994), 1: 274, 276; Lieutenant General Han Huaizhi (deputy chief of the PLA General Staff, 1985-1992), *Dangdai zhongguo jundui de junshi gongzuo* [Military Affairs of Contemporary China's Armed Forces] (Beijing: Zhongguo shehui kexue chubanshe [China Social Sciences Press], 1989), 1: 70, 540, 557; Xiao Shizhong, "An Important Military Operation to Put Out War Flames in Indochina: How China Aids Vietnam and Resists the U.S.," in *Junqi piaopiao; xinzhongguo 50 nian junshi dashi shushi* [PLA Flag Fluttering; Facts of China's Major Military Events in the Past 50 Years], ed. Military History Research Division, China Academy of Military Science (CAMS) (Beijing: Jiefangjun chubanshe [PLA Press], 1999), 2: 451.
2. Major General Qu Aiguo, Bao Mingrong, and Xiao Zuyue, Introduction to *Yuanyue kangmei; zhongguo zhiyuan budui zai yuenan* [Aid Vietnam and Resist America; China's Volunteer Forces in Vietnam], ed. Qu, Bao, and Xiao (Beijing: Junshi kexue chubanshe [Military Science Press], 1995), 12.
3. Among Chinese forces in Vietnam were 150,000 AAA troops of the PLAAF. Their statistics show that Chinese anti-aircraft units shot down 1,707 planes and damaged 1,608 U.S. airplanes in 1965-1968. American official sources say that the United States lost approximately 950 aircraft in North Vietnam between 1965 and 1968. Col. Jerry Noel Hoblit (U.S. Air Force, ret.), interviews by the author at Lubbock, TX, in October 2006 and again at Edmond, OK, in April 2009. Capt. Hoblit was an American pilot who flew F-105F in the 357th Technical Fighter Squadron, 355th Tactical Fighter Wing, USAF, during the Rolling Thunder campaign in 1966-1967. See also George Moss, *Vietnam: An American Ordeal*, 6th ed. (Upper Saddle River, NJ: Prentice Hall, 2010), 187.
4. Han, *Dangdai zhongguo jundui de junshi gongzuo* [Military Affairs of Contemporary China's Armed Forces], 1: 562-63.
5. Zhang, *Zhongguo renmin jiefangjun* [The PLA], 1: 276-77.
6. The term "Viet Cong" was used by President Diem to label the NLF, meaning "Vietnamese Communists," to discredit it. The South Vietnamese Communists and the NLF never used the term "Viet Cong" to

describe themselves. The People's Liberation Army of Vietnam (PLAVN) was the armed force of the NLF. For their publications on NVA and PLAVN in English, see Colonel Dinh Thi Van (NVA, ret.), *I Engaged in Intelligence Work* (Hanoi: Gioi Publishers, 2006); General Hoang Van Thai (PLAVN, ret.), *How South Viet Nam Was Liberated* (Hanoi: Gioi Publishers, 2005); General Phung The Tai (NVA, ret.), *Remembering Uncle Ho; Memories in War Years* (Hanoi: Gioi Publishers, 2005).

7. Jung Chang and Jon Halliday, *Mao: The Unknown Story* (New York: Knopf, 2005), 357.
8. Lorenz M. Luthi, *The Sino-Soviet Split: Cold War in the Communist World* (Princeton, NJ: Princeton University Press, 2008), 340-41.
9. Xiaoming Zhang, *Deng Xiaoping's Long War: The Military Conflict between China and Vietnam, 1979-1991* (Chapel Hill: University of North Carolina Press, 2015), 92-93.
10. Chen Jian, *Mao's China and the Cold War* (Chapel Hill: University of North Carolina Press, 2001), 120.
11. Qiang Zhai, *China and the Vietnam Wars, 1950-1975* (Chapel Hill: The University of North Carolina Press, 2000), 131.
12. Le Duan, "Le Duan and the Break with China," in *Behind the Bamboo Curtain: China, Vietnam, and the World beyond Asia*, ed. Priscilla Roberts (Stanford, CA: Stanford University Press, 2006), 469.
13. Mao's quote from Zhang Baijia, "'Resist America and Aid Korea' and 'Aid Vietnam and Resist America'," in *Duikang, boyi, hezuo: zhongmei anquan weiji guanli anli fenxi* [Confrontation, Calculation, and Cooperation: Case Studies of Security Consideration and Crisis Management between China and the United States], eds. Zhang Tuosheng and Shi Wen (Beijing: Shijie zhishi chubanshe [World Knowledge Press], 2000), 86-89.
14. Zhang, *Zhongguo renmin jiefangjun* [The PLA], 1: 273, 276; Han, *Dangdai zhongguo jundui de junshi gongzuo* [Military Affairs of Contemporary China's Armed Forces], 1: 70, 540, 557; Senior Colonel Long Guilin, "Show the Valor and Spirit Again," in *Yuanyue kangmei* [Aid Vietnam and Resist the U.S], eds. Qu, Bao, and Xiao, 71. Long was commander of the First Division of the CVFAV in Vietnam in 1965-1966.
15. Military History Research Division, CAMS, *Zhongguo renmin jiefangjun de 70 nian, 1927-1997* [Seventy Years of the PLA, 1927-1997] (Beijing: Junshi kexue chubanshe [Military Science Press], 1997), 585-89.
16. Li Ke and Hao Shengzhang, *Wenhua dageming zhong de renmin jiefangjun* [The PLA in the Cultural Revolution] (Beijing: Zhonggong

dangshi ziliao chubanshe [CCP Central Committee's Party Historical Document Press], 1989), 423.

17. Han, *Dangdai Zhongguo jundui de junshi gongzuo* [The Military Affairs of Contemporary China's Armed Forces], 1: 550.
18. *Ibid.*
19. Zhang, *Zhongguo renmin jiefangjun* [The PLA], 1: 275.
20. Wang Dinglie, *Dongdai Zhongguo Kongjun* [Contemporary China's Air Force] (Beijing: Shehui kexue chubanshe [Social Science Press], 1989), 397; Han, *Dangdai Zhongguo jundui de junshi gongzuo* [The Military Affairs of Contemporary China's Armed Forces], 1: 551.
21. Military History Institute of Vietnam, Socialist Republic of Vietnam (SRV), *Victory in Vietnam: The Official History of the People's Army of Vietnam, 1954-1975,* trans. Merle L. Pribbenow (Lawrence: University Press of Kansas, 2002), 96, 165.
22. Major General Qu Aiguo, "Military Operations of the Chinese Supporting Forces in Vietnam's Battleground," in *Zhongguo yu yindu zhina zhanzheng* [China and the Indochina Wars], ed. Li Danhui (Hong Kong: Tiandi Tushu [Heaven and Earth Books], 2000), 50. Qu began serving as deputy chief of the War Theory and Strategic Research Division of the China Academy of Military Science (CAMS) in 2012.
23. Military History Institute of Vietnam, SRV, *Victory in Vietnam,* 189.
24. Tucker, *Vietnam,* 120.
25. CIA, "Current Chinese Communist Intentions in the Vietnam Situation" (SNIE 13-66), in *Tracking the Dragon; National Intelligence Estimates on China during the Era of Mao, 1948-1976,* ed. National Intelligence Council (Pittsburgh, PA: US Government Printing Office, 2004), 411.
26. CCP Central Archival and Manuscript Research Division, *Zhou Enlai Nianpu, 1949-1976* [A Chronological Record of Zhou Enlai, 1949-1976] (Beijing: Zhongyang wenxian chubanshe [CCP Central Archival and Manuscript Press], 1997), 2: 657.
27. Shuguang Zhang, "Beijing's Aid to Hanoi and the United States-China Confrontations, 1964-1968," in Roberts, *Behind the Bamboo Curtain,* 280-81.
28. Wang Taiping, *Zhonghua renmin gongheguo waijiaoshi, 1957-1969* [A Diplomatic History of the PRC, 1957-1969] (Beijing: Shijie zhishi chubanshe [World Knowledge Press, 1998]), 2: 35.
29. Chen, *Mao's China and the Cold War,* table 1, 228.
30. Major General Chen Huiting, "Establishing A Vietnamese Surface-to-Air Missile Regiment," in Qu, Bao, and Xiao, *Yuanyue kangmei* [Aid Vietnam

and Resist the U.S.], 34. Chen was the head of the Chinese Missile Training Group in Vietnam from 1972 to 1973.

31. Wang Xiangen, *Zhongguo mimi da fabing: yuanyue kangmei shilu* [The Secret Dispatch of Chinese Forces: The True Stories of Aiding Vietnam and Resisting the U.S.] (Ji'nan: Ji'nan chubanshe [Ji'nan Publishing], 1992]), 137.
32. Wang Xiangen, *Yuanyue kangmei shilu* [True Stories of Aiding Vietnam and Resisting the U.S.] (Beijing: Guoji wenhua chubangongsi [International Culture Publishing Co.], 1990), 130-31.
33. Mao's instruction is cited in Zhang, "Beijing's Aid to Hanoi and the United States-China Confrontations, 1964-1968," 285n41.
34. Mao, "Instruction on the Meeting Minutes of the Southern Vietnamese Leaders' Conversation with the Chinese News Team," in *Jianguo yilai Mao Zedong wengao* [Mao Zedong's Manuscripts since the Founding of the State] (Beijing: Zhongyang wenxian chubanshe [CCP Central Archival and Manuscript Press], 1993), 11: 478-79.
35. The military supply agreement was signed between the PLA Kunming Regional Command and NLF Logistics Service on June 11, 1967. For more details, see Li and Hao, *Wenhua dageming zhong de renmin jiefangjun* [The PLA in the Cultural Revolution], 410-11.
36. Zi Ding, *Li Qiang zhuan* [Biography of Li Qiang] (Beijing: Renmin chubanshe [People's Press], 2004), 262.
37. Zhang Shihong, Zhang Yanping, and Wu Di, *Hu zhiming xiaodao shang de 701 Tian: Zhongguo jizhe Yuezhan jianwenlu* [701 Days through the Ho Chi Minh Trail: The Vietnam War in My Eyes] (Beijing: Jiefangjun wenyi [PLA Literature Press], 2007), 34-36.
38. Zi, *Li Qiang zhuan* [Biography of Li Qiang], 276.
39. Zhang, Zhang, and Wu, *Hu zhiming xiaodao shang de 701 Tian* [701 Days on the Ho Chi Minh Trail], 328, 338.
40. Zi, *Li Qiang zhuan* [Biography of Li Qiang], 274-75.
41. *Ibid.*, 284-89.
42. Wang, *Zhongguo mimi da fabing* [The Secret Dispatch of Chinese Forces], 129-30.
43. Zi, *Li Qiang zhuan* [Biography of Li Qiang], 259-60.
44. General Creighton Abrams' quote in Michael Kelley, *Where We Were in Vietnam: A Comprehensive Guide to the Firebases, Military Installations, and Naval Vessels of the Vietnam War* (Central Point, OR: Hellgate Press, 2002), F-33.

45. Zhang, "Beijing's Aid to Hanoi and the United States-China Confrontations, 1964-1968," 281.
46. Military History Research Division, CAMS, *Zhongguo renmin jiefangjun de 70 nian* [Seventy Years of the PLA], 593.
47. Ilya V. Gaiduk, *The Soviet Union and the Vietnam War* (Chicago, IL: Ivan R. Dee, 1996), 59, 61-62.
48. SNIE, "Probable Communist Reactions to a U.S. Course of Action, September 22, 1965," in NIC, *Estimative Products on Vietnam*, 294-96.
49. Among the total were 447,900 tons of aids sent to Vietnam by sea, and the rest was shipped over railroads through China. For the details of the Soviet aid, see Li Danhui, "The Sino-Soviet Dispute over Assistance for Vietnam's Anti-American War, 1965-1972,"4-5. Her source is from Foreign Trade Bureau, "Minutes of Meeting between Chinese and Vietnamese Transportation Delegates," July 26, 1965, International Liaison Division Records, *PRC Ministry of Railway Administration Archives.*
50. Gaiduk, *The Soviet Union and the Vietnam War*, 59.
51. Guo Ming, *Zhongyue guanxi yanbian 40 nian* [Deterioration of the Sino-Vietnam Relations in the Past 40 Years] (Nanning: Guangxi renmin chubanshe [Guangxi People's Press], 1992), 103.
52. CIA Memo, "The Vietnamese Communists' Will to Persist—Summary and Principal Findings only, 26 August 1966," in NIC, *Estimative Products on Vietnam*, 365.
53. Major General Robert J. Kodosky (KGB, ret.), interviews by the author at the International Conference on "Intelligence in the Vietnam War" at the Vietnam Center, Texas Tech University, Lubbock, TX, on October 20-22, 2006.
54. Mr. B (KGB, ret.), interviews by the author at Silver Spring, Maryland, in September 2007. He worked as a KGB agent in Russian Embassy in Hanoi in 1966-1968. He wishes to remain anonymous in the publication of his personal story.
55. Mr. B, "Russian Spies in Hanoi," in Li, *Voices of the Vietnam War*, 96-97.
56. Col. Konstantin Preobrazhensky (KGB, ret.), interviews by the author at the International Conference on "Intelligence in the Vietnam War" at the Vietnam Center, Texas Tech University, Lubbock, TX, on October 20-22, 2006. Col. Preobrazhensky worked as a KBG agent in the Russian embassy at Tokyo in the Cold War.
57. Director of Central Intelligence, "SNIE 10-11-65: Probable Communist Reactions to a U.S. Course of Action, September 22, 1965," in National

Intelligence Council (NIC), *Estimative Products on Vietnam, 1948-1975* (Washington, DC: Government Printing Office, 2005), 294-96.

58. Major T (Strategic Missile Force, Soviet Union, ret.), interviews by the author at Kyiv, Ukraine, in July 2005. Maj. T served as a training instructor at the SAM Missile Training Center of the NVA in North Vietnam from 1966 to 1968. He wishes to remain anonymous in the publication of his personal story.
59. According to the American military reports, the U.S. armed forces lost 950 planes during the Rolling Thunder from March 2, 1965 to October 31, 1968. For more details, see Moss, *Vietnam*, 182, 187.
60. Major T, interviews by the author at Kyiv, Ukraine, in July 2005. See also Maj. T, "Russian Missile Officers in Vietnam," in *Voices of the Vietnam War: Stories of American, Asian and Russian Veterans*, Xiaobing Li (Lexington: University Press of Kentucky, 2010), 65-68.
61. Gaiduk, *The Soviet Union and the Vietnam War*, 61-62.
62. Mark Clodfelter, *The Limits of Air Power: The American Bombing of North Vietnam* (New York: Free Press, 1989), 141.
63. Ronald B. Frankum, Jr., *Like Rolling Thunder; the Air War in Vietnam, 1964-1975* (Lanham, MD: Rowman & Littlefield, 2005), 64.
64. The U.S. Air Force lost another F-111 on April 22, 1968. Col. Jerry Noel Hoblit (U.S. Air Force, ret.), interviews by the author at Lubbock, TX, in October 2006 and again at Edmond, OK, in April 2009.
65. Frankum, Jr., *Like Rolling Thunder*, 30-32; Zi, *Li Qiang zhuan* [Biography of Li Qiang], 267.
66. Maj. T, "Russian Missile Officers in Vietnam," 71.
67. Lieutenant Wang Xiangcai, interviews by the author in Harbin, Heilongjiang, on August 20-21, 2003. Wang served in the First Battalion, Third Regiment, Sixty-first AAA Division. Also see Marshal Xu Xiangqian, "The Purchase of Arms from Moscow," in *Mao's Generals Remember Korea,* trans. and eds. Xiaobing Li, Allan R. Millett, and Bin Yu (Lawrence: University Press of Kansas, 2001), 143-46.
68. Director of Central Intelligence Agency (CIA), "Special National Intelligence Estimate: Current Chinese Communist Intentions in the Vietnam Situation, August 4, 1966," in *Estimative Products on Vietnam*, 344-45.
69. Chen Pai, *Yuezhan qinliji* [My Personal Experience in the Vietnam War] (Zhengzhou: Henan renmin chubanshe [Henan People's Press], 1997), 22.
70. Gaiduk, *The Soviet Union and the Vietnam War*, 16-18, 34-37.

71. Li, "The Sino-Soviet Dispute over Assistance for Vietnam's Anti-American War, 1965-1972," 1. Accessed on August 18, 2017 at http://www.shenzhihua.net/ynzz/000123.htm
72. Mao, "Faith in Victory Is Derived from Struggle," conversations with a party and government delegation from the DRV on October 20, 1965, in Ministry of Foreign Affairs and Party Archives and Manuscript Research Center of the CCP Central Committee comps., *Mao Zedong on Diplomacy* (Beijing: Foreign Languages Press, 1998), 435.
73. Zhai states, "After the opening of the Paris peace talks and the Johnson administration's suspension of the American bombing of the DRV in November 1968, China began to pull back its support troops from the DRV." Zhai, *China and the Vietnam War*, 179. Also see Christian G. Appy, *Patriots: The Vietnam War Remembered from All Sides* (New York: Viking, 2003), 461-69; George C. Herring, *America's Longest War: The United States and Vietnam, 1950-1975*, 3rd ed. (New York: McGraw Hill, 1996), 276-78.
74. Xinhua News Agency, *China's Foreign Relations: A Chronology of Events, 1949-1988* (Beijing: Foreign Languages Press, 1989), 461-67.
75. After the Soviet invasion of Czechoslovakia in 1968, Moscow reinforced its border forces from seventeen divisions to twenty-seven divisions in 1969 along the Russo-Chinese borders. See Xiaobing Li, "Sino-Soviet Border Disputes," in *MaGill's Guide to Military History*, ed. John Powell, 4: 1423.
76. Zhou quoted in Westad, Chen, Tonnesson, Nguyen, and Hershberg, eds., "77 Conversations between Chinese and Foreign Leaders on the War in Indochina, 1964-1977," 130.
77. Among the recent publications on the rise and demise of the Sino-Soviet alliance in English are Zhihua Shen and Yafeng Xia, *Mao and the Sino-Soviet Partnership, 1945-1959* (Lanham, MD: Lexington Books, 2015); Odd Arne Westad, ed. *Brothers in Arms: The Rise and Fall of the Sino-Soviet Alliance, 1945-1963* (Washington, DC and Stanford, CA: Woodrow Wilson Center Press and Stanford University Press, 1998); Gordon H. Chang, *Friends and Enemies: The United States, China, and the Soviet Union* (Stanford, CA: Stanford University Press, 1990).
78. Li, "Sino-Soviet Border Disputes," 4: 1424.
79. Nicholas Khoo, *Collateral Damage: Sino-Soviet Rivalry and the Termination of the Sino-Vietnamese Alliance* (New York: Columbia University Press, 2011), 23.
80. *Ibid.*, 39.

81. Niu Jun, "Historical Change in China's Policy toward the United States in the late 1960s," in Li, *Zhongguo yu yindu zhina zhanzheng* [China and the Indochina Wars], 103.
82. Khoo, *Collateral Damage,* 3.
83. Xiaobing Li, "Sino-Soviet Border Disputes," in Powell, *MaGill's Guide to Military History,* 4: 1424.
84. Han, *Dangdai Zhongguo jundui de junshi gongzuo* [Military Affairs of Contemporary China's Armed Forces], 1: 639-42; Military History Research Division, CAMS, *Zhongguo renmin jiefangjun de 70 nian* [Seventy Years of the PLA], 580-81.
85. Han, *ibid.*, 1: 643-44; Military History Research Division, CAMS, *ibid.,* 582.
86. *Ibid.*
87. Yang Kuisong, "From the Zhenbao Island Incident to Sino-American Rapprochement," *Dangshi yanjiu ziliao* [Party History Research Materials], no. 12 (1997), 7-8; Thomas Robinson, "The Sino-Soviet Border Conflicts of 1969; New Evidence Three Decades Later," in *Chinese Warfighting: The PLA experience since 1949,* eds. Mark A. Ryan, David M. Finkelstein, and Michael A. McDevitt (Armonk, NY: M. E. Sharpe, 2003), 198-216.
88. CIA, "National Intelligence Estimate 11/13-69, the USSR and China, August 12, 1969," in *Tracking the Dragon:,* 549.
89. Khoo, *Collateral Damage,* 23.
90. John L. Gaddis, Forward in *China and the Vietnam Wars,* by Qiang Zhai, x.
91. Lorenz Luthi, "Chinese Foreign Policy, 1960-1979," in *The Cold War in East Asia, 1945-1991,* ed. Tsuyoshi Hasegawa (Stanford, CA: Stanford University Press, 2011), 162-63.
92. Mao, "We Agree with Vietnam's Policy to both Fight and Negotiate," in Ministry of Foreign Affairs and Party Archives and Manuscript Research Center of the CCP Central Committee comps., *Mao Zedong on Diplomacy,* 442-43.
93. Mao quoted in "Mao's Conversation with Pham Van Dong, November 17, 1968," in "77 Conversations between Chinese and Foreign Leaders on the Wars in Indochina, 1964-1977," trans. and eds. Odd Arne Westad, Chen Jian, Stein Tonnesson, Nguyen Vu Tungand, and James G. Hershberg, *Cold War International History Project, Working Paper No. 22* (Washington, DC: Woodrow Wilson International Center for Scholars, 1998), 138-46.

94. Xiaobing Li, *The Cold War in East Asia* (London: Routledge, 2018), 150, 152.
95. Han, *Dangdai Zhongguo jundui de junshi gongzuo* [Military Affairs of Contemporary China's Armed Forces], 1: 550.
96. Khoo, *Collateral Damage*, 76.
97. Gaiduk, *The Soviet Union and the Vietnam War*, 215, 231.
98. Chen Jian and Xiaobing Li, "China and the End of the Cold War," in *From Détente to the Soviet Collapse; The Cold War from 1975 to 1991*, ed. Malcolm Muir, Jr. (Lexington: Virginia Military Institute, 2006), 122-24.
99. Chen and Li, "China and the End of the Cold War," 124.
100. Khoo, *Collateral Damage*, 4.
101. Han, *Dangdai Zhongguo jundui de junshi gongzuo* [Military Affairs of Contemporary China's Armed Forces], 1: 659-60.
102. Xie Guojun, "Maintain the Peace and Safety along the Sino-Vietnamese Border," in Military History Research Division, CAMS, *Junqi piaopiao* [PLA Flag Fluttering], 2: 624-25; see also Xiaobing Li, *The Cold War in East Asia* (New York: Routledge, 2017), 179.
103. Deng's conversations are quoted from Tian Fuzi, *Zhongyeu zhanzheng jishilu* [Factual Records of the Sino-Vietnam War] (Beijing: Jiefangjun wenyi chubanshe [PLA Literature Press], 2004), 16-18.
104. Tian, *ibid.*, 18.
105. Zhang, *Deng Xiaoping's Long War*, 118-19.
106. Chen and Li, "China and the End of the Cold War,", 124.

The Role of a Military Advisor in Vietnam

Ron Milam

> Well, let's be honest about what a captain with less than six months in grade or about six months in grade, what kind of advice I've got to offer some regimental commander like Colonel Tieb of the 52nd Regiment who had been fighting for 25 years. Let's be honest, what I had was a U.S. Army nametag that made me the embodiment of the U.S. commitment to support the South Vietnamese and I had a radio that allowed me to talk to artillery, TAC air and attack helicopters. And that's primarily what my function was.[1]

So expressed Jim Willbanks when reflecting on his role as a U.S. Army advisor in Vietnam in 1971. His candor is indicative of how American soldiers sometimes had to deal with the myriad of roles that advisors had to play in a war that involved many various jobs and experiences, depending on when and where one served. Willbanks went on to be heavily involved in one of the great battles of the war at An Loc in the spring of 1972. For his service, he was awarded the Silver Star; thus, recognizing that he was more than just a guy with a "U.S. Army nametag."[2]

For the purpose of full disclosure, the author of this chapter served as a Mobile Advisory Team Leader (MAT), and Assistant Team Leader of MAT Team 38, District Team 36 in Phu Nhon District, Pleiku Province, Republic of Vietnam in 1970-1971. Like Jim Willbanks, I was a young lieutenant and would experience combat for the first time in my role as an advisor. And while we were trained well, as will be discussed in this chapter, we could not possibly have accumulated the experience in our short lives that so many of our allies had earned through years of combat either with or against the Viet Minh, the Viet Cong, and the soldiers from the north. But there we were as advisors, representing the United States of America.

And Americans as advisors are perceived differently than those from other countries. We are the ones who bring technology, who bring attitudes of American exceptionalism, and who sometimes believe that we have answers to every problem. We must constantly remind ourselves that it is *their* war, and that we are *their* allies— not the other way around. In training, we were taught that we must never lead in an operation, that we must offer suggestions, opinions, and options, but that we must never make a decision, or override a decision made by our counterpart. This is very difficult for those who were commissioned through the Reserve Officer Training Corps (ROTC), Officer Candidate School (OCS), or the United States Military Academy (USMA or West Point). We were taught to be decision makers, not followers, and it was particularly difficult for those who had prior service in Vietnam, in American units. And for career non-commissioned officers, they had, in many cases, "seen it all." For all of these reasons, being an advisor in Vietnam was not an easy assignment, notwithstanding the difficulty of being in combat in a controversial war.

To understand how Americans performed the various functions of advisors, one must first recognize that the advisory role changed from 1954 to 1973 as the war itself changed. The very first advisors actually were sent to Vietnam in 1951 to train and support Vietnamese soldiers aiding the French military. Organized as the Military Assistance Advisory Group (MAAG), these soldiers trained Vietnamese in counterinsurgency techniques, but were there mostly to provide logistical and financial assistance.[3] Advisors were usually field-grade officers or senior non-commissioned officers who had not been specifically trained for the tasks to which they had been assigned. There was no defined mission for the United States in the French Indochina War as America was supporting an ally while also protecting our monetary investment.

As America replaced the French in 1954 and Vietnam was divided into the State of Vietnam, (later the Republic of Vietnam – RVN) and the Democratic Republic of Vietnam (DRV) by agreement at the Geneva Convention, America occupied the country south of the 17th parallel.[4] Militarily, the Dwight D. Eisenhower administration and later the John F. Kennedy administration began an "advisory build-up." Both presidents believed financial aid was not enough to discourage communist attacks on the Ngo Dinh Diem government and the rise in insurgent attacks by the newly organized National Liberation Front (Viet Cong or "VC"). It would be the need for an effective counter-insurgency program that would cause President Kennedy to deploy over 16,000 advisors to Vietnam by the time of his assassination in November 1963. This would also be the beginning of re-organization for what would become the main operational unit during the war: Military Assistance Command, Vietnam (MACV).[5]

Because of the nature of counter insurgency operations, both Presidents Eisenhower and Kennedy believed a special kind of soldier must be selected, trained, and deployed to Vietnam. This soldier must possess language skills, be more "culturally sensitive," and possess skills that supersede those of regular combat soldiers. President Kennedy would designate the Special Forces soldiers as "Green Berets" and authorize them to wear that special headgear and to "wear the beret proudly, it will be a mark of distinction and a badge of courage in the difficult days ahead."[6] Organized into twelve-man teams consisting of specialists in operations, intelligence, communications, demolitions, weapons, and medicine, each team was led by a commander, usually a captain, and an executive officer, usually a 1st lieutenant. The detachments known as "A-Teams" would be among the first advisory units sent to Vietnam.[7] As the first Medal of Honor recipient in the Vietnam War, Roger Donlon stated, "As the senior advisor in the district, everything was my concern, whether it was military, economic, political, agricultural or even social."[8]

In Donlon's Special Forces camp on the Laotian border, his Detachment A-726 was overrun by a Viet Cong reinforced battalion consisting of sappers, mortar men, and heavy weapons insurgents who had effectively re-conned the target and successfully entered the compound. Three of these Green Beret advisors were killed, all others wounded. Fifty-five "friendlies" of the Mung indigenous peoples were killed and seventy-five wounded. In Captain Donlon's memoir of the battle, he writes about the cultural challenges when one of the Vietnamese nurses was wounded with shrapnel in her butt. Not willing to let an American man work on her wound, the medic said, "Now wait a minute, girl... You come over here. Captain Donlon's my boss and he can tell me to go away and I'll go. But I'm your boss, and I'm telling you I'm going to fix up that wound. And if I say you can go back to work you'll go. And if I say you can't, you'll be flat on your back with the rest of the wounded. And that's all there is to it."[9] Advisors had to be aware of the cultural differences, even while a firefight was happening.

These early advisors did their job as they were trained. These A-Teams would be assigned to strategic locations all over Vietnam, particularly at border points, river crossings, and mountainous areas to work with local village leaders to organize militias to combat the rising Viet Cong units. After President Kennedy's death, they would be trained at the U.S. Army John F. Kennedy Special Warfare Center at Fort Bragg, North Carolina.[10]

But it was not only Green Berets who were trained at the John F. Kennedy Special Warfare Center and School. In this "first advisory period," the Kennedy and Johnson administration believed the Army of the Republic of Vietnam (ARVN) needed the support and advice of American soldiers who would be trained to understand both Vietnamese history, culture, and language. Unlike the Green Berets who were assigned both security and training responsibilities, MACV advisors were assigned to ARVN units to advise and support military operations. The presidents told Congress and the American people that these advisors were not to participate in combat operations, or at least that they were not to use their weapons unless fired upon, but that was a difficult directive for these field-grade and senior non-commissioned officers. One of the first advisors in this early advisory period was Captain Colin Powell who writes in his memoir of the frustration of teaching even non-combat procedures:

> The ARVN soldiers were courageous and willing but not always easy to train. I instructed. They smiled, nodded, and often ignored what I said. I drilled them for hours on how to unload a helicopter. The key was speed. The helicopter was vulnerable. It drew fire. We needed to unload it as fast as possible. The quickest way was for two men to jump inside the aircraft as soon as it landed and start throwing out the cargo. The rest of the squad should form a line from the helo into the jungle, passing the supplies from man to man, bucket-brigade style, and stockpiling them under cover of the trees. I scratched an outline of a helicopter into the dirt, and we drilled again and again. Aircraft lands. Two men inside. Others form line. Pass supplies. Over and over.
>
> The next day, a resupply helicopter put down inside our perimeter. I gave the unloading crew the signal, and the whole squad raced for the doorway, all trying to climb inside the aircraft at once. They were uncomplaining as I began drilling them all over again, and finally, they got it.[11]

One of the first major encounters for these advisors was in January 1963 in the rice paddies 60 km south of Saigon at Ap Bac, a tiny hamlet. There, three American advisors and air crew were killed, and eight more were seriously wounded doing what they had trained to do— offer advice and support to the ARVN units.[12]

Being assigned as an advisor to an ARVN unit in these early days of the war was an adventure in that there were not any real training programs that had been designed from any battlefield experience. Lt. Col. John Paul Vann had been assigned as senior advisor to the ARVN 7th Infantry

Division. He had spent a lot of time in the field working with ARVN leaders and generally had respect for their command over their troops. He was concerned, however, that MACV leadership in Saigon was not pressing ARVN leadership as hard as they should, and he was particularly bothered by what he perceived as a lack of respect for the Viet Cong. As writer and war correspondent Neil Sheehan writes in *A Bright Shining Lie*, "General Harkins and his Saigon staff regarded the Viet Cong with the contempt conventional soldiers from great powers usually display toward the guerrillas of small nations."[13] Thus, Vann was one of the few advisors who recognized the skill and power of the enemy, and the need for better leadership of the ARVN. The mission of Vann's 7th Infantry Division was to take on the 261st Main Force National Liberation Front battalion who had taken over the local radio transmitter. Vann liked the mission because it was an operation that intelligence indicated would require his ARVN troops to attack a set location with overwhelming force and technology and with superior numbers. And since the Viet Cong had a reputation for never standing and fighting, Vann assumed this would be the morale booster needed to encourage both enlistment and retention. Observing from the back seat of an L-19 aircraft, Vann was shocked to see that the ARVN did not use their helicopters, artillery, or M-113 armored personnel carriers (APC) effectively, nor did the Viet Cong retreat as in previous battles. Instead, they effectively neutralized the APCs, and shot down five helicopters. Even a late parachute assault failed to dislodge the Viet Cong entrenched unit when the paratroopers landed directly in front of the VC force, either by mistake or by deliberate action by a Communist sympathizing pilot.[14]

While John Paul Vann was critical of the ARVN leadership in this battle, ARVN soldiers had great respect for Vann. While the U.S. Army concentrated on the use of technology and firepower, even in these early days of the war, Vann believed the secret to success in the war was in the training and motivation of the common soldiers who were "peasants like their guerrilla opponents, and who were potentially good soldiers who deserved to win their war and not have their lives wasted."[15] For advisors, how your ally responds to your support or direction is critical to your success.

The aftermath of Ap Bac is generally considered by Vietnam War scholars to be the beginning of the "credibility gap," caused by General Harkins' positive assessment of the results and LTC Vann's negative report. Thus, this senior advisor to the 7th Infantry Division reported what he saw, experienced and measured, and other reporters accepted the advisor's conclusion. From this day forward, reporters made every effort to see for themselves what happened in the field and learned to not rely on the general's briefings. With advisors being assigned to most of the ARVN units, they became the voice of progress or lack thereof in Vietnam. Ap Bac also aided the NLF and even the PAVN who were not even there. Neil Sheehan writes:

> Ap Bac came at the most propitious moment and was a drama ready-made for the purposes of Ho Chi Minh and his disciples. It was exactly the sort of event they needed to infuse the building of a Viet Cong army with the patriotic emotion they had aroused and poured into the creation of the original Viet Minh. In March, with their assessment completed and their preparations made, they seized on the battle and turned Ap Bac into the rallying cry of the revolution in the South. Posters, professionally printed in color, began to appear in the Delta extolling the victory and the fighters who had attained it. The Hanoi Politburo had the Central Committee of the National Liberation Front announce the first three-month round of 'the Ap Bac Emulation Drive' that was to continue for the next two years. Everything started to move ahead full speed. Harkin's intelligence section thought that infiltration from the North during the 1962-63 southwest monsoon dry season was running at approximately the same level as the 1961-62 season, about 6,000 infiltrators on an annual basis... Subsequent evidence showed that in an act of faith rewarded by Ap Bac, Hanoi had doubled the flow from an average of 850 men coming down the trails each month during the 1961-62 season to about 1,700 a month during the current season. The infiltrators were former southern Viet Minh who had gone to the North in 1954, 'autumn cadres'

> to join the 'winter cadres' who had survived Diem's terror and launched the rebellion in 1957.[16]

On March 8, 1965, 3,500 Marines "stormed" the beaches at Da Nang, but instead of being met by enemy soldiers entrenched in fortified bunkers, they were met by beautiful Vietnamese women in traditional "ao dais."[17] America's role in Vietnam changed drastically in that "Americanization" of the war had happened. Thus, the advisor's role would also change.

The influx of American troops signaled to the South Vietnamese government and to the ARVN that the Johnson administration had lost confidence in their ability to effectively wage war against the Viet Cong. Furthermore, the DRV was beginning to move People's Army of Vietnam (PAVN) troops into South Vietnam, along with supplies and heavier armaments, anticipating that it would take large elements of conventional troops to hold back America's support for the ARVN. General William Westmoreland who had replaced General Harkins as Commander U.S. Military Assistance Command Vietnam (COMUSMACV) believed certain ARVN units were capable of effective combat missions, but others were not. Thus, Rangers, Marines, and some other units were given the responsibility of conducting combat operations, often alongside American units. Other units were given the responsibility of "pacification." While a definition of this term is difficult, and many leaders would define it differently, generally the term means "winning the hearts and minds of the people."[18] It was this "soft power" responsibility that was given to the ARVN. Theoretically, this makes sense, because their soldiers had language skills, were sensitive to cultural issues, knew the territory, and generally could navigate their way through the bureaucracy of the South Vietnamese government. But some ARVN officers took offense to the "Americanization" of the war; specifically, the attitude American leaders had toward the ARVN's military capabilities and ability to get the job done.

For the period that Vietnam War scholars have named "the era of big battles," advisors were sent mostly to elite ARVN units.[19] It was also during this period that President Johnson decided to focus more attention on the pacification effort by creating an organization with the formidable title of Civil Operations and Revolutionary Development Support (CORDS). The "Revolutionary" term was later changed to "Rural" to account for Vietnamese sensibilities, but the responsibilities were the same— manage pacification or as President Johnson proclaimed it, "the other war."[20]

This new CORDS organization would cause significant change in the role of the advisor and also increase the number of them sent to Vietnam. While CORDS included many functions such as the Phoenix program which was designed to identify, capture, imprison, or execute members of the Viet Cong infrastructure, its program for security and operations against the Viet Cong had the greatest impact on the advisory effort.[21] Led by Robert Komer, each of the forty-two provinces in South Vietnam was organized under a South Vietnamese province chief who would have an American Provincial advisor assigned to him, usually a colonel. This advisor would usually be a military man, but he might be a civilian who had risen through the ranks of the Department of State. If the Provincial advisor was a civilian, his deputy would be a military man and vice versa.

Below the province level was the district, with a South Vietnamese district chief and a district senior advisor, usually a major in rank. The district advisory team consisted of an intelligence officer, a medic, and a communications non-commissioned officer. Each district team also consisted of at least one Mobile Advisory Team (MAT) whose members included a team leader, usually a captain, an assistant team leader, usually a 1st lieutenant, a light weapons non-commissioned officer, a heavy weapon non-commissioned officer, and a medic.[22] These five-man teams were "mobile" in that while they were usually headquartered at a district compound, they traveled throughout the hamlets and villages of the district. It was on these MATs that most American advisors served during the "era of big battles," and beyond as men assigned to American units were deployed back to the states.

The selection and training of the MAT members began at least six months prior to deployment to Vietnam. Once selected, the soldier was sent to the John F. Kennedy Special Warfare Center and School where he was enrolled in the Military Advisory Training (MATA) program which consisted of twelve weeks of training designed specifically for advisors. Topics in this intense course were: weapons, air operations, communications, tactics, evasion and survival, sanitation, first aid, and demolition.[23] The course handbook was actually published prior to the development of CORDS, thus there is no reference to the culture and language training that would eventually become important. However, instructors were flexible and sometimes changed instruction to meet current needs. Philip Brady, a Marine advisor stated:

> Well, the MATA course was the only training I had prior to that outside, of course, the basic school. My on-the-job-training and the division which I served in prior the assignment. The specific preparation in the MATA course had some facets of which were good and other facets were not. The language was good. That has been expanded. That is valuable. Secondly, the background on the individual personality. The Vietnamese personality, their customs, traditions, is valuable. That was included. Outside of that, there is nothing else of value for a battalion advisor. It would be assumed that one being assigned there was a working practical knowledge of small-unit tactics, which is what he needs to know. The rest of it was an orientation for the role of USOM, the role of many facets, the big picture in other words. It did not concern you as the battalion advisor. I found it, for the most part, useless.[24]

For MAT team personnel, these first months of training would be followed by three months of language training at a Defense Language Institute (DLI) program at either the Presidio in Monterey, California, or at Fort Bliss, Texas. Vietnamese women taught these language courses and they were extremely intense, with eight hours of instruction, six days per week.

After six months of training, advisors were sent to Vietnam where they would be assigned temporarily to a "repo-depot" at Cam Ranh Bay,

Da Nang, or Tan Son Nhut where they would be assigned to a district.[25] The advisor would then be assigned to a base camp at Di An where he would spend two weeks in intense weapons, tactics, and culture training before he left for his assigned district.

MAT teams performed many tasks in Vietnam, but they were particularly involved with advising local Popular Forces (PF) which were organized into squad and platoon-sized units at the district level and to Regional Forces (RF) which were organized into company-sized units at the province level. They were collectively referred to as "Ruff-Puffs" and were responsible for the security of hamlets, villages, and district and province headquarters. There were also, in some districts, Peoples Self-Defense Forces (PSDF) which often consisted of men younger than eighteen and over forty-five who participated in local security, essentially a village militia.[26]

These "local militias" were trained by MAT teams, which included instruction on how to effectively fire and clean the M-16 rifle, the M-60 machine gun, the M-79 Grenade Launcher, and the M-72 Light Anti-Tank Weapon (LAW). The PSDF were trained to use World War II vintage weapons such as the M-1 Garand, the M-2 Carbine, the Thompson .45 Caliber Sub Machine Gun, the Browning Automatic Rifle (BAR), and the Stevens 12 Gauge single-shot shotgun. They were also trained to set up ambushes around their hamlets and villages, to effectively avoid ambushes, and to understand the advantages of supporting the South Vietnamese government, which was a challenge. These propaganda sessions usually took place in the afternoon and were usually monitored by local Viet Cong cadre. Attendance was often poor, particularly among the PSDF. MAT Teams also had to perform administrative duties as if they were clerks.[27] David Donovan writes:

> Some of the attempts to apply American technology to Vietnamese problems would be funny if they had not been so damned frustrating to deal with. The Hamlet Evaluation System and the territorial Forces Evaluation system, referred to as HES and TFES, were

> two examples of such ill-advised Americanisms. The HES and TFES were computer printout lists of standardized questions sent monthly to every district senior advisor in the country. Among other things, the HES report had us determine how many televisions were in each village and hamlet (none— hell, we didn't even have electricity!), how many were in business, how many houses had tin roofs, etc., etc.... TFES wanted to know about the troop strength, morale, weapons, and equipment of the local district and village militia organizations. The intent of these reports was good, but like so many good bureaucratic intentions, the idea was weakest at the point of practical application... The Vietnamese authorities wanted all TFES HES reports to be glowing and upbeat. The HES reports, for instance, formed the basis for the countrywide system of classifying areas as 'pacified,' 'contested,' or 'Viet Cong controlled.'[28]

One of the persistent myths that exists about the role of advisors in Vietnam is that they were not involved in combat as much as soldiers assigned to American units. Because advisors were usually one of only two Americans on an operation, it was imperative that he be physically and mentally prepared to not only offer advice and support to his Vietnamese counterparts, but also that he be prepared to defend himself. And unlike officers assigned to American units, advisors served twelve months in combat rather than six. Also, the extent to which he is in charge, rather than just advising, was always important. David Donovan wrote of his experience on a night ambush:

> I was the last man on the right of our ambush position; the enemy were approaching from the left. That meant I could wait until the first man of the enemy column was in front of me before I triggered the ambush. When I opened fire, everyone would let loose at the two or three Viet Cong closest to him. With this group bunched up like they were, we should easily be able to get them all. It should all be over in less than a minute. Later, after successfully executing the ambush, Donovan writes: 'Shee-it *Trung Uy,* we really kicked their ass, didn't we?' 'You're goddam right we did!' I replied, the excitement of triumph rising in my own voice. 'This'll be worth

> a beer and a night's sleep when we get back to the compound.' 'Dammed right', he chuckled. 'The others are going to shit when they see all this stuff! The other three Americans on our team were going to be green with envy.'[29]

When operating with only a five-man team, each American was critical to the operation. Yet those they advised had to carry the burden of the fight. And, as if combat was not enough to keep MAT leaders busy, they had to deal with basic needs. Donovan observed:

> One of my major headaches now was trying to find supplies, not only military and civilian supplies for the Vietnamese villagers, but even subsistence supplies for my own team of Americans. MACV had made the decision that since MAT teams were to teach the local village and hamlet defense forces how to make the Vietnamese government and military system work, then the MAT teams should be provided for primarily by that same Vietnamese system. That would supposedly heighten our desire to make the system proficient. When we came in-country the army issued us our initial TA-50 equipment, an M-16 rifle, and a basic load of ammunition. After that we were supposedly on our own to survive with the Vietnamese. That made life in general, and combat in particular, a very different thing than what we'd been taught at the Infantry Officer Basic Course.[30]

The CORDS organization was very important to assisting the U.S. military effort during the "era of big battles" by improving the living conditions in the villages and rural areas of South Vietnam. However, after January 30, 1968, when almost all of South Vietnam came under attack, including the American embassy in Saigon, the pacification of the rural areas became less important to President Johnson than just regaining control of the cities. Virtually all of them were attacked by PAVN and Viet Cong units, and Hue was under siege for three weeks.[31] This came as a shock to Americans. General Westmoreland and others had led them to believe that the war was at least winding down in the cities even if the rural areas were not yet pacified to the degree that

CORDS Director Robert Komer had expected. Furthermore, with Johnson deciding not to run for re-election, political turmoil was expected in Washington. Thus, 1968 was a period when the "era of big battles" ceased and stalemate began to frustrate the military. The PAVN and organized NLF units refused to be enticed into large battles and both the South Vietnamese government and the leaders in Hanoi watched Washington, to try to determine whether America would change its Vietnam policy as a result of the election of Richard Nixon.[32]

"Vietnamization" became known not only to Americans, but to both ARVN and PAVN troops. American soldiers would benefit by having their year-long tours of duty reduced by a few days in 1969-1970, then weeks and months after that. This would obviously change the dynamics on the battlefield as the ARVN would have to assume the burden previously borne by American units. So began the "second advisory period" as Americans began to assign more specific projects not only to elite ARVN units, but even to those which had previously been ignored because they were not considered to be militarily ready for extensive combat. And the "Ruff-Puffs" would have to assume more responsibilities at the province and district levels, which would require more MAT teams with competent American leadership and district teams that could build-up the South Vietnamese Regional and Popular Forces. With many of those units still using World War II era weaponry, an urgent plea went out for M-16s, heavy weapons such as 60MM and 81MM mortars, and .50 caliber and M-60 machine guns. Thus, at the district levels, American military planners believed the focus of the PAVN would be to take over local headquarters in their efforts to eventually reach Saigon. With President Nixon's new administration seeming to focus on bombing North Vietnam into submission, or at least enticing them to become more serious at the negotiation table in Paris, the ground war seemed to become less important. This was frustrating for the South Vietnamese government as it required them to "beef up" their recruitment of ARVN soldiers at a time when success on the battlefield was not apparent, which undoubtedly hurt their efforts to acquire new blood for the fight.[33]

In 1970 and 1971, American units began to re-deploy. Many soldiers who still had time on their tours were re-assigned to MACV district headquarters and some to MAT teams. Intelligence reports were providing evidence that the PAVN were going to launch more offensive operations and America's response was to provide logistical and air support wherever possible, but not to commit large numbers of soldiers to the fight. One of the first big tests of "Vietnamization" would be in neighboring Laos.[34]

President Nixon had wanted to prove to the American people that the ARVN could bear the combat role in Vietnam, the one previously shouldered by Americans and an operation called Lam Son 719 would provide such evidence, if successful. U.S. troops provided artillery support from 175MM guns firing from great distances in Vietnam, U.S. helicopters carried ARVN troops into Laos, and logistical support was provided along Route 9. Because of the passage of the Cooper-Church amendment as a response to America's invasion of Cambodia in May, 1970, American ground troops and even advisors were precluded, however, from entering the sovereign nations of Cambodia and Laos.[35] This congressional action was among the first indications that American involvement in Vietnam was beginning to unfold and banning advisors from participating with their ARVN units affected their performance, or at least, hampered some logistical support that could have occurred.[36] The operation was not successful, many Americans were killed supporting the operation on the South Vietnamese side of the border, and 102 helicopters were destroyed and 601 damaged.[37] Lam Son 719 proved that American advisors were critical for success in large scale operations, particularly when PAVN troops were at full-strength and had supply chains readily available, as was the case with the adjacent Ho Chi Minh Trail.

ARVN and South Vietnamese people's reaction to Lam Son 719 was that America had decided to let the Vietnamese "go it alone" by not allowing advisors to accompany their troops into battle. Anti-America demonstrations were held in Saigon, and a poster emerged depicting Nixon standing over a pile of dead South Vietnamese soldiers, with a message that Vietnamization meant that the United States would fight to the last South Vietnamese.[38]

Major General Nguyen Duy Hinh, an ARVN infantry division commander who was tasked with analyzing ARVN performance as "Vietnamization" was taking place wrote:

> Lam Son 719 was a combined RVNAF-US operation conducted under several constraints. No U.S. ground combat troops were allowed to cross the border into Laos. There was no joint command for the control of operations. Both the ARVN I Corps commander, who directed the operational effort in Laos, and the Commanding General, U.S. XXIV Corps, his senior adviser, worked together on an equal footing in keeping with the principle of cooperation and coordination. In contrast to the usual practice, ARVN forces went into combat without their advisers; neither could they expect a helping hand from U.S. or other Allied infantry troops while on Laotian soil. On the other hand, U.S. combat support for the offensive effort was greatly increased in terms of firepower and helilift.[39]

President Nixon came into office with plans for rapid troop withdrawals, and he (as well as the president's COMUSMACV, General Creighton Abrams) was consequently faced with the huge questions regarding how to best use ARVN troops, and whether they could take on additional combat responsibilities. Large American bases such as Camp Holloway, which housed the 4th Infantry Division in Pleiku, and the 25th Infantry Division's home at Cu Chi, were turned over to ARVN units. By 1972, most American combat units had returned to the United States. CORDS was beginning to wind down and Mobile Advisory Teams were beginning to change their missions to logistic support rather than the advisement of "Ruff-Puff" units. Meanwhile, the DRV and its PAVN military units had not yet achieved their goals of reunification of the country; as such, while the American presence slowly dissipated, they fixed their sights on Saigon.[40]

General Vo Nguyen Giap said, "he who controls the Central Highlands controls Vietnam." On March 15, 1971, he sent elements of the PAVN HQ 95B Regiment to attack the Phu Nhon District Headquarters in Pleiku Province which was also the location of the MACV district team and two MAT teams. Sappers broke through the wire of the compound, destroying the ammo bunker, the fuel bunker, the non-commissioned officer barracks, and temporarily overran the compound. For four hours, sappers detonated satchel charges at will, destroying a considerable amount of infrastructure and killing one American and seventy ARVN and RF/PF soldiers.[41] Over the ensuing five days, nearly 400 enemy soldiers were killed by air and artillery strikes. This battle was fought by American personnel on two MAT teams and one district team, thus requiring skills that have nothing to do with pacification, "winning hearts and minds," or filling out Hamlet Evaluation Forms (HES). Instead, these two MAT teams did what soldiers had been doing for six years in Vietnam: they used the military skills they had been taught in Basic Combat Training (BCT), Advanced Individual Training (AIT), Airborne, Officer Candidate School, Non-Commissioned Officer Academy, Ranger School, or any other training they may have received to destroy the communist enemy. This author was at that battle, survived, and lived to fight another day.

By spring of 1972, Vietnamization had taken hold throughout Vietnam with only advisors working in South Vietnam as combat troops. Only 5,416 advisors were in-country and most of them were on division staffs.[42] Some air assets were available to these advisors, and Operations Linebacker and Linebacker II kept pressure on the DRV to negotiate earnestly in Paris.[43] But ARVN troops and "Ruff-Puffs" continued to make contact with Communist troops throughout South Vietnam. PAVN leaders believed they had made substantial gains during the "Easter Offensive," and set their sights on Saigon. If they could effectively get close to South Vietnam's capital, they could at least threaten to launch raids into South Vietnam's largest city, and maybe gain some bargaining strength in Paris. The stage was set for a large battle at a village called An Loc.

Located ninety miles west of South Vietnam's capital, An Loc was targeted by the DRV as the place from which the PAVN could launch attacks on Saigon. As the capital of Binh Phuoc Province, it was targeted by the PAVN during the Easter Offensive not only because of its proximity to Saigon, but also because it was located near the Cambodia border, therefore American bombing raids had to be careful not to execute missions that would cross into the sovereign nation, which had become a critical issue in the rhetorical battlefield being waged in Congress over the prosecution of the war. It was a logical choice for the attackers, and the ARVN and their American advisors knew it.[44]

B-52s carrying 500-pound bombs would be used tactically on PAVN positions which helped neutralize the overwhelming force advantage held by the combined PAVN and VC forces. The ARVN were supplemented by RF/PF and even PSDF forces, but the difference in the battle would be the ability of American advisors to call in airstrikes, including the tactical use of B-52s, as opposed to their normal strategic use. PAVN units used frequent artillery barrages, and even Vietnamese T-54 tanks to try to overrun the village. They were not successful and for the sake of South Vietnam, this was important. Political Scientist and Viet Cong scholar Douglas Pike called An Loc "the single most important battle of the war."[45]

General Tran Van Nhut expressed the frustration of many ARVN officers that in these late stages of the war, there were not enough American advisors to take care of all the military needs:

> The situation persisted, day after day, month after month. The casualty count, dead and wounded, rose to almost fifty soldiers. In spite of this fact, morale remained high and never wavered. Many times during my radio conversations with the outpost, I almost broke down in tears because everything they needed was beyond my capabilities to provide. All I could do was call on U.S.

> air power through my American advisor because there was no advisor at Minh Thanh.[46]

Vietnamization was taking its toll even on the advisory effort, as there were fewer soldiers to perform these important functions. Both air and helicopter assets had been left in-country, but the ARVN allies relied on American advisors to "call it in." By 1972, frustration in the ability to use those assets began to sit in with ARVN officers.

Two battles separated by nine years and both involving ARVN and U.S. advisors— Ap Bac in 1963 and An Loc in 1972— were critically important: each transformed the war effort. Ap Bac was impacted by advisors who were critical of the ARVN effort; yet they worked hard to improve the quality of their allies' fighting abilities. At An Loc, nine years of fighting experience made the ARVN better fighting units, but it still required American advisors to bring in the appropriate air assets that allowed these troops to at least have a chance to be successful against overwhelming numerical superiority.

How do we assess the role of advisors in America's most controversial war? President Kennedy relied heavily on them believing that they could work effectively with the ARVN, and that it would not be necessary to send in ground troops if "advisors" did their job correctly. And that idea seems to be prevalent throughout American military history: that advisors can be effective by using American technology in combat situations. As Captain Willbanks remarked at the beginning of this chapter, with a radio and access to air power and artillery, an advisor can be an effective asset to an army.

Yet, advisors continued to be used even after ground troops had been deployed in March, 1965. Military planners believed the performance of ARVN troops was improved by the presence of American advisors, probably because communications with air assets was improved if it was an American on the other end of the phone line or radio.

Oral histories of advisors who have served with ARVN units have generally been more positive about their performance than Americans who served with American units. Several Texas Tech graduate students conducted research in this area and have written papers that are not yet published, but the general thesis seems to be that there was a direct correlation between how close one served to the ARVN and the degree of confidence in their performance. And as America continues to fight wars around the globe, the general consensus of military planners seems to be that advisory efforts are always the first stage of the conflict. Iraq, Afghanistan, Syria, and other countries have been the recipients of American advisory efforts, often accompanied by statements that "we must stay long enough to be certain our ally is trained sufficiently to take on the burden of battle."[47] In Vietnam, we used those words in the beginning and again toward the end. And after America pulled troops out in 1973, the Communist forces succeeded because they believed that ARVN troops without American advisors to handle the technology would fail— as they had in Lam Son 719.

But American advisors were critical to the military, diplomatic, political, and social aspects of the Vietnam War, both before, during, and after American ground troops were deployed. That they were usually among the most experienced and mature soldiers and Marines, and that they worked closely with all elements of the Vietnamese military and civilian personnel: ARVN, RF, PF, PSDF, district and provincial chiefs, and South Vietnam government officials would not ultimately make the difference. But their efforts should be recognized by anyone who seeks to understand what happened in Vietnam, both on and off the battlefield.

Notes

1. Interview with James H. Willbanks, 20 September 2000, Cold Storage, James Willbanks Collection, The Vietnam Center and Archive, Texas Tech University, Accessed August 14, 2017. https://vva.vietnam.ttu.edu/repositories/2/digital_objects/35743
2. Ibid.
3. George C. Herring, *America's Longest War: The United States and Vietnam, 1950-1975* (New York: McGraw Hill, 2002), 27-30.
4. Marilyn B. Young, *The Vietnam Wars, 1945-1990* (New York: Harper Perennial, 1991), 52-58.
5. Herring, 103-4.
6. Robin Moore, *The Green Berets* (New York: Avon Books, 1965), 16.
7. Roger H.C. Donlon, *Beyond Nam Dong* (Leavenworth, Kansas: R&N Publishers, 1998), 76-77.
8. Donlon, 115-16.
9. Donlon, 164.
10. Moore, 13.
11. Colin L. Powell, *My American Journey* (New York: Random House, 1995), 95.
12. Robert K. Brigham, *ARVN: Life and Death in the South Vietnamese Army* (Lawrence: University Press of Kansas, 2006), 78.
13. Neil Sheehan, *A Bright Shining Lie: John Paul Vann and America in Vietnam* (New York: Vintage Books, 1989),204.
14. Sheehan, 201-67.
15. Brigham, 84.
16. Sheehan, 311-12.
17. James S. Olson and Randy Roberts, *Where the Domino Fell: America and Vietnam, 1945-1995* (Malden Massachusetts: Blackwell Publishing, 2008), 122.
18. Gerald C. Hickey, *Window on a War: an Anthropologist in the Vietnam Conflict* (Lubbock, Texas: Texas Tech University Press, 2002), 12.
19. Ron Milam, "The Era of Big Battles in Vietnam," *New York Times,* January 10, 2017.
20. John Prados, *Vietnam: The History of an Unwinnable War, 1945-1975*(Lawrence, Kansas: University Press of Kansas, 2009), 321.

21. Dale Androde & James Willbanks, "CORDS/Phoenix: Counterinsurgency Lessons From Vietnam for the Future," *Military Review, (March/April, 2006),* 77-91.
22. David Donovan, *Once a Warrior King: Memories of an Officer in Vietnam* (New York: Ballantine Books, 1985), 37.
23. "MATA Handbook for Vietnam" U.S. Army Special Warfare School, Fort Bragg, North Carolina.
24. Interview with Philip Brady, No Date, U.S. Marine Corps History Division Oral History Collection, The Vietnam Center and Archive, Texas Tech University. Accessed August 18, 2017. https://www.vietnam.ttu.edu/virtualarchive/items.php?item=USMC0023 .
25. Ron Milam, *Not a Gentleman's War: An Inside View of Junior Officers in the Vietnam War* (Chapel Hill: University of North Carolina Press, 2009), 80-81.
26. Prados, 322.
27. Author's personal experience as a MAT team leader. Visual depictions of these soldiers and weaponry can be seen at https://vietnam.ttu.edu/repositories/2/digital_objects/246609 in the documentary *Going Back.*
28. Donovan, 157.
29. Donovan, 6.
30. Donovan, 102.
31. Herring, 225-27.
32. Young, 240-42.
33. Prados, 388-95.
34. James H. Willbanks, *A Raid Too Far: Operation Lam Son 719 and Vietnamization in Laos* (College Station, Texas: Texas A&M *University* Press, 2014), 4.
35. Herring, 295.
36. Prados, 410-20.
37. James Willbanks, 215.
38. George Donelson Moss, *Vietnam: an American Ordeal* (Saddle River, New Jersey: Prentice Hall, 2010), 305.
39. Nguyen Duy Hinh, "Lam Son 719" *Indochina Monographs* (Washington, D.C.: U.S. Army Center for Military History, 1979), 162.
40. James H. Willbanks, *The Battle of An Loc* (Bloomington: Indiana University Press, 2005), 14.
41. "After Action Report" Phu Nhon Relief Operation, 29 April 1971. Prepared by the 1/92nd Field Artillery Association – Vietnam.
42. Willbanks, 10.

43. Prados, 473.
44. Willbanks, 1-13.
45. Willbanks, xviii.
46. General Tran Van Nhut, *An Loc: The Unfinished War* (Lubbock: Texas Tech University Press, 2009), 148.
47. Author's general paraphrase of current military thinking.

The Natural Environment and the American Military Experience in Vietnam

Matthew M. Stith

> They carried diseases, among them malaria and dysentery. They carried lice and ringworm and leeches and paddy algae and various rots and molds. They carried the land itself— Vietnam, the place, the soil— a powdery orange-red dust that covered their boots and fatigues and faces. They carried the sky. The whole atmosphere, they carried it, the humidity, the monsoons, the stink of fungus and decay, all of it, they carried gravity.
>
> —Tim O'Brien[1]

Overlooked Ubiquity

In 1965, Marine Lt. Philip Caputo gazed at what hundreds of thousands of American combatants would soon see: a frustrating, miserable, deadly, and impenetrable wilderness loaded with mysterious animals and tangled plants that played havoc on American fears and served as a primary ally for the outnumbered and outgunned Viet Cong (VC) and North Vietnamese Army (NVA). Perhaps the best-known writer to convey the American military experience in Vietnam, Caputo later related with eloquent horror what he and his fellow Marines were up against. Standing before a stretch of wilderness into which he had been ordered to search for and destroy the enemy, Caputo looked in shock at what he had been warned was "that humid wilderness where the Bengal tiger stalked, and the cobra coiled beneath its rock and the Viet Cong lurked in ambush." Reflecting on just how ridiculous the situation seemed, he concluded: "I half expected those great mountains to shake with contemptuous laughter at our pretense."[2]

Caputo's fear and uncertainty regarding Vietnam's complex natural environment reflects anxieties shared by nearly every combat soldier who entered the country, and it exemplifies the primary struggle for the larger American war. Indeed, the natural environment impacted the course and consequences of America's war in Vietnam as much or more as in any other conflict in modern history. While military and environmental historians have certainly acknowledged nature in the context of the Vietnam War, the environment has yet to emerge as a *principal* character in the story of America's most enigmatic and troubling conflict. The natural environment— terrain, weather, flora, fauna— and American attempts to leverage it to their advantage, or make war against it, shaped the course and outcome of the war as much as any other factor, and it indelibly marked, and marred, the American experience in Indochina in both history and memory.[3]

That terrain, and the environment generally, dramatically and conclusively shape warfare is nothing new. In his classic *On War*, Carl von Clausewitz put it simply and conclusively when he argued that terrain in a time of war has a potential three-fold affect: "as an obstacle to the approach, as an impediment to visibility, and as cover from fire." All warfare, guerrilla, conventional, or both, is affected by at least one of these factors. In South Vietnam, they were *all* at play, almost all the time. The NVA and VC knew this well. They based their strategy and survival on using the terrain to hinder American movements, hide from American eyes, and avoid American firepower. Clausewitz's nineteenth century tactical and strategic wisdom did not end there. In what some might consider an ominous foreshadowing to the literal and figurative quagmire

American forces found in Vietnam, Clausewitz argued that in heavily forested or swampy ground, the attacker "will hardly be in a position to impress the omnipresent enemy with the superior weight of his numbers. This is without doubt one of the worst situations in which an attacker can find himself."[4] American forces found themselves in a terrain far more difficult than even Clausewitz had envisioned. Instead of European forests and lowlands, which informed the military strategist's mindset, American soldiers slogged through some of the most ecologically and geographically diverse and difficult landscapes on Earth.

South Vietnam's natural beauty and rugged immensity struck most Americans when they arrived in-country. Indeed, nature consumed the American experience, often before they exited the airplane. For Mary Emeny, a humanitarian aid worker who arrived in 1967, the view though the airplane window was striking. "We could detect the thick, thick jungle," she wrote, "occasional potholes left over from someone's work, and then as we approached we began to see Saigon, with the huge Mekong river bending around it."[5] Airforce mechanic Larry Wasserman was also moved by Vietnam's natural beauty, and his job was to keep the airplanes in the air so the pilots taking part in Operation Ranch Hand could destroy it with herbicide in order to expose the enemy. Like Emeny, Wasserman was impressed by the view from the air. He recalled the "mountain areas were beautiful. Flying over it is very nice... You'd find occasional lakes and waterfalls." In sum, Wasserman said, "if you stayed off the ground it's a beautiful country." Once on the ground, it was "Hot. Hot and wet, hot and dry."[6] The intense heat and humidity Wasserman so succinctly described greeted most soldiers immediately upon arrival. "My first impression of 'Nam was typical," U.S. Army Sergeant Robert Forrest remembered. After arriving at Cam Ranh Bay, Forrest was "overwhelmed by the smells, thick humid air, and the heat." Forrest and millions more found themselves in a quagmire. Their war went far beyond high-level politics and diplomacy. They became immediately enveloped instead by ubiquitous and intense natural forces.[7]

Image 9. Sergeant Robert Forrest from the 1st Infantry Division stands in front of his bunker at Fire Support Base (FSB) Dominate, November 19, 1969

Source: Courtesy of Robert Forrest, Charlottesville, VA.

This chapter, then, explores what Americans like Caputo, Emeny, Wasserman, and Forrest faced while in-country: the heat, humidity, insects, jungles, wild animals, and host of other natural factors that both helped to determine the war's ultimate outcome and dramatically shaped their daily experience. The environment's powerful and thorough impact on American combatants in Vietnam, together with how those combatants attempted to *control* the natural environment, has been inexplicably relegated to the margins of Vietnam War historiography. Vietnam's remarkable environmental complexity provided a brutally diverse set of obstacles for American soldiers to adapt or succumb to as they fought an increasingly exasperating war against a foe who leveraged the environment as a chief ally.[8]

One cannot fully understand or appreciate the American military experience in Vietnam without coming to terms with the world in which, and through which, soldiers lived, marched, slogged, and fought. Few American soldiers did not, at some level, comment on the difficult terrain in which they plied their trade, and fewer still were able to separate the war from the jungles, mud, and rain, which consumed and plagued them far more than enemy bullets. The enemy knew this well. General Vo Nguyen Giap, one of the most articulate and outspoken North Vietnamese commanders, recognized that the massive and powerful American military would struggle. As Giap declared, American forces would face "great difficulties due to unaccustomed terrain and climate, and to the considerable needs in supply and logistics." At its heart, this is that story.[9]

Contextualizing Nature and War

Recent studies of the war have moved beyond the discussion of military, social, political, and diplomatic actors to focus on the other war being waged in Vietnam. Namely, the war on its environment. Such an overlooked ubiquity as the environment— which shaped every facet of the conflict— is slowly coming into focus. In recent years, scholars have analyzed the American war against the dense Vietnamese foliage with chemical defoliants like "Agent Orange." Other historians have explored the devastating effects on both plants and humans of incendiary weapons such as napalm. Historian Greg Bankoff, in particular, has shown the dramatic impact of the war on animals and their habitat— a valuable avenue of research that gets to the heart of the conflict's totality. And countless, perhaps all, first-hand and scholarly studies of the conflict have been balanced at some level by South Vietnam's ever present, and ever confounding, climate and terrain. A notable contribution to this topic is historian David Biggs's *Quagmire: Nation-Building and Nature in the Mekong Delta*. Biggs makes a much needed and valuable contribution to the environment-as-agent scholarship. Yet, Biggs's treatment on the American war in Vietnam is relegated to only one chapter.[10]

This promising and growing research, however, largely focuses on how American chemical and conventional weapons devastated the environment. Or, put more generally, how the natural and built environments were altered or destroyed by war. Chemical defoliation, napalm, and a myriad of other weapons, for instance, dramatically impacted Vietnam's flora and fauna. These impacts are still felt throughout Southeast Asia. It is equally important, however, to explore how the natural environment impacted American soldiers and how the Viet Cong and North Vietnamese Army

used the natural environment as a key ally in their eventual success against the American military, the Army of the Republic of Vietnam (ARVN), and their collective allies. It is time to situate the environment alongside the other threads of historiographical discussion where it sorely belongs.[11]

Vietnamese combatants used the countryside as a buffer and an ally for centuries. The Chinese, Japanese, and French all fought as much against the climate, flora, and fauna as they had against the Vietnamese. The French, most famously, struggled to control Vietnam throughout the first half of the twentieth century in an effort that ultimately culminated in their defeat in the First Indochina War. The 1954 French military disaster at Dien Bien Phu— a military outpost in the mountains and forests of northern Vietnam— proved not only the Viet Minh's intense will to fight and, equally importantly, provided startling evidence of their ability to harness the natural environment to their benefit against a modernized, well-equipped military force. In the absence of overwhelming force up to and including nuclear weapons and full occupation, the people and countryside of Vietnam had proved itself theretofore invincible.[12]

Meanwhile, Americans were not wading into the struggle blindly when it came to environmental concerns. As the primary financial backer of the failed French escapade in Vietnam, they were cognizant of the problems that the environs of the country posed. By the late 1950s and early 1960s, the United States had invested enormous amounts of money and resources to help South Vietnam control and perfect its *built* environment in the hopes that such tactics might form a foundational element in its nation-building efforts. The Michigan State University Group (MSUG), U.S. Operations Mission (USOM), and other programs focused much of their effort on agrovilles, strategic hamlets, and sustainable agriculture. The United States recognized the built and natural environment's underlying role in Vietnamese life, but civilian and military authorities underestimated how paramount these environmental factors would be for the Viet Cong and North Vietnamese Army.[13]

Environment and American Military Strategy

American decision makers at the highest levels were aware of the problems that faced the feeble Republic of Vietnam and ARVN prior to significant American military presence. But the United States nevertheless fell precipitously into the political and environmental quagmire of Vietnam. Just months before significant American military build-up commenced in the summer of 1965, Ambassador Maxwell Taylor sent a top secret telegram to Secretary of State Dean Rusk with regard to the Viet Cong's threat to American and ARVN control in the South. Although inferior in number to ARVN forces, Taylor explained, the VC held one of the most valuable advantages in a guerrilla war— the ability to choose when and where to fight. The VC, Taylor said, "can achieve temporary local superiority at times and places of their selection." While ARVN troops were in largely "static missions" centered on resource protection, the VC and NVA had the ability to move throughout the countryside and marshal their resources on specific targets, then disappear quickly back into the landscape. "The Viet Cong thus enjoy the initiative in that they can choose the time, conditions, and place of engagement," Taylor ominously warned the State Department. As it turned out, Taylor's words foreshadowed the very problem that would plague the nascent American ground support. Hundreds of thousands of American soldiers in-country with the benefit of constant air support and the most technologically advanced and destructive weaponry, it turned out, could not stop the VC and NVA's ability to wage an effective guerrilla war using the devastatingly effective blend of politics and nature to their advantage.[14]

Intelligence regarding the difficult, if not intractable, military problems associated with fighting in South Vietnam was well-publicized among the U.S. military. As early as 1966, the Department of Defense distributed an informational booklet titled "Know Your Enemy: The Viet Cong." The authors attempt to define the nature and purpose of the Viet Cong by focusing attention on the natural environment in which they waged their war. "Vietnam as a whole," the booklet acknowledges, "is very nearly ideal for the type of warfare the Viet Cong is waging." The thick jungles provided "ideal concealment to secret installations and troop movements" and the people were "well suited to this kind of war... accustomed to hard work, meager rations, and an absolute minimum of material comforts." The Viet Cong and NVA leveraged their lifestyle and environment to give their guerrilla war enough strength to stretch the politicized and limited American response to the eventual breaking point. This is not to suggest that the United States had no chance for a compromised peace or even victory, if such a thing could be defined as the protection and perpetuation of South Vietnam. But whether or not this might have happened, it could *not* have happened given the notoriously unprepared and ill-conceived strategic and tactical notions employed by American commanders. For Military Assistance Command-Vietnam (MACV) Gen. William Westmoreland and the majority of American military strategists, the answer to victory in Vietnam was the same as it had been in World War II and Korea: overwhelming firepower.[15]

With even a seemingly clear understanding that the built and natural environments underscored Vietnamese society, American military forces made an early and confident decision to focus their efforts on what they knew best: technological warfare in force. Westmoreland's war of attrition by way of large, technological forces in the air and on the ground made sense only so far as those military technologies could reach through the forests, swamps, and mountains of South Vietnam. As historian Greg Bankoff has shown, the American military dumped as much as 85 percent of its firepower on landscapes— jungles, mountains, and any other terrain feature *thought* to shelter the enemy.[16] Furthermore, American forces failed to fully adapt to the guerrilla style of warfare – a kind of fighting that tied down countless thousands of American combatants and support personnel who came to South Vietnam chiefly in support of their war against the NVA and VC. American military officials counted on superior American firepower and technology to defeat the less advanced and supplied North Vietnamese. They discounted the impact of the VC in the South, and, most of all, they worried more about implicit Chinese and Soviet support than the more direct and ubiquitous alliance provided by the jungles, mountains, and creatures that marked the South Vietnamese countryside. For historian Loren Baritz, the American reliance on conventional warfare in Vietnam was both consistent with what the United States military knew best, and counter to what was needed for an effective fight against the VC and NVA. Counterinsurgency, ultimately, became mixed with established military doctrine. In general, the key to Westmoreland's strategy for the American war effort in South Vietnam rested on quantity. According to Baritz, the American doctrine was that "quantity would overcome." But massing destructive resources and technology against a people and an army merged with the forests and dirt, and who resorted to exceedingly effective guerrilla warfare, proved a large factor in America's undoing in Vietnam. The environment, and its ability to absorb and obfuscate American firepower and those soldiers who wielded it, shielded the relatively poorly equipped but psychologically steeled VC and NVA. The environment, in essence, gave teeth to Ho Chi Minh's promise of a lengthy, destructive, but ultimately successful engagement against the Americans.[17]

America's fight against the VC and the NVA did not happen in a level vacuum, and many perceptive combatants and witnesses drew distinct environmental metaphors to explain the American military's inability to win. The U.S. in Southeast Asia wielded superior firepower, technology, communications, and most other facets needed to wage and win a modern war. Or, put differently, the American military's size and capabilities compared to North Vietnam and its southern supporters was, in Stanley Karnow's words, like "a microbe facing a leviathan." For reporter Malcom Browne, the overwhelming force with which the U.S. military hit pockets of resistance "was like a sledgehammer on a floating cork." American firepower was often dramatically effective in the short-term, but never enough to permanently sink the enemy. The United States was ultimately unsuccessful, and, like so many microbes, the Vietnamese resistance slowly and methodically wore down the uninoculated American will to fight. Or, as Marine Brian McKinsey put it, it was like "the tiger and the elephant, take a little bite out here, take a little bite out there... finally they kill that elephant."[18]

Since the end of the conflict, veterans, politicians, scholars, and Americans generally have struggled to understand why. The answers are most often, and correctly, mired in politics, diplomacy, and military strategies. Strategic intransience diverted necessary resources from effective counterinsurgency measures that might have proven more successful. But there were other reasons, chief among them the natural environment. Nature's impact on American forces and the larger war effort was no less important to the American military experience in Vietnam than were high-level politics and diplomacy. Indeed, when in the thick of it, or even when in the relative safety of a well-defended base, American combatants' most immediate and persistent notions centered on the consuming environmental conditions. The ubiquity of natural forces on the physical and psychological existence of soldiers in South Vietnam defined their experience, and it must find more definition in our scholarly understanding of the conflict.

Image 10. Soldiers from 35th Infantry move along a small stream while on patrol north of Duc Pho, Vietnam. The natural environment served as the most important medium through which, and sometimes against which, combatants fought.

Source: Courtesy U.S. Army and Heritage Center, Carlisle, PA.

Nature as Ally and Enemy

Vietnamese soldiers and guerrillas leveraged nature to their advantage against the Americans, and they recognized its importance to their success. One NVA soldier exemplified the physical and emotional reliance they had on the natural environment. After weeks of struggling through South Vietnamese and Laotian forests, he confided to his diary: "The green jungle covers and cools the human heart. It covers the enemy's eyes and ears, it covers our soldiers." The landscape impacted the Vietnamese just as it did U.S. soldiers, but the former recognized its paramount role in their success. "The heat almost burns the mountains and jungles," the NVA soldier wrote, "but it cannot stop us." They snaked through heavily forested valleys and trudged over mountains, sometimes up and down slopes as steep as eighty-five degrees, careful to travel through areas off the main corridors and trails to avoid American planes and patrols. When they came closer to American and ARVN forces, the going got worse. Moving at night, often under the cover of heavy rain and through dense mud, they hid in the most unlikely areas and traveled as many as twelve hours per day through heat, mud, and hordes of biting ants.[19]

Even in the midst of the harshest and most dangerous conditions, American soldiers generally held a guarded respect for the ability of the NVA and VC to leverage the environment to their advantage against otherwise overwhelming technology and firepower. "As to the NVA or VC," Sergeant Robert Forrest of the 1st Infantry Division remembered, "I knew they were tough soldiers, poorly equipped but creative in that they used everything at their disposal to build weapons." For so many, they also had a psychological advantage because they had nature on their side. "The ground was always in play, always being swept," war correspondent Michael Herr wrote with a horrible eloquence, "underground was his, above it was ours." The ground, though, belonged to anyone. Herr continued, "We had the air, we could get up in it but not disappear in *to* it, we could run but we couldn't hide, and he could do each so well that sometimes it looked like he was doing them both at once." By using the environment as both a hiding place and a tool of war, the VC and NVA often subjugated the minds of the Americans sent to find, chase, and kill them. Nowhere was completely safe, and most places were completely treacherous. "You could be in the most protected space in Vietnam," Herr continued, "and still know that your safety was provisional, that early death, blindness, loss of legs, arms or balls, major and lasting disfigurement— the whole rotten deal— could come in on the freaky fluky as easily as in the so-called expected ways."[20]

American forces found themselves in an almost perpetual hunt for the enemy in hostile, mysterious, and arduous terrain. Often, their biggest fight was not against the human enemy but their environmental foe. "The main environment advantage the VC had," Sgt. Robert Forrest remembered, "was the great cover the jungle provided." Top military strategists had centered American military goals on killing enough of the enemy quickly enough so that they could not adequately replace them. This "body count" strategy meant constant, blind, and dangerous patrols into the bush. American soldiers, then, had to continually adapt in their quest to seek and destroy the enemy. In 1970, Forrest was stationed at Fire Support Base "Lorraine," located approximately forty miles north of Saigon. Forrest recalled the omnipresent role played by the natural world in their patrols:

> Thick jungle is a natural barrier and we either had to chop our way through it or walk on paths already available. The first option made a lot of noise and was slow going. Walking on existing trails was dangerous because of the threat of booby traps or ambush. The VC moved primarily at day break and dusk as it was cooler at these times. We would set up ambushes and try to catch the VC on the move. Once engaged, we would call in artillery and mortar strikes... The terrain in this part of the country was relatively flat, crisscrossed with small streams and rivers... The VC were very good at camouflaging their positions and themselves. Using the plants and leaves available, the enemy would break up their profiles so as to mask their movement.[21]

Thousands of NVA soldiers and support personnel moved themselves and their supplies into South Vietnam by way of the Ho Chi Minh Trail, which ran north and south just west of the Vietnamese border in Laos and Cambodia. Humans, elephants, bicycles, ox carts, and trucks traversed the trail, bringing with them thousands of pounds of ammunition, weaponry, and other war supplies. Vietnamese laborers lugged packs of war supplies weighing fifty to sixty pounds by foot alongside beasts of burden and motorized vehicles. A constant stream of human, animal, and vehicle traffic coursed up and down the trail network, often with little interference save for the harsh natural terrain, seasonal rains, and the very environmental conditions that helped shield and protect them. Short of secretive special operations missions and heavy, but often inaccurate, aerial bombing, the load-bearers continued apace for the remainder of the American presence in Southeast Asia.[22]

Image 11. Even in the dry season, undergrowth throughout much of South Vietnam was dense and unrelenting. Here a helicopter lands to evacuate Sgt. Robert Forrest and others.

Source: Courtesy of Robert Forrest, Charlottesville, VA.

Gen. William Westmoreland and other Military Assistance Command, Vietnam (MACV) leadership soon focused their attention on shutting down the Ho Chi Minh Trail, which snaked through incredibly difficult terrain. Concealed from the air by dense foliage, and inundated with caves, supply posts, and tunnels, Vietnamese porters and soldiers could often move with relative impunity to American air attack and limited ground assaults. "When I frequently scanned the region from helicopters in the 1960s," war reporter Stanley Karnow wrote, "nothing was discernible, even at low altitudes, beneath the green canopy that seemed to stretch on endlessly." But they also had to negotiate increasing numbers of bomb craters, cross rivers, and trudge through buffalo wallows. As the war evolved and grew, so did the trail. By 1967, nearly 70 percent of all weapons and ammunition used by VC forces had been transported on the trail. The NVA, VC, and countless civilian laborers had turned an old, unreliable trail into the very lifeline of the southern war effort. The Ho Chi Minh Trail was among the most important factors that led to American and ARVN defeat. By 1967, MACV had formulated a plan to cut off the trail and, in effect, suffocate resistance in the South. Operation Plan *El Paso* would choke off a key sector of the trail near the old French airbase at Tchepone just as the Monsoon season came to an end in November or December. American and ARVN forces would seal off the supply route in the dry season when the trail was busiest and maintain their block until the rains resumed in the spring. But *El Paso* suffered from enormous logistical complications, which involved supplying an army for an extended time in one of the most remote and difficult environments on earth. Also, Tchepone (like most of the trail) was in Laos— a political liability as Lyndon Johnson's presidency gave way to Richard Nixon's. In the end, *El Paso* never happened, for both political *and* environmental reasons. American forces struggled to control North Vietnam's lifeline into the South, and they ultimately failed.[23]

Air Force Gen. Merrill McPeak reflected the thoughts of thousands more when he compared the Ho Chi Minh Trail to a living, breathing organism – one that quickly regenerated itself no matter the damage. "More a maze than a road," McPeak later wrote, "the trail disappeared, returned to view, dissolved, emerged, contracted, expanded, split, reunited, vanished, materialized." The VC lifeline was ever moving, ever evolving. No matter how many thousands of tons of ordnance McPeak and others dropped on it, the corridor remained, seemingly and unnervingly stronger than before. The Ho Chi Minh Trail, McPeak wrote, "itself the enemy, was always there. Killing it was like trying to put socks on an octopus."[24]

SOLDIERS AND THEIR WAR WITH FLORA AND FAUNA

Harsh environmental conditions quickly took a toll on the Americans who endlessly searched the jungles and mountains for the enemy they concealed. Jungle boots, ponchos, and combat uniforms deteriorated at a rapid pace, and replacements were not always guaranteed. After days or weeks on an operation, soldiers would come back with their gear and clothes in tatters. As for the uniform, "you didn't come in and get them washed," Brian McKinsey recalled, "you just took them off and put them in a burn barrel. I mean they had been pissed in or shit in accidentally, X amount of times... you just burned them."[25] Sergeant Bob Forrest remembered the futility of maintaining any level of cleanliness. The rain and mud in the wet season and the dust and sweat in the dry season yielded a constant muck spread over the soldiers. "You couldn't stay clean," Forrest remembered, "and anyway we only got a change of clothes once every three or four days... dry socks were important, and no one wore underwear, as it was too tight and sweaty." All soldiers, Forrest recalls, had towels around their necks "to wipe off the never-ending sweat." [26]

Life in Vietnam was a relentless fight for comfort and survival against the sky and earth in addition to the enemy. The wet season, especially, brought with it a constant struggle against rain, mud, chills, and misery. "I live with mud, the damned, ever present clay," Lieutenant James Coan confided to his diary. "It clogs your boots up to the ankles and is the same color as melted Hershey bars." The constant, unrelenting downpours, he wrote, made it impossible to ever really be dry. "Your head, armpits, crotch, and chest itch constantly," Coan lamented, "and all you can do is scratch or douse foot powder on the itchy spots." And, in a particularly cruel twist, a state of perpetual wetness gave soldiers cold chills even in what was otherwise a hot and humid environment. Sgt. Bob Forrest said the continual rains transformed the ground into "a soupy mess." Ponchos, Forrest remembered, were sometimes the only barrier between soldiers and the soaking mud.[27] In the end, as Marine Lieutenant and writer Philip Caputo made clear, American combatants were under a constant, unyielding, and oppressive assault by the environment:

> Everything rotted and corroded there: bodies, boot leather, canvas, metal, morals. Scorched by the sun, wracked by the wind and rain of the monsoon, fighting in alien swamps and jungles, our humanity rubbed off of us as the protective bluing rubbed off the barrels of our rifles.[28]

Beyond the environment's physical toll on soldiers' bodies, clothes, and equipment, the brush, and all the creatures in it, further taxed soldiers' psychological well-being as well. From large, dangerous animals to parasites and bugs, American soldiers fought a constant physical and psychological battle against Vietnamese fauna. The Walter Reed Army Medical Center noted many of the smaller but no less dangerous entomological and zoological dangers found in South Vietnam, including a preponderance of "cobras, vipers, leeches, rats, lice, fleas, spiders, [and] scorpions." Another publication warned of the mighty and elusive tiger and a host of other large creatures soldiers might encounter, including "wild oxen, buffalo, elephants, panthers, and a variety of poisonous snakes."[29]

Not only did the Viet Cong and North Vietnamese Army haunt the forests, but rumors (and realities) of dangerous wildlife also abounded. Indochinese Tigers (*Panthera tigris corbetti*) were perhaps the most evocative of all. Tigers had roamed the highlands and valleys for centuries, but they had always been elusive. By the time of the Vietnam War, they were exceedingly rare. Their population dropped sharply in the late twentieth century, and very few American soldiers ever encountered them. But the perception of these beautiful and dangerous creatures lurking in the same forests VC and NVA soldiers hid in only added to the danger and mystique permeating the physical and mental landscape through which they trudged. Instruction manuals distributed to American troops added to the psychological uncertainty of what lurked in the dark forests. One such booklet warned:

> It may seem strange to say in the second half of the 20th century, when most people see them only in zoos, that tigers are one of the dangers faced by servicemen in the Republic of Vietnam. But, for men on patrol in the upland jungles they still represent a threat.[30]

The duration and severity of the war resulted in an unintended consequence for the tiger population, however. Not only had the war rearranged or destroyed vast swaths of the environment, it had also uprooted hundreds of thousands of Vietnamese from their villages and farms. This, in turn, had opened new territory and more relative safety for roaming tigers. They found food to be more easily attainable, too, in the form of feral livestock set free by the war's devastation. Some accounts even suggest tigers consumed human remains and became attracted to the sound of gunfire for such purposes, although these rumors are difficult to substantiate. Authentic or not, the very perception that tigers might have haunted the dark jungles ready to feast on American soldiers, dead or alive, played no small role in the environment-based psychological war, which plagued their thoughts.[31]

Tigers did exist, and they became increasingly bold as the war dragged on. Some soldiers became rare and unlucky exceptions when they encountered aggressive tigers. While patrolling a section near "Razorback Ridge" in South Vietnam, a nearby helicopter pilot radioed to American soldier Gonazalo Baltazar and his men, telling them he had spotted a tiger straight in front of them. At first, Baltazar believed the pilot to mean an ambush since "tiger" was sometimes code for a trap. The chopper pilot soon clarified that a real tiger was skulking in front of the troops. "That was more scary than an ambush to me," Baltazar remembered, "because a tiger can rip you apart." Soon, the helicopter moved closer to the tiger to scare it away, and the now ever more leery troops moved forward.

For Baltazar, an ambush by the enemy might have been preferable to a run-in with an Indochinese Tiger.[32]

Not all tiger encounters ended so peacefully. Marines at a remote outpost in the northwestern section of South Vietnam had been warned of dangerous wildlife in the area including elephants and, ominously, tigers. Two Marines stationed at the far end of the line became victims not of the NVA or VC but a particularly aggressive tiger. "One night," Marine Keith Erdman recalled, "all we heard was a blood-curdling scream and then nothing, quiet..." After daylight, a small patrol went to check on the outpost and found nothing but what they thought were tiger tracks. So far as Erdman and his fellow Marines knew, the two had been killed and "taken away."[33] Except for the exceptional stories that are difficult to fully substantiate, South Vietnamese tigers affected soldiers at more of a psychological level than a realistic one.

Other animals played a far more direct and pervasive role in the American experience in South Vietnam. Monkeys, rats, snakes, water buffalo, pigs, chickens, and a wide variety of wild and domesticated animals became a daily occurrence for most troops. Snakes, especially, caused considerable anxiety and occasional pain among soldiers in the strange and ecologically unique environment. Venomous bamboo vipers were especially feared by American GIs. Stories spread throughout the ranks of especially cruel encounters with the dangerous snakes. According to one soldier, a green bamboo viper, hanging in a tree, dropped and "bit one of the guys... in the face." The unfortunate soldier would have almost certainly died had the viper bit him in the neck. As it was, his face was undoubtedly mangled from the intense swelling as a medevac helicopter evacuated him from the bush— a casualty of the environment.[34]

Rats also plagued the minds and realities of soldiers. Perhaps more than any other animal, rats thrived on the widespread destruction and dislocation of flora, fauna, and humans in South Vietnam during the war. As millions of refugees fled to urban areas, the overcrowded and often unsanitary cities became ideal breeding grounds for rats. So, too, did the multitude of small and large American bases that emerged throughout the countryside, giving rats a constant and reliable source of food and shelter.[35] They infested barracks, firebases, and the dirt and mud. They were everywhere. "I haven't said much about the rats here," Marine Lt. James Coan wrote in his diary, "every bunker I've lived in has had its share of shrieking, skittering creatures." When not hiding from mortar rounds or trying to sleep, soldiers stayed busy catching and killing the creatures. Coan caught "over 50 rats" during the first half of his year-long tour. How Ordnance Specialist Randall Kunkleman spent his turn at nighttime guard duty was contingent upon the rats residing in the protective bunker intended to shield him, and anyone else on guard duty, from harm. Fearing the undoubtedly aggressive rats more than the human enemy, Kunkleman would often wrap himself "in a poncho liner and lay on top of the bunker [with his] M-16 kind of holding it like a teddy bear." One night, a Rocket Propelled Grenade nearly blew him off the top of the bunker. Thereafter, Kunkleman recalled, "I was off the top of that and down inside that bunker and I had zero fear of those rats at that particular moment." He continued his time on guard duty braving the rats rather than risking the RPGs. The nasty and bellicose creatures "would be rubbing against my legs, my arms, and just moving in their nightly journeys."[36]

Coan and Kunkleman had good reason to hate and fear rats, beyond the rodents' nasty demeanor. In 1967, the 221st Signal Company and the Army Pictorial Center went so far as to produce a short informational film titled "Waging War on Rats." It was distributed to troops in Saigon and Binh Hoa. A summary transcript of the film warned that "another enemy... more widespread than the Viet Cong is the rat population of Viet Nam." These unnerving creatures spread a variety of diseases, the film transcript says, including and especially the plague— a rat-riding, flea-born disease, which afflicted Vietnam as much or more than the rest of the world "combined." The film cautioned Americans to spray flea-killing insecticide in and around rat traps and, where possible, capture rats alive "so that the fleas and other insects on them will still be on the rats." If killed, the disease-carrying parasite will look for new hosts, including humans.[37]

Military health official James Schill dedicated a great deal of his time to the rat problem in South Vietnam, specifically where it concerned disease-carrying fleas. For Schill and others, the goal was not to simply control the rat population, which was nearly impossible, but to make sure the rats were "clean" of their plague-carrying riders. They used vast amounts of Dichloro-diphenyl-trichloroethane (DDT) to spray areas with large rat densities in hopes of killing the fleas atop them. The primary threat, Schill said, was pneumatic plague— a highly contagious and deadly strain, which occasionally broke out in Saigon and other population areas.[38]

More than animals, a menagerie of insects consumed soldier life. Mosquitoes, giant centipedes, ants, and a host of other bugs impacted daily life regardless of whether soldiers were in the bush or at base. Mosquitoes, especially, were universal. As early as 1965, the *U.S. News and World Report* announced a new strain of especially dangerous Malaria had been added to "the variety of diseases that make Vietnam a virtual pest hole." Over 400 cases had already been reported, and the Surgeon General's office predicted more to come. One instructional manual warned soldiers to take precautions in order to avoid mosquito-borne illnesses such as Malaria and Encephalitis: "Take your anti-malaria pill every week without fail; Sleep under a mosquito net, no matter how hot and inconvenient it is."[39] Guard duty for most soldiers was marked by tedium and the hum of mosquitoes. According to one soldier, "we just kept our eyes open and watched for rats and swatted mosquitoes and tried to stay awake." The "turkey size mosquitoes," as he described them, wreaked havoc as the miserable lookouts stared into the darkness for signs of the enemy. They infiltrated the sleeping quarters to harass hot, wet, and exhausted soldiers. Helicopter pilot Ray Foley suffered dearly from the mosquito menace. Foley neglected to patch his mosquito net and fell asleep. "The next morning I get up," he recalls, "and I'm eaten alive... I must have had 150 bites and both of my eyes had swelled closed so I had to pry my eyes open to see." According to Foley's experience, the mosquitoes were drawn to the "tender" parts of the face, focusing their relentless attacks against the eyes and mouth. American soldiers were often as focused on fighting mosquitoes as their human enemies. Ray Foley explains:

> The only way you could get them is if you were lucky enough to get a spray bomb of that DDT stuff... you could get one of those and hide it, keep it, and horde it and fight for it and threaten life and limb of anybody who tried to steal it from you, and before you got into that mosquito net... you could spray the net, the bunk, everything down, jump in, fold it around you... if your arm went over against that net they would, by the zillions, they would bite you there on that fleshy area that they could reach and they would just annihilate your arm. You'd wake up with a huge whelp where they'd chewed on you there sucking your blood. They were ridiculous, those damn mosquitoes. [40]

Mosquitoes, of course, hardly held an entomological monopoly with regard to the ongoing and vicious conflict between American soldiers and Vietnamese bugs. South Vietnam was full of "centipedes, big centipedes, big bugs," Marine Steve Harding remembered, "especially when you're digging underground." According to Harding, some of the centipedes were so big that the Korean allies he fought with made temporary pets out of them, going so far as to put them in leashes. "Insect life was phenomenal," recalled Marvin Mathiak, who was in awe of the vast abundance of colorful and often pernicious bugs. Mathiak remembered seeing more than one massive black scorpion— so big that, when uncurled, "would be about a foot from the tip of its tail to its claws. It's an enormous thing." He also encountered numerous "giant millipedes" that he estimated to be close to eight inches long, along with vast numbers of spiders.[41]

There were also leeches. The slimy blood sucking creatures lived throughout much of South Vietnam and were especially prevalent in the jungles. They did not just live in water. They would drop from trees onto soldiers, or attach to their clothes as they moved through the forest of tangles. "Every time we stopped for a break," one soldier lamented, "we had to pick leeches off of ourselves." Most soldiers carried insect deterrent that they called "bug piss," and they would often use a drop of it to get the leeches off. When in a rush or out of repellent, a lit cigarette would do. At times, leeches would become much more than a minor nuisance. After wading across a small river, Marvin Mathiak and his fellow soldiers were covered by the dark, viscous blood suckers, each about two inches long. "I had 47 on me," Mathiak remembered, "and another guy had 120 something on him... they were omnipresent." David Shows, a Long Range Reconnaissance Patrol (LRRP) soldier, found leeches almost intolerable. Even when on mountaintops a long way from standing water, swarms of the blood-sucking parasites besieged Shows and his fellow soldiers. "Every time we would stop," he recalls, "you could see the leeches coming at you like little inch worms from all directions." Even the resilient, native Montagnards who helped American soldiers and who were intimately familiar with the jungle and life in it, grew weary of the parasites. Shows was surprised "that the Montagnards who were never bothered by anything hated the leeches at least as much as the G.I.'s did." The key to controlling leeches, Shows said, was to soak the ground with repellant wherever to ward off the masses of leeches inching toward them.[42]

The incessantly hot, wet, and muddy conditions in South Vietnam made even the smallest wounds potentially deadly, and leeches only exacerbated the problem. "The combination of heat, humidity, and dirt can cause infection in small cuts and abrasions within hours," cautioned a health book distributed to troops. "In this manner," the warning continued, "leeches are a particular problem since they secrete an anticoagulant which delays blood clotting and leaves an open wound when they are removed." Once leech-free, soldiers were advised to immediately clean and disinfect wounds and keep them as dry as possible.[43] Leeches were not the only worm problem soldiers faced. A booklet distributed by the Walter Reed Army Medical Center cautioned that "hookworm disease is almost universal among the rural population, and the proportion of people infected with roundworms is extremely high [and] the pork tapeworm is common." Soldiers who consumed undercooked food or bad water were potentially host to innumerable parasitic, bacterial, and viral infections. Dysentery and hepatitis were considered "major threats."[44]

Conclusion

Some American combatants felt a deep sense of nostalgia with respect to Vietnam's natural environment— the same diverse ecological quagmire that had been so difficult, indeed impossible, to control in their fight against the NVA and VC. American pilot Peter Faber saw South Vietnam at the beginning of the American build-up in 1965, and he saw it again at the end in the early 1970s. "When I was over there in '65," Faber recalls, the jungle "was gorgeous and the wildlife and actually seeing a tiger and seeing wild elephants and things like that... and the monkeys and everything that was there." The subsequent seven or eight years saw American military strategy bent on fighting not just the NVA and VC but also, and significantly, their chief ally: the jungle itself. The American war against South Vietnam's natural environment destroyed much of what Faber had seen. "I don't want to remember what it looked like in the 70s," Faber continues, "when they'd gotten done with defoliation and bombing because they pretty much changed a beautiful country into something like a tornado went through a place."[45]

As Faber conveys, combatants then knew well the reality of America's war on the environment, and the topic receives a great deal of scholarly attention now. That Americans and Vietnamese alike recognized the intentional environmental destruction wrought by the United States military shows, among other things, that the natural environment was a strategically and tactically critical player during the Vietnam Conflict. In addition to the larger forces of climate and topography, the most mundane and miserable environmental factors like rain, mud, heat, mosquitoes, snakes, rats, and even the occasional tiger wreaked havoc on the minds and bodies of American soldiers. The NVA and VC leadership knew it, and they effectively leveraged South Vietnam's beautiful and terrible flora and fauna as a significant ally in what otherwise should have been an objectively futile effort against the world's greatest military power. High level politics, diplomacy, and civil unrest notwithstanding, it was the seemingly endless jungles and mountains, drenched in rain or heat or both, along with all the creatures in them, that helped the NVA and VC survive and ultimately win.

NOTES

1. I would like to offer my sincerest thanks to co-editor and friend Geoffrey W. Jensen for his patience, keen editorial eye, and encouragement. Thanks, also, to Vietnam veteran Robert Forrest who lent his time and memories to this project. Tim O'Brien, *The Things They Carried* (1990; Boston: Mariner Books, 2009), 14.
2. Philip Caputo, *A Rumor of War* (New York: Henry Holt and Co., 1996), 82.
3. Soldier interaction with nature plays no small part in numerous films and cultural depictions of the conflict. See, especially, experiential elements of the soldier-nature relationship in *Apocalypse Now*, directed by Francis Ford Coppola, Zoetrope Studios, 1979, and *Platoon*, directed by Oliver Stone, MGM, 1986.
4. Carl von Clausewitz, *On War*, ed. and transl. by Michael Howard and Peter Paret (Princeton, NJ: Princeton University Press, 1984), 348-49; 544. Ancient military strategist Sun Tzu also commented on terrain, classifying it into six distinct types with respect to warfare: accessible ground, entangling ground, temporizing ground, narrow passes, precipitous heights, and positions at a great distance from the enemy. By Tzu's definition, American soldiers in Vietnam faced both entangling and temporizing ground. See Sun Tzu, *The Art of War*, transl. Samuel L. Griffith (New York: Oxford University Press, 1963), 124-29.
5. Diary of Mary Emeny, 26 August 1967, Folder 02, Box 01, Mary Emeny Collection, The Vietnam Center and Archive, Texas Tech University. https://www.vietnam.ttu.edu/virtualarchive/items.php?item=0840102001, accessed September 25, 2017.
6. Interview with Larry Wasserman, 02 December 2002, Cold Storage, Mr. Lawrence H. Wasserman Collection, The Vietnam Center and Archive, Texas Tech University. https://www.vietnam.ttu.edu/virtualarchive/items.php?item=OH0245, accessed 25 September 2017.
7. Robert Forrest, Sergeant, First Infantry Division, Interview by Matthew M. Stith (Author), Transcript, August 20, 2017.
8. For the best and most comprehensive study of Vietnam's natural environment, see Eleanor Jane Sterling, Martha Maud Hurley, and Duc Minh, *Vietnam: A Natural History* (New Haven: Yale University Press, 2006).

9. Vo Nguyen Giap, *The Military Art of Peoples War*, ed. Russell Stetler (New York: Monthly Review Press, 1979), 259; See also Winters, *Battling the Elements*, 106.
10. Greg Bankoff, "A Curtain of Silence: Asia's Fauna in the Cold War," in J.R. McNeill and Corinna R. Unger, eds., *Environmental Histories of the Cold War* (New York: Cambridge University Press, 2010): 203-26; David Biggs, *Quagmire: Nation-Building and Nature in the Mekong Delta* (Seattle: University of Washington Press, 2010), 197-225. For the most thorough study on napalm in Vietnam and other wars, see Robert M. Neer, *Napalm: An American Biography* (Cambridge: Harvard University Press, 2013). For recent and useful examinations of chemical weapons used against Vietnamese forests and their lasting effects on those soldiers and civilians in the vicinity, see Peter Sills, *Toxic War: The Story of Agent Orange* (Nashville: Vanderbilt University Press, 2014), Edwin A. Martini, *Agent Orange: History, Science, and the Politics of Uncertainty* (Amherst: University of Massachusetts Press, 2012), and David Zierler, *The Invention of Ecocide: Agent Orange, Vietnam, and the Scientists Who Changed the Way We Think About the Environment* (Athens: University of Georgia Press, 2011).
11. Military history and environmental history have long been complimentary but rarely have they been combined. Recent work, however, is slowly mending this oversight. For some of the more helpful scholarship that blends military and environmental history, see J. R. McNeill and Corinna R. Unger, eds., *Environmental Histories of the Cold War* (New York: Cambridge University Press, 2010), Charles E. Closmann, ed., *War and the Environment: Military Destruction in the Modern Age* (College Station: Texas A&M University Press, 2009), Harold A. Winters, *Battling the Elements: Weather and Terrain in the Conduct of War* (Baltimore: Johns Hopkins University Press, 1998), and Richard P. Tucker and Edmund Russell, eds., *Natural Enemy, Natural Ally: Toward an Environmental History of War* (Corvallis: Oregon State University Press, 2004).
12. John Prados, *Vietnam: The History of an Unwinnable War, 1945-1975* (Lawrence: University Press of Kansas, 2009), 26-34. For the rich history Vietnamese warfare in the decades before American intervention, see, especially, Fredrik Logevall, *Embers of War: The Fall of an Empire and the Making of America's Vietnam* (New York: Random House, 2012); Marilyn Young, *The Vietnam Wars, 1945-1990* (New York: Harper Perennial, 1991); Mark Atwood Lawrence, "Explaining the Early Decisions: The United States and the French War, 1945-1954," in Mark Philip Bradley

and Marilyn B. Young, eds., *Making Sense of the Vietnam Wars: Local, National, and Transnational Perspectives* (New York: Oxford University Press, 2008), 23-44. For the best short treatment of Dien Bien Phu as an environmental battle, see Harold A. Winters, *Battling the Elements: Weather and Terrain in the Conduct of War* (Baltimore: Johns Hopkins University Press, 1998), 242-47. For a focus on the travails of guerrilla warfare and counterinsurgency with respect to Dien Bien Phu, see Max Boot, *Invisible Armies: An Epic History of Guerrilla Warfare from Ancient Times to the Present* (New York: W.W. Norton, 2013) 357-63.

13. For the United States role in nation building with regard to agriculture and the *built* environment in South Vietnam, see Jessica Elkind, *Aid Under Fire: Nation Building and the Vietnam War* (Lexington: University Press of Kentucky, 2016), 93-131.
14. Telegram From Saigon To Secretary Of State: Viet Cong, 05 June 1965, Folder 01, Box 02, Larry Berman Collection (Presidential Archives Research), The Vietnam Center and Archive, Texas Tech University. https://www.vietnam.ttu.edu/virtualarchive/items.php?item=0240201028, accessed 19 Sep. 2017.
15. "Know Your Enemy: The Viet Cong," 01 January 1966, Folder 04, Box 02, Dr. Calvin Chapman Collection, The Vietnam Center and Archive, Texas Tech University. www.vietnam.ttu.edu/virtualarchive/items.php?item=0380204001, accessed 23 September 2017; Boot, 417-18.
16. Greg Bankoff, "A Curtain of Silence: Asia's Fauna in the Cold War," in McNeill and Unger, *Environmental Histories of the Cold War*, 204.
17. Loren Baritz, *Backfire: A History of How American Culture Led Us into Vietnam and Made Us Fight the Way We Did* (William Morrow and Co., 1985), 319.
18. Stanley Karnow, *Vietnam: A History* (New York: Viking Press, 1983), 435. Malcom W. Browne, *Muddy Boots and Red Socks: A Reporter's Life* (Time Books, 1993), 180. See also Gregory A. Daddis, *Westmoreland's War: Reassessing American Strategy in Vietnam* (New York: Oxford University Press, 2014), 118-119; Interview with Brian McKinsey, 14 April 2002, Cold Storage, Mr. Brian McKinsey Collection, The Vietnam Center and Archive, Texas Tech University. https://www.vietnam.ttu.edu/virtualarchive/items.php?item=OH0135, accessed 25 September 2017.
19. Diary of a North Vietnamese Infiltrator, 16 August 1973, Folder 11, Box 05, Douglas Pike Collection: Unit 05 - National Liberation Front, The Vietnam Center and Archive, Texas Tech University. https://www.

vietnam.ttu.edu/virtualarchive/items.php?item=2310511005, accessed 25 September 2017.

20. Interview with Robert Forrest; Michael Herr, *Dispatches* (1968; New York: Vintage, 1977), 14.
21. Interview with Robert Forrest.
22. John M. Collins, *Military Geography: For Professionals and the Public* (Washington, D.C.: National Defense University Press, 1998), 368.
23. Stanley Karnow, *Vietnam: A History* (1983; New York: Penguin Press, 1997), 347; Collins, *Military Geography*, 368; 375; Boot, *Invisible Armies*, 419.
24. Merrill A. McPeak, *Hangar Flying* (Lake Oswego, OR: Lost Wingman Press, 2012).
25. Interview with Brian McKinsey, The Vietnam Center and Archive, Texas Tech University.
26. Interview with Robert Forrest.
27. Ibid.; Typed Version of the Con Thien Diary, 29 August 1967, Folder 02, Box 01, James Coan Collection, The Vietnam Center and Archive, Texas Tech University. https://www.vietnam.ttu.edu/virtualarchive/items.php?item=11370102002, accessed 19 September 2017.
28. Caputo, *Rumor of War*, 217.
29. New Health Hazard For GI's In Vietnam, 13 December 1965, Folder 18, Box 02, Dr. Calvin Chapman Collection, The Vietnam Center and Archive, Texas Tech University. https://www.vietnam.ttu.edu/virtualarchive/items.php?item=0380218007, accessed 18 September 2017; Health Problems of Soldiers in Vietnam and Prevention Measures, No Date, Folder 01, Box 01, 1st Battalion, 8th Artillery, 25th Infantry Association Collection, The Vietnam Center and Archive, Texas Tech University. https://www.vietnam.ttu.edu/virtualarchive/items.php?item=0030101010, accessed 17 September 2017.
30. Health Problems of Soldiers in Vietnam and Prevention Measures, No Date, Folder 01, Box 01, 1st Battalion, 8th Artillery, 25th Infantry Association Collection, The Vietnam Center and Archive, Texas Tech University. https://www.vietnam.ttu.edu/virtualarchive/items.php?item=0030101010, accessed 17 September 2017.
31. Bankoff, "A Curtain of Silence," 221.
32. Sterling, et al., *Vietnam*, 118; Interview with Gonzalo Baltazar, 23 March 2001, Cold Storage, Gonzalo Baltazar Collection, The Vietnam Center and Archive, Texas Tech University. https://www.vietnam.ttu.edu/virtualarchive/items.php?item=OH0152, accessed 25 September 2017.

33. Interview with Keith Erdman, 26 February 2001, Cold Storage, Keith Erdman Collection, The Vietnam Center and Archive, Texas Tech University. https://www.vietnam.ttu.edu/virtualarchive/items.php?item=OH0085, accessed 25 September 2017.
34. Interview with Steve Harding, 11 April 2002, Cold Storage, Steve Harding Collection, The Vietnam Center and Archive, Texas Tech University. https://www.vietnam.ttu.edu/virtualarchive/items.php?item=OH0133; Interview with Keith Erdman, OH0085 TTU, accessed 25 September 2017.
35. Bankoff, "A Curtain of Silence," 221-22.
36. Typed Version of the Con Thien Diary, 29 August 1967, Folder 02, Box 01, James Coan Collection, The Vietnam Center and Archive, Texas Tech University. https://www.vietnam.ttu.edu/virtualarchive/items.php?item=11370102002, accessed 19 Sep. 2017; Interview with Randall Kunkleman, 01 October 1999, Cold Storage , Randall Kunkleman Collection, The Vietnam Center and Archive, Texas Tech University. https://www.vietnam.ttu.edu/virtualarchive/items.php?item=OH0108, accessed 19 September 2017.
37. Motion Picture Summaries Waging War on Rats, 01 August 1968, Folder 08, Box 01, William Foulke Collection, The Vietnam Center and Archive, Texas Tech University. https://www.vietnam.ttu.edu/virtualarchive/items.php?item=10400108005, accessed 19 September 2017.
38. Interview with James Schill, 10 April 2001, Cold Storage, James Schill Collection, The Vietnam Center and Archive, Texas Tech University. https://www.vietnam.ttu.edu/virtualarchive/items.php?item=OH0155, accessed 19 September 2017
39. New Health Hazard For GI's In Vietnam, 13 December 1965, Folder 18, Box 02, Dr. Calvin Chapman Collection, The Vietnam Center and Archive, Texas Tech University. https://www.vietnam.ttu.edu/virtualarchive/items.php?item=0380218007, accessed 18 September 2017; Health Problems of Soldiers in Vietnam and Prevention Measures, No Date, Folder 01, Box 01, 1st Battalion, 8th Artillery, 25th Infantry Association Collection, The Vietnam Center and Archive, Texas Tech University. https://www.vietnam.ttu.edu/virtualarchive/items.php?item=0030101010, accessed 17 September 2017.
40. Health Problems of Soldiers in Vietnam and Prevention Measures, No Date, Folder 01, Box 01, 1st Battalion, 8th Artillery, 25th Infantry Association Collection, The Vietnam Center and Archive, Texas Tech University. https://www.vietnam.ttu.edu/virtualarchive/items.php?item=0030101010, accessed 17 September 2017; Interview with Willis F.

Marshall, OH0269 TTU; Interview with Ray Foley, 04 May 2000, Cold Storage, Ray Foley collection OH0101, The Vietnam Center and Archive, Texas Tech University. https://vva.vietnam.ttu.edu/repositories/2/digital_objects/37467, accessed 7 July 2018.

41. Interview with Steve Harding, OH0133 TTU; Interview with Marvin Mathiak, TTU
42. Interview with Marvin Mathiak, 08 August 2000, Cold Storage, Marvin Mathiak Collection, The Vietnam Center and Archive, Texas Tech University. https://www.vietnam.ttu.edu/virtualarchive/items.php?item=OH0011, accessed 25 September 2017; Firsthand account - Snippets I remember from missions with Don Glover, 01 January 1968, Folder 03, Box 01, The LRRP/Rangers of the First Cavalry Division During the Viet Nam War Collection, The Vietnam Center and Archive, Texas Tech University. https://www.vietnam.ttu.edu/virtualarchive/items.php?item=21610103004, accessed 17 September 2017.
43. "Health Problems of Soldiers in Vietnam and Prevention Measures," No Date, Folder 01, Box 01, 1st Battalion, 8th Artillery, 25th Infantry Association Collection, The Vietnam Center and Archive, Texas Tech University. https://www.vietnam.ttu.edu/virtualarchive/items.php?item=0030101010, accessed 17 September 2017.
44. "New Health Hazard for GI's In Vietnam," 13 December 1965, Folder 18, Box 02, Dr. Calvin Chapman Collection, The Vietnam Center and Archive, Texas Tech University. https://www.vietnam.ttu.edu/virtualarchive/items.php?item=0380218007, accessed 18 Sep. 2017.
45. Interview with Peter Faber, 29 April 2000, Cold Storage, Peter Faber Collection, The Vietnam Center and Archive, Texas Tech University. https://www.vietnam.ttu.edu/virtualarchive/items.php?item=OH0024, accessed 25 September 2017.

Part III

Remembering Vietnam

The 'Nam Comics

Remembering the American War in Viet Nam

Susan L. Eastman

At the turn of the century, the field of Vietnam War studies focused on the inclusion of the Vietnamese and civilian experiences, as well as the experience of women; a significant shift from previous decades. Cultural scholarship broadly recognizes an evolution in the American national memory of the war from a sense of guilt in the 1970s, a revisionist refighting of the war in the 1980s, and "kicking" the "Vietnam Syndrome" in the 1990s. With so many books and articles about the conflict, it may seem there is little left to say about the war representations, particularly those produced during the 1980s. This seems especially true of war films produced during that period. Oliver Stone's critically acclaimed *Platoon* (1986) and Stanley Kubrick's *Full Metal Jacket* (1987) provide visceral cultural representations of the conflict grounded in historical reality.[1] The popular appeal of Sylvester Stallone as John Rambo in the *Rambo* franchise and Chuck Norris as Colonel James Braddock in the *Missing in Action* series,[2] depict an effort for the characters, America generally, to go back, refight, and "win" the war. This is what Susan Jeffords calls the "Remasculinization of America" in President Ronald Reagan's Cold War America.[3] Many scholars emphasize the revenge-plot revisionism found in literary and cinematic representations of the war throughout the 1980s.[4] But not all literature and film fell into this revisionist category. One of the cultural productions that provided a different view in the era dominated by Vietnam-cultural revisionism was a comic book series called *The 'Nam.*[5]

Comic books are a genre traditionally considered either childish or deviant, and certainly not the medium for such serious topics as history, trauma, and memory. However, comics provide audiences with what one reader of the series referred to as a remedy for "pernicious tendency in the popular media today to trivialize what was a very traumatic issue."[6] One need only consider critics' surprise upon the overwhelmingly positive reception to Art Spiegelman's *MAUS* (1986),[7] a graphic novel about his parents' experiences during the Holocaust.[8] Indeed, Spiegelman's *MAUS* is credited to the changing perception of comics and graphic novels as not only an appropriate, but a widely accessible medium for representing history, war, and atrocity.[9] Perhaps the success of *MAUS* unlocked the potential of broader audiences for *The 'Nam.*

The 'Nam, a new war title, arrived on newstands and in comic book shops during Marvel Comics' 25th anniversary. The title was written in the vernacular one might hear from a Vietnam veteran, and it served as a signpost for the authenticity series readers could expect. *The 'Nam* (1986-1993) follows the 23rd Infantry and boasts a reputation as a veteran-created, reality-based comic. Initially envisioned as a twelve-issue, year-long series, the comic primarily follows draftee Private First Class (PFC) Edward Marks's tour of duty with the 23rd infantry in Vietnam through the first thirteen issues. The eventual seven-year lifespan of the series intended to parallel the historical period between 1966 and 1972.[10]

Vietnam dominated the cultural imagination in the 1980s, and many veterans found broad and diverse audiences receptive to their stories. *The 'Nam* provided an important cultural outlet for these stories, which now included children, the primary consumer of comic books. Although there were several changes in artists and writers throughout the series, Vietnam War veterans Larry Hama and Doug Murray created the comic and remained with the project for its duration. Murray believed the series would be short-lived, lasting for twelve issues— that one tour of duty; however, it sold quite well.[11] In fact, the first issue outsold the popular *X-Men* comic the month it came out. [12] Moreover, *The 'Nam* was nominated for the Best New Series category of the 1987 Jack Kirby Awards.[13]

Despite the seemingly positive response, reception to the series was mixed and remained so throughout its run. Vietnam veteran and author William Broyles, Jr. praised the "gritty reality" of the comics, whereas Jan Scruggs, founder of the Vietnam Veterans Memorial Fund, criticized it for trivializing the war.[14] The very first readers' letters in issue number three reflect this discussion. There is no shortage of praise for *The 'Nam*, particularly in comparision with other war comics. One reader states that when compared to war comics set during World War II, such as *Sgt. Rock* or *Sgt. Fury*, *The 'Nam* avoids "simplistic combat action and one demensional characters who exist only to blow the enemy away."[15] There are many similar assessments from readers, especially in the early issues.

Although the comic was popular in its early years, little has been written about the series. There are a few news pieces about *The 'Nam* from 1986 and some interviews published on online comic websites, but the only scholarly text to mention the series is *Cord Scott's Comics and Conflict: Patriotism and Propaganda from WWII through Operation Iraqi Freedom (2014).*[16] Due to the lack of scholarly attention, in addition to debates about the genre and the series, readers are left with questions about how *The 'Nam* represents the war in history and memory. Does the very genre trivialize the war? Is it historically accurate? Does it have a political message? Is it revisionist history? The comic series does not simpy portray the war as a quagmire, but rather endeavors to fulfill an educational mission of authenticity. Moreover, the letters from readers provide insight into cultural attitudes toward the war in the 1980s and 1990s. As might be expected with any attempt to represent the pyschic aftereffects of violence, however, the series does not maintain an apolitical position.

The creators aimed for historical reality insofar as the series attempts to follow the historical movements and moments of the 23rd Infantry in Vietnam between 1966 and 1972. As they noted on the last page of issue number one, "every action, every firefight is based on fact."[17] In addition, the series takes on a broad range of representations of the war, which include, but are not limited to the use of white phosphorus, incursions into Cambodia, prisoners of war (POWs) on both sides, love interests, racial tension among American military personnel, an occasional homefront scene or issue, the anti-war movement, and representations of Vietnamese allies, civilians, and foes. For example, the series' depiction of female nurses mirrors the complexity of women's involvement in the war as they appear as love interests, friends, and mediators between the wounded and brisk doctors.[18] Likewise, the series illustrates major events such as the attack on the American embassy in Saigon during the TET Offensive, minor moments such as singer Chris Noel's United Service Organizations (USO) show in Vietnam, and the various complexities of the war.

This conglomeration of experiences creates a collected cultural memory. "Collected" memory is distinct from "collective" memory. In *Texture of Memory* (1993), James Young explains, "collective memory" signifies cohesion, whereas "collected memory" suggests the contentious nature of cultural memory.[19] The use of the term arises from the insufficiencies of the phrase "cultural memory" in that memories of the war do not always coincide with the predominant thoughts of society. Thus, the combination of "collective" and "cultural" results in a collected cultural memory. The terminology also imports the cultural emphasis of collected memory found in Marita Sturken's theory of cultural memory as shared outside formal historical discourse and situated among culturally mediated negotiations, such as textual and visual narratives.[20] Most importantly, a collected cultural memory is a culturally mediated gathering of contradictory memories, which reject unification of memory. However, privileging "collected," as opposed to "collective" cultural memory does not preclude political leanings or revisionist history.

The 'Nam appeared after the dedication of the national Vietnam Veterans Memorial (1982), after *First Blood* (1985), and during the Gulf War (1990-1991). Because the series ran from the late 1980s through the early 1990s, that specific cultural context informs the memory of the war, which the comic storyline depicts, while the letters from audience members demonstrate the cultural attitudes of the era. The comic contained an "Incoming" section at the end of each issue containing readers' responses. Written by a demographically varied audience, they included letters from contemporary military personnel, Vietnam veterans, and people closely associated with veterans. While there are letters written by both male and female teens, there do not seem to be any by children as one might find in other comics. The cultural commentary in the "Incoming" section of each issue provides insight into audience attitudes toward the war, toward its representation in the comic, and the broader collected cultural memory of it during the 1980s and 1990s.

In the 1980s, healing became synonymous with revising memories of the war. The desire for recuperation became a sought after "cure" for the "Vietnam Syndrome," a misnomer President Reagan coined to categorize anti-war sentiments as an illness in need of a treatment, and has come to define the national post-war wariness of military intervention in the developing world.[21] Indeed, the president attempted to provide a "cure" in his 1980 Veterans of Foreign Wars convention campaign speech wherein he claimed that "for too long, we have lived with the 'Vietnam Syndrome'... [claiming the war] was, in truth, a noble cause... [and] we dishonor the [memory of the dead] when we give way to feelings of guilt as if we were doing something shameful."[22]

In the post-Cold War era of the 1990s, Americans could seemingly relegate Reagan's "Vietnam Syndrome" to the past. Yet, media representations and popular responses to the Gulf War (1990-1991) conveyed sentiments of victory and the virtue and exceptionalism of American military operations to its citizenry. This also gave President George H.W. Bush an opportunity to announce in 1991 that America had "finally kicked the Vietnam Syndrome." [23] Several scholars have addressed the Persian Gulf War's influence on American memory of the war in Vietnam. Pease and Kaplan's *Cultures of U.S. Imperialism* (1993), for example, include essays that contrast the Gulf War with the American War in Vietnam, often emphasizing the Persian Gulf War's role in "finally kick[ing] the Vietnam Syndrome."[24] As literary scholar Lynda Boose aptly noted, the Persian Gulf War produced "the parades, the cheers, the public excitement over military hardware, and... a revivified militarism."[25] Moreover, memories of World War II and its attendant victory dominated the American cultural imagination during and after the 50th anniversary celebration of it. Such transformation in cultural attitudes influenced audience responses to *The 'Nam*, both in the letters and in the eventual decline in sales.

Not only does *The 'Nam* boast a reputation as a veteran created, historically based comic, its narrative is also set in real-time— when thirty days passed for a reader (the span of one issue), thirty days also passed for the characters. As noted at the end of issue number one, the original plan was to "rotate" the characters back to the states after one year, or twelve issues, to parallel a tour of duty for a grunt drafted into the war.[26] At the suggestion of one reader, Murray and team added a note about the month and year, and often the location, for each issue.[27] Their commitment to a time-based reality comic quietly diminished without comment, however, as the series progressed and the aformentioned dates eventually disappeared.

The real-time structure of each issue and the series as a whole is significant due to its rarity. Murray explained his intentions behind the real-time setup by saying he did not want to anthologize the war or the series. He explained that when he served in Vietnam, the "short-time concept" made a lasting impression because "everybody had a calendar that kept track of how long they had to go in-country."[28] His conceptualization for the series reflected that reality: "the characters would arrive in Vietnam and a certain number of issues later would go home."[29] He argues that in a traditional comic book format, "there's no correspondence in time," noting, "It becomes far too easy to do six months on the Tet Offensive."[30] He did not want to create "six issues on the same incident that actually took place in a day or so."[31] Instead, he "wanted to make it snappier and maybe more accessible to readers where [they] could pick up a book and each book was essentially a separate story."[32] Of course, the cast of characters would also change when their tours of duty ended and they returned to the United States.

Ed Marks, the main character of the first thirteen issues, experiences this short-term concept, and his character provides the typical "innocence-to-experience" war narrative. In issue number one, before Ed arrives in-country, he and the readers experience the hustle of drill sergeants, vaccinations, general issue, and other matters related to boot camp and training.[33] Readers ride along with Ed during his flight to Vietnam and witness the chaos of landing under fire. Once Ed is assigned, he, and always the readers, meet the other main characters who often introduce themselves based on that perpetual calendar to which Doug Murray had referred. Furthermore, Mike, a soon to be popular character, guides Ed through his initial "green" weeks. For example, he helps Ed adjust to the M-16 rifle and shows him what a booby trap looks like. While reflecting on the military training issues of the era, namely training with one rifle (M-14), only to arrive in country and having to adjust to another (M-16), *The 'Nam* joined in on the long-held criticism of the weapon.[34] Mike says of the M-16, "you can tell it's Mattel. It's swell."[35] The weapon was infamous for being ill-suited to the jungle climate and for jamming in high-pressure situations. *The 'Nam*'s representation of issues with training and weaponry did not simply depict historical reality, it also participated in propagating memories of the war engaged with popular arguments of the 1980s; arguments claiming "the United States could have won the war if..." These stipulations and qualifications demonstrate a cultural memory that continued to struggle with the historical reality that the technologically superior United States military did, indeed, lose a war to an agrarian society, albeit one that received substantial material support from China and the Soivet Union. Thus, audiences are likely left believing the United States could have won the war, *if only*. However, Ed's experiences are not limited to the context of the Vietnam War, but also represent the experience of fighting in war more broadly. He is overwhelmed during his first firefight and experiences difficulty firing his weapon, like many soldiers throughout the twentieth century.[36]

As the series progressed, so too did Ed's education in Vietnam. He discovers the dangers of tunnel complexes, snipers, and weak armor on Armored Personnel Carriers. Ed also begins to understand the seedy underworld of Saigon prostitutes, the black market, tensions among ranks, bribery, corruption, and the death of those close to him. The once innocent Ed is now seasoned and, upon his return home in issue number thirteen, becomes disillusioned. He is surprised by the lack of a homecoming at the airport and shocked by the anti-war movement's presence.[37] Ed's homecoming reflects the cultural memory of veterans' treatment upon their return home from Vietnam. Numerous studies, particularly in the 1980s explored this issue, and their titles are often telling: *No Victory Parades, Strangers at Home, Long Time Passing: Vietnam and the Haunted Generation, Walking Wounded, Discarded Army Veterans After Vietnam.*[38] The image of the Vietnam veteran as victim took hold. For example, David E. Bodnar's edited collection *The Vietnam Veteran: A History of Neglect* (1984) accuses the media, various presidents, and Congress of failing to help Vietnam veterans adjust to civilian life.[39] The war is known for the quick transition between the warzone and the homefront: two extremes of the human experience divided only by a flight from Vietnam to California. Ed's homecoming experiences are fairly typical; either he, or his former friends, had changed too much to reconnect or he is staggered by the media coverage of the war stressing the negative consequences.[40] Nonetheless, Ed, who is still in the service, finds his purpose in training new troops to help them prepare for the war.[41]

Ed's character serves as just the beginning of the comics' educational undertaking. In the first few issues, the instructive enterprise is clear to contemporary readers, especially those aware of the trope of the audience learning alongside a main character. For example, in issue number one, when Ed Marks learns how to blast a landing zone (LZ) for a helicopter, so too does the audience.[42] In a later issue, near the end of Ed's tour of duty, he becomes the educator, this time for civilians on the homefront. He writes home to his parents and gallingly explains every moment of slang or jargon to his mother in the letter, even if he just explained it a few sentences earlier. For example, he writes "we have to move right into our LZ's (that's Landing Zones, Mom)" and two lines further down in the letter he again defines LZ, followed by "remember, Mom?"[43] This letter speaks to the division, particularly along gender lines, between civilians on the homefront and military personnel serving in combat zones.

In several later issues, the educational undertaking becomes clear once again when the editors include a page of informational and historical context outside of the story. These included, but were not limited to the Ho Chi Minh Trail, Airmobile, and Long-Range Reconnaissance Patrol (LRRPs). Often, the tone of these pages emphasized setting the story right. For example, in issue number sixty, the page about the Ho Chi Minh Trail claimed, "during the war, most Americans' conception of the [Trail]... was that of a broad highway carrying tucks and followed by columns of marching troops. Nothing could have been further from the truth." It seems doubtful that something dubbed a "trail" was misperceived as a highway; however, considering the masses of North Vietnamese troops and equipment transported through the country on this "trail," audiences may be confused about how American firepower could not stop or significantly stymie the flow. Because the Ho Chi Minh trail varied from a footpath weaving through mountains and over rock formations to a dirt road that traversed through neighboring Cambodia; it was difficult to locate and disable, unlike an American "highway." These examples demonstrate concern about the memories of the war, particularly those held by the post-Vietnam war generation. Although the mantra of the series was couched in the daily lives of American foot soldiers, it seems *The 'Nam* team also wanted their audience to gain a broader feel of the war.

Though the series was considered a reality-based comic, some reality is missing due to it being a Comics Code-approved series. This is addressed at the end of issue number one. Murray acknowledges that they "had to make some compromises. The real language used by soldiers in the field can be quite raw. The most common appellation for a new troop was not 'greenie.' The word itself was printable, but the explanation gets a bit touchy."[44] The comic is, after all, as the very first line of this endnote indicates, "as close to the real thing as [they could] get– in a newsstand comic bearing the Comics Code seal."[45] Clearly, the swearing and slang are sanitized in the series, and often humorously. "CRIPES" seems to be a favorite and in issue number five, "pound those suckers" stands in for more explicit language.[46] Yet in the same issues, there are self-reflexive, humorous moments wherein a soldier calls the main character, Ed Marks, an "altar boy" for his language being "almost a curse" when he uses "cripes."[47] Not only are the writers having a little fun here, they are creating a subtle acknowledgement that soldiers in Vietnam were no longer innocent.

Further still, in issue five, a letter Murray recieves and his response to it debates the choice of language and adherence to the code. One writer accuses him of taking the language censorship so far that it "detract[s] from the realism."[48] In his response, Murray notes the series is "meant as a sort of primer on the Vietnam War to anyone who will read it. This includes the kids" and that he does not believe they have "compromised too much" in order to reach this younger audience.[49] Even though the comics code restricted some reality, with both audience accessibility and authenticity in mind, there is a glossary in the back of each issue that typically lists definitions of acronyms and slang in the issue. The glossary makes a significant effort to educate readers while maintaining historical accuracy and authenticity.

Maintaining this commitment to realism, one of the main characters, Mike Albergo, is killed as early as issue number nine. Murray noted this character was based on "Mike Vergo ...a real person... a friend of [Murray's] brother," [50] Not only was Mike a primary character starting with the first issue, he took the main character, Ed Marks, and thus the readers, under his wing. Mike was a friendly, likable character and Murray believed his death might impart some of the impact of actual American deaths during the war. Murray said, "everybody was in equal danger" and that "there was no warning when someone was killed... which is why so many people didn't form friendships or the ones that did had real problems."[51] He admits that Mike's death had no relevance to the story line, but that "it just happened" as death does in war and in life. As evidenced in letters following Mike's death, it had the intended impact on a sorrowful and shocked audience.[52] For example, readers asked how they could kill Mike, accused the team of being "cruel," and shared how difficult it was "to say goodbye" to Mike after "knowing" him for nearly a year.[53] Murray's response to these letters is more developed than his reflection on Mike's death in the interview. He wrote, "we got dozens of letters talking about the death of Mike and how readers felt... in real war, men died just like Mike did– suddenly, unexpectedly, tragically. It always had other effects as well, on the friends of those who died."[54] Reminding readers not just of the realism mission of the series, Murray carefully notes that if readers responded this way, we might imagine the greater impact an actual death in war would have.

Realism certainly stands at the center of these "Incoming" letters published at the back of each issue. Reality, facts, and the comics code create a sustained debate in the letters through the entire first year (twelve issues) of the series and never seem to disappear throughout the years and over eighty issues. For example, many letter writers request Murray and team write outside the comics code to maintain the highest level of realism. Each time Murray responds with his need to reach the largest possible audience. He continually defends this choice as a minor sacrifice of language in exchange for this broader audience and the likelihood that the series would continue. Murray always answered these criticisms with an emphasis on audience. In an interview, he was asked about the importance of younger audience members having access to the series. He responded by noting many veterans including himself, "were uncomfortable talking about experiences... Especially people who were parents, they didn't talk about it to their kids."[55] He further clarifies, "working outside the code... would have denied [him] a substantial audience that [he] really wanted to get to."[56]

Some letters, seemingly hand-picked, even testify to *The 'Nam* fostering bonding experiences between the younger generation and their Vietnam veteran relatives, whether they be a brother, father, or uncle. There are many letters written by children of Vietnam veterans, and some written by veteran fathers. One letter written by a Vietnam veteran in issue number eleven thanks *The 'Nam* team for the comic. As he explains, he was "a Vietnam casualty, not physically, but mentally" and that he hopes his "twelve-year-old son who, through reading THE NAM (sic) can possibly begin to understand what his dad went through."[57] Murray is clearly touched by this letter. He writes, "When we here read that some of our readers are helped or brought together by our comic, it really makes the work worthwhile."[58] The educational efforts of the series intersect with inter-generational memory and understanding.

Of course, not all letters are positive and even the critical letters seem specifically chosen for their negative assessments. Murray responds to some critical letters by citing others from younger readers who say they would have never learned about the war if it were not for *The 'Nam*. Repeatedly, these readers stress that now they "understand." It is disconcerting that the next generation would now believe they understand the war based solely on the representations provided in the comic. This is likely the root of debate over the realism of the series. If comics portray a sanitized version of the war, what memories of the war will these readers hold? Still, the comic breaks the silence many maintained about the war. One young reader wrote, the series "tells [him] what adults won't."[59] Additionally, other readers defend the choice to reach this larger, younger, audience noting their Vietnam veteran fathers like the series or that Vietnam veteran they have spoken with about the series acknowledge similar experiences.[60] Thus, the audience also defends the authenticity of the series.

Unfortunately, the comics code stymied depictions of the harsh realities of the war such as fragging, drug use, prostitution, and rape. This results in a limited memory of the war for a generation who may have relied solely on *The 'Nam* as a realistic depiction of the war. Murray and Hama certainly received no shortage of criticism about depicting the war within the comics code constraints. The disapproval becomes more stringent in issue number eleven when one letter writer who is "disgusted by" the series claims *The 'Nam* "promises realism and delivers fluff."[61] This reader, however, is not referencing the language sanitation but the content, specifically the censorship of rape, drug use, and fragging. This was in 1987 and Murray continued to defend adherence to the code and to defend their choice to portray the ordinary day-in-the-life of the average foot soldier. Considering that their younger readers had most likely also encountered the numerous films about the war that emphasized these bitter realities, their exposure to a variety of mediated representations of the war would help foster a collected, rather than collective– or unified – memory of the war.

Once the authenticity of experience is attacked, however, Murray's response to criticism about the code and the content of the series shifts. In issue number fifty-nine in 1991, a Vietnam veteran, Vince Lacouzze, sent in a long letter criticizing an unnamed issue he read for "being written as if somebody who wrote it really wasn't there and just gave the story a glossing over."[62] To any reader aware of stolen valor controversies and authenticity of experience debates, this letter would be considered quite fierce. Taking them to task further, Lacouzze accused Murray of "cop[ing] out" when he previously responded to this concern by saying "fragging was not an everyday occurrence" in response to a letter in issue number eleven.[63] Relying on his own authenticity of experience as a veteran who served in the 101st Airborne Division in 1968, Lacouzze writes about atrocities he witnessed in Vietnam, including rape, drug use, and fragging.[64]

Murray takes on a distinctly different tone in his response to this letter compared with his repeated defense of staying within the code to reach the broadest possible audience. He admits to being stymied by the code. For example, he writes "we are forced to [portray the war] within the confines of the comics code authority, which... can be somewhat limiting, to say the least."[65] Murray and his team fully acknowledge the difficulty of portraying the war within the code. The response further explains that the series "portray[ed] a fragging" in issue number six.[66] However, they only depicted an attempted fragging, not the actuality, and not a death. Still, Murray continued, when they later attempted to include a fragging "it was decided at the last minute" that the scene would be cut because it was not "appropriate at the time to the story."[67] Consider the passive tone here, "it was decided," with no mention of who made the decision. Years later, Murray shares his frustration about writing within the comics code in an interview. He explained the effort to portray a fragging was cut because the officer was black and the subordinate attacker was white.[68] He said, "In fact, they cut page twenty-two out of a book that had already gone to the printer to prevent it, even though it made the story make no sense."[69] Obviously, the comics code held greater sway over the content of the series than Murray alluded to in his responses to reader's letters.

While the series does not overtly represent such moments, there are hints of fragging, prostitution, and drug use in the series. As early as issue number three, Ed Marks and the readers encounter prostitutes while on R&R in Saigon. One of the prostitutes drugs Marks and it seems she is about to steal from him and possibly even hurt or kill him, but his comrades saved him just before she has the opportunity. While this is likely an attempt to depict the difficulty of determining the enemy among civilians, young readers also encounter a sexualized enemy that could further propagate the misogyny of the war.[70]

There are certainly instances of grisly violence in the series, but these are typically reserved for the images, thus requiring a close-reading to perceive. In issue number twelve, a helicopter lands directly on a villager who was not able to move out of the way in time.[71] There is no mention of this in the dialogue or text; instead, the savvy reader must notice the gruesome violence of the moment. Despite letters praising movies such as Oliver Stone's *Platoon* (1986) depicting atrocities, while accusing *The 'Nam* of ignoring them, the series does not ignore the horrors of war. While the comic may rarely explicitly address such issues, they are often apparent to the reader of images. It is, after all, a comic book, and visuals convey far more than text in this genre. Consider, for example, silent comic book series such as the nearly silent *Owly* or the famous, yet unintentionally, silent issue of *G.I. Joe*: *Real American Hero* issue number twenty-one (1984). *G.I. Joe* released another silent comic years later in issue number 214, a memorial service for one of the main characters, Snake Eyes, is depicted.[72]

Continuous debate about the realism of the comic erupted in many letters comparing *The 'Nam* to movies, particularly Oliver Stone's *Platoon* (1986). A letter in issue number eleven by the reader who was "disgusted" by *The 'Nam's* "fluff" previously addressed, makes his argument about the comic in relation to *Platoon* and the television mini-series *A Rumor of War* (1980) based on Philip Caputo's 1977 memoir by the same name.[73] Murray responds to this letter, comparisons with *Platoon*, and the film more generally by writing that many other readers who mentioned the film in their letters did not arrive at "the same conclusions."[74] Sharing his assessment of the film, Murray writes,

> [the film] is a very realistic looking movie; however, it is *not* a totally realistic portrayal of the Vietnam War! Fraggings, rape, destruction of villages, all of the stuff the TV and newspaper reporters made such a big thing out of were not, I repeat, *not* the everyday affairs of life in the Vietnam war (sic). Atrocities did happen, officers and NCOs were fragged, but this was the exception, not the rule. Reality may not be as exciting and titillating as entertainment— but it does exist.[75]

Murray is frustrated by the comparisons to other mediums of entertainment, and to *Platoon* in particular. Yet, there is a serious reveal in this response, one that indicates his political leanings as he essentially accuses the so-called liberal media of following the old, "if it bleeds, it leads" stereotype. Indeed, Murray did not attempt to mask his politics in interviews. For example, in one interview, he voiced one of his concerns "about the comic industry these days, and even the *Buyer's Guide* being very skewed towards a liberal view of the world, which [he's] not convinced is the right view."[76]

Still, Murray is not alone in his critique of *Platoon* or other movies of the period. Between 1986 and 1988, there was an ironically cartoonish abundance of Vietnam films inspired by the popularity of the *Rambo* and the *Missing in Action* series of films, in addition to the successes of *Platoon* and *Full Metal Jacket.*[77] This was also the year of *Hamburger Hill, Good Morning Vietnam,* and *Hanoi Hilton.*[78] As Jack Hunter notes in his book *Search and Destroy,* the number of *First Blood* (1982) and *Rambo: First Blood II* (1985) imitations alone were overwhelming with *Strike Commando, Strike Commando II, Double Target* and *Angel Hill: Ultimate Mission* all of which were released between 1986 and 1988.[79] The comics code restrictions on *The 'Nam* and the very genre itself may seem childish to some readers, particularly today, considering twenty-first century digital advancements, printing, and paper quality; yet the irony is that the comic series is far more realistic than the miasma of juvenile films about the war in the 1980s.

Murray's concern about media bias also provides insight into the entanglement in the series concerning historical reality and authenticity of experience. Hama and Murray said they wanted to circumvent politics and focus on the war from the average foot soldier's point of view. Murray believed the comic was "a pretty accurate view of the way the average soldier looked at the war. It was outside ordinary experience. The world was elsewhere."[80] Asserting such authenticity of experience can have a profound influence on audiences who might believe that the comic must truly portray the war as it happened. This could, thereby, mislead them into believing there is an *absolute* truth in war and in representations of war. Indeed, as the subtitle of Ken Burns and Lynn Novick's documentary, *The Vietnam War* (2017), notes "there is no single truth in war."[81] Unfortunately, critics of *The 'Nam* have since propagated this authenticity of experience argument.[82] For example David Brothers, a Series Editor for Image Comics, claims *The 'Nam* makes "no grand political statements," but rather focuses on "real" stories "based on [veterans'] accounts."[83] Thus, Brothers tries to reassure his audience that there is an authenticity of experience inherent in *The 'Nam* series that makes it distinct from the "John Rambos with guns blazing." [84] Instead, Brothers claims the series is about "a lot of scared kids."[85]

However, the political leanings of the series become apparent considering the prisoner of war issues— number sixteen, fifty-nine, and sixty. In an interview about this matter, Murray was asked if he still thought there were American POWs in Vietnam as he indicated in one letter. His answer was yes. He further commented that he believes "the government wrote them off years ago because they're politically embarrassing... because they force people to look at the fact that this war never really ended and that we gave up these people."[86] Murray's commentary, however, is not historically accurate.

The Prisoners Of War/Missing In Action controversy began before the war even ended under the Nixon administration. It served as a means of uniting a country divided by the war, wherein both those who supported the war and those who called for a swift end to the war could come together to honor and remember those who were taken prisioner or missing.[87] This effort literally materialized in the POW/MIA bracelettes.[88] Further still, with the signing of the Paris Peace agreements in 1973, many Americans believed the high number of military personnel missing in action, must horridly, and actually be prisoners of war.[89] These beliefs held great sway over the American imagination during the 1980s only to be reinforced by the popular rescue-return films of the decade. Attempts to debunk myths over the POW/MIA debate have yet to take hold among many Americans, despite studies such as Bruce H. Franklin's *MIA: Mythmaking in America* (1992) and Michael J. Allen's *Until the Last Man Comes Home: POWs, MIAs, and the Unending Vietnam War* (2009).[90] Yes, the second study was published after Murray's 2001 interview, but his contributions to American cultural memory of The POW/MIA mythology and disagreement continued to be a source of contention. This was especially true among veterans and their families, who were concerned by normalizing relations with Vietnam in the 1990s. This was particularly the case during President Bill Clinton's administration, who himself was accused of being a draft-dodger via his graduate studies in England.[91]

Before normalization of relations, the Persian Gulf War influenced attitudes toward the Vietnam War. During the build-up, course, and aftermath of that conflict, readers of *The 'Nam* might have expected to see "Incoming" letters from military personnel serving in the Gulf War, and later, veterans of that war writing in. It was, after all, a brief conflict with a clear mission. Moreover, as then President George H.W. Bush claimed at the time, this conflict would not be "another Vietnam" and that indeed, the United States had now "kicked" the so-called Vietnam Syndrome.[92] Likely due to these factors, the Persian Gulf War only made a small impact on *The 'Nam*. Throughout the series, the letters frequently provide a lens through which readers today can view how readers remembered the Vietnam War then, within the cultural context of the Cold War and the Persian Gulf War. That being said, explicit connections to the

Persian Gulf War are limited. Issue number fifty-one (December 1990) includes an innocuous letter from a Marine stationed in Saudi Arabia who describes the weather, shares hopes that he will soon return home, and invites other readers to write him.[93]

A more interesting letter in issue number fifty-five (April 1991) provides some insight into cultural attitudes toward the contrast between the Vietnam War and the Persian Gulf War. One young man noted the shift in respect for military personnel and attributes it to the Persian Gulf War and the slew of representations of the Vietnam War, including *The 'Nam.*[94] He explains that his "parents think... people out there want to make up for the shame of the Vietnam veterans' homecoming."[95] Embracing the American support of the military, he notes that *The 'Nam* "is a part of this effort... and should be proud."[96] There are a few such moments wherein readers will praise the series for what sounds like propaganda or revisionism while being seemingly unaware that this is what they are doing. These moments may provide insight into how the series influences memories the war for the post-Vietnam War generation. The letters certainly reflect a collected conglomeration of cultural memories. Responding to the Persian Gulf War in this same issue, *The 'Nam* team provided a promotional "Subs for Soldiers," a 50 percent discount for anyone willing to purchase a subscription of *The 'Nam* for military personnel participating in Operation Desert Storm.[97] While they sought a potential burgeoning audience among military personnel serving in war, this call did not appear in earlier issues. The United States military was still in the Middle East, but the offer appeared too late (April 1991) as the war had already been "won."

During the Persian Gulf War, the sales of the series declined. Several issues during the time reflect this in their lack of letters. Issues fifty, fifty-two, and fifty-six through fifty-eight contain no letters from readers. Instead, the issues included promotional material for future issues, something that did not exist in the early years. This later promotion typically consisted of a brief synopsis of the upcoming story, an image of the cover, and a panel or two from the issue. They further shifted these promotions from black-and-white to color for a greater impact. Readership and engagement with the series must have declined quite seriously, because the editors started asking for letters. In issue number fifty-two (an issue without letters but with promotional materials for the next two issues) they wrote that they "expect that the current Punisher two-issue crossover will inspire a torrent— nay, a flood" of letters.[98] In addition to promoting a new writer for the series, the editors nearly pled for letters, writing, "Now, even more than ever, [they] want to hear [readers'] feedback! Hate us, love us, but write us!" As discussed previously, hate mail they did, indeed, receive.[99]

Yet this seeming desperation is quite mild compared to the "Gun Shots" they encouraged and requested in subsequent issues. In issue number sixty, one letter-writer sent in a photo of himself holding two different handguns to demonstrate that they do look distinct from one another.[100] Accuracy debates appear in many issues throughout the series. However, these are the only photographs to appear in the entire series. Not only would it be striking for that very fact, but of course because they are of a serious looking man holding a gun. If that was not enough, *The 'Nam* team actually responded to the photographs by encouraging other readers to send in their own so-called "Gun Shots."[101] The first time they call for these in this very same issue, readers might have thought it sarcastic or humorous when they wrote "If you've got your own 'family portraits' of yourself and your favorite small arms (or heavy ordinance, tanks, helicopters, battleships, etc.) [they would] love to see them. If [they] get enough responses, a 'Gun Shots' photo gallery might become a regular feature."[102] The editors' call for "heavy ordnance" and "family portraits'" seems excessive and thereby amusing. They remind readers of this request in the following issue, number sixty-one, noting they would "be glad to print them." Considering the likely audience of Vietnam veterans, military personnel, and people interested in military history, the debate over photographs of a gun are not that surprising. Likely, the team was attempting to curry favor and audience members from the National

Rifle Association set (NRA), a demographic likely to overlap with those who believed there were still American POWs in Vietnam. Despite a focus on potential audience, however, this request that equates firearms with family members is excessive, particularly considering Murray's early responses about young audience members in relation to the comics code.

The 'Nam team employed promotional techniques on their covers around this time as well. The covers started to include tantalizing text in an attempt to hook potential readers. For example, issue number forty-seven depicts two American soldiers, one black and one white, in a physical fight while they are surrounded by a circle of enemy guns. The text on the cover reads "Can they kill each other before the N.V.A does?"[103] To emphasize the drama and excitement, the cover and story not only includes racial violence among American soldiers, but also promises potential death, a certain battle, and perhaps even a prisoner of war scenario. Another such example is the cover of issue number fifty-nine illustrating a massive explosion at the top of the page and a pilot dropping from the sky just before his parachute opens. In case readers did not know, the text on the cover informs them, "You are now entering North Vietnam."[104] The use of the pronoun "you" signifies an experiential reading adventure. Readers will learn about North Vietnam along with the character who is taken prisoner. As they responded to waning sales, the series began to portray the Vietnam War as one of drama and action. Certainly, these representations would influence audience members to form memories of the war and of the day-to-day life of the average foot soldier according to Murray's own definition. Such memories would not be historically accurate.

Diminishing sales finally compelled Marvel to place the then-popular character the Punisher in several guest appearances in *The 'Nam* during the early 1990s. The Punisher "Invades *The 'Nam*" as the covers indicate, in issue number fifty-two and fifty-three. The Punisher certainly did "invade" Vietnam with his impressive sharpshooter skills and swaggeringly rough persona, going so far as to call an enemy sniper a "monkey" at the very end of issue number fifty-three.[105] The "Punisher Invades *The 'Nam*" story arc is not entirely suprising. He is, afterall, Sergant Frank Castle, who served in the Vietnam War. Like many comic book characters, the Punisher is a military veteran. While his origin story is not seated in the war, but in the death of his family after the war, many comic book characters do find their origins in war.[106] For instance, not only did Captain America essentialy win World War II, the war gives birth to his character and his super-human strength. Morover, crossovers are common for the Punisher who appears in comics ranging from *Spiderman* and *Batman* (D.C. comic franchise) to *The Hulk* and *Daredevil.* He even makes an appearance in Riverdale, when "Archie Meets the Punisher," (1994). He saves Archie and friends from "Red," an infamous drug dealer.[107] Moreover, the Punisher is currently on American television, though now he is protrayed as an Iraq War veteran.[108]

Attempts to resurrect *The 'Nam* after the Punisher's visit included the promotional techniques previously discussed; namely, the five-part story arc, "The Death of Joe Hallan," wherein one of the main characters dies a psychological death, much to the chagrin of several readers as evidenced by subsequent letters. These promotional efforts failed and the Punisher made yet another invasion into *The 'Nam* in issues sixty-seven through sixty-nine. The series ended before the story was complete, but a conclusion appeared in a special edition entitled *The Punisher in The 'Nam: Final Invasion.*[109]

It is difficult to precisely determine why *The 'Nam* series ultimately failed. A conglomeration of forces likely contributed to the decline in readership. Children who grew up pretending to be Rambo while inundated by G.I. Joe in cartoons, in public service announcements, and in the comics, were in high school or beyond by this time. The Cold War was over, the United States "won" the Persian Gulf War and "kicked the Vietnam syndrome." Movies about the Vietnam War also significantly declined at the time and were replaced by the generational *Forrest Gump* and Disney's family-friendly *Dumbo Drop.*[110] The American public seemed far more interested in World War II or in simply forgetting the Vietnam War altogether.

Comics code restrictions may have limited some realism; however, *The 'Nam* certainly did not trivialize the war. Within the code, the series portrays corruption in the US military, sudden death in war, racial tensions, and violence. With few exceptions, the series maintained its mission of historical accuracy. Unfortunately, these moments when the *The 'Nam* deviates from its own standard of authentic experience and historical reality also reveals occasionally biased political messages that the series promulgates. The series is not apolitical. Moreover, readers' letters provide insight into the debates about the war, which endured throughout the 1980s and 1990s. They reveal cultural attitudes that sought the certainty of accuracy and authenticity. It seems audience members were grasping for certitudes in their memories and attitudes toward the war that were difficult to solidify in the face of such a complex conflict. Even so, *The 'Nam* fulfilled an educational undertaking for its younger audience members— often children of Vietnam veterans. This, in turn, helped to bridge gaps between military personnel, their families, and civilians interested in grasping this period of American history.

NOTES

1. Stanley Kubrick, Director, *Full Metal Jacket* (1987).
2. Ted Kotcheff, Director, *Rambo First Blood* (1982) and Joseph Zito, Director, *Missing in Action* (1984).
3. Susan Jeffords, *The Remasculinization of America: Gender and the Vietnam War* (Bloomington: Indiana University Press, 1989).
4. See Rick Berg and John Carlos Rowe, *The Vietnam War and American Culture* (New York: Columbia University Press, 1991), Jeffery Walsh and James Aulich, *Vietnam Images: War and Representation* (London: Macmillan, 1989), and Fred Turner, *Echoes of Combat* (New York: Anchor/Doubleday, 1996).
5. Doug Murray and Larry Hama, et al., *The 'Nam*, Issues 1-84, (New York: Marvel Comics, 1986-1993).
6. Murray, *The 'Nam,* issue 6.
7. Art Spielman, *Maus: A Survivor's Tale.* (New York: Pantheon Books, 1986).
8. Stephen Weiner, *Faster than a Speeding Bullet: The Rise of the Graphic Novel* (Broomfield, CO: NBM Publishing, 2003).
9. Joseph Witek, *Comic Books as History: The Narrative Art of Jack Jackson, Art Spiegelman, and Harvey Pekar* (Jackson: University Press of Mississippi, 1989).
10. Doug Murray, *The 'Nam,* issue 1.
11. "*The 'Nam,*" comicvine. https://comicvine.gamespot.com/the-nam/4050-19757/25 February 2017. Accessed on June 9, 2017.
12. "*The 'Nam,*" comicvine.
13. Ibid.
14. Paula Span, "Vietnam: The Comic Book War," *The Washington Post,* September 10, 1986.
15. Murray, *The 'Nam,* issue 3.
16. Cord Scott, *Comics and Conflict: Patriotism and Propaganda from WWII through Operation Iraqi Freedom* (Annapolis, MD: Naval Institute Press, 2014).
17. Murray, *The 'Nam,* issue 1.
18. See, for example, Murray, *The 'Nam,* issue 21. For more about the roles of American servicewomen see Heather M. Stur, *Beyond Combat: Women*

and Gender in the Vietnam War Era(New York: Cambridge University Press, 2011).

19. James E. Young, *The Texture of Memory: Holocaust Memorials and Meaning* (New Haven: Yale University Press, 1993), xi–xii.
20. Marita Sturken, *Tangled Memories: The Vietnam War, The AIDS Epidemic and the Politics of Remembering* (Oakland, CA: University of California Press, 1997).
21. For more about the Vietnam Syndrome, see Fred Turner, *Echoes of Combat: The Vietnam War in American Memory* (New York: Anchor/Doubleday, 1996) and Donald E. Pease, "Post-National Spectacles," *Cultures of United States Imperialism*, Amy Kaplan and Donald E. Pease eds. (Durham, N.C.: Duke University Press 1993), 557-80.
22. Turner, 63.
23. Ibid., 120.
24. Amy Kaplan and Donald E. Pease eds., *Cultures of United States Imperialism* (Durham, N.C.: Duke University Press 1993).
25. Lynda Boose, "Techno-Muscularity and the 'Boy Eternal' From the Quagmire to the Gulf," *Cultures of United States Imperialism,* Amy Kaplan and Donald E. Pease, eds. (Durham, N.C.: Duke University Press, 1993), 584.
26. Murray, *The 'Nam,* issue 1.
27. Murray, *The 'Nam,* issue 8.
28. *Brian Jacks,* "Interview: Doug Murray," *Slushfactory.* http://www.slushfactory.com/features/articles/052502-murray.php *May 25, 2002. Accessed on* 9 June 2017.
29. Ibid.
30. Ibid.
31. Ibid.
32. Ibid.
33. Murray, *The 'Nam,* issue 1.
34. Thomas L. McNaugher, *The M-16 Controversies: Military Organizations and Weapons Acquisitions* (Praeger Publishers, 1984) and Gordon L. Rottman, *The M16* (London: Bloomsbury Publishing, 2011).
35. Murray, *The 'Nam,* issue 1.
36. Dave Grossman, *On Killing: The Psychological Costs of Learning to Kill in War and Society* (London: Little Brown, 1996).
37. Murray, *The 'Nam,* issue 13.
38. Murray Polner, *No Victory Parades: the Return of the Vietnam Veteran* (New York: Holt, Rinehart and Winston, 1971); Charles R. Figley,

Strangers at Home: the War, the Nation and the Vietnam Veteran (New York: Praeger, 1980); Myra. MacPherson, *Long Time Passing: Vietnam and the Haunted Generation* (NewYork: Doublday, 1984); Steve Trimm, *Walking Wounded*: Men's Lives During and Since the Vietnam War (Norwood, NJ: Ablex, 1993); and Paul Starr, *Discarded Army Veterans After Vietnam: the Nadar Report on Vietnam Veterans and the Veterans Administration* (New York: Charterhouse, 1973).

39. David E. Bodnar, ed., *The Vietnam Veteran: A History of Neglect* (New York: Praeger, 1984).
40. Murray, *The 'Nam,* issue 13.
41. Ibid.
42. Murray, *The 'Nam,* issue 1.
43. Murray, *The 'Nam,* issue 12.
44. Murray, *The 'Nam,* issue 1.
45. Ibid.
46. Murray, *The 'Nam,* issue 5.
47. Ibid.
48. Ibid.
49. Ibid.
50. Jacks, "Interview: Doug Murray".
51. Ibid.
52. Ibid.
53. Murray, *The 'Nam,* issue 12.
54. Ibid.
55. Jacks, "Interview: Doug Murray".
56. Ibid.
57. Doug Murray, *The 'Nam,* issue 11.
58. Ibid.
59. Murray, *The 'Nam,* issue 7.
60. Murray, *The 'Nam,* issue 8.
61. Murray, *The 'Nam,* issue 11.
62. Dog Murray, *The 'Nam,* issue 59.
63. Ibid.
64. Ibid.
65. Ibid.
66. Ibid.
67. Ibid.
68. Jacks, "Interview: Doug Murray."
69. Ibid.

70. J. E Lawson, "'She's a Pretty Woman… for a Gook': The Misogyny of the Vietnam War," *Journal of American Culture* 12 (1989): 55–65.
71. Murray, *The 'Nam,* issue 12.
72. Mike Thaler, and David Wiesner, *Owly* (New York: Scholastic, 2000) and Larry Hama, S. L. Gallant, Ron Wagner, Gary Erskine, J. Brown, Shawn Lee, and Neil Uyetake, *G.I. Joe: A Real American* Hero. *Issue 21* (Marvel, 1984) and *Issue 214* (IDW Publishing, 2016).
73. Philip Caputo, Director, *A Rumor of War* (1995), and Philip Caputo, *A Rumor of War* (New York: Holt, Rinehart and Winston, 1977).
74. Murray, *The 'Nam,* issue 11.
75. Ibid.
76. Jacks, "Interview: Doug Murray."
77. Stanley Kubrick, Director, *Full Metal Jacket* (1987).
78. John Irvin, Director, *Hamburger Hill* (1987), Barry Levinson, Director, *Good Morning, Vietnam* (1987), and Lionel Chetwynd, Director, *The Hanoi Hilton* (1987).
79. Jack Hunter, *Search & Destroy* (London: Creation Books, 2003).
80. *Span, "Vietnam: The Comic Book War."*
81. Ken Burns and Lynn Novick, *The Vietnam War* (2017).
82. *Span, "Vietnam: The Comic Book War."*
83. David Brothers, "*The 'Nam*: A War Comic about People." Comics Alliance. http://comicsalliance.com/the-nam-a-war-comic-about-people/30 May 2011. Accessed on June 9, 2017.
84. Brothers, "*The 'Nam*: A War Comic about People."
85. Ibid.
86. Jacks, "Interview: Doug Murray."
87. Bruce H. Franklin, *M.I.A., or, Mythmaking in America* (New Brunswick: Rutgers University Press, 1993) and Michael J. Allen, *Until the Last Man Comes Home: POWs, MIAs, and the Unending Vietnam War* (Chapel Hill: UNC Press, 2009).
88. Ibid.
89. Ibid.
90. Ibid.
91. Michael S. Foley, *Confronting the War Machine: Draft Resistance During the Vietnam War* (Chapel Hill: UNC Press, 2003).
92. Fred Turner, *Echoes of Combat* (New York: Anchor/Doubleday, 1996).
93. Murray, *The 'Nam,* issue 51.
94. Murray, *The 'Nam,* issue 55.
95. Ibid.

96. Ibid.
97. Ibid.
98. Murray, *The 'Nam,* issue 52.
99. Ibid.
100. Murray, *The 'Nam,* issue 60.
101. Ibid.
102. Ibid.
103. Murray, *The 'Nam,* issue 47.
104. Murray, *The 'Nam,* issue 59.
105. Murray, *The 'Nam,* issue 53.
106. Scott, 86.
107. Batton Lash, John Buscema, and Stan Goldberg, *The Punisher Meets Archie* (Marvel, 1994).
108. Steve Lightfoot, Creator, *The Punisher* (2017).
109. Don Lomax, Alberto Saichann, and Joe Kubert, *The Punisher in The 'Nam: Final Invasion* (Marvel, 1994).
110. Robert Zemeckis, Director, *Forrest Gump* (1994), and Simon Wincer, Director, *Operation Dumbo Drop* (1995).

Claiming the Flag

Patriotism and the Nixon White House

Sarah Thelen

"Put Out More Flags," pleaded the editors in a June 1970 article in the *Evening Star*, a Washington, D.C. paper. They hoped that convincing more citizens to display the flag would prevent it from being "grossly distorted" by the political actions of both sides of the domestic debate over the Vietnam War. In their eyes, "the flag, once the emblem of national unity, is well on its way to becoming a symbol of national division." The article does not take sides. In fact, it blames both "the extremists of the New Left" and "the violent counter protesters of the far right" for "diminishing the flag."[1] White House officials, however, rejected the idea that anti-war protesters and other critics were in any way patriotic. Rather, Special Counsel to the President Charles Colson and other White House officials shared the view that not only was internal opposition diplomatically unhelpful and domestically dangerous, but that it was inherently suspect and essentially un-American. In this context, the extreme lengths to which the administration went to isolate and undermine their opponents— a story ably told elsewhere— was entirely justified and, indeed, laudable in their eyes.[2] White House officials did not set out to politicize the flag and patriotism, but their efforts to rally supporters behind Nixon's Vietnam War policies effectively framed both as symbols of unquestioning, uncritical support for the nation, the president, and official policy.

In doing so, White House officials benefitted from the lack of consensus about what, exactly, makes someone or something "American." Then, as now, Americans define patriotism in terms of their own values and perspective. For some, it is rooted in the radical dissent of the "Founding Fathers" while others define it as a celebration of the nation's ideals, history, and potential. Still others embrace the self-reliance and morality of the Puritans. Indeed, there seem to be as many patriotisms as there are Americans and they tend to fall into two broad categories: one which emphasizes unquestioning loyalty and national pride, and another which seeks to see the nation live up to its ideals, even if doing so sometimes requires harsh critique. Even as scholars and theorists debate what to call these different strands, with some differentiating between patriotism and nationalism, others between different types of patriotism or nationalism, and still others arguing that "civil religion" is the more accurate label.[3] The domestic debates over the Vietnam War exacerbated these tensions and the decision of many critical, idealistic patriots to join the peace movement and, in extreme cases, to reject the flag and other patriotic symbols, facilitated White House efforts to promote a patriotism emphasizing support for the president and opposition to his critics.[4] Woden Teachout's history of the U.S. flag offers a useful way to distinguish between the patriotism of dissenters and that which was promoted by the Nixon administration. Arguing that opposition movements and critical citizens were 'humanitarian patriots," Teachout contrasts this celebration of national ideals with a "nationalist patriotism," which prioritizes loyalty to the nation.[5] Similarly, Anatol Lieven frames them as the "American Creed" promoting US ideals and lofty rhetoric and its "Antithesis" of bellicose, chauvinist nationalism.[6] As administration officials from President Nixon down primarily framed their efforts in terms of patriotism rather than nationalism, Teachout's construction is the more useful approach in this context. Even though Nixon and his supporters would likely have challenged the idea that there was anything "patriotic" about the anti-war movement.

Attacks on the critical, humanitarian patriotism of the anti-war movement were rooted in both its inherent conflict with the unquestioning loyalty of nationalist patriotism, but also in a deeper fear. As a nation of immigrants held together by shared ideals, the United States is particularly vulnerable to uncertainty about what and who is truly "American."[7] And when pro-war forces claimed the flag with patriotic demonstrations in 1969 and 1970, the war's opponents surrendered a powerful symbol. Just as concerns over flag desecration rose during times of upheaval and uncertainty— after the Civil War, World War I, during World War II, and Vietnam— conflicts over patriotism and national identity are most intense when there is no consensus over their definitions[8] While not as overt as the 1844 nativist riots in Philadelphia, or the World War I "outbreak of forced flag kissings," the White House campaign to promote domestic support of the president's policies had a similar goal: namely to use patriotic appeals to elevate one group of citizens at the expense of another.[9] Administration efforts to promote the Silent Majority in 1969 and 1970 consistently denied the validity of humanitarian patriotism, stressing the incompatibility of dissent and patriotism.[10] At the same time, they actively promoted nationalist patriotism both as a counterweight to the anti-war movement and as a way to mobilize and control supporters.

"A Series of Patriotic Rallies"

Much of this approach came from Nixon's own combative political style, but it was also rooted in the lessons he learned from watching President Lyndon Johnson's struggles with the anti-war movement.

Having benefitted from domestic opposition to Johnson's Vietnam policies, Nixon recognized the importance of domestic public opinion and arrived in the White House in January 1969 determined to undermine and isolate the opposition. He ultimately did so by giving voice to the "silent majority" of citizens, both with his speech on November 3, 1969, and by actively encouraging patriotic demonstrations in the subsequent days and weeks.[11] Fortunately for White House officials, grassroots activists had similar plans. As Nixon's staff prepared for an outpouring of support following his speech, the Committee for a Week of National Unity and the National Committee for Responsible Patriotism organized a series of local and national events centered around Veterans' Day on November 11 and the "Mobilization" anti-war protest on November 15. Based on Committee for a Week of National Unity founder Edmund Dombrowski's view that many "believed that the president was doing all he could to end the war, but did not want to have to parade in the streets to show their support," the majority of National Unity Week activities centered on smaller and more local displays of support.[12] Proposed events such as "marches of policemen and firemen" and a "series of patriotic rallies throughout the country" would be complemented by "increased display of American flag[s] (offices, homes, automobile bumpers and windshields, lapel pins, etc.) ...of porch lights and automobile headlights [on] during daylight hours."[13] These local efforts ensured that those who could not come to Washington, D.C., for the major rallies could still actively participate in the counter-protest. White House officials, in turn, framed participation in these local and national events as demonstrations of support for Nixon and collaborated with local and national organizers to ensure maximum participation and coverage.

In reporting on the week of protests, *Newsweek* concluded that "America's antiwar (*sic*) dissidents had no monopoly on last week's demonstrating" and claimed the prior week included "the most widespread patriotic demonstrations in recent history."[14] In addition to gatherings at the Washington Memorial and in major cities across the country, the article covered much smaller protests and demonstrations, not all of which required significant effort on the part of the Silent Majority. *Newsweek* reporters highlighted one such initiative in which a small town mayor paid $360 (just under $2,500 in 2017 dollars) for 20,000 flag lapel pins for the residents of New Britain, Connecticut. The pins provided supporters with an easy way to take part in the National Unity Week activities: even if they changed nothing else about their daily routine, the badge showed clearly that they were patriotic Americans who opposed the anti-war movement. Similarly, White House staff were told, "they would be conspicuous without displaying an American Flag on their dresses or coat lapels."[15] Echoing White House claims, *Newsweek* reported, "flag-waving citizens" participated in pro-Vietnam activities to "honor the dead of Vietnam and other wars and reaffirm their faith in the U.S., its government and the ultimate rightness of the nation's course." For most, there was no room for compromise or a loyal opposition: "AMERICA, read the ubiquitous signs, LOVE IT OR LEAVE IT." Conveniently for White House officials, the article explicitly linked these activities with the President's November 3 speech and highlighted the fact that for many participants, the popularity of the Silent Majority label proved "traditional values controlled the destiny of the republic." Worries about their nation's future and believing their silence had given the anti-war movement undue authority led many to participate in rallies, marches, and other demonstrations during the second week of November. Organizers emphasized that these protesters were part of the Silent Majority invoked in Nixon's speech— "The silent majority has become very vocal indeed"— and despite media portrayals to the contrary, argued, "there are more of us patriotic Americans than those pro-Hanoicrats." The article recognized that at least some of these protests were shaped by the 100,000 "Veterans' Day kits" mailed out by the Department of Defense and the Veterans Administration, but was careful to point out that many participants "turned out without any nudge from official Washington."[16]

The *Newsweek* journalists did not condemn efforts by "official Washington" to encourage participation in these patriotic events, but they certainly saw such efforts as distinct from those organized by local individuals or grassroots organizations. That media coverage differentiated between those who participated because of governmental "nudges" from those who participated on their own initiative encouraged White House officials— who were already inclined to be secretive— to protect the official distance between themselves and their outside allies. They therefore decided against a proposal to use press conferences by the committees behind National Unity Week to publicize the letters and telegrams sent to the White House after the president's speech. While doing so would have strengthened the link between Nixon's Silent Majority and the myriad patriotic celebrations, aides feared "the risk of White House exposure would be too great."[17] They were concerned such exposure would undermine their larger plans to use these events to isolate and marginalize the anti-war movement. After all, if the Silent Majority idea could be dismissed as White House propaganda, there was a very real risk that the project would thwart their intentions and weaken the president's position instead. Aides would, of course, continue to support and advise their outside allies, but always with the understanding that they had to remain deep in the background. This determination to maintain a meaningful distance between the White House and its outside collaborators would occasionally result in tension and frustration on both sides, but aides understood the real strength of their patriotic program lay in its apparent grassroots origins.

This made the massive participation in National Unity Week all the more gratifying. Chief of Staff H.R. Haldeman's assistant, Alexander P. Butterfield, reported at least five to six million people participated in the patriotic events and stressed that this was a conservative estimate.[18] Combined with the many letters, telegrams, and petition campaigns from which Butterfield calculated a "grand total of known supporters" of 208,886 named individuals, such activity was "proof positive" of support for Nixon and his policies.[19] These numbers were certainly encouraging, but aides would likely have been happy with smaller totals as long as those who participated did so publicly. Indeed, White House planning repeatedly emphasized the importance of making sure supporters were visible and had a unified message even as these same plans explicitly stated "there should be no specific goal in terms of numbers." Their goal was "not to compete with the protesters; it is merely to get across the point that not all of the crowd is anti-Administration."[20] The active and enthusiastic participation of so many people in the local and national events strengthened the claim that Nixon, not the anti-war movement, represented national opinion on the war. The next step, of course, was to turn these individual participants and counter protesters into a viable counterweight to the anti-war movement. The close association between the idea of a "Silent Majority" and patriotism would prove critical to their success as it provided a way to publicly support Nixon, and the nation, without explicitly endorsing specific policies.

"Love for the Only Flag We Have"

In promoting the idea of a Silent Majority of pro-war, pro-president citizens, White House officials strove to balance their desire for visible, public support with the need to ensure that as many people as possible saw themselves as part of the newly vocal group. Aides knew that if the idea was too closely tied to any single Nixon policy, it risked losing the support of people who opposed that particular policy despite otherwise identifying with the administration's interpretation of nationalist patriotism. But, at the same time, they needed to be able to rally support around specific issues or the Silent Majority would not realize its political potential. White House officials, therefore, took a proactive role in defining and promoting the idea of the Silent Majority after Nixon's November 3 speech. Chief of Staff H.R. Haldeman justified the active White House role in the creation and promotion of the Silent Majority saying its members "weren't... activists, so you needed to help them along."[21] Cooperating with projects such as National Unity Week was certainly useful, but aides were not willing to leave the political effectiveness of the Silent Majority to chance. They therefore endeavored in the weeks and months following the president's speech to inextricably link the White House with the increasingly popular idea. Aides were told to "make a consistent effort"[22] and that "as a general rule," all public opinion projects "should be tied to the 'Silent Majority' over and over... always."[23]

White House officials did as they were ordered and for a short time, the Silent Majority dominated their efforts to organize the president's supporters. But as they were not, as Haldeman noted, "activists," many felt they had done their part by speaking out after the speech. They soon returned to their usual pursuits, leading the president to observe in February 1970 that "it seems our silent majority group has lost its steam."[24] Nixon suggested "another demonstration" as a way to reenergize them, but aides struggled to recreate the alchemy of the November speech and while the Silent Majority did not disappear completely in early 1970, it was certainly much quieter, perhaps in part because the anti-war movement was quiet as well. Both groups, however, would rediscover their voices in response to Nixon's April 30, 1970, announcement of American and South Vietnamese "incursions" into Cambodia. Protesters took to the streets in response and gathered on college campuses in opposition. On May 4, a group of National Guardsmen fired into a nonviolent protest at Kent State University in Ohio injuring nine and killing four students. As schools closed and protesters poured into Washington, D.C., members of the New York Construction and Building Trades surged down Wall Street on May 8 to confront students and anti-war activists attending a vigil in honor of the Kent State victims.

The resulting clash was a violent show of support for Nixon and initiated almost two weeks of marches and demonstrations by the pro-Nixon workers culminating in a well-organized and remarkably peaceful march and rally on May 20. The stark contrast between anti-war activists and the so-called "hard hats"— pro-war, pro-Nixon white ethnic construction workers— strengthened administration efforts to promote patriotic loyalty and the flag as a symbol of support for both Nixon and the Vietnam War. Agreeing "that love of country and love and respect for our country's flag are not as old-fashioned and as out of date as the 'know-it-alls' would have us believe," between 60,000-150,000 construction workers took to the streets on May 20, 1970, in a powerful display of support for Nixon, the war in Vietnam, and opposition to the anti-war movement.[25] Organizers explicitly invited the participation of all Americans, "students and Workers— long hair or short— bald or bearded" as long as each brought "love for the only flag we have."[26] The Hard Hat emphasis on nationalist patriotism allowed them to avoid endorsing all of Nixon's policies while demonstrating that "patriotism and love and respect for our flag is not dead."[27] These workers supported Nixon, yes, but primarily as Commander-in-Chief.

This distinction was very important for both the Hard Hats and for the administration. In planning their May 26 White House visit, officials reminded the president that the Hard Hats "have been very careful to say that they back the President and back the country without necessarily endorsing all Administration policies." [28] Nixon therefore emphasized "country rather than this Administration" when meeting with Peter Brennan, President of the New York Building and Construction Trades Association, and other New York workers. At the same time, aides publicly pointed to the Hard Hat endorsement as further proof of popular support for Nixon. Their efforts to do so were aided by the Hard Hats themselves. In remembering the May protests, Eugene Shafer, one of a group of Hard Hats interviewed by Diana Lurie with *New York Magazine*, frankly acknowledged that he viewed the elite students in the anti-war movement with a "sort of jealousy" and explained his participation in both the May 8 riot and the May 20 rally on his belief that "anybody who raises an enemy flag in our country is a traitor."[29] Taken together, these two comments reflect the effectiveness of White House efforts to promote an uncritical, nationalist patriotism and isolate the anti-war movement. But even as Schafer echoed White House rhetoric, it is worth noting he kept to vague generalities when interviewed, expressing loyalty to Nixon as "our president" and referring to Vice President Agnew as "a prince." More importantly, Schafer implicitly cast the war's opponents, a minority of whom were known to wave the North Vietnamese flag, as unpatriotic and un-American.[30] In this way, he and other Hard Hats used their nationalist patriotism to ignore the Nixon policies they opposed and the White House used that same nationalist patriotism to organize and mobilize supporters without addressing substantive policy issues.

Even as they recognized they would likely never get blanket Hard Hat support for Nixon's policies— workers and their unions were particularly critical of the administration's economic policies— aides were enthusiastic about the public opinion potential of these new allies. Yes, their violence was a problem and the "near riot" on May 4 complicated the White House narrative of a law-abiding Silent Majority opposed to a violent and radical anti-war movement, but as one aide observed, "those portions that emphasize support and respect for the President and patriotism, are positive and constructive."[31] Furthermore, the Hard Hat protests provided the White House with a valuable opportunity to solidify their preferred interpretation of patriotism as belonging to "an America where people work for a living, where they respect the flag, where they appreciate what they have."[32] The Hard Hats' very public embrace of the President and his foreign policies bolstered White House efforts to delegitimize the idea of patriotic dissent and make the flag a symbol of both the United States and uncritical embrace of Nixon's foreign policies. Aides therefore worked to cultivate friendly union leaders in the spring and summer of 1970 even as they planned another national patriotic celebration for the Fourth of July.

"A Sea of Red, White, and Blue"

Unaware of these plans and, like the Hard Hats, disgusted by the mounting domestic opposition to Nixon's Vietnam policies, Maryland Legionnaire Fred Rohrer wrote to the National Commander of the American Legion berating the organization for its inaction in the face of domestic protests. Urging the National Executive Committee to "get off of your posteriors and stand up and be counted," he pushed the Legion to sponsor "a massive 24 hour parade (*sic*) in Washington, D.C. on July 4,

1970, in support of our God, President and patriotism for our country." Forwarding his telegram to President Nixon, Rohrer urged him not to "listen to the Neville Chamberlains in our Congress and Senate" and likely hoped for a presidential endorsement of his proposed parade.[33] Instead, Special Counsel to the President Charles Colson replied a month later thanking him on behalf of the president and urged Rohrer to join the existing effort to organize a Fourth of July celebration in Washington, D.C.[34] This event, dubbed Honor America Day, was closely, if covertly, controlled by the White House and was the culmination of administration patriotism promotion efforts since the president's November 3 speech. These efforts had attempted to harness patriotic sentiment and transform it into support for the president and his Vietnam policies.

In this context, Honor America Day functioned as both a patriotic Fourth of July celebration and as a massive endorsement of the president. Although officially nonpartisan and apolitical, Honor America Day was very much a Nixon administration production.[35] By mid-May 1970, White House officials had lined up major names for the steering committee to serve as the public face of the Fourth of July event. These included Bob Hope, Billy Graham, George Meany, and Ross Perot, in addition to outside groups such as the AFL-CIO, VFW, YAF, as well as other patriotic and business groups.[36] Co-Chairmen Bob Hope and Billy Graham announced Honor America Day a month later at a June 5, 1970, press conference. Organizers claimed the occasion was "not designed to rally support either for the war in Vietnam or against it," but rather would "show the world that 'Americans can put aside their honest differences and rally around the flag to show national unity.'"[37] Planners therefore avoided specific references to Vietnam and sought the visible participation of as many of the President's outside supporters as possible.

And so, even though some members of the organizing committee complained the "Hard Hats [were] making too much noise publicly re the 4th of July," Colson and other staffers refused to ask them to be quiet, passive participants.[38] Instead, Colson told Jeb Magruder, "there is no middle ground. Either the Hard Hats are going to come and make a significant display on July 4th or we better tell them to do nothing."[39] Most likely because Hard Hat support had become a central part of White House planning– particularly the promotion of the Silent Majority– Colson suggested that if members of the organizing committee were unable to work with the Hard Hats, "let's get someone else to run the show."[40] That Colson could so cavalierly propose the administration replace the official organizers for the event less than a month before it was to take place speaks to the control White House officials had over the ostensibly nonpartisan and apolitical event. Not only that, but their influence, in turn, suggests the bulk of the actual planning took place in the White House rather than at the initiative of the official committee. Colson further recommended that "dealings with the Hard Hats be handled by me directly," which would have the dual benefit of distancing committee members, many of them prominent businessmen, from the President's working class supporters as well as ensuring even greater White House sway over the upcoming event.[41]

On the whole, Honor America Day was a "splendid success" from the Administration's perspective, with between 400,000 and 500,000 people participating in the day and evening events.[42] The program included prayers, speeches, and celebrity performances as well as an "Old Glory Marathon," a National Salute during which "whistles, bells, horns and carillons across the nation will proclaim Honor America Day," an aerial salute filled the sky with "tiny American Flags," and a "Procession of flags" ending at a "huge" American flag surrounded by state and territorial flags at the White House Ellipse.[43] There, Boy Scouts distributed "100,000 miniature American flags" which participants then placed in a large "USA" carved into the grass.[44] The elaborate pageant effectively cemented the administration's claim on the flag and was an effective endorsement of its promotion of nationalist patriotism. The humanitarian patriotism and dissent of the anti-war movement had no place in the lavish celebration and aides saw the high attendance as proof that "most Americans continue to support American principles, that they have not given up on the system."[45] In its effort to "rekindle the American spirit of patriotism," Honor America Day organizers succeeded largely by ignoring many of the substantive issues dividing the country.[46]

And yet, despite these successes, White House officials were frustrated by the failure of some of their allies to turn out as expected. Specifically, "literally none" of the promised "thousands of hard hats" were in Washington, D.C., on July 4.[47] Although as puzzled as Haldeman was by the "inexplicable" lack of Hard Hat participation in Honor America Day, Colson confidently assured him that "we are dealing with the right labor leaders" and blamed minimal Hard Hat participation in Honor America Day on a combination of personal conflicts and miscommunication rather than diminishing support for the president.[48] Specifically, Colson acknowledged that he and others, from both the committee and the White House, had ignored advice from Brennan and other labor leaders, which might have adjusted their expectations for Hard Hat participation. Not only had Brennan warned Colson "at the outset" that it would be "exceedingly difficult to get a large group" of Hard Hats to come down to Washington, D.C. for the Fourth of July— often the only weekend they took off all summer— but other Hard Hats had been "offered double pay to work on a holiday."[49] Colson argued the blame for the failure of the Hard Hats to turn up in significant numbers lay not in White House planning, but rather in the fact that "Hard Hats turn out because of spontaneous events" and "react more to the negative than to the positive."[50] Consequently, Colson reluctantly concluded that an event such as Honor America Day might not motivate them as much as a "fist fight with the students on Wall Street."[51] All the same, Colson was confident that as long as they took care in the future not to "reject their leaders' instincts," the Hard Hats could provide useful political assistance.[52] Despite this disappointment, aides were generally pleased with Honor America Day and saw it as a useful model for future organizing since, mistakes with the Hard Hats aside, White House officials had successfully maintained covert control over the event and in doing so, ensured the event reinforced the administration's nationalist patriotic rhetoric.

POLITICIZED PATRIOTISM AFTER NIXON

Although not a primary goal, administration efforts to rally domestic support for the Vietnam War deepened the growing divisions in the nation and politicized both patriotism and its symbols (such as the American flag). Beyond rallying domestic support for Vietnam and his policies, Nixon's repeated invocations of patriotism and his ostentatious embrace of the flag further exacerbated domestic tensions over patriotism and national identity. Indeed, administration aides strove to make flag lapel pins a de facto symbol of Nixon's 1972 re-election campaign. White House guidance insisted that not only should "all of our people... be wearing American Flags," but "they should be on all our speakers."[53] Furthermore, "each speaker should have a supply of them to give to the people who ask for them."[54] In this way, the flag– a traditional symbol of the nation– would be explicitly linked with Nixon. He later explained his decision to wear a flag lapel pin "come hell or high water" as an effort to push back against what he saw as a concerted attempt by liberals and other critics to "undermin[e] the traditional concept of patriotism."[55] He insisted, "this was not a politically motivated prejudice on my part," but recognized the risks commenting in his diary, "Of course, this must be carefully done so that there is no indication of throwing doubts on the patriotism of people who are on the other side."[56] Which, of course, was exactly what the very well-publicized celebration of the flag by pro-war and pro-Nixon groups ultimately accomplished. That said, partisan patriotic appeals declined somewhat following Nixon's resignation during the Watergate scandal. Coming into office after Nixon's resignation, Gerald R. Ford sought to distance himself from the disgraced president, which included moving away from overt displays of nationalist patriotism. For instance, he chose not to wear a flag pin and there was a brief shift away from such partisan patriotism during his and Jimmy Carter's administrations.

Ronald Reagan's presidency marked a return to the nationalist patriotism of the Nixon years, reflecting a change in the national mood.[57] In electing Reagan in 1980, the nation turned its back on the decline and failures of the 1970s— the Watergate scandal, the humiliating and disorganized evacuation from the U.S. Embassy in Saigon in 1975, the 1973 and 1979 oil crises, and the Iranian hostage crisis— to instead celebrate a nostalgic and optimistic patriotism rooted in uncomplicated ideas of national greatness. Reagan appealed to voters' nostalgia and pride in the nation's past, and his campaign slogan— "Let's make America great again"— explicitly asked them to join him in restoring the nation's lost status. Reagan soundly defeated Carter in 1980 winning forty-four states and just over 50 percent of the popular vote. Nixon's Silent Majority had rediscovered their voices and Reagan did not disappoint them. His public statements echoed and reinforced nationalist patriotism and by 1984, Reagan campaigned on this record and on the idea, in the words of one campaign advertisement, that it was "Morning in America" in a subtle reminder to viewers— and voters— that the work of reviving the nation had only just begun. The ad emphasizes beginnings from the first image of a quiet port at dawn, to men and women headed to work, to a family moving into a new house, to a wedding celebration, and ending with images of Americans of all ages raising the U.S. flag.[58] Given the importance of patriotism in Reagan's mystique and rhetoric, it is perhaps surprising there are so few flags in this popular ad— flags only appear in the last ten seconds— with the focus instead on soft-palette depictions of an idealized "American way of life." Yet, the association between nationalist patriotism and a particular vision of the United States more broadly meant that Reagan did not have to make his patriotism explicit in the ad; his target audience would associate the nostalgic images of U.S. citizens— most of them suburban, middle class whites— with the nationalist patriotism championed by Nixon during the Vietnam era. For many in Nixon's Silent Majority, the flag was a symbol of the nation, yes, but it was also a symbol of the way of life they either had or, in the case of the working class Hard Hats, aspired to: the lifestyle on display in Reagan's "Morning in America" ad. Indeed, the official title for the spot is "Prouder, Stronger, Better," making Reagan's promise to his voters clear and apparent.

Adding urgency to these nostalgic and patriotic appeals was a growing domestic debate over the American flag. On August 22, 1984, Gregory Lee Johnson, a member of the Revolutionary Communist Party, set an American flag on fire as part of a larger protest at the Republican National Convention in Dallas, Texas. Johnson was arrested and convicted of violating a Texas law prohibiting "desecration of a venerated object."[59] Johnson's case made its way to the Supreme Court, which ruled in 1989 that the Texas law violated the First Amendment and was therefore unconstitutional. Congress quickly passed legislation in response, but the 1989 Flag Protection Act was also struck down, which led the bill's supporters to push for a Constitutional amendment. While they were unsuccessful, the project is often revived in response to domestic protest, thus strengthening the links between the flag, nationalist patriotism, and opposition to protest. Doing so makes the flag a potent symbol for extremist dissidents who reject all that the United States represents, but the linkage further distances humanitarian patriots and more gentle critics, thus cementing the partisan associations of patriotism and its symbols. This division was initially possible because moderate anti-war activists and other critics opted not to challenge Nixon administration efforts to claim the flag for the president. They did so, of course, not because they rejected the flag itself or even U.S. ideals, but because they were so disheartened by what they saw as their nation's failures that they felt the flag was no longer theirs— thus facilitating Nixon's efforts to claim it. This distance from the flag would be intensified by Reagan's patriotic politics as well as the campaigns to make flag desecration not only illegal, but unconstitutional. By the end of the twentieth century, it was rare indeed to see a U.S. flag at a protest march or demonstration even though such actions were central to the nation's history and founding.

This pattern would continue through George H.W. Bush's presidency, particularly in the response to the 1990-91 Persian Gulf War. Learning from the Vietnam War, Bush and his aides were determined to prevent an anti-war movement from forming and quickly framed opposition to official policy as opposition to and criticism of the U.S. troops fighting in

Iraq and Kuwait. The proliferation of yellow ribbons across the country signified both their original meaning— that someone connected to the household was on active duty— as well as a silent indication that the residents "supported the troops." In this way, the yellow ribbon's intended function was nearly identical to the flag lapel pins during the Nixon years: they were a visible symbol of patriotic support for the president and his official policies. Conflating patriotism and pro-military views, therefore, helped insulate Bush and his policies from serious criticism as any questioning of policy could now be framed as an effort to undermine troops in the field. The strategy worked and the yellow ribbons, combined with a very short period of active fighting, limited domestic opposition to the conflict. Those who did speak out were charged with being un-American, unpatriotic, and, most damning of all, against the troops. This kind of public prosecution encouraged others with doubts about the policy to keep quiet. At the same time, Bush's decision to wrap himself and his policies in the flag meant the flag was yet again closely associated with a pro-war position, with the Republic Party, and, more broadly, with an uncritical and celebratory patriotism. These associations, in turn, further encouraged humanitarian patriots, anti-war activists, and others uncomfortable with the Bush administration's rhetoric to see the flag as representing some other group of Americans. In this way, even as Bush claimed that victory in the Persian Gulf meant that "by God, we've kicked the Vietnam syndrome once and for all," his approach to wartime public opinion meant the politicization of patriotism Nixon started during Vietnam was firmly entrenched within U.S. society.[60]

And, up until September 11, 2001, it looked like that was the way things were going to stay. Although voters rejected President Bush's efforts to paint then-Governor William Jefferson Clinton as unpatriotic and therefore unelectable in the 1992 campaign, Clinton's victory cannot be taken as a shift in the popular approach to patriotism. Rather, debates over patriotism would become part of the larger "culture wars" of the 1990s in which traditionalists and conservatives squared off against Clinton directly and liberalism more generally. With few liberals attempting to reclaim the flag or patriotism, the debate centered on conservative culture warriors such as Pat Buchanan and Phyllis Schafley and their attacks on what they saw as moral decline represented by abortion, the women's movement, gay liberation, and other social movements and changes. Patriotism was invoked as part of a broader definition of an idealized "American way of life" to which the conservatives hoped to return. In this context, the American flag was practically the exclusive property of the Republican Party and few outside that group seemed inclined to mount a serious challenge. However, after the September 11, 2001, attacks, there was a surge in bipartisan patriotism. Members of Congress and politicians from both parties took to wearing flag lapel pins and neighborhoods not known for enthusiastic patriotism such as Boston's Beacon Hill sprouted flags practically overnight.[61] Even so, this nonpartisan embrace of the flag soon began to echo earlier efforts to use the flag to separate "them" from "us." As Americans displayed flags purchased from the corner store, gas stations, bookstores, and even Tiffany's, those less prepared scrambled to find some way of showing their solidarity, or at least of silencing their neighbors' implicit critiques. Remembering the sudden proliferation of flags in the days following what he describes as "the Horror," novelist David Foster Wallace describes "a weird accretive pressure to have a flag out. If the purpose of a flag is to make a statement, it seems like at a certain point of density of flags you're making more of a statement if you *don't* have a flag out."[62] Although unsure of what, exactly, this statement would be, the pressure demonstrates the effectiveness of Nixon's efforts to politicize the flag in support of his Vietnam policies. Indeed, President George H.W. Bush would combine Nixon's politicization of the flag with his father's yellow ribbon campaign during the Persian Gulf to silence dissent by further conflating support for the troops with nationalist patriotism.

This deeper politicization of the flag and patriotism led at least one Senator to stop wearing a flag pin as the pressure mounted for the United States to go to war with Iraq. Years later, on October 3, 2007, Senator Barack Obama, then a presidential candidate, explained in an interview that he had stopped wearing the pins because in the months leading up to the Iraq war, doing so "became a substitute for, I think, true patriotism."[63] Obama was careful not to reject the pins in their entirety— "sometimes I wear one, sometimes I don't"— but instead emphasized that he saw actions as more important evidence of patriotism. Thus, Obama told voters at an Independence, Iowa, event that he was "less concerned about what you're wearing on your lapel than what's in your heart."[64] Obama did not seek to spark a national debate about patriotism and its symbols, but rather hoped to diffuse a potential campaign issue by advocating a patriotism beyond sartorial accessories. Even so, hard line nationalist patriots framed his decision as, at best, an anti-war statement and, at worse, an outright rejection of patriotism. And as pundits such as Sean Hannity on Fox News insisted that Obama "said he's doing it as a political statement about the war,"[65] the candidate himself repeatedly sought to clarify his position. Unable to do so, he described it as a "phony" issue during an April 2008 Democratic primary debate but, by May 2008, was wearing a flag pin far more often.[66] Even so, the issue— both the pins specifically and his patriotism more generally— would follow him throughout both the campaign and his presidency. While his supporters saw his willingness to acknowledge flaws in U.S. policy as a return to an earlier, humanitarian patriotism, one which celebrated the country's strengths while recognizing its failures, his opponents saw Obama's rejection of the conventional norms and symbols of nationalist patriotism as a direct attack on themselves and their vision of the country. These voters— and politicians— would challenge Obama at almost every turn during his eight years in office and many would enthusiastically support Donald J. Trump in the 2016 campaign. This new, self-proclaimed Silent Majority was even more vocal than Nixon's and Trump came into office on a wave of populist enthusiasm and nationalist patriotism.

These voters saw Trump's chauvinist nationalist patriotism as a return to an earlier era, before "political correctness" and immigration transformed the nation. Trump's embrace of this perspective energized his base as did Nixon's patriotic appeals during the Vietnam War. And after his inauguration in January 2017, Trump, like Nixon, used divisive patriotic appeals to mobilize his base without any apparent regard for the ways in which such politicized patriotism can divide the country. Indeed, fanning the flames of these divisions enabled Trump to avoid engaging with substantive criticism on a host of domestic and international policies. In this way, appeals to nationalist patriotism rooted in a white, Christian vision of the United States repeatedly enabled Trump to reshape domestic debates. Furthermore, this rhetoric undermined protest more generally by framing any criticism as an attack on the nation and, recalling both George H.W. Bush and George W. Bush, the troops. Take, for instance, the 2017 debate over the decision of professional athletes, particularly those in the NFL led by former San Francisco 49er quarterback, Colin Kaepernick, to "take a knee" during the National Anthem as a way to bring attention to systemic racism and police brutality. While then-President Obama defended their right to do so in 2016, President Trump attacked them less than a year later.[67] In turn, many journalists, pundits, and commentators followed Trump's lead and rather than exploring the reasons for the demonstrations, instead debated whether or not protest and protesters could be "American" or "patriotic." Just as Nixon sought to delegitimize his opponents by questioning their Americanness and the legitimacy of protest, Trump argued that protesters were "disrespecting" the anthem, the flag, veterans, and, of course, the nation.

CONCLUSION

President Trump's 2017 success in reframing protests *during* the National Anthem as protests *of* the National Anthem benefitted from Nixon's own efforts to use patriotism for political ends. By branding his opponents and critics as un-American, Nixon ensured that domestic debates over the Vietnam War reached beyond the conflict and, essentially, made patriotism contingent upon uncritical support of the president and official policies. While not entirely successful in silencing his opponents, Nixon's patriotic appeals effectively linked the flag with the presidency and, by extension, with approval for official policy. Transforming support for the president into an act of patriotism, rather than one of partisanship, Nixon and his aides hoped to counterbalance his critics despite growing impatience with the Vietnam War. At the same time, they knew patriotism alone would not have the necessarily political effects. Thus, while White House officials were content to leave the details of National Unity Week up to the grassroots organizers in October and November of 1969, they insisted on much greater influence over Honor America Day just under a year later. This increased control and in turn, reflected the growing political importance of such events to White House officials. In November 1969, it was sufficient to have patriotic displays which could be linked to the president after the fact, but by early summer 1970, aides were determined to ensure that the proposed patriotic events matched larger White House goals. They were no longer satisfied with pointing to grassroots activism as proof that the president spoke for the majority, but support now also had to complement detailed White House plans. Specifically, public demonstrations had to have both the right messaging and the right participants to further White House political ambitions.

Aides were largely successful in their political goals: the anti-war movement never regained the broad participation of the October 1969 protests, the Silent Majority became a force in domestic politics, Nixon was handily re-elected in 1972, and he announced the Paris Peace Accords ending U.S. involvement in Vietnam in January 1973. While certainly good news for Nixon, these successes came with a high price. They demonstrated that unity was not necessary for electoral victory and, indeed, that divisive appeals were quite effective in the U.S. political system. His promotion of the Silent Majority and embrace of patriotic symbols, particularly the flag, transformed it into a "bitter symbol of tremendous loss" for many in the anti-war movement.[68] They therefore turned away from the flag and other symbols linked to Nixon's patriotic rhetoric. They would remain distant through Reagan's nostalgic political appeals, during pleas from both Presidents Bush to "support the troops" in 1991 and 2001, but would start to reengage with the conventional symbols of patriotism as Obama drew national attention to a different sort of patriotism. Starting with his attempts to explain why he did not wear a flag lapel pin and later in his 2009 speech in Cairo, Obama offered an alternative to the patriotism preeminent since Nixon's time in the White House. During his administration, Obama's patriotism, which celebrated American ideals even as he recognized that the nation had made mistakes in the past, slowly challenged nationalist patriotism for control of popular symbols and ideas. But even as flags became a common sight at protests— on the left, now, as well as on the right— those who saw themselves in Nixon's Silent Majority rejected this patriotism and found an enthusiastic standard bearer in Donald Trump.

At first glance, Trump's patriotism in both the 2016 campaign and the 2017 anthem protests echo Nixon's appeal to the Silent Majority during the Vietnam War. Like Nixon, he did not try to unite the country behind either his policies or his rhetoric and sought to benefit from the resulting tension and division. However, the larger political climate was very different for the two men and unlike Nixon, Trump faced concerted opposition in his attempts to use patriotism for political gain. Not only did former President Obama offer a visible alternative, but even those in Trump's own party challenged his efforts to further narrow the boundaries of U.S. patriotism and identity. Notably, Senator John McCain (R, AZ), publicly rebuked Trump, although not by name, in criticizing a "half-baked, spurious nationalism cooked up by people who would rather find scapegoats than solve problems" during an October 2017 speech.[69] That journalists and pundits alike took McCain's critique seriously speaks to both his personal status as well as the fracturing of the domestic consensus around patriotism. More broadly, such attacks highlight an important limitation on presidential efforts to shape and politicize patriotism: the need for an enthusiastic and receptive audience. Nixon succeeded in politicizing patriotism because many citizens saw themselves in the Silent Majority and because the anti-war movement chose not to contest his claim to the flag. At the same time, there are limits to even this politicized patriotism. After all, even though the patriotism Nixon promoted made it easier for presidents to rally support for military interventions abroad, it also created rhetorical— and sometimes sartorial— constraints. Looking back on the evolution of politicized patriotism from Nixon to Trump, it would behoove any politician to remember its costs as well as its potential advantages.

NOTES

1. "Put Out More Flags," *Washington Star*, June 18, 1970.
2. See, for example: Charles DeBenedetti, *An American Ordeal: The Antiwar Movement of the Vietnam Era* (Syracuse, NY: Syracuse University Press, 1990); Melvin Small, *Johnson, Nixon, and the Doves* (New Brunswick, NJ: Rutgers University Press, 1988); Tom Wells, *The War Within: America's Battle Over Vietnam* (Berkeley, CA: University of California Press, 1994).
3. John E Bodnar, *Remaking America: Public Memory, Commemoration, and Patriotism in the Twentieth Century* (Princeton, N.J.: Princeton University Press, 1991); John E. Bodnar, *The Transplanted: A History of Immigrants in Urban America* (Bloomington: Indiana University Press, 1985); Robert Justin Goldstein, *Saving Old Glory: The History of the American Flag Desecration Controversy* (Boulder, CO: Westview Press, 1995); Michael G Kammen, *People of Paradox: An Inquiry Concerning the Origins of American Civilization* (New York: Knopf, 1972); Kevin M. Kruse, *One Nation Under God: How Corporate America Invented Christian America* (New York: Basic Books, 2015); Anatol Lieven, *America Right or Wrong: An Anatomy of American Nationalism* (Oxford University Press, 2005); Maurizio Viroli, *For Love of Country: An Essay on Patriotism and Nationalism* (Oxford; New York: Clarendon Press ; Oxford University Press, 1995).
4. Woden Teachout provides a thorough discussion of her conception of these two types of patriotism in Woden Teachout, *Capture the Flag: A Political History of American Patriotism* (New York, NY: Basic Books, 2009), 4–9, 229–30, 232–33. Scholarly studies of American patriotism have tended to focus on the Revolutionary and New Republic periods, with sometimes a brief discussion of the 1976 Bicentennial, but more recent works by Richard M. Fried, Robert Justin Goldstein, Teachout, and Arnaldo Testi analyze and contextualize debates over patriotism and the flag throughout the nineteenth and twentieth centuries, paying particular attention to the Cold War and the Vietnam War periods. Benedict R. O'G Anderson, *Imagined Communities: Reflections on the Origin and Spread of Nationalism* (London: Verso, 1991); John Fousek, *To Lead the Free World: American Nationalism and the Cultural Roots of the Cold War* (Chapel Hill: University of North Carolina Press, 2000); Richard M. Fried, *The Russians Are Coming! The Russians Are Coming!: Pageantry and Patriotism in Cold-War America* (New York: Oxford University Press,

1998); Goldstein, *Saving Old Glory*; Kammen, *People of Paradox*; Michael G Kammen, *Mystic Chords of Memory: The Transformation of Tradition in American Culture* (New York: Knopf, 1991); Cecilia Elizabeth O'Leary, *To Die For: The Paradox of American Patriotism* (Princeton, N.J.: Princeton University Press, 1999); Robin Deich Ottoson, "The Battle Over the Flag: Protest, Community Opposition, and Silence in the Mennonite Colleges in Kansas During the Vietnam War," *Journal of Church and State* 52, no. 4 (Autumn 2010): 686–711; Teachout, *Capture the Flag*; Arnaldo Testi, *Capture the Flag: The Stars and Stripes in American History* (New York: New York University Press, 2010); Len Travers, *Celebrating the Fourth: Independence Day and the Rites of Nationalism in the Early Republic* (Amherst, Mass.: University of Massachusetts Press, 1997); David Waldstreicher, *In the Midst of Perpetual Fetes: The Making of American Nationalism, 1776-1820* (Chapel Hill: Published for the Omohundro Institute of Early American History and Culture, Williamsburg, Virginia, by the University of North Carolina Press, 1997).

5. Teachout, *Capture the Flag.*
6. Lieven, *America Right or Wrong.*
7. Kammen, *People of Paradox*; Lieven, *America Right Or Wrong.*
8. Kammen, *People of Paradox*, 4.
9. Goldstein, *Saving Old Glory*, 82, 91–93; Teachout, *Capture the Flag*, 46–50, 54–72.
10. This gradual delegitimization of opposition and dissent is an underlying narrative in much work on U.S. patriotism; see, e.g., Fousek, *To Lead the Free World*; Goldstein, *Saving Old Glory*; Teachout, *Capture the Flag.*
11. Sarah Thelen, "Helping them Along: Astroturf, Public Opinion, and Nixon's Vietnam War," *49th Parallel* no. 37 (2015); Sarah Thelen, "Mobilizing a Majority: Nixon's 'Silent Majority' Speech and the Domestic Debate over Vietnam," *Journal of American Studies* 51, no. 3 (August 2017): 887–914.
12. Sandra Scanlon, *The Pro-War Movement: Domestic Support for the Vietnam War and the Making of Modern American Conservatism* (Amherst, MA: University of Massachusetts Press, 2013), 190.
13. "Alex Butterfield to Richard Nixon," November 12, 1969, 1, Memoranda for The President's File (November 1969); Box 138; WHSF: SMOF Haldeman, NPLM, College Park, MD.
14. "Love It or ... ... Leave It," *Newsweek*, November 24, 1969.

15. "Alex Butterfield to H.R. Haldeman [2]," November 11, 1969, 1, Memos/Alex Butterfield (November 1969); Box 54; WHSF: SMOF Haldeman, NPLM, College Park, MD.
16. "Love It or ... ... Leave It."
17. "Alex Butterfield to H.R. Haldeman [2]," November 12, 1969, Memos/Alex Butterfield (November 1969); Box 54; WHSF: SMOF Haldeman, NPLM, College Park, MD.
18. "Alex Butterfield to H.R. Haldeman [1]," November 19, 1969, Memos/Alex Butterfield (November 1969); Box 54; WHSF: SMOF Haldeman, NPLM, College Park, MD.
19. "Alex Butterfield to H.R. Haldeman," November 18, 1969, Memos/Alex Butterfield (November 1969); Box 54; WHSF: SMOF Haldeman, NPLM, College Park, MD.
20. "Game Plan for the President's November 3rd Speech on Vietnam, Master Copy," n.d., 10, Silent Majority; Box 1; WHCF: SMOF Butterfield, NPLM, College Park, MD. Emphasis in the original
21. Wells, *The War Within*, 386.
22. "H.R. Haldeman to Jeb Magruder," January 13, 1970, Memos/Jeb Magruder (January 1970); Box 56; WHSF: SMOF Haldeman, NPLM, College Park, MD.
23. "H.R. Haldeman to Jeb Magruder [2]," November 21, 1969, Memos/Jeb Magruder (November 1969); Box 54; WHSF: SMOF Haldeman, NPLM, College Park, MD.
24. "John Brown to H.R. Haldeman," February 20, 1970, H.R. Haldeman A-G Memo Feb 1970; Box 57; WHSF: SMOF Haldeman, NPLM, College Park, MD.
25. Homer Bigart, "Huge City Hall Rally Backs Nixon's Indochina Policies: Thousands at Rally Here Back Nixon on Vietnam," *New York Times* (New York, N.Y., May 21, 1970); "Advertisement: Official Building Trades Rally," *Daily News*, May 18, 1970.
26. "Advertisement: Official Building Trades Rally."
27. "Thomas Nolan to International Union of Operating Engineers," May 18, 1970, Hard Hats; Box 69; WHSF: SMOF Colson, NPLM, College Park, MD.
28. "Memorandum to Richard Nixon," n.d., 2, Hard Hats; Box 20; WHSF: SMOF Colson, NPLM, College Park, MD.
29. Diana Lurie, "Underneath the Hard Hats: A Political Symposium," *New York Magazine*, November 2, 1970, 32.
30. Ibid.

31. "Longshoremen, Construction Workers Support U.S. on Vietnam," *Longshore News*, June 10, 1970; "Steve Bull to Charles Colson," May 22, 1970, Hard Hats; Box 69; WHSF: SMOF Colson, NPLM, College Park, MD.
32. "Tom Huston to Bryce Harlow, Harry Dent, Lyn Nofziger, Murray Chotiner, H.R. Haldeman, and John Ehrlichman," May 15, 1970, 5, HRH Memoranda For The President May 1970; Box 139; WHSF: SMOF Haldeman, NPLM, College Park, MD.
33. "Fred Rohrer to Richard Nixon," May 14, 1970, Cambodia-Letters, Telegrams and Correspondence; Box 42; WHSF: SMOF Colson, NPLM, College Park, MD.
34. "Charles Colson to Fred Rohrer," June 8, 1970, Cambodia-Letters, Telegrams and Correspondence; Box 42; WHSF: SMOF Colson, NPLM, College Park, MD.
35. DeBenedetti, *An American Ordeal*, 288; Sandra Scanlon, "The Pro-Vietnam War Movement During the Nixon Administration" (Thesis (Ph.D.), University of Cambridge, 2005), 165–66; Wells, *The War Within*, 459.
36. Other members of the steering committee: Norman Vincent Peale, Cardinal O'Boyle, Hobe Lewis, John Connally, Irving Feist, Stan Musial, Clarence Mitchell, Henry Ford, Arthur Ashe, Glen Campbell, Clem Stone, William Paley, Johnny Cash, and Arnold Palmer. Additional sponsors were to include: the Chamber, the Jaycees, DAR, AL, Boy Scouts of America, Girl Scouts, Amvets, Jewish War Veterans, the Catholic War Veterans, NAACP, ministers, League of Women Voters, American Society of Association Executives, NAM, UAW, Voluntary Action Group, the Elks, the Kiwanis Clubs, the Rotary Clubs, the Congress, the Legion, construction workers, ASG. "Charles Colson," n.d., "I Love America" July 4th [1970]; Box 73; WHSF: SMOF Colson, NPLM, College Park, MD.
37. Paul Hodge, "Washington Post," *Washington Post*, June 5, 1970.
38. "Memorandum to Charles Colson," n.d., "I Love America" July 4th [1970]; Box 73; WHSF: SMOF Colson, NPLM, College Park, MD.
39. "Charles Colson to Jeb Magruder," June 11, 1970, "I Love America" July 4th [1970]; Box 73; WHSF: SMOF Colson, NPLM, College Park, MD.
40. Ibid.
41. Ibid.
42. "Jeb Magruder to H.R. Haldeman, Herb Klein," July 6, 1970, 2, "I Love America" July 4th [1970]; Box 73; WHSF: SMOF Colson, NPLM, College Park, MD; "Jeb Magruder to H.R. Haldeman and Herb Klein," July 13, 1970, 1, HRH May-Aug 1970 Magruder; Box 62; WHSF: SMOF Haldeman, NPLM, College Park, MD; John MacLean, "400,000 in Capital Join

in 'Honor America Day'',''' *Chicago Tribune (1963-Current file); Chicago, Ill.* (Chicago, Ill., United States, Chicago, Ill., July 5, 1970), sec. 1; Murray Seeger and Rudy Abramson, "America Honored in Capital With Speech, Song, Symbol: Tradition and Protests Mark July 4 Ceremony," *Los Angeles Times (1923-Current File); Los Angeles, Calif.* (Los Angeles, Calif., United States, Los Angeles, Calif., July 5, 1970), sec. A.

43. "Fact Sheet - Honor America Day," n.d., "I Love America" July 4th [1970]; Box 73; WHSF: SMOF Colson, NPLM, College Park, MD; Glen Elsasser, "Flags Will Be Highlight of Fete in Capital Today," *Chicago Tribune (1963-Current file); Chicago, Ill.* (Chicago, Ill., United States, Chicago, Ill., July 4, 1970), sec. 1; Arnold R. Isaacs, "Honor America Day Rites Held," *The Sun (1837-1992); Baltimore, Md.* (Baltimore, Md., United States, Baltimore, Md., July 5, 1970); "Honor America Day Schedule Announced," *The Washington Post, Times Herald (1959-1973); Washington, D.C.* (Washington, D.C., United States, Washington, D.C., July 4, 1970); John Herbers, "Thousands Voice Faith in America at Capital Rally," *The New York Times*, July 5, 1970; Seeger and Abramson, "America Honored in Capital With Speech, Song, Symbol"; MacLean, "400,000 in Capital Join in 'Honor America Day''.'"
44. "Honor America Day Schedule Announced"; Seeger and Abramson, "America Honored in Capital With Speech, Song, Symbol."
45. "Jeb Magruder to H.R. Haldeman, Herb Klein."
46. "1970/07/04," 2.
47. "H.R. Haldeman to Charles Colson," July 8, 1970, HRH-July-August 1970--Staff Memos - Cole-D; Box 61; WHSF: SMOF Haldeman, NPLM, College Park, MD.
48. "Charles Colson to H.R. Haldeman," July 9, 1970, 1, HRH-July-August 1970--Staff Memos - Cole-D; Box 61; WHSF: SMOF Haldeman, NPLM, College Park, MD.
49. Ibid., 3.
50. Ibid.
51. Ibid.
52. Ibid.
53. "Gordon Strachan to Jeb Magruder," September 12, 1972, WHSF: SMOF: H. R. Haldeman: Strachan Chron. M-Z July 1972; Box 14; NPRMC: WHSF: Contested Materials, NPLM, Yorba Linda, CA. Emphasis in original.
54. Ibid.
55. Richard M Nixon, *RN: The Memoirs of Richard Nixon* (London, UK: Sidgwick and Jackson, 1978), 763. In a diary entry extracted in his memoirs,

Nixon remembers that he and Haldeman had been discussing the association between negative characters and flag lapel pins in the recent films *The Man* and *The Candidate.*

56. Ibid.
57. Teachout, *Capture the Flag*, 201-2.
58. Hal Riney and The Tuesday Team, "Prouder, Stronger, Better," *The Living Room Candidate (Museum of the Moving Image)*, September 17, 1984, http://www.livingroomcandidate.org/commercials/1984/prouder-stronger-better.
59. *Texas v. Johnson*, 155 (United States Supreme Court 1989).
60. George Bush, "Remarks to the American Legislative Exchange Council," March 1, 1991, Online by Gerhard Peters and John T. Woolley, The American Presidency Project. http://www.presidency.ucsb.edu/ws/?pid=19351.
61. George McKenna, *Puritan Origins of American Patriotism* (Yale University Press, 2007), 351.
62. David Foster Wallace, "The View from Mrs. Thompson's," in *Consider the Lobster and Other Essays* (New York: Little, Brown, 2005), 130.
63. Jeff Zeleny, "The Politician and the Absent American Flag Pin" (New York, N.Y., United States, 2007), http://search.proquest.com.proxyau.wrlc.org/hnpnewyorktimes/docview/848043651/abstract/138ABBC61BD2466065A/1?accountid=8285.
64. Ibid.
65. "Was Barack Obama Shunning the American Flag?" rush transcript, posted online, *Hannity & Colmes*, October 4, 2007, http://www.foxnews.com/story/2007/10/05/was-barack-obama-shunning-american-flag.html.
66. Jeff Mason, "Obama dons flag pin again, says it's a 'phony issue,'" *Reuters Blogs*, n.d., http://blogs.reuters.com/talesfromthetrail/2008/05/14/obama-dons-flag-pin-again-says-its-a-phony-issue/; "Obama returns to the flag after Republicans attack his patriotism | The Independent," n.d., http://www.independent.co.uk/news/world/americas/obama-returns-to-the-flag-after-republicans-attack-his-patriotism-828309.html; "Breaking News: Obama caves! Flag pin returns to his coat lapel," *LA Times Blogs - Top of the Ticket*, April 16, 2008, http://latimesblogs.latimes.com/washington/2008/04/obamaflagpinlap.html; "ABC Defends the Obama Flag-Pin Question," *Vanity Fair*, April 2008, https://www.vanityfair.com/news/2008/04/abc-under-fire; Jay Newton-Small, "Obama's Flag Pin Flip-Flop?," *Time*, May 14, 2008, http://content.time.com/time/politics/article/0,8599,1779544,00.html.

67. "Obama defends Kaepernick's anthem protest - CNNPolitics," September 29, 2016, http://edition.cnn.com/2016/09/28/politics/obama-colin-kaepernick-nfl-national-anthem-presidential-town-hall-cnn/index.html.
68. Woden Teachout, *Capture the Flag: A Political History of American Patriotism* (New York, NY: Basic Books, 2009), 8.
69. John McCain, "Remarks by Senator John McCain as 2017 Liberty Medal Ceremony," October 16, 2017, https://www.mccain.senate.gov/public/index.cfm/press-releases?ContentRecord_id=3E879161-766F-4E0B-8FC9-F446A9F341F5.

Provisional Healing

Vietnam Memorials and the Limits of Memory

William Thomas Allison

There is a 1955 Chevy two-door sedan painted to honor American prisoners of war and missing in action in Vietnam, which appears at special events around the United States.[1] A fully restored and operational dragster, this auto-memorial is a labor of love for a small group of Vietnam veterans in northern California. The car itself is a brilliant, polished black, just like the National Vietnam Veterans Memorial (NVVM, otherwise known as "The Wall") on the National Mall in Washington, D.C. While working inside veteran Max Loffgren's garage in Willow, California, volunteers painstakingly placed 3,578 names in raised vinyl lettering on the car before adding a protective, clear coating. The entire process took over 500 hours to complete. Loffgren and his friends had a purpose behind their design. The names are arranged in neat rows on both sides of the car so that people would not have to kneel to read them. Despite the thick, clear coating, the lettering— each letter one-quarter inch in size and each name spaced one-quarter inch apart, with three-eighths of an inch between each row of names— is raised so that visitors can feel the names, just as they can at The Wall. And like The Wall, there is little context of the war on the car. Other than the names, it only displays the phrase, "POW/MIA," on both sides of the enormous dragster air intake atop the hood as well as along its front.

The car is Loffgren's brainchild. A retired firefighter, Loffgren served in Vietnam in the 23rd Infantry "Americal" Division of the United States Army from 1969 to 1970. Looking for a way to honor veterans of the Vietnam War, Loffgren naturally turned to his hobby of building and racing classic dragsters. While the idea dates to the early 1990s, the 1955 Chevy's current iteration dates from 2002, when Loffgren formed a nonprofit organization tellingly named Never Forgotten, Inc., to manage the expense of maintaining the car and transporting it to events around the United States. Dozens of individuals, businesses, and organizations in northern California have supported Never Forgotten, including several veterans' organizations. Loffgren's goal is to use the car more to "educate than race." On Never Forgotten's Facebook page, Loffgren claims "The car speaks for itself… People understand it."[2]

But who understands it, and why should this Chevy be understood? No doubt Vietnam veterans understand the symbolic nature of the car and are grateful for the attention it brings to their service. Loffgren's 1955 Chevy is The Wall on wheels and was intentionally designed as such because people would, or should, know what it represents. Families of prisoners of war and those still listed as missing in action understand what they are looking at when they see the car at an airshow, or county fair, or Veterans Day celebration. But do people, in general, get it? At the very least, the car evokes recognition if one is familiar with the NVVM. Veterans, of course, will never forget, but will the American people?

The 1982 dedication of the NVVM sparked a memorial-building frenzy across the United States. Memorials commemorating a seemingly endless list of people, events, identities, and causes sprung up around the country. More directly, the NVVM inspired an explosion of Vietnam memorials, including the Never Forgotten POW/MIA car. While around forty Vietnam memorials existed before 1982, hundreds of monuments of various types have been erected since that year on the grounds of state capitols, in city parks, and in other public and private spaces in just about every corner of America. By some counts, there are over 500 memorials of some form or fashion associated with the American war in Vietnam.[3] Many are stand-alone permanent monuments built of granite or marble. Dozens are part of memorials that honor those who served in all wars. Several include statuary and static displays (the ubiquitous UH-1 "Huey," for example), while still others are temporary or mobile, such as the various traveling "Walls," or Loffgren's Chevy.

Some of these memorials received public funding, but most were the result of volunteerism: private donations and fundraising events alongside governmental provisions of space for the memorial. These monuments' installations typically began with a veteran, or groups of veterans, who identified an alignment of opportunity and civic concerns to help create a permanent remembrance of their war. These costly undertakings took tremendous effort and dedication on the part of countless volunteers to organize, fund, design, build, dedicate, and maintain.

Collectively, these Vietnam memorials offer a fascinating study of memory, civic art, and the shaping of a narrative for a war the United States lost: a war that remains unsettled in the American public consciousness. Who builds these memorials? What motivates people to undertake such a task? Why do individuals, civic organizations, and businesses spend hundreds of thousands of dollars to memorialize a lost war Americans are still trying to forget? What form do these memorials take and what do their designs symbolize? What is the intended purpose or objective? Do Vietnam memorials have longevity? What do these questions reveal about the evolution of the memory of the Vietnam War and about war memory itself?

The irony of war memorials, or any memorial, lies in their "permanent temporary" condition. While their structure may be imperishable, their meaning can be less so despite the intentions of those who establish them. Memorials and monuments are, in the words of author and professor of creative writing Michael Martone, "actuarial tables in stone... the preferred material for casting the illusion of time immemorial."[4] The historian Jay Winter concurs, contending that "historical remembrance" is indeed dependent upon "space and time."[5] Memorials should give a sense of a specific present, one that future generations of visitors of a culture or society should at least recognize regardless of how far along the stream of time they are from both the memorialized event and the moment the memorial was dedicated. As members of that culture or society, visitors at any moment in time should be able to relate to what stands before them. This enhances the necessary emotional sense of belonging and community that war memorials symbolize and instill. Otherwise, memorials become objects of poorly understood curiosity, residing as artifacts of a bygone time. "Memorials," the American Studies scholar Erika Doss agrees, "embody the histories and feelings that respective Americans choose to remember at particular moments."[6] Such is the case with many American war memorials, particularly those for Vietnam.

War memorials bind citizens to their nation. Through the memorialization of a collective, wartime sacrifice to the nation, lasting national memories are established among its citizens. For the citizen, this connection helps shape a national identity, which as Winter suggests, should transcend space and time. From this identity stems nationalism, the ultimate expression of the willingness of a citizenry to participate in state-sanctioned violence against another state. The concepts of justified killing and honorable death at the behest of a nation's leaders are at the very heart of maintaining a national identity. Americans today seldom reflect on this ultimate demand of citizenship in their daily lives unless they are in the military or have family members or other loved ones who serve. A visit to a war memorial, however, ought to bring this concept abruptly to the forefront. These places of national remembrance serve as emotional reminders of this willingness to sacrifice by honoring those citizens who fought and died in the name of national identity— for the nation.[7]

For this to work and have the most meaningful impact, war memorials must portray a memory (preferably an accurate one though not necessarily so). The sociologist Jeffrey Olick makes a good case for the importance of this process in his study on national retrospection. That is, national memories are necessary to enhance national identity, but to have a national identity the nation must have memories. Memories of sacrifice in war are among the most crucial in joining a citizen with their nation.[8]

While war memorials provide critical links between the citizen and the nation, such connections are perilously fragile, because national memory can be so easily manipulated. Recall the collective trauma left behind by the First World War, and how the National Socialists weaponized those wounds in Germany during the 1930s. Recall the cult of Stalin in Russia: how one tyrant utilized nationalism to bolster his seat of power. Recall the continued— if increasingly tenuous— survival of the Confederate Lost Cause mythology throughout the deep south of the United States. The political or social needs of a given time can override authentic memories to create a misleading link with the past. It does not take much to sway a national narrative in favor of an ulterior motive. If Samuel Johnson's 1758 lament that "Among the calamities of war may be justly numbered the diminution of the love of truth, by the falsehoods which interest dictates and credulity encourages," is correct, then perhaps it is equally so in the memory of war.[9]

How do war memorials, then, shape such memories? Memorials cannot over-emphasize the trauma of war. Otherwise, citizens may conclude that killing and dying for the nation is a sacrifice too far. Political scientist Jenny Edkins suggests the nation, therefore, must deemphasize state-sanctioned horror into a "linear narrative of national heroism" throughout the course of its national story, and war memorials work toward that end.[10] When done effectively, war memorials hide war trauma while emphasizing heroism and sacrifice, which enhances nationalism among citizens. If, however, the war in question does not fit the national narrative, it can be forgotten, leaving those who sacrificed and those who were victims of a tragically misguided state policy denied their due recognition, stripped of their legitimacy, and absent from the national memory.[11] In reminding citizens of their national identity and of their role within the nation, there is an inherent tension between the trauma and heroism of war. This is especially true in the case of Vietnam. Since the end of the war, as American Studies scholar Julia Bleakney notes, the practice of memorializing Vietnam has gradually moved from the collective to the individual, remaining predominantly conservative, and becoming over time increasingly divorced from the facts of the war. As Bleakney puts it, "How the war is remembered has shifted from national soul-searching toward personal identity and recovery." Thus, the war has been reinvented or restyled around healing and absolution on the one hand and "the war as a noble cause and its veterans as heroes" on the other.[12] With Vietnam memorials, Americans chose to honor those who fought and died while patently ignoring the implications of the war in which they fought.

But of what are we to be reminded? What ought to be memorialized? Are memorials meant to restore the glory of the nation, or to confirm the justness of the cause? Are we recognizing unrecognized service? Is the sacrifice of the dead at risk of being forgotten? Do memorials warn future generations against foolhardy intervention in foreign civil wars? Are these memorials for "them," the veterans, or for "us," the broader citizenry? Can they not be for both? At the level of local government, can these memorials also be the result of civic competition? After all, if the county two counties over has a veterans memorial, we had better get one, too, lest we seem unsupportive of our veterans, or worse still, miss out on tourist dollars. Does civic pride not demand a piece of civic art to help legitimatize the civic polity? What better way to jump on the community bandwagon of memory and unquestioning patriotism than to have a war memorial?

What veterans and other volunteers have erected across the United States in state capitals, counties, and burgs must compare to the NVVM on the Washington Mall. The idea of a national memorial originated from veteran Jan Scruggs, who spearheaded the effort along with his Vietnam Veterans Memorial Fund (VVMF). As has been well documented, the challenges presented by the establishment of a national Vietnam memorial were immense.[13] Commemorating a war defeat, especially one that had divided the nation so deeply, would not be easy. Scruggs wanted no overt political statement in the design, fearing the potential polarization of such a monument between the conservative "politicians wouldn't let us win the war"-types and the leftist radicals of the sixties who still rabidly opposed what they considered to be an immoral war. To minimize or undercut such controversy, the primary requirement for design submissions was that the monument had to list the names of the over 58,000 American service members who died in Vietnam and be "reflective and contemplative in nature."[14] The design guidelines, in the words of art historian Harriet F. Senie, "intended from the start to separate the dead from the undeclared war in which they disappeared or perished."[15] The design committee received over 1,400 submissions, an astonishing number revealing substantial interest for some sort of national reconciliation over Vietnam. Numerous public and private stakeholders jockeyed for influence on the final design decision, which in the end was reached through compromise to partially satisfy veterans, the various federal bureaucracies that managed the National Mall, and the design winner, the twenty-one-year-old Yale student of Asian descent, Maya Lin.

Lin's winning design incited immediate and intense controversy, but once The Wall was completed, it would become the most visited memorial in the United States. Lin brilliantly condensed the enormously complex and conflicted emotions of the war, still fresh and raw in the early 1980s, into a flawlessly simple concept that honored the dead of what many Americans considered a dishonorable war and provided an almost purifying healing to those who had survived it. That veterans had come to perceive their own service in such a war as also dishonorable is a fascinating evolution in the way veterans saw themselves during the years following Vietnam.[16]

Very few anti-war protesters had a go at the soldiers themselves, as the peaceniks tended to view those who served in Vietnam as victims of an immoral policy. It was only after the war that the myth of the sullied veteran began to develop, but the myth stuck and became the new reality for the way veterans viewed themselves by the late 1970s. Whether they needed it or not, veterans wanted absolution, recognition, and dignity for their service in Vietnam. As veterans accepted this construct, it became embedded in the American national psyche. By the late 1970s, this was part of the Vietnam narrative.[17]

According to the art and architectural historian Kirk Savage, Lin created the first American memorial to serve as a sort of therapy couch for both veterans *and* the American national identity. Hers was a memorial designed "expressly to heal a collective psychological injury" inflicted on the American national psyche by the nightmarish ordeal of the Vietnam War.[18] Scruggs even titled his account of getting the National Vietnam Memorial established *To Heal a Nation.*

Was it about healing a nation, or healing veterans? In her design, Lin boldly tried to do both, as Scruggs had intended when he first envisioned a national memorial. She described her creation as an "anti-monument" that represented the dead and missing in a cemetery *in absentia.*[19] As Senie put it, Lin "embedded her memorial into the earth and created an aggregate tombstone. She saw the Vietnam Veterans Memorial as an impermeable membrane separating the living from the dead."[20] Heavily influenced by her study of funerary architecture and earthen sculpture at Yale, Lin employed both in her design. The entire concept relies on a passage of remembrance into the ground, flanked by the long polished black granite panels listing the names by year of death going down each side, meeting at a 125-degree apex ten-feet deep into the ground. The apex was key to the original design concept. Two connecting panels list the first and last casualties, which Lin intended the visitor to approach head-on to realize the timeline of the war from the beginning on one flank and the end on the other, providing emotional closure at the apex.[21]

Practical challenges, however, initially blurred Lin's vision of the visitor experience. Drainage concerns and crowd movement dictated the addition of a pathway to funnel visitors down either flank and out the other. This change enhanced Lin's original idea. As one travels downward toward the apex, the horrific cost of Vietnam weighs on the visitor. Then, coming up out of the depths along the other panel, the visitor should feel the transition from grief to healing. It is as if Lin is taking the visitor into darkness, but provides a means of escape into light, an apt metaphor for the American experience in Vietnam. Thus, the monument entices the visitor to take a journey, albeit an uncomfortable one. But, perhaps that was the point. One had to experience pain before one could heal, be it as an individual or as a nation. If the primary purpose of the national memorial was to absolve and heal both the veteran and the nation, then Lin's design seemed to do both.[22]

Before that healing could begin, the design itself drew the ire of omnipresent critics. Many objected to the stark nature of the design, which ran visibly counter to the classical architectural style of the other monuments on the Mall. The long black row of panels meeting deep in the earth, critics cried, resembled an open wound. Veterans protested that the design implied their service had been dishonorable, symbolized in perpetuity now by a dark "gash of shame." Black, darkness, and evil, even racial overtones seem to stand out to the critics. Lin responded, explaining she chose polished black granite for its reflective qualities, and appropriate to a piece of funerary architecture, black was the traditional color of mourning. Nevertheless, veterans and other critics demanded alterations that highlighted their honorable service. They wanted a traditional "war" monument, *a la* the Iwo Jima Memorial.[23]

As a compromise, the Commission on Fine Arts, the bureaucratic entity charged with overseeing the design, added Frederick Hart's Three Servicemen statue, the American flag (which had been absent in Lin's design submission), and later Glenna Goodacre's Pietà -like sculpture as the Vietnam Women's Memorial. The presence of the American flag symbolically legitimized service in the war. Both sculptures focused more on sacrifice, trauma, and healing than heroism.[24] The Wall, the Three Soldiers, the Vietnam Women's Memorial, and the flag– the core components that make up the NVVM complex– became base fixtures for future Vietnam memorials around the United States.

As soon as the NVVM opened to the public, visitor reactions at the site fascinated observers. Visitors posed for photographs in front of the statues where there was little solemnity but then fell into a mournful tone at The Wall.[25] Facing the panels of names, people behaved, according to Senie, "reverentially, as if they were at a cemetery, largely because the presence of bodies is implied by the list of names" on the polished black panels. Few anticipated the phenomena of the rubbing of engraved names and offerings of remembrance, which continue to this day over thirty-five years removed from the dedication and over forty-five years after the United States withdrew from South Vietnam.[26] Even naming the memorial required negotiation and compromise. Ultimately Scruggs' vision became the "Vietnam Veterans Memorial" rather than the "Vietnam War Memorial," which is revealing in and of itself. The monument is about veterans of that war and those who lost their lives in Vietnam. It is not about the *war.*

Contrary to the naysayers who criticized the design, the NVVM was, for want of a better term, a hit. With the tumultuous end of the war, the resignation of a president because of scandal, the economic difficulties of the 1970s, and the general malaise of the post-Vietnam years, The Wall gave Americans exactly the sort of therapy they believed they needed. It helped cleanse the guilt over the war and national shame over its cost in lives and to its survivors. Just as significant, the NVVM unleashed what Doss later called "memorial mania" at the national, state, and local levels.[27]

Image 12. Tokens of remembrance at the base of the Vietnam Veterans Memorial on the day before its official dedication, November 12, 1982

Source: National Archives and Records Administration.

But, why? Why did this urge to memorialize appeal so abruptly to Americans around the country? Doss offers a compelling explanation, suggesting Lin had unintentionally provided a mass release of anxiety, which had arguably always been present in the American national conscience but had been contained, even hidden, in response to the pressures of conformity and superficial patriotism. Vietnam had brought it to the surface, and then Lin unintentionally let the pot boil over with her monument. Doss suggests by listing the names of the dead and thereby making the cost of Vietnam both individual and collective, The Wall gave license for all sorts of voices to be heard, to share their narratives, to reveal "individual memories" and even settle "personal grievances." Many were sincere, many others less so, as competing social and political narratives fought to "harness those anxieties and control particular narratives about the nation and its publics." Far from healing the nation, the NVVM instead caused a philosophical riot over who could share their memories as well as who would control them. According to Doss, "Driven by heated struggles over self-definition, national purpose, and the politics of representation, memorial mania is especially shaped by the affective conditions of public life in American today; by the fevered pitch of public feelings such as grief, gratitude, fear, shame, and anger."[28]

Absolution and healing remain steadfast as core themes of these new Vietnam memorials. Veterans finally received the nation's recognition that they believed they deserved. They could grieve, while the nation apologized for ostracizing them, for failing to give them a meaningful "welcome home." President Ronald Reagan "nobly" recognized their service and the war in which they fought, but also embraced the prevailing "healing" theme. Reagan's November 1984 speech marking the transfer of the NVVM to the care of the federal government none-too-subtly emphasized healing and forgiveness in the interest of unity, of moving on from the national nightmare of Vietnam. After all, there was still a Cold War to be won. Nevertheless, neither Reagan nor the memorial the federal government now had in its care confronted the moral questions of American involvement in Vietnam, which so many Americans doubted and protested during the war, and which still divided the nation. The American Studies scholar Patrick Hagopian agrees: "If the memorial did bring its visitors to a stark confrontation with a roster of the dead, we find no comparable honesty about American wrongdoing in Vietnam: not in the rationale behind the memorial's founding, not in the monument itself, and not in the speechmaking surrounding it."[29]

The new Vietnam memorials erected around the United States followed a similar thematic path as the NVVM in origination, organization, design, and purpose. In fact, there is little variation in Vietnam memorials. The core components of walled panels listing the dead and contemplative or traumatic rather than heroic statuary dominate design concepts. The themes remain consistent as well. Designs focus on the sacrifice of the dead and honorable service of the veteran while avoiding political comment or even the historical context of the war itself.[30]

Following the 1982 dedication of NVVM, traveling replica Walls appeared around the United States. These are portable, scale replicas of Lin's memorial built by individuals and organizations with the intent of giving people who cannot travel to Washington, D.C., the opportunity to grieve and heal closer to home. There are at least four replicas currently in operation, which can cost as much as $4,000 to set up in a town for several days. Veteran John Devitt's Vietnam Combat Veterans organization manages two replica Walls. Initially a critic of Lin's design for the NVVM, Devitt was emotionally overwhelmed by its impact on himself and other veterans after visiting The Wall in 1982. From that experience, Devitt built the first of two "Moving Walls," which debuted in Tyler, Texas, in 1984. In 1996, Service Corporation International (SCI), a major funeral service provider and cemetery management firm, approached Jan Scruggs at the VVMF about establishing another traveling Wall. Knowing that earlier, Devitt had rejected a partnership with SCI, Scruggs jumped at the opportunity. Calling his replica "The Wall That Heals," the VVMF (along with SCI until 2007 when SCI created its Dignity Memorial Vietnam Wall) toured the replica around the country, building somewhat of a rivalry with Devitt's Moving Walls. Both The Wall That Heals and the Moving Wall occasionally even appear in the same city at the same time![31]

For local veterans especially, it is a major event to have one of these traveling Walls visit for a few days. Schools bring busloads of students and often hundreds of people travel from miles around to stand before a replica of the real thing. If organized well, veterans are on hand to speak with young people. As with the permanent memorials, local fundraising pays for these temporary exhibits rather than tax dollars. One can debate the merits of these Walls versus visiting the real one, but interestingly people respond much the same way as visitors do in Washington, D.C. There is a sense of reverence, if not grief, but one wonders how much of this behavior is routinized by observing behavior at the original Wall through film and television, and even online. Bleakney suggests visitors to these replica Walls have been conditioned in this way "without fully understanding what they are doing and why— without knowing, in other words, the significance of touching a name etched onto granite." Visitors take rubbings of names (The Wall That Heals offers "virtual" rubbings, while the Moving Wall allows visitors to take actual rubbings), and leave offerings of remembrance just as they do at the original Wall. Afterward, veterans remember when "The Wall" came to town. These visits are moments of civic commemoration, temporary though they may be, as well as sources of civic pride, which hopefully do some good while just as easily feeding "uncritical patriotism." Millions of people have visited, and continue to visit, these moving Walls, but once Vietnam veterans are gone, will these traveling memorials still maintain their attraction? Sadly, probably not.[32]

A recent visit of "The Wall That Heals" in Kalispell, Montana, shows the popularity of the traveling Walls. Members of the local chapter of the Vietnam Veterans of America organized the visit, which included raising funds to pay for the four-day display. Rosauers Supermarket near the Kalispell Airport provided space. The display was open to the public twenty-four hours per day. Vietnam veterans on motorcycles escorted the display transport into town. A half-scale replica of the real Wall, "The Wall That Heals" includes a mobile education center, which "teaches the history of the Vietnam War." Its visit to Kalispell from September 7-10, 2017, was its second in the area since 2013. Interestingly, that 2013 visit in nearby Whitefish, Montana, spurred the creation of Northwest Montana Vietnam Veterans of America Chapter 1087, which the *Flathead Beacon* claims is one the most active veterans group in Montana. John Wise, a veteran who helped organize the event in Kalispell, tried to describe for nonveterans what it meant to see the names even on this traveling Wall: "It brings out of a lot of emotions for veterans. It's really hard to explain the experience." For local veteran Lee Heser, the traveling Wall's second visit to the region was extraordinary: "Lots of cities and towns wait and wait and wait to get the Wall for the first time, and this is our second time, so we are quite privileged."[33] This event was an extraordinary moment for veterans, and probably for the community as well.

Like the NVVM and the traveling replicas, many state and local memorials list names of the fallen, often on dark polished granite or stone native to the region. The effect on the visitor is similar— quiet, reflective, somber, as if the dead are contained within the panels. There are dozens of useful examples at the state and local level. The Maryland Vietnam Veterans Memorial lists 1,046 Marylanders who died in Vietnam, plus thirty-eight listed as missing in action, on polished stone panels in a large semi-circle. Veterans initiated the project through the private Maryland Vietnam Veterans Memorial Commission and helped raise over $2,250,000 to pay for the memorial. The State of Maryland's Veterans Commission took responsibility for the site upon its dedication in 1989.[34] Oregon's Vietnam Veterans Memorial occupies a more park-like setting, which Scruggs originally envisioned for the NVVM in Washington, D.C. Located in a Portland city park, in a grassy bowl lined with native trees, shallow, black granite panels listing Oregon's Vietnam dead border a 1,200-foot long spiral path in what had been a large amphitheater in one of Portland's city parks. Local veterans began the project after visiting the NVVM in 1982, raising more than $1 million to pay design and construction costs. The Oregon Vietnam Veterans Memorial Fund maintains the site, even though it is on city property.[35] The State of Washington Vietnam Veterans Memorial in Olympia, Kansas City's Vietnam Veterans Memorial Fountain, the Philadelphia Vietnam Veterans Memorial, a brick and granite Wall in Texarkana, Texas, among many others, have a similar story and design.[36]

The California State Vietnam Memorial in Sacramento and Western Slope Vietnam War Memorial Park in Fruita, Colorado, are typical of Vietnam memorials established through civic/private partnerships. The California State Vietnam Memorial began in 1983, just less than a year after the dedication of the NVVM, at the behest of Vietnam veterans in Sonoma and Marin counties. Although authorized by the California legislature in September 1983, the memorial itself took five years from that point to complete. While the state provided space on the grounds of the California State Capitol complex in Sacramento, funding for the memorial came entirely from private donations totaling $2.5 million. The physical structure includes twenty-two polished black granite panels listing over 5,000 Californians killed in Vietnam or listed as missing in action, arranged in a circular complex. In the center is a statue of a bareheaded, seated combat soldier, holding his M-16 rifle in one hand and a letter from home in the other, while staring emptily into the distance. The dedication plaque in part reads: "The people of the State of California dedicate this Monument to the memory of those Californians who died, or remain missing, in the Vietnam War 1959-1975 and in doing so Honor all the men and women who served during that war. All Gave Some, Some Gave All."[37]

The Western Slope Vietnam Memorial Park's Welcome Home Memorial was founded by Jim Doody, whose brother Thomas Doody was killed in action as a helicopter pilot in Vietnam in 1971. Doody's intent was to both honor his brother but also "make up for the welcome home that so many Vietnam veterans didn't get to enjoy" (another common theme of the veteran experience). Doody organized much of the labor and materials gratis from the Associated Builders and Contractors of America, while donations and fundraisers provided for other costs. The city of Fruita, Colorado, designated a plot of land as part of the city parks system, but still required Doody to provide an additional $10,000 for maintenance of the site. The memorial itself includes black granite panels that list not only the names of the fifty-five Vietnam casualties from the Western Slope region of Colorado but also the names of all veterans of all wars from that area. A bronze statue set depicts a soldier returning home, greeted by his parents. Because Doody's brother was a helicopter pilot, he included a static Huey perched high above the panels. Like the California memorial, there is little context beyond the listed names. The City of Fruita gained a monument not only for Vietnam but for all wars and had to do next to nothing for it. Doody and his volunteers did the demanding hard work that made the memorial possible.[38]

School children have even initiated Vietnam memorials. The Connecticut Vietnam Veterans Memorial in Coventry, Connecticut, dedicated in 2008, arose from a middle school history class project on the 612 Connecticut service members killed in Vietnam. In 2001, teacher Thomas Dzicek had his history class at Captain Nathan Hale Middle School in Coventry compile mini-biographies of each service member from Connecticut who died in the war. The project took over one and a half years to complete, resulting in a locally printed book aptly titled *612.* Jean Risely, a sister of Robert Tillquist, a combat medic from Connecticut who was killed in action at Pleiku in 1965, helped with the project but wanted more than the book to honor the 612. Risely formed the Connecticut Vietnam Veterans Memorial Committee, which by 2006 had secured the moral support of the Coventry town council and began raising funds. The town council provided space in Veterans' Memorial Green in downtown Coventry, which had served as the militia training ground during the American War for Independence and the War of 1812 and where several other monuments reside. Risely organized fundraising events, including dinners put on by students and the local chapter of American Legion

Riders, as well as solicited support from veterans' organizations and businesses not only in Coventry but from across the state of Connecticut.

The Connecticut Vietnam Memorial's design is simple. It is, in essence, a four-paneled replica of Lin's Wall. Two polished black granite panels listing the 612 engraved names come together at a slightly offset angle, mimicking the apex of The Wall. The seals of each military service dot the base of the monument, while across the top are the dates 1959-1975 and the standard "All Gave Some, Some Gave All" salute. On the left side of the base is engraved "Connecticut Vietnam Veterans Memorial." At the far end of each flank are etchings of the Three Soldiers statue and National Women's Vietnam Veterans Memorial. Behind the memorial are three flag poles, flying the Connecticut state flag, the United States flag, and the ever-present black POW/MIA flag. Hundreds of people attended the dedication in May 2008.

The memorial's website reveals the intended dual purpose of establishing the monument: "It is hoped that this memorial will make the Veterans [of] Coventry and the State of Connecticut proud and remind future generations of their sacrifices," and to "welcome home our Vietnam veterans."[39] The memorial represents tremendous local effort. It is also typical in that it says very little about the Vietnam War itself. Much like the POW/MIA 1955 Chevy, there are only subtle suggestions that this memorial is about the Vietnam War. Still, veterans had been honored with a monument built mainly by veterans and their loved ones. Lin's design appeared to have achieved perfection. The mantra seemed to be that it was hard to improve upon her basic concept, so other than adding a helicopter-on-a-stick here and there, why change it? It told a story and established a narrative veterans wanted. The politics and history of the war had largely been set aside. What happens when there are no more Vietnam veterans to visit this place of remembrance? How will visitors fifty years from now interpret this memorial and those in Sacramento and Fruita?

When all the hoopla and good feeling fades away, ultimately the local government gets a memorial that others worked hard to establish. A charitable view would point to the community spirit built by diverse groups of people coming together in this effort with the cooperation of local government to create a meaningful space of remembrance for the town. A more cynical view might suggest that local government, stretched thin on resources, is glad to allow this to happen because of the return on sales tax revenues from people visiting the town to see the memorial, which cost them very little to build. Cities incur slight risk for a decent return on not investing much. Few would argue over the sincerity of those involved, but it does seem to work both ways.

Statuary is frequently part of these memorial complexes, often mimicking both sculptures at the NVVM in depicting suffering and sacrifice while deemphasizing heroism. The faces often have a standard expression— one that seems to ask "why?" One of the earliest Vietnam monuments did exactly that when erected in 1967. World War One veterans in Placer County, California, wanted a memorial for all soldiers of all wars, but the times dictated the design. A Vietnam soldier looks skyward as he holds a dying comrade, asking the heavens for an explanation for the high cost of war; the base of the statue asks the obvious to the less informed: in all caps, "WHY?" Sculpted in bright stone, the statue sits in front of the Placer County Administration Center, facing a cemetery. There is an eternal flame, which is not surprising since 1967 was only a few years removed from John F. Kennedy's burial at Arlington National Cemetery. After the war ended in 1973, the flame went out at the Placer County Veterans Memorial and remained that way for over twenty years.[40]

A similar statue appears on the grounds of the Texas state capitol in Austin, which depicts a group of ethnically diverse combat infantrymen in a defensive position just after a fire-fight. They are exhausted, fearful, yet vigilant as one of their number receives attention from a medic. The statue is one the few Vietnam memorials formally referred to as a "monument" rather than a memorial.[41] The Faces of War Memorial in Roswell, Georgia, is haunting in its bronze relief of a combat soldier reaching out across space to touch the hand of his daughter back home. The bronze statue of the little girl is separate from the relief wall, enhancing its three-dimensional effect.[42] The Arkansas Vietnam Veterans Memorial includes a bronze soldier, titled "The Grunt," standing with his helmet in one hand and M-16 rifle in the other. "The Grunt" stares not at the black panels listing the names of the dead, but rather toward the Arkansas State House, toward the politicians, in a subtle yet poignant political statement. Interestingly, the Arkansas memorial is a rare example of government matching funds raised by private donations dollar for dollar.[43]

Westchester County's Vietnam Veterans Memorial in New York has one of the more striking statue groupings. Set among boulders and trees, a soldier emerges dramatically from the rocks carrying a wounded comrade, clearly in extreme pain. The long slender figure of the shirtless, wounded warrior recalls Renaissance paintings depicting the lowering of Christ from the cross. Some yards away, a female nurse hurries toward the pair to give aid. The setting and statues are quite moving; even photos of the monument will get one's heart racing a bit. The soldier's face is laced with fear; the wounded man's expression is one of agony; the nurse's face reveals feminine compassion.[44] The Vietnam Veterans Memorial of San Antonio has a similar look, minus the nurse. A radioman looks skyward in desperation for the medevac chopper to arrive, while using his hand to stop the bleeding from the neck of his wounded comrade. The realism is stunning.[45] The Inland Northwest Vietnam Veterans Memorial in Spokane, Washington, dedicated in 1985, includes a bronze statue of a sitting soldier, holding a letter from home, looking exhaustedly into space.[46] Whether revealed in solitary reflection or caring for a wounded fellow soldier, regardless of race, ethnicity, or gender, emotional anguish is the common theme. What these statues say on behalf of veterans is, to quote Hagopian, "Vietnam is not something we did; it is something that happened to us and that did things to us."[47] They all ask "why?"

An occasionally overlooked means of honoring those who served in Vietnam is the one-memorial-fits-all approach often found at the county or municipal level. Not to be left out of "memorial mania," but either short on funds or reluctant to sink a lot of money into a memorial honoring a lost war, why not give a shoutout to all veterans? These memorials combine the World Wars, Korea, Vietnam, the Gulf War, and even recent conflicts to commemorate a locality's collective contribution to the nation. Catch-all memorials are often the most interesting and most safe. They connect local service and sacrifice to the national narrative. They list local dead or list all who served or both. They can cost a lot of money but can make a place like Sulphur Springs, Texas, a destination— see the Hopkins County Veterans Memorial on the town square, taste our wines, eat our food, buy from our shops. The Hopkins County Veterans Memorial is quite impressive and was initiated and funded by the efforts of local veterans and generous planning assistance from city and county officials who recognized the civic and economic value of having such a memorial as a centerpiece of a revitalized downtown square.[48] The same is found in College Station, Texas, which is home to the still under construction Brazos Valley Veterans Memorial. A long-term project that is dependent entirely upon private donations, the memorial will ultimately include statues of soldiers representing all periods of American military history, in addition to listing the names of all veterans from the College Station-Bryan-Brazos River Valley region. It is an ambitious undertaking, and since beginning work in 2000, organizers have raised millions of dollars, which should come as no surprise considering the rich military tradition of nearby Texas A&M University. It almost seems, however, more of a tourist attraction rather than a place for somber reflection.[49] Ohio Veterans Memorial Park in Clinton, Ohio, is also a typical example of the catch-all memorial, complete with Walls, static displays, memorial benches, and other forms of commemoration.[50]

For Vietnam, these combo memorials avoid discomforting questions and conflicted emotions. All veterans can feel good about themselves and their service, and the community can honor them, regardless of the nature of the war in which they served. Vietnam is balanced by the presence of World War II, which in turn is made less triumphant because of the presence of Vietnam. They are meant for multiple audiences, are sources of civic pride, and are uncontroversial. It appears everyone involved wins, but do they? And, for how long?

A third and perhaps least creative and meaningful Vietnam memorial is the static display of the helicopter-on-a-stick or tank-on-blocks variety. Indeed, who does not enjoy a piece of military equipment? But while the Huey is a ubiquitous symbol of the Vietnam experience for veterans of that war, how does it achieve broader commemoration or lasting memory? There are several around the country, including a Huey that flew in the war at the Lower Alabama Vietnam Memorial in Mobile, Alabama, which also includes a bronze statue of a veteran holding a dog tag, looking at the panels of names as if searching for a dead comrade.[51] The Kent County Veterans Memorial Park in Dover, Delaware, also has a static Huey that saw service in Vietnam.[52] There are dozens of these types of displays that are part of Vietnam memorials. Without any context, they risk becoming objects of mere curiosity divorced from their original intent.

Despite these concerns about longevity, some Vietnam memorials may achieve lasting meaning. For example, the most distinctive and poignant Vietnam memorial in the United States actually predates NVVM on the National Mall. The Vietnam Veterans Memorial State Park in Angel Fire, New Mexico, has a unique origin, and, as luck would have it, also a helicopter-on-a-stick. In 1968, Victor and Jeanne Westphall lost their son David in Vietnam. Using David's life insurance policy as seed money, the Westphalls began building a mid-century, sail-like, white adobe chapel in the Moreno Valley in New Mexico in memoriam to their son. Completed in 1971, this unique structure is the centerpiece for what became a no-fee state park in 2005. Operated by the David Westphall Veterans Foundation and the Vietnam Veterans Memorial State Park Friends Group, the chapel complex now has a water garden with a deeply moving bronze statue called "Dear Mom and Dad," depicting a seated soldier writing a letter home. And the helicopter-on-a-stick is also a veteran of Vietnam: damaged by ground fire in 1967 then returned to the United States for repair where it ended up with the New Mexico National Guard, which ultimately donated it to the park. There is even a scale model of Santa Fe resident Glenna Goodacre's National Vietnam Women's Memorial. At an elevation of 8,500 feet, the chapel is an awe-inspiring site. That the Westphalls first built it for their son but gladly let it evolve into a community memorial makes its history unique. And that community extended beyond New Mexico, indeed beyond the United States. In addition to displaying photographs of his son and other Americans killed in Vietnam, Victor Westphall exhibited pictures of Vietnamese people— North, South, Viet Cong— who lost their lives in the war. Angel Fire became a memorial for all who fought and died in Southeast Asia, not just Americans. Most Vietnam memorials in the United States ignore South Vietnam and other allies. Laudable as the Westphalls' universality was, this all but killed any chance of Angel Fire becoming the National Vietnam Veterans Memorial as they had at one time hoped. The American national narrative on Vietnam could not cope with honoring any dead other than American dead. David Westphall's father and mother passed away in 2003 and 2005 respectively. They now rest behind the chapel they originally built to memorialize their son.[53]

Image 13. The Peace and Brotherhood Chapel at Vietnam Veterans Memorial State Park, Angel Fire, New Mexico.

Source: Courtesy of the David Westphall Foundation.

Vietnam memorials are meant to offer some permanent reminder of war, of collective and individual sacrifice, and of a conflict's role in shaping national identity. Largely, however, they propagate national myths, fail to address the war itself, and fall short in establishing permanence. The problem is that their desired permanence cannot be attained. While their physical structure may remain unaltered, society and its perception of the past changes around them, which may enhance a memorial's intended meaning or erode it. Moreover, one day Vietnam veterans will be gone. What do these walls, statues, and static displays mean to the rest of us, especially those who have no connection to Vietnam? What will they mean fifty years from now?[54] Is it any wonder that Jan Scruggs and the VVMF have led the push to establish a $115 million interpretive center at the NVVM? They fear the story of their war will vanish once they are gone. But what story is at risk of being lost? Is it a thoughtful, introspective examination of their war and their role in it, or an effort to whitewash Vietnam so that it fades into the heroic narrative, which dominates the mythologically triumphant American military past? It remains to be seen.[55]

For a nation that did little to memorialize its wars for over two hundred years, why did the United States wait until after its worst defeat to build a memorial to honor the dead of that defeat? Why did the U.S. then embark on a Vietnam memorial-building frenzy? Guilt. To forget. To move on.[56] These memorials are physical places of remembrance of the dead and those who served. They are universally called "Vietnam Veterans Memorials" rather than "Vietnam War Memorials." They choose the citizen over the state, individuals over national policy, or great armies, or campaigns. Names engraved on polished stone walls and bronze statues of service members attest to their sacrifice less as citizens of the nation, and more as individuals with family, friends, and loved ones. Rare is an explanation of why the United States sent these men and women to Southeast Asia over fifty years ago, or why 58,000 of them died. Rare is mention of campaigns, commanders, or the home front; nowhere are allies honored; rarer still is recognition of the hundreds of thousands of

Vietnamese who perished. These memorials are about veterans rather than the nation. And yes, that implies a very selfish view of the Vietnam War, one that still avoids answering the question on the bronzed faces of so many Vietnam memorial statues– why? If Lin's brilliant design inspired so many others, and was intended to heal, then an unintended consequence of that healing is avoiding "why?"[57] Healing allows us to put Vietnam behind us. These memorials, then, may have the unintended consequence of allowing us to forget the war, to avoid moral reflection, to avoid an honest confrontation with what the nation did to its youth in the 1960s, to feel better about it than perhaps we should.[58]

Or, maybe the existence of recognition is enough for the veteran; not a parade or "welcome home," as one photo book of Vietnam memorials is subtitled, but simply recognition that whether the policy was just or morally wrong, they went, suffered, and over 58,000 of them died. They did their duty that the national tradition of the time demanded of its youth. If so, then these 500 or so memorials are rightfully for them, not for "us." Apparently, we are content to let veterans build their memorials, then pat them on the back and say, "thank you for your service," and leave them to their places of remembrance. Perhaps that is enough for them, but in time fewer veterans will visit their places of remembrance, which they worked so hard to establish because there will be fewer veterans. Visitors, then, may also visit in smaller numbers. Then these places will be forgotten– places where veterans promised each other and their fallen comrades they would "never be forgotten."[59]

NOTES

1. This essay is an expanded version of a paper delivered at the 2017 annual meeting of the Society for Military History. The author is grateful to Andrew Wiest, Heather Stur, Justin Hart, Ron Milam, James Willbanks, and Eugenia Kiesling for their comments on that paper, and to Geoffrey Jensen and Matthew Stith for their helpful critique of this essay. That said, the interpretations and errors therein are mine alone.
2. Welcome to *Never Forgotten, Inc.*: Home of the POW-MIA 1955 Chevy Dragster Tribute Car, http://www.neverforgotteninc.org, accessed September 2, 2017; The POW/MIA Car – Never Forgotten, Inc., https://www.facebook.com/POW-MIA-Car-Never-Forgotten-Incorg-140960845914272/, accessed September 2, 2017.
3. The American Studies scholar Patrick Hagopian personally documented 461 Vietnam memorials erected in the United States as of 2009. I have found through online searches at least thirty memorials established between 2009 and 2017, but there are undoubtedly many more. Patrick Hagopian, *The Vietnam War in American Memory: Veterans, Memorials, and the Politics of Healing* (Amherst: University of Massachusetts Press, 2009), 5. For this essay, "memorial" and "monument" are used interchangeably.
4. Michael Martone, "Permanent Temporary," *The Southern Review* 41:4 (Autumn, 2005): 878-79.
5. Jay Winter, *Remembering War: The Great War Between Memory and History in the Twentieth Century* (New Haven: Yale University Press, 2006), 135.
6. Erika Doss, *Memorial Mania: Public Feeling in America* (Chicago: University of Chicago Press, 2010), 59-60.
7. Kirk Savage, *Monument Wars: Washington, D.C., the National Mall, and the Transformation of the Memorial Landscape* (Berkeley: University of California Press, 2009), 10-11; William Thomas Allison, "War Mall: Civic Art, Memory, and War on America's National Public Space," in Derek R. Mallett, ed., *Monumental Conflicts: Twentieth Century Wars and the Evolution of Public Memory* (New York: Routledge: 2018), 39-40.
8. Jeffrey Olick, ed., *States of Memory: Continuities, Conflicts, and Transformations in National Retrospection* (Durham: Duke University Press, 2003), 3.

9. Samuel Johnson, *The Ilder* No. 3 (November 11, 1758), Yale Digital Edition of the Works of Samuel Johnson, http://www.yalejohnson.com/frontend/sda_viewer?n=107593 (accessed October 11, 2017), 95.
10. Jenny Edkins, *Trauma and the Memory of Politics* (Cambridge: Cambridge University Press, 2003), 16-19.
11. Allison, "War Mall," 40.
12. Julia Bleakney, *Revisiting Vietnam, Memoirs, Memorials, Museums* (New York: Routledge, 2006), 3-5.
13. For a thorough retelling of the NVVM saga, see Jan C. Scruggs and John Swerdlow, *To Heal a Nation: The Vietnam Veterans Memorial* (New York: Harper Collins, 1985), Robert W. Doubek, *Creating the Vietnam Veterans Memorial: The Inside Story* (Jefferson, North Carolina: McFarland, 2015), and James Reston, Jr., *A Rift in the Earth: Art, Memory, and the Fight for a Vietnam Memorial* (New York: Arcade Publishing 2017).
14. Robert Wagner-Pacifici and Barry Schwartz, "The Vietnam Veterans Memorial: Commemorating a Difficult Past," *The American Journal of Sociology* 97:2 (September 1991): 377.
15. Harriet F. Senie, *Memorials to Shattered Myths: Vietnam to 9/11* (New York: Oxford University Press, 2016), 11.
16. Wagner-Pacifici and Schwartz, "The Vietnam Veterans Memorial": 389; Lewis, "Mumbling Monuments": 51; Senie, *Memorials to Shattered Myths*, 13.
17. Jerry Lembcke, *The Spitting Image: Myth, Memory, and the Legacy of Vietnam* (New York: New York University Press, 1998), 81; Robert D. Schulzinger, *A Time for Peace: The Legacy of the Vietnam War* (New York: Oxford University Press, 2006), 73-93.
18. Savage, *Monument Wars*, 266-67.
19. Doss, *Memorial Mania*, 43-44, 127-29; Seine, *Memorials to Shattered Myths*, 17-19.
20. Senie, *Monuments to Shattered Myths*, 17.
21. "Vietnam Veterans Memorial: America Remembers," *National Geographic*, vol. 67, no. 5 (May 1985): 557.
22. Savage, *Monument Wars*, 271-75; Senie, *Memorials to Shattered Myths*, 14-15.
23. Savage, *Monument Wars*, 276; Senie, *Memorials to Shattered Myths*, 19-20.
24. Senie, *Memorials to Shattered Myths*, 21-22.
25. Ibid., 25-27.

26. Ibid., 28-33; Kristen Ann Hass, *Carried to the Vietnam Veterans Memorial: American Memory and the Vietnam Veterans Memorial* (Berkeley: University of California Press, 1998), 83-120.
27. Allison, "War Mall," 45-49. See also Doss, *Memorial Mania.*
28. Lewis, "Mumbling Monuments": 52; Doss, *Memorial Mania*, 2.
29. Patrick Hagopian, *The Vietnam War in American Memory*, 402-4.
30. There is a growing body of work on this phenomenon. Doss, *Memorial Mania*, and Patrick Hagopian, *The Vietnam War in American Memory: Veterans, Memorials, and the Politics of Healing* (Amherst: University of Massachusetts Press, 2009) are noteworthy. Two useful photo-book resources are Albert J. Nahas, *Warriors Remembered: Vietnam Veterans – Welcome Home* (Indianapolis: IJB Book Publishing, 2010) and Ronny Ymbras, Matt Ymbras, and Eric Rovelto, *Fallen Never Forgotten: Vietnam Memorials in the USA* (Poughkeepsie, New York: 2016).
31. Bleakney, 75-91; Hagopian, *The Vietnam War in American Memory*, 386-91.
32. Bleakney, *Revisiting Vietnam*, 90-96; Hagopian, *The Vietnam War in American Memory*, 390-97. In Spring 2017, my senior seminar course at Georgia Southern University was on "The Vietnam War in Your Hometown." During their research, several students discovered that one of the traveling Walls had visited their hometown at some point. Local veterans interviewed by students frequently recalled the event, emotionally so in some cases. Some even helped organize the visit. Local newspapers from the time confirm the importance to civic pride that one of these Walls had visited their town.
33. Justin Franz, "Vietnam Veterans Group Brings 'The Wall That Heals' Back to Montana," *Flathead Beacon*, September 5, 2017, flatheadbeacon.com, accessed September 7, 2017; "The Wall That Heals Arrives in Kalispell," KPAX, September 7, 2017, kpax.com, accessed September 7, 2017; Vietnam Veterans Memorial Fund – The Wall That Heals, http://www.vvmf.org/twth, accessed October 10, 2018.
34. Ymbras, et al., *Fallen, Never Forgotten*, 104.
35. Vietnam Veterans of Oregon Memorial, City of Portland Parks and Recreation Division, https://www.portlandoregon.gov/parks/finder/index.cfm?action=ViewPark&PropertyID=835, accessed September 5, 2017; Ymbras, et al., Fallen, Never Forgotten, 196-99.
36. Ymbras, et al., *Fallen, Never Forgotten*, 246-49; Washington State Vietnam Veterans Memorial, http://www.des.wa.gov/services/facilities-leasing/capitol-campus/memorials-and-artwork/vietnam-veterans-memorial,

accessed September 5, 2017; Vietnam Veterans Memorial Fountain, http://kcparks.org/fountain/vietnam-veterans_-memorial-fountain-2/, accessed September 5, 2017; Philadelphia Vietnam Veterans Memorial, http://www.pvvm.org/index, accessed September 5, 2017; Texarkana Korea/Vietnam Memorial, http://www.vva278.org/memorial.html, accessed September 5, 2017.

37. California State Capitol Museum: Vietnam Memorial, http://capitolmuseum.ca.gov/the-museum/vietnam-memorial, accessed August 10, 2017; Ymbras, *Fallen, Never Forgotten*, 24.
38. Western Slope Vietnam War Memorial Park, http://www.field-of-dreams.org/, accessed August 10, 2017; Ymbras, et al., *Fallen, Never Forgotten*, 40.
39. Official Site of the Connecticut Vietnam Veterans Memorial, Inc., http://www.cvvm.org/index.htm, accessed September 1, 2017.
40. Hagopian, *The Vietnam War in American Memory*, 6-7. If the local gas company can make it work, an eternal flame is a must for a local war memorial.
41. Texas Capitol Vietnam Veterans Monument, http://tcvvm.org/, accessed August 10, 2017.
42. Ymbras, *Fallen, Never Forgotten*, 58-62; Faces of War Memorial, http://www.roswellmemorialday.com/faces-of-war-memorial/, accessed September 2, 2017.
43. Nahas, *Warriors* Remembered, 134-35; Arkansas Vietnam Veterans Memorial, http://www.vietvet.org/arkbkgnd.htm, accessed August 20, 2017.
44. Westchester County Government, Veterans Memorial and Museum, https://veterans.westchestergov.com/veterans-memorial-and-museum/, accessed August 28, 2017; Nahas, *Warriors Remembered*, 26-27.
45. Vietnam Veterans Memorial of San Antonio, http://vietnamveteransmemorialofsanantonio.com/, accessed September 3, 2017; Nahas, *Warriors Remembered*, 152-53.
46. Nahas, *Warriors Remembered*, 88-89.
47. Hagopian, *The Vietnam War in American Memory*, 268-308.
48. Hopkins Country Veterans Memorial, http://www.sulphurspringstx.org/visitors/veteran_s_memorial.php, accessed September 15, 2017. In the interest of full disclosure, I was born and raised in Sulphur Springs, Texas, but I'm not just saying the memorial is impressive because I'm from there and my father was instrumental in the effort to establish it. He's a Vietnam veteran, by the way.

49. Brazos Valley Veterans Memorial, http://www.bvvm.org/, accessed September 12, 2017.
50. Ohio Veterans Memorial Park, http://www.ovmp.org/, accessed August 10, 2017.
51. Ymbras, et al., *Fallen, Never Forgotten*, 8-9; The American Legion: Lower Alabama Vietnam Memorial, https://www.legion.org/memorials/238093/lower-alabama-vietnam-veterans-memorial, accessed September 10, 2017.
52. Ymbras, *Fallen, Never Forgotten*, 48-49.
53. Hagopian, *The Vietnam War in American Memory*, 8-9; Nahas, *Warriors Remembered*, 128-31.
54. Martone, "Permanent Temporary," 878-85.
55. Kirk Savage, "The 'Education Center' at the Vietnam Veterans Memorial," http://www.kirksavage.pitt.edu/?p=368, accessed September 1, 2017.
56. The National Park Service web page for the NVVM is titled "The Wall That Heals." See Vietnam Veterans, Memorial, District of Columbia, https://www.nps.gov/vive/index.htm, accessed September 10, 2017.
57. Hagopian, *The Vietnam War in American Memory*, 399-405.
58. Bleakney, *Revisiting Vietnam*, 7-10.
59. Hagopian, *The Vietnam War in American Memory*, 396-432.

They Got Out of That Place

Understanding the Vietnam War through the Music-Based Memories of Vietnam Veterans

Doug Bradley

Well the music is your special friend
Dance on fire as it intends
Music is your only friend
Until the end
Until the end
Until the end

John Densmore & Ray Manzarek of the Doors

Vietnam. The word comes camouflaged in music: rock and roll, soul, pop, and country; Jimi Hendrix, Johnny Cash, Aretha Franklin, and

Creedence Clearwater Revival (CCR). *I fell into a burning ring of fire. Take another little piece of my heart. Nowhere to run, baby, nowhere to hide.* "I Feel-like-I'm-Fixin'-to-Die" and "Fortunate Son," and the song more than one Vietnam veteran has called "our national anthem": "We Gotta Get Out of This Place," by the Animals, all connoted powerful meanings and memories for those involved in the Vietnam quagmire.

For those who watched the war unfold on the evening news, the music of Vietnam blurred with sounds rising from American streets during a time of momentous challenge and change. For those born after the last helicopters sank beneath the waves of the South China Sea, movies, documentaries, and T.V. shows have repeatedly used music as a sonic background for depicting Vietnam as a tug-of-war between war hawks and peace doves.

But for the men and women who served in Southeast Asia, music was what inexorably linked them to their generation. They sang along to the Beatles, Nancy Sinatra, Marty Robbins, and the Temptations *before* they went to war, and they listened to them *after* they came back home. Music was more than just background for Vietnam veterans. It was their lifeline, a link to their existence "back in the world," connecting them with the things that enabled them to "keep on keeping on." From the peaks of the Central Highlands and the rice paddies of the Mekong Delta to the "air-conditioned jungles" of Da Nang and Long Binh, Vietnam soldiers used music to build community, stay connected to the home front, and hold on to the humanity the war was trying to take away. And once they returned home, music became essential to their healing.

In this chapter, I'll draw upon twelve years of interviews and research my University of Wisconsin-Madison colleague Craig Werner and I conducted for *We Gotta Get Out of This Place: The Soundtrack of the Vietnam War*, which tells the story of the Vietnam War through the music-based memories of those who were there.[1] These conversations and published sources underscore a significant, yet often overlooked fact that there is no such thing as *the* typical Vietnam experience. Every

Vietnam soldier and veteran had his or her own individual story, and that story is dependent on what Craig and I refer to as the "**3 W's**" – **W**hen you were in Vietnam; **W**here you were stationed; and **W**hat you did (i.e., your military job in Vietnam).

Take my Vietnam service, for example. I was stationed in Vietnam from November 1970 to November 1971 (**when**), a relatively "quiet" period of the war when the troops' mantra was "nobody wants to be the last GI killed in Vietnam." I worked in a corporate-esque, shine and polish public information office at the U. S. Army's headquarters at Long Binh (**where**), a safe "rear echelon" location jokingly referred to as "the air-conditioned jungle" because the Army brass for whom I toiled wanted to work in comfortable surroundings. Finally, as an Army "journalist" (**what**), I carried a pen and not a rifle, reporting, writing, editing, and publishing Army newspaper and magazine articles intended to boost the morale of the soldiers in the field doing the fighting and dying.

Now, contemplate the myriad permutations of the three variables at any particular time: 200 different military "jobs" and eleven to twelve years of jungle/guerrilla warfare across an area of 67,000 square miles. The possibilities are inexhaustible! Point being, there is no *one* Vietnam story; rather, there are almost three million of them, one for every service member who was there.

And if one takes the time to listen respectfully to what veterans of that misunderstood war have to say, they will frequently find a song at the heart of what they remember. Music is indispensable to understanding and appreciating the Vietnam soldier and veteran experience and how it serves as the crucible for community, connections, comradery, love, loss, despair, understanding, and, most importantly, healing. It is also important to address how soldiers were able to access music in Vietnam and how the various kinds of music played and heard in Vietnam changed over the course of the war. Finally, this chapter will close with a tribute to the power of song to help heal the soul.

Historians have increasingly recognized music as a lens for understanding movements, attitudes, and opinions. Nowhere is this more evident than in the iconic music of the 1960s and early 1970s. The power of that extraordinary, generation-defining music, combined with the memories associated with it by Vietnam veterans, provides a truer, deeper story of what Vietnam meant, and continues to mean.

With the crucial exception of combat situations, music was just about everywhere in Vietnam, reaching soldiers via albums, cassettes, and tapes of radio shows sent from home; on the Armed Forces Vietnam Network (AFVN); and on the legendary underground broadcasts of Radio First Termer. Soldiers played it in their hooches on top-of-the-line tape decks they purchased cheap at the PX or via mail order from Japan and over headphones in helicopters and planes. Sometimes the music was live: soldiers strumming out Bob Dylan and Curtis Mayfield songs at base camps; Filipino bands pounding out "Proud Mary" and "Soul Man" at Enlisted Men's Clubs and Saigon bars; touring acts from Bob Hope and Ann-Margret to Nancy Sinatra and James Brown granting momentary calm during the military storm. AFVN blanketed Vietnam with songs from stateside Top 40 stations. Soldiers in remote areas maneuvered their transistor radios in hopes of catching the week's countdown of stateside hits, while radio helped helicopter crews fill the empty hours crisscrossing the airways above the endless forests and rice paddies. [2]

The songs troops listened to were the same ones their friends were listening to back home, radio being the Vietnam generation's Internet, but the music took on different and often deeper meanings in Vietnam. For example, Nancy Sinatra's "These Boots Are Made for Walkin'" became an anthem to the "grunts" who humped endless miles on patrol in the jungles thanks to their all-important "boots," adding layers of meaning to the story of a young woman turning the tables on her cheating boyfriend. No one listening to the Jimi Hendrix Experience's "Purple Haze" in a college dorm room was likely to associate the LSD-suggestive title with the color of the smoke grenades used to guide helicopters into Vietnam landing zones. "Ring of Fire," "Nowhere to Run," and "Riders on the Storm" all shifted shape in relation to the war.

The songs and stories that form the chorus at the center of *We Gotta Get Out of This Place: The Soundtrack of the Vietnam War* are intensely individual. While there is no such thing as a typical Vietnam vet, the songs come together in a shared story of what music meant, and means, to the young men and women who shouldered their country's burden during a period of dizzying change. Most of them belonged to a generation that, probably more than any other, was defined by its music: Elvis, the Beatles, and Dylan; Aretha, James Brown, and the Supremes; Jimi Hendrix, Creedence, and Johnny Cash.[3]

Like other members of their generation, those who served in Vietnam shaped the music they loved to fit their own needs, a process that continued after they returned to the United States. As Michael Kramer observes in *The Republic of Rock*, the music of the 1960s and early 1970s gave the younger generation "a sonic framework for thinking, feeling, discussing, and dancing out the vexing problems of democratic togetherness and individual liberation."[4] While music in Vietnam did not deliver a preordained set of meanings to the troops, the songs afforded a set of overlapping fields for making, sharing, and, at times, rejecting meaning. Songs and styles signified something particular to one group and something very different to another; the tensions were especially clear in relation to country music and soul, at times the catalyst for battles over the jukebox in Vietnam, but they show up again and again.

For example, radically divergent responses to Sgt. Barry Sadler's "The Ballad of the Green Berets," a singular Vietnam song that was revered by many Vietnam soldiers yet vilified and satirized by as many more, are as much a reflection of the shifting politics of the war and the soldiers fighting in it as they are about changes in musical tastes. Likewise, "For What It's Worth" by the Buffalo Springfield, the song frequently played to accompany film depictions of anti-war protests, had nothing to do with Vietnam *per se*, yet was as treasured by scores of soldiers as it was by protestors in America.[5]

The meaning of songs often changed for individual vets whose personal, and in several cases, political, perspectives underwent seismic shifts in the years during and after the war. The dynamic was complicated by music's peculiar status as *both* a center of political or cultural resistance *and* a manifestation of America's hi-tech supremacy. Building on Thomas Frank's history of the rise of "hip capitalism" in the 1960s, Michael Kramer argues that, especially in the later years of the war, music in Vietnam was part of a "hip militarism" designed to reduce the disruptive potential of generational conflict.[6] Soldiers who identified deeply with the iconoclastic messages of the Jefferson Airplane and/or James Brown simultaneously accepted their place in the highly-technological, commercial culture that defined American society. Rather than resolving the tensions, however, Vietnam's material surroundings, painstakingly detailed in Meredith Lair's *Armed with Abundance: Consumerism and Soldiering in the Vietnam War,* often intensified the sense of what Kramer calls "the blurred lines between official and unofficial knowledge."[7]

Thus, music never arrived in an unmediated form in Vietnam; even the most emotionally direct or politically provocative songs were part of a music industry delivered through technological channels that shaped responses, even if only subconsciously. As Lair points out, "The widespread availability of popular music, by way of soldiers' personal stereos but, more consistently, through radio, made a year in Vietnam less isolating and more manageable." [8]

The soundscape of Vietnam unfolded in distinct movements, musical and military. As the war changed, the music changed with it. Or maybe it was the other way around? Without question, however, individual understandings of the music changed over the course of time. A song like the Monkees' "Last Train to Clarksville," with its refrain of "*I don't know if I'm ever comin' home*," meant one thing to a recruit saying goodbye to his family or sweetheart as he left for boot camp but frequently took on new, sometimes painfully ironic meanings to a soldier or marine serving twelve, thirteen, or more months in the field. According to Dennis McQuade, a mortar infantryman in Vietnam in 1966-67, "Last Train to Clarksville" was "dedicated to us" because "our last train could come any day" in Vietnam. "We never knew for sure that we were ever coming home."[9]

Image 14. U.S. soldiers in Vietnam purchased more than 178,000 reel-to-reel tape decks in 1969-1970

Source: Photo provided by Doug Bradley.

Similarly, the sound of a voice or guitar that once evoked a connection with comrades in Vietnam could ignite intense feelings of sorrow back home. As Jim Roseberry, a native of Chico, California, who served as a supply clerk in Vietnam in 1969-70, told me: "I think the hardest thing for a soldier is being frozen in a moment. You feel like the world is passing you by and you're stuck, you're stuck in the Army. I still have that feeling every time I hear the Simon & Garfunkel song 'Scarborough

Fair.' That was me and my then girlfriend's favorite song. It kept me alive. It kept me going emotionally. It connected me to my girlfriend, UC-Berkeley, the summer of love, the Fillmore, my generation, everything... The song still triggers connections for me— romance, loss, life lessons actually..." Like Roseberry, many of the veterans we talked with testified that music has an inexplicable, yet distinctive, power to unlock deeply buried memories. [10]

Although the cultural memory of Vietnam-era music centers on songs that questioned or protested the war, the first wave of Vietnam-related songs to be played on the radio expressed an unquestioning belief that the Cold War stakes justified the sacrifices of the soldiers and their families. One of the best known of the many Vietnam-themed songs that began to appear on country radio in 1965 and 1966, Johnnie Wright's number one country hit "Hello Vietnam," follows in the footsteps of songs from the era of World War II and Korea like "Remember Pearl Harbor," "Praise the Lord and Pass the Ammunition," and "(Heartsick Soldier On) Heartbreak Ridge," the latter a huge country and western hit by both Gene Autry and Ernest Tubb. [11]

Today, "Hello Vietnam" is best remembered as the music playing over the title sequence of Stanley Kubrick's film *Full Metal Jacket.* "Hello Vietnam" hardly shares Kubrick's fiercely anti-war sentiments, but it does not celebrate the war, either. Adapting the familiar persona of a soldier saying goodbye to his sweetheart, Wright sings that he does not "*suppose this war will ever end.*" But he does not doubt the sacrifice is worth it. If we do not stand up to Communism in Vietnam, he sings, our "*freedom will start slipping through our hands.*" [12]

"Hello Vietnam" typifies the genre of so-called pro-war songs, many of them sentimental ballads centered on the separation of soldiers from their families. They outnumbered protest songs on the radio by a wide margin until at least 1967. The first songs to mention Vietnam were simply adding a specific locale to the soldier-away-from-home lyrics of songs like the Shirelles' "Soldier Boy" and Bobby Vinton's "Mr. Lonely," the lament of a soldier "*away from home through no wish of my own.*" In "Dear Uncle Sam," Loretta Lynn pleaded that she needs her man much more than the Pentagon does. The emotional textures varied from song to song, but none of them questioned the closing lines of the Powell Sisters' 1963 release, "Our Daddy's in Vietnam": "*Without their Daddy, tall and strong, we'd lose our freedom's land.*"[13]

As the anti-war movement became more vocal and more visible, however, songs such as Ernest Tubb & the Texas Troubadours' "It's for God, and Country, and You Mom (That's Why I'm Fighting in Viet Nam)" and Jerry Reed's "Fightin' for the U.S.A." gave evidence that the war needed to be defended in ways that had not been necessary during World War II. Dave Dudley's "What We're Fighting For," which, like "Hello Vietnam," was written by the ace country songsmith Tom T. Hall, sounded an even more confrontational note. Best known for hard-driving honky-tonker ballads like "Six Days on the Road" and "Truck Drivin' Son-of-a-Gun," Dudley's letter-writing narrator vows to his mother, "*another flag would never fly above our nation's door.*" Dudley's follow-up single, "Vietnam Blues," written by Kris Kristofferson, was even more angry and bitter. That vitriol was echoed in Stonewall Jackson's "The Minute Men (Are Turning in Their Graves)," which struck near-apocalyptic tones, warning that the anti-war demonstrators were at best naïve and quite possibly traitorous, an attitude that became the centerpiece of Merle Haggard's late 1960s hits "Okie from Muskogee" and "The Fighting Side of Me." [14]

World War II–style patriotism smacked up against the iconoclastic irreverence that would become a central part of Vietnam musical culture in the skirmishes surrounding Sgt. Barry Sadler's "The Ballad of the Green Berets," by far the best known of the patriotic hits of the Vietnam era. Co-written by Sadler and Robin Moore, whose semiautobiographical novel *The Green Berets* is more morally ambiguous and complex than either the song or the movie it gave rise to, "The Ballad of the Green Berets" was *the* most popular song of 1966, surpassing "We Can Work It

Out," "Paint It Black," the Association's "Cherish," and a host of Motown classics, including the Four Tops' "Reach Out, I'll Be There" and the Supremes' "You Can't Hurry Love." And while Sadler's anthem became the driving force for thousands of young men going off to the jungles of Southeast Asia, it quickly became the most parodied and derided song in the extensive Vietnam playlist. "*Frightened soldiers from the sky,*" intones one "Ballad of the Green Berets" parody, "*Screaming, 'Hell, I don't wanna die / you can have my job and pay / I'm a chicken any old way.*'"[15]

During the early years of U. S. presence in Vietnam, folk music comforted many soldiers, much of it performed by in-country songsters whose accouterments included guitars as well as rifles. Like the folk-oriented groups at home, these individual troubadours played an important role in forming the musical culture of Vietnam. In *Singing the Vietnam Blues: Songs of the Air Force in Southeast Asia*, Joseph Tuso, a weapons systems officer aboard an F-4D phantom who flew 170 missions over Vietnam, catalogs more than 200 songs, which reworked familiar melodies, popular and traditional. Tuso's list includes "The Wabash Cannonball," "The Battle Hymn of the Republic," "The Ballad of the Green Berets," "The Yellow Rose of Texas," "Ghost Riders in the Sky," "Folsom Prison Blues," "I've Been Workin' on the Railroad," "Red River Valley," "Puff the Magic Dragon" (in honor of the AC-47 "Spooky" Gunship), "On Top of Old Smoky," "Pop Goes the Weasel," "MTA" (known in-country as "The Man Who Never Returned"), "Bye Bye Blackbird," and just about every Christmas carol you can imagine.

Army aviator Marty Heuer, who spent two tours in Vietnam, played in a folk group of fellow officers dubbed The High Priced Help. "Music was our way of combating loneliness," Heuer recalled, alluding to a folk repertoire that included songs by Peter, Paul and Mary and the Kingston Trio, along with original material. "Everyone thought we were there to win," he explained about those early war years. "But as time passed and the war ground on, that concept went to hell in a hand basket."[16]

Almost from the beginning, however, that folk music hand basket included songs critical of the war and its conduct sung by the likes of Bob Dylan, Joan Baez, Buffy St. Marie, and Pete Seeger. Vietnam soldiers responded to the politically-oriented folk music in a variety of ways; for example, some simply enjoyed the sound of the music, even when they actively disagreed with the politics. Infantryman Leroy Tecube did not share Barry McGuire's politics, but he used several lines from McGuire's tune "Eve of Destruction" to introduce his memoir, *Year in Nam: A Native American Soldier's Story*:

> It was hard to understand how the adult system worked, wrote Tecube. A popular song of the time said, 'You're old enough for dyin', but not for voting.' Young men in the prime of their lives were dying, in a far-off country, before they could vote.[17]

Similarly, Gary Blinn, a native of Valentine, Nebraska, and a Naval Academy graduate who served as a patrol craft captain in the Mekong Delta in 1967 and 1968, admitted listening to Joan Baez despite her association with the anti-war movement. "I have to confess I enjoy Joan's folk songs. I know Joan was probably in exactly the same camp, but she just wasn't as obnoxious as Jane Fonda."

For some younger soldiers, the folk music scene was less a sign of political commitment than part of a generational rite of passage. Mike Morea, who served as a forward air controller at Tan Son Nhut Air Base from 1966 to 1967, a time when the Vietnam soundtrack was changing, had attended college in New York City and made occasional trips to Greenwich Village:

> A lot of times after hours, after class, or on a Friday night or what not, we'd wind up down in the Village in one of the more famous old places where there was, relatively speaking at least, a lot of radical thought, says Morea. But we were more interested in the atmosphere than in the substance. We'd rather go to a place where maybe a young Joan Baez was singing and nobody had ever heard of her, but there she was, or maybe a Woody

> Guthrie... [We were there to] have a few beers rather than really take anything seriously.

As the singers' repertoires shifted from folk ballads to topical songs about civil rights and nuclear war, Morea remembered feeling shocked to realize that:

> these people were serious, where we were just sort of having a good time. The attitude was almost like, 'Hey, lighten up, relax and enjoy life, what are you getting all excited about?' Of course, we didn't understand their point of view. I guess I'm painting a not-too-pleasant picture of what we were: just kind of scatterbrained college kids having a good time, but that's probably pretty accurate.

Others took the folk music messages more seriously. John Hubenthal, a physician, and conscientious objector, chose to fulfill his service obligation as an army medic in Vietnam. He said that folk music played "a tremendously important role" in shaping his awareness. "I wrote poetry avidly from about fourteen or fifteen right on through into my twenties and aspired to be a poet," Hubenthal explained, "so good lyrics were very important to me and, frankly, served to reinforce my political and social views, given the music that I listened to. A lot of Bob Dylan..."[18]

For Hubenthal, the folk idiom, and the rock music it inspired, marked a rebellion against what he saw as the naïveté of commercial rock 'n' roll. He pointed to the television show *Hootenanny* as a cultural breakthrough. "I loved it. The Limelighters, Peter, Paul, and Mary, and some of the older singers— Pete Seeger and people like that. Woody Guthrie songs. It was, 'Oh, my God! Good music!' That led me later on into Bob Dylan, Joan Baez... only after that when we got into the Beatles and Rolling Stones did actual rock 'n' roll start to appeal to me..."[19]

Tecube, Morea, and Hubenthal belonged to a generation of Vietnam veterans who were byproducts of their fathers' triumphant return home from World War II. Although most were weaned on the same patriotic ethos as older soldiers like Marty Heuer and Barry Sadler, the cohort that went to Vietnam in the years following the 1964 Gulf of Tonkin incident included many who were either drafted or grudgingly enlisted. Some chose to enlist because they knew they were very likely to be drafted. Volunteering gave them, at least in theory, a broader set of options for their eventual military assignment. [20]

As Christian Appy points out in his book *Working-Class War*, the working-class youth who volunteered for service did not do so out of any John Wayne–type patriotic fervor. Rather, a large-scale survey in 1964 found that the single biggest reason for volunteering was to avoid being drafted.[21] In his book, *American Soldiers*, Peter Kindsvatter elaborates: "At that time, volunteering meant three years of service as opposed to two years of service [as a draftee]. So, some volunteers signed up so they could pick a specialty to teach them a skill, or perhaps just to try and keep themselves out of a foxhole."[22]

Regardless, music served as a lifeline to the home front for draftees and enlistees alike. By the late 1960s American popular music was changing at a dizzying rate, changes that could be heard in the American enclaves of Vietnam as well as back home in "the world." It was there in the difference between "I Get Around" and "Good Vibrations"; "She Loves You" and "Sgt. Pepper's Lonely Hearts Club Band"; "Please Please Please" and "Say It Loud— I'm Black and I'm Proud"; "Come See About Me" and "Cloud Nine"; the Shangri-Las and Grace Slick. Whereas the soldiers of the JFK-era war (1961-63) identified primarily with their service branch or unit, the arrivals during the Vietnam war years of Lyndon Johnson (1964-68) and Richard Nixon (1969-73) confronted a more complex set of musical choices for shaping their sense of identity, many of them coupled with the newly emerging musical styles.[23]

Shaped by the racial tensions in America that were becoming ever clearer in the North and West as well as in the South and the emergence of a newly assertive counterculture, the musical communities formed by soldiers in Vietnam would have been almost unrecognizable to the generation who served in World War II, Korea, or, for that matter, pre-

Gulf of Tonkin Vietnam. Black GIs clustered around the soul music that charted the transition from the interracial civil rights movement to Black Power. The white soldiers who proudly claimed the title of redneck or rebel, many of them from the rural West, the Midwest, or the South, embraced Merle Haggard, Buck Owens, and George Jones. Soldiers of all races experimenting with the drug culture that linked the home front to Vietnam plugged in with the psychedelic sounds of Iron Butterfly, Cream, the Doors, and, especially, Jimi Hendrix.[24]

Adding to the cacophony and confusion, the soldiers in Vietnam during the later stages of the war were also aware that a growing number of returning veterans voiced their opposition to the conflict, most notably through the Vietnam Veterans Against the War (VVAW) and songs like "Bring the Boys Home" by Freda Payne. If their brothers-in-arms stateside had experienced the war and were convinced of its futility, why should they put their lives on the line in the service of a lost cause?[25]

Realizing they were losing their grip on the war and their soldiers, the military fought back with one of its few remaining weapons: stuff. Lots and lots and lots of it. As Michael Kramer reminds us in *The Republic of Rock*, while the anger and rebellion expressed in the ranks increased, the military made it easier for the soldiers to hear the music that articulated their feelings. Modeling its approach on the cooptation of the counterculture by the "hip capitalism" that had become a central feature on the home front, the military developed a "hip militarism" based in large part on the musical culture, which set itself in clear opposition to the war.[26] As Meredith H. Lair writes in *Armed with Abundance*, "The U.S. military sought to raise morale not by resolving soldiers' doubts about the war but by improving their material circumstances." She notes specifically that military authorities made sure there was music all the time in order to boost morale, pointing out that by 1969, one-third of American soldiers listened to the radio more than five hours a day, a figure that rose to 50 percent for soldiers between the ages of seventeen and twenty.[27] Similarly, the elaborate sound systems that became a defining feature of life in the rear were both a means of releasing GI frustration and yet another manifestation of America's technology-driven presence in Vietnam.

In fact, as Lair explains, AFVN radio broadcast twenty-four hours a day, including FM broadcasts during afternoon and evening hours. With permanent studios in Saigon and additional transmitters in Pleiku, Cam Ranh Bay, Da Nang, and Qui Nhon, AFVN reached the more than 99 percent of U.S. military personnel in Vietnam who owned or had access to a radio by 1970. In 1969 and 1970 alone, GIs purchased nearly 500,000 radios, 178,000 reel-to-reel tape decks, and 220,000 cassette recorders. In effect, Lair concludes, "American soldiers adjusted their John Wayne expectations to demand comfortable living conditions, time for leisure activities, abundant recreational facilities, and easy access to mass-produced consumer goods."[28]

Maybe soldiers were benefiting from the new hip militarism, but they were still in Vietnam and there was still a war. Just as there were riots back home, there were riots in Vietnam; just as there was racism at home, there was racism in Vietnam; just as there were drugs back in the world there were drugs in-country, too. Amid all this mayhem, music could be a balm, an inspiration, an ironic commentary, and sometimes all three at once. "Most of all," Lair writes, "it [music] offered reassurance to American soldiers far, far from home that they were still a part of the world they remembered before they left for Vietnam."[29]

As the war ground on and the causalities mounted, music became even more essential for the soldiers/veterans to express their feelings and attempt to understand the politics of the war, and politics in general. The burgeoning GI resistance movement, which joined forces with the anti-war movement stateside, had its share of advocates in Vietnam. One anonymous soldier, quoted in *Life* magazine, stated, "Many soldiers regard the organized antiwar movement campaign in the United States with open and outspoken sympathy."[30]

Some of the political transformations were smaller and more personal. For Mike Berto, a helicopter crew chief at Camp Evans in 1969, the change in attitude was a result of what he saw and what he heard from soldiers coming back from the field. "I decided this is crazy and told them I couldn't justify my part in the war," said Berto, who had arrived in Vietnam prepared to carry out his assigned military duties. "They didn't believe me, so I made a couple of boo-boos, nothing that would kill anybody, and they put me on permanent guard duty. That," he continued with a wry laugh, "was when I became part of Crosby, Stills, Nash, and Young." [31]

Berto's metamorphosis began when he made friends with three other soldiers on guard detail. "It was a unique experience because we were so close," he said. "We'd stay up all night partying. I bought a telescope, and we were looking at Jupiter and Saturn and Mars. There was a drugstore in Hue which had amphetamines, we'd do that and go kind of crazy." Not surprisingly, Berto and his friends attracted the attention of the brass, which is when they assumed the identities of the rock super group, CSN&Y.[32]

"We had name tags made and sewed on our uniforms. I was Stills," Berto said, laying claim to the mantle of the star whose breakthrough hit "For What It's Worth," recorded when he was a member of Buffalo Springfield, became an anthem for the counterculture at home and for many GIs in Nam. "The other guys were Crosby, Nash and Young. Every time we went out on guard duty we were supposed to meet at battalion headquarters so we'd show up in our new threads. 'All right, your shoes aren't clean enough, Mr. Stills,'" Berto mimicked. "'Trim that hair, Mr. Young.' We always had a good time with that, and they never did catch on."[33]

Even the military hierarchy itself was not immune to the changing musical culture. Mike Subkoviak, a native of Tonawanda, New York, who went to Vietnam with an Reserved Officer Training Corps (ROTC) commission, worked with engineering units assigned to building Highway 1 before being reassigned to work as a statistician on the staff of a three-star general at Long Binh. "The music at the officers' parties provided a way of trying to push war out of your mind for a few hours," Subkoviak said. "The further you got from Saigon, the more relaxed things were. Some of the dances were like Grateful Dead concerts, where people just stood up and moved. I remember one party in the unit where there was a Joe Cocker tape blaring. 'Feelin' Alright,' 'A Little Help from My Friends.' There were officers, enlisted men, even some Vietnamese. Everybody was having a good time in the middle of the war." [34]

Image 15. U.S. soldiers in Vietnam playing music in a band

Source: Photo provided by Doug Bradley.

Of course, for most of the men and women who served in Vietnam, it was difficult, albeit impossible, to have a good time. That is where inebriants played a major role. Drugs and alcohol were plentiful in Vietnam. Jeff Dahlstrom, who began his tour of duty in October 1970 driving what he called a "Follow Me" truck, which guided incoming airplanes at Tan Son Nhut airfield, remembered Vietnam as "the best time of my life," due, in large part, to music and marijuana.[35]

"Almost everybody smoked pot," he observed, portraying pot as the connecting tissue of military culture. "We had army guards, warrant officers, pilots did it. Every night we'd listen to music," he continued:

> That was our ritual. I couldn't have lived without the music over there. *Every night.* We'd go out behind the barracks along this little ditch, smoke some dope, and drink some beer, and then we'd go listen to the James Gang, Derek and the Dominos' "Layla," lots of Hendrix. Somebody brought back the Doors' "L.A. Woman" from R&R in Hawaii. "Riders on the Storm," the whole album blew me away.

Taking drug use and musical taste as touchstones, Dahlstrom offered a concise breakdown of base culture:

> There were three groups of guys— the guys who just played cards, the hippies, and the guys who did heroin," he observed. They'd smoke it all the time, and they never came outside. Nothing was funny to them, and mostly they listened to instrumental stuff. For some reason the guys on heroin were really into *Jesus Christ Superstar.* All the blacks were in their own world. We had one black guy who hung with us, he was a Hendrix guy. But mostly we just saw the blacks in the chow line, where they'd do their (dap) handshakes and ceremonies.

Music played a major part in the sensory overload of Saigon, where Dahlstrom went frequently. "It was smoky and there were a million smells," he said. "A different smell around every corner. The city was beautiful, the temples, and the Buddhas. We basically stayed stoned and had them drive us around in the front of the cyclos. There was music everywhere. They had a Saigon version of Woodstock. Vietnamese girls in short black skirts, Filipino and Vietnamese bands. They played a lot of Creedence and, of course, 'We Gotta Get Out of This Place.'"[36]

Rick Berg, who grew up on Chicago's rough West Side before becoming a marine in 1966, described another set of slightly surrealistic scenes that developed around the connection between music and drugs:

> There was this guy connected to helicopters, I was never quite sure what he did, but he'd move around the country setting up things with helicopters and landings. He was a friend of one of the guys in the company, Berg recalled. We had a hooch with three of us that the officers wouldn't bother. He'd show up, and he was like Santa Claus because he could fly around country and buy albums; he'd pull out of his bag all the latest albums; we had the dope, he had the albums. One day he pulled out the landing lights for a helicopter and sets them in the room, and we sat there mesmerized. So, we plug these things in. One time he brought back sparklers. It sent the stoned marines into some other world; as if we didn't have enough fireworks. In retrospect, Berg recognized the risks he and his friends were taking. Some guy brought back the Stones' *Their Satanic Majesties Request* from R&R. I took it down to the beach. We'd hook up long extension cords to the tape decks and put on headphones. I'm sitting down there light years from anywhere. If we'd been hit... I was nowhere near where I was supposed to be.

Berg was one of many GIs who associated music with their political awakening. "I was into music but there was a lot I hadn't heard," he said. "Paul Revere and the Raiders had a song out when I was drafted. '*Kicks just keep getting harder to find.*' That song stayed in my head during Marine Corps boot camp." Upon arriving in Vietnam, Berg began listening to folk music. "My hooch mate had these two albums, and I listened to them over and over and over. I think they were the only two albums he had. One of them was by the Pozo Seco Singers, two girls and a guy. 'Ribbon of Darkness.' The other one was by Judy Collins, kind of soft hippie music." Berg credited Collins's version of "Poor People of Paris" from *Marat Sade,* a trippy, experimental 1963 play written by Peter Weiss, with initiating a process he was not aware of at the time:

> A while later I recognized the irony to that, admits Berg. I'm listening to French revolutionary songs! The Viet Cong gave me my first lesson in Marxism, and I had the soundtrack. The lesson was a bit overdetermined. I figured it out in a hole one day. The VC are fighting for poor people; the Vietnamese are poor; I'm poor; I'm on the wrong side. [37]

In his memoir... *and a hard rain fell*, the Vietnam vet John Ketwig, an outspoken critic of the war, recounts a musical moment which crystallized his developing political feelings:

> Back at the bungalow I put on a record, poured another Coke, and did another pipe of grass. I couldn't sleep. Rock had married brass, and Blood, Sweat and Tears and a band called the Electric Flag were at the center of the ceremony. I was listening to an Electric Flag album I had picked up at the PX and grown to love. There was silence, then Lyndon Johnson's familiar drawl boomed, 'I speak tonight for the dignity of man, and the destiny of mankind...' interrupted by a burst of laughter and the scream of tortured guitars. 'For the dignity of man.' LBJ was sitting on his ranch, in the very undignified position of having been forced out of the White House by public protests in the streets. There is no dignity, no glory, in mud up to your ass with bullets overhead.[38]

Even soldiers who did not identify with the politics or lifestyle of the counterculture often responded to its music. Bill Peters, who believed strongly in the U.S. mission in Vietnam, recounts his initiation into the hippie scene when his girlfriend convinced him to accompany her to a concert in San Francisco, about forty miles from the rural community of Livermore where he had grown up. "The Fillmore Auditorium, not far from the San Francisco Haight-Ashbury district, the center of hippie activity, reverberated with the music of the Jefferson Airplane," Peters wrote in his memoir, *Sunrise at Midnight*. "Grace Slick, the Plane's lead singer, was barely visible in the smoky haze that filled the ancient music mecca. She began to moan her way through her hit song 'White Rabbit.' Hippies and straight kids filled the dance floor, creating an incredible atmosphere that knew no race, color, or creed. The music of the Sixties somehow bridged that gap for a generation that was being torn apart by Vietnam."[39]

As Peters makes clear, the music meant something different in Vietnam than it had in the Haight. He describes being in an LZ which had caught fire from the bombs dropped to clear the space, despite a warning from the officer in charge of the mission:

> There was no celebration from Grim Reaper, only thousand-yard stares as the chopper gained altitude and headed south toward An Hoa. Drenched in their own sweat, the strong smell of smoke coming off them, and their equipment, the marines sat on the floor of the chopper. [The officer] was furious when he learned that the bombs that had prepped Grim Reaper's LZ had also started the fire. His appeals to change the insert policy had fallen on deaf ears. Someone up the command structure of the wing was not budging on the issue. The words to a Janis Joplin song, 'Freedom's just another word for nothing left to lose,' were blaring from our tent.

As Peters's disillusionment with the conduct of the war, always distinct in his mind from its purpose, deepened, he began to share his feelings with his fellow marines. Again, music played a key role in working things through. "We were warriors, not politicians," he concluded. "That evening we chased away the political demons with some beer and a new tape by Creedence Clearwater Revival. Randy Champe trashed the Janis Joplin tape, and 'Bad Moon Rising' replaced 'Bobby McGee.'" [40]

Craig Werner and I closed *We Gotta Get Out of This Place* with an entire chapter devoted to the many ways music helped Vietnam veterans to get back home and to heal. From the songs of Marvin Gaye and Bruce Springsteen to the music Vietnam vets like Billy Bang, Kimo Williams, and numerous others created themselves, music became the emotional touchstone for connecting vets with the wounded parts of themselves. In a searing "solo" written specifically for *We Gotta Get Out of This Place*,

Vietnam veteran Arthur Flowers recalled how listening to Marvin Gaye's iconic album "What's Going On" turned his life around:

> It was like nothing I had ever heard before or since, he observed, and it just didn't let go, wasn't no break between the songs, it didn't let go, it just kept taking me higher and deeper and further every song... and this worldview he was forging note by note in my soul and my consciousness, and it was like he had write it specially for me, speak for me speak to me, and I could feel my plan, my contribution to black folks' freedom taking shape...

Perhaps even more powerfully, these kinds of moments occurred frequently in Vietnam, the music enabling soldiers to hold out, and hold on. One poignant example will suffice.

At the height of the Tet (Lunar New Year) Offensive in early 1968, thousands of North Vietnamese and Viet Cong troops launched a series of surprise attacks inside South Vietnam, striking more than one hundred towns and cities, including thirty-six of forty-four provincial capitals, five of the six autonomous cities, and Saigon itself, the capital of South Vietnam. Nowhere was the fury of the Tet Offensive felt more intensely than at Khe Sanh, a marine outpost near the Demilitarized Zone (DMZ).

For seventy-seven uninterrupted days, the NVA pounded away at the marine encampment at Khe Sanh– making it one of the longest battles of the war. CBS news reporter John Laurence was there with the Marines and asked one young man from Bravo Company of the 3rd Recon Battalion, with dirt, grime, and sweat caking his face, "How do you keep your spirits going?"[41]

"I guess we play cards and sing at night," the young man responded quietly. Then, in a heartbreaking segment shown on the CBS evening news, a half dozen marines under siege at Khe Sanh sit on a bunker strumming guitars and singing "Where Have All the Flowers Gone?," a song written by the World War II veteran and pacifist Pete Seeger. "*Where have all the soldiers gone, long time passing?*" The segment faded out as the marines sang the lines "*Where have all the soldiers gone? / Gone to graveyards every one. / When will they ever learn? / When will they ever learn?*" Watching that heartbreaking news clip almost half a century later, you can still hear the song echo in the jungle air, see the fear in the singers' eyes, and feel the comfort and resilience the ballad provides.

For those marines at Khe Sanh and the more than three million other men and women who served in Vietnam, music provided release from the uncertainty, isolation, and sometimes stark terror surrounding them. But the sounds offered more than just simple escape. Music was a lifeline connecting soldiers to their homes, families, and parts of themselves they felt slipping away. It was the glue that bound the communities they formed in their hooches, base camps, and lonely outposts from the Mekong Delta to the DMZ. Both in-country and "back in the world," as the troops called the United States, music helped them make sense of situations in which, as Bob Dylan put it in a song that meant something far more disturbing and haunting in Vietnam than it did back in the USA, they felt like "*they were on their own with no direction home.*"

And if they were fortunate enough to return home from Vietnam, music echoed through the secret places where they stored memories and stories they did not share with their wives, husbands, or children for decades. Music was the key to survival and a path to healing, the center of a meaningful human story that is too often lost in the haze of politics and myth that surrounds Vietnam.

NOTES

1. Much of the material in this chapter, especially the direct quotes by Vietnam veterans, are taken from Doug Bradley and Craig Werner, *We Gotta Get Out of This Place: The Soundtrack of the Vietnam War* (Amherst: University of Massachusetts Press, 2015).
2. Referenced in *We Gotta Get Out of This Place: The Soundtrack of the Vietnam War*, p.2. Meredith Lair also underscores the importance of music and its omnipresence in her book, *Armed with Abundance: Consumerism and Soldiering in the Vietnam War* (Chapel Hill: University of North Carolina Press, 2011), 189-95.
3. Bradley, 3; Michael Kramer makes much the same point in *The Republic of Rock: Music and Citizenship in the Sixties Counterculture* (New York: Oxford University Press, 2013).
4. Kramer, 127.
5. More than one veteran we interviewed told us this, but perhaps none more so than Mike Berto— see Bradley, 108.
6. Ibid., 138.
7. Ibid.
8. Lair, 87.
9. From an interview with Dennis McQuade by Doug Bradley, June 2006.
10. From an interview with Jim Roseberry by Doug Bradley, October 2007.
11. Bradley, 31.
12. Ibid.
13. Ibid., 32.
14. Ibid.
15. Ibid., 36. Lydia Fish uncovered many of these musical tidbits in her work, "Songs of Americans in the Vietnam War." http://faculty.buffalostate.edu/fishlm/folksongs/americansongs.htm, accessed on January 23, 2009.
16. Bradley, 28.
17. Leroy Tecube, *Year in Nam: A Native American Soldier's Story* (Lincoln: University of Nebraska, 1999), 2.
18. Bradley, 39.
19. Ibid.
20. Bradley, 44. Christian Appy drives home this point in *Working-Class War: American Combat Soldiers and Vietnam* (Chapel Hill: University of North Carolina Press, 1993).

21. Appy, 47.
22. Peter Kindsvatter, *American Soldiers: Ground Combat in the World Wars, Korea, and Vietnam* (Lawrence: University of Kansas Press, 2003), 61.
23. Bradley, 45.
24. Ibid.
25. Ibid, 94.
26. Kramer, 127.
27. Lair, 188.
28. Ibid., 133.
29. Ibid., 10.
30. Ibid., 108.
31. Ibid.
32. Ibid.
33. Ibid.
34. Ibid. 109.
35. Ibid.
36. Ibid, 109-10.
37. Ibid., 111.
38. John Ketwig, *...and a hard rain fell* (New York: Macmillan, 1985), 271.
39. Bill Peters, *First Force Recon Company: Sunrise at Midnight* (New York: Ballantine, 1999), 22.
40. Ibid., 222.
41. CBS Evening News, John Laurence reports from Vietnam, "Marines comment on the war through songs and words," February 19, 1968.

Contributor Biographies

William Thomas Allison is Professor of History at Georgia Southern University. He is the author of *Military Justice in Vietnam: The Rule of Law in the An American War* and *My Lai: An American War Crime*, among other works. He is a past Vice President and Trustee of the Society for Military History and was the 2012-2014 General Harold K. Johnson Visiting Chair in Military History at the U.S. Army War College.

Doug Bradley is a Vietnam veteran and distinguished lecturer and academic staff emeritus, University of Wisconsin-Madison. He has written and taught extensively about his Vietnam, and post-Vietnam, experiences. Most notably, he is the is the co-author of *We Gotta Get Out of This Place: The Soundtrack of the Vietnam War* (Amherst: University of Massachusetts Press, 2015).

Martin G. Clemis is Assistant Professor of History and Government at Valley Forge Military College and a part time lecturer at Rutgers University, Camden. Martin is the author of *The Control War: The Struggle for South Vietnam, 1968-1975* (University of Oklahoma Press, 2018). He is also a contributing author in *Drawdowns: The American Way of Postwar* (New York University Press, 2017) and *War and Geography: The Spatiality of Organized Mass Violence* (Ferdinand Schoningh, 2017). Martin has also had articles published in *Army History* and *Small Wars and Insurgencies.*

Susan L. Eastman is an Assistant Professor of English at Dalton State College. Her scholarship addresses memory and war of the twentieth and twenty-first century found in memorials, literature, film, and culture. In 2016, she participated in an NEH Summer Institute, Veterans in Society at Virginia Tech, where she began conducting research on War on Terror memorials, literature, and films. In her recent book, *The American War in Viet Nam: Cultural Memory at the Turn of the Century* (University of

Tennessee Press, 2017), Eastman analyzes veteran, civilian, American, Vietnamese, Vietnamese American, and Philippine memorial, literary and cinematic representations of the war produced at the turn of the twenty-first century.

Geoffrey W. Jensen, co-editor of the volume, is an Associate Professor of History in the College of Security and Intelligence at Embry-Riddle Aeronautical University, Prescott. He is also the editor of *The Routledge Handbook of the History of Race and the American Military* (2016). On several occasions, Jensen has presented on the matter of race in the military, including presentations at the Society for Military History Annual Meeting. He is a former West Point Summer Seminar Fellow (2012). His research has received support from the Harry S. Truman and Lyndon B. Johnson Presidential Libraries and Embry-Riddle Aeronautical University. Jensen is currently at work on a manuscript examining the Cold War racial integration of the American Armed Forces.

Xiaobing Li is a Professor in the Department of History and Geography and Director of the Western Pacific Institute at the University of Central Oklahoma. Among his recent books are *The Cold War in East Asia* (Routledge, 2017), *Modern China* (ABC-CLIO, 2015), *China's Battle for Korea* (Indiana University Press, 2014), *China at War* (ABC-CLIO, 2012), and *Voices from the Vietnam War* (University Press of Kentucky, 2010). He served in the People's Liberation Army (PLA) in China.

Ron Milam is an Associate Professor of History at Texas Tech University where he teaches courses on military history, World War II, and the Vietnam War. After a lengthy career in the Oil & Gas industry, he earned a Ph.D. in history at the University of Houston. Ron is the author of *Not a Gentleman's War: An Inside View of Junior Officers in the Vietnam War*, and the editor of *The Vietnam War in Popular Culture*. Ron is a Fulbright Scholar to Vietnam and he serves on the Content Advisory Committee for the Vietnam Veteran's Memorial Education Center at "The Wall." He is the Interim Executive Director for the new Institute for Peace and Conflict (IPAC) at Texas Tech which includes the world-renowned

Vietnam Center and Archive, and he was recently inducted into the Army's Officer Candidate School (OCS) Hall of Fame at the National Infantry Museum at Fort Benning, Georgia. He is a combat veteran of the Vietnam War where he served as an infantry advisor to Montagnard forces in Pleiku, Republic of Vietnam.

Geoffrey C. Stewart is an Assistant Professor of History at the University of Western Ontario. His research focuses on the intersection of decolonization with the Cold War in the developing world. He specializes in the history of Vietnam's Wars, twentieth century international relations, and the United States in the world. He has published in the *Journal of Vietnamese Studies* and written book reviews for H-Diplo, *Cross-Currents* and the *Journal of Asian Studies.*

Matthew M. Stith, co-editor of the volume, is Associate Professor of History at the University of Texas at Tyler. He is the author of *Extreme Civil War: Guerrilla Warfare, Environment, and Race on the Trans-Mississippi Frontier* (Baton Rouge: Louisiana State University Press, 2016) in addition to articles and book chapters that explore the intersection between warfare and the environment.

Heather Marie Stur is General Buford Blount Professor of Military History at the University of Southern Mississippi and a fellow in USM's Dale Center for the Study of War & Society. Her first book, *Beyond Combat: Women and Gender in the Vietnam War Era*, was published by Cambridge University Press in 2011. She is also co-editor of *Integrating the U.S. Military: Race, Gender, and Sexuality Since World War II*, which was published by Johns Hopkins University Press in 2017. She is currently writing two books: *Saigon at War: South Vietnam and the Global Sixties*, forthcoming from Cambridge University Press, and *Reflecting America: U.S. Military Expansion and Global Interventions*, forthcoming from Praeger/ABC-CLIO. She is the author of numerous articles, which have been published in the *New York Times*, the *National Interest*, the *Orange County Register*, *Diplomatic History*, and other journals and newspapers. In 2013-2014, Stur was a Fulbright scholar in Vietnam, where she was a visiting professor in the Faculty of International Relations at the University of Social Sciences and Humanities in Ho Chi Minh City.

Sarah J. Thelen lectures in U.S. history at University College Cork and has published several articles on the Silent Majority and other aspects of the domestic debates over the war in Vietnam. She holds a Ph.D. from American University in Washington, D.C. and is writing a monograph on White House efforts to rally support for the U.S. war in Vietnam. Her research also explores the changing nature of patriotism, nationalism, and American identity in the twentieth century.

Jeffrey A. Turner earned his Ph.D. at Tulane University and teaches at St. Catherine's School in Richmond, Virginia. He is the author of *Sitting In and Speaking Out: Student Movements in the American South, 1960-1970* (Athens: University of Georgia Press, 2010).

Nengher N. Vang is Assistant Professor of Transnational American History at the University of Wisconsin-Whitewater. He teaches the Vietnam War, U.S. foreign relations and empire, and Hmong American historical and contemporary issues. His research interests include American imperialism, U.S.-Asia relations, and refugee migration and politics. His research focuses on the diaspora or transnational politics of refugee and immigrant communities in the U.S. with an emphasis on the Hmong.

Index